iMedia

OCR Level 2 Certificate and Diploma

RUKSANA PATEL
YVONNE OAKES

www.payne-gallway.co.uk
✓ Free online support
✓ Useful weblinks
✓ 24 hour online ordering

01865 888070

Payne-Gallway is an imprint of Pearson Education Limited, a company incorporated in England and Wales, having its registered office at Edinburgh Gate, Harlow, Essex, CM20 2JE. Registered company number: 872828

www.payne-gallway.co.uk

First published 2007

12 11 10 09 08 07
10 9 8 7 6 5 4 3 2 1

British Library Cataloguing in Publication Data is available from the British Library on request.

ISBN 978 1 904467 99 1

Edited by Ros Davies
Designed by Wooden Ark
Typeset by TechType
Original illustrations © Pearson Education Ltd. 2007
Picture research by Helen Reilly
Cover photo/illustration © Jupiter Images
Printed in Scotland by Scotprint

Websites
The websites used in this book were correct and up-to-date at the time of publication. It is essential for tutors to preview each website before using it in class so as to ensure that the URL is still accurate, relevant and appropriate. We suggest that tutors bookmark useful websites and consider enabling students to access them through the school/college intranet.

Ordering Information
Payne-Gallway, FREEPOST (OF1771),
PO Box 381, Oxford OX2 8BR
Tel: 01865 888070
Fax: 01865 314029
Email: orders@payne-gallway.co.uk

ACKNOWLEDGEMENTS

Ruksana Patel would like to thank Stephe Cove and Abdul Patel for carefully working through units 1, 2 and 3, for providing honest, invaluable feedback and for their help and support. Thank you to my family Abdul, Fayaz and Fozia Roked for their continued patience, encouragement and support. Thank you to Lewis Birchon and Kate Wigley at Heinemann, for their patience, and for their input and support which has improved the quality of the book.

Yvonne Oakes would like to thank James Benedito for all his encouragement and support.

The authors and publisher would like to thank the following individuals and organisations for permission to reproduce photographs (t = top, b = bottom, mt = middle top, mb = middle bottom):

p.1: © Arnos Design Ltd.
p. 4: © Stephe Cove
p. 6: © Corbis
p. 7: (t) © Canon; (m) © istock/Richard Cano; (b) © Arnos Design Ltd.
p. 8: © Sony
p. 13, 24: © Ruksana Patel
p. 29: © Stephe Cove
p. 37, 38: © Ruksana Patel
p. 40: Courtesy of Adobe Photoshop
p. 49: © Ruksana Patel
p. 51, 64, 103, 110: © Arnos Design
p. 154, 159: © istock/Gaby J Albert, Stas Perov, Andrey Zyk, Heiko Etrodt, Andrey Stenkin
p. 158: © Cumulus/Photodisc & Old Computers.com
p. 161: © Wifi
p. 162: © Bluetooth
p. 197, 207: © istock/Lisa Kyle Young
p. 203: © Audacity
p. 205: (t) © istock/Kevin Russ; (mt) © Fujinon; (mb) © istock/Luis Camargo; (b) © Sony
p. 206: (t) © Sony; (b) © istock/Roberto A Sanchez
p. 239, 248: © JVC
p. 247: (t) © Arnos Design Ltd.; (b) © istock
p. 249: (t) © JVC; (mt, m, mb) © Sony; (b) © Nokia
p. 251: istock/Emrah Turudu
p. 255: (t) © istock/Polushkin Ivan; (t2) © istock/Tomas Kraus; (t3) © istock/Christine Balderas; (m) © istock/Adivin; (mb) © Getty/Stone/Dream Pictures; (b) © Fotolia/Vladimir Kirichuk
p. 257: © istock/Sang Nguyen

Every effort has been made to contact copyright holders of material reproduced in this book. Any omissions will be rectified in subsequent printings if notice is given to the publishers.

CONTENTS

INTRODUCTION

This book is suitable for anyone working towards the OCR Level 2 Certificate or Diploma for iMedia Users. It can be used by learners as a self-study workbook or in tutor-assisted workshops or tutor-led groups. It is also suitable for anyone wanting to learn practical skills in using Adobe Photoshop, Macromedia Dreamweaver, Macromedia Flash, Audacity and Windows Movie Maker.

HOW TO USE THIS BOOK

You may select the chapter for any unit – the units need not be completed in any particular sequence. However, you **must** work through a chapter for a unit in sequence and refer to the 'Common Skills' chapter where instructed. This will teach you the skills in the order in which you will need them. It will also help you to understand the relevant theory and the knowledge and understanding required in the syllabus.

For the practical, hands-on skills, 'HOW TO' guidelines are given. These are intentionally not referenced to any particular file so that you can refer to these 'HOW TO' guidelines whilst working on any task or assignment. You are advised to work through each step in the 'HOW TO' guidelines using any practice file – you should not simply read the guidelines.

TERMS AND SYMBOLS USED IN THIS BOOK

TERM	ICON	EXPLANATION
Resource toolkit	RESOURCE TOOLKIT	Guidelines for the hardware and software you will need for each unit
Information		Further information about the topic/skill
Key term	Key terms	Definition of a term used in the book or in the syllabus
Practical task	PRACTICAL TASK 1.1	A 'hands-on' task that you should work through. As subsequent tasks may require you to continue working on a file, you must save all the files you create in these tasks using appropriate filenames. Ensure that your files are organised into folders.
Student review	Student review	An activity, including questions, that you should complete to help reinforce your knowledge and understanding
Refer to		Refer to the page, section, figure or table indicated, for more detail on a topic or for a topic/skill already covered elsewhere in the chapter or book
Warning		Things to avoid or to be aware of
Tip	TIP!	Helpful hints or alternative ways of doing something
	→	Indicates that another instruction follows, i.e. the option from the menu should be selected. For example: **File** menu → **Open** means that you should click on the **File** menu, then click on the **Open** option from the menu.

SCHEME CODE 05580

This book has been designed to cover the syllabus for the following units of the OCR Level 2 Certificate/Diploma for iMedia Users:

- Unit 1 Digital Graphics
- Unit 2 Web Authoring
- Unit 3 Digital Animation
- Unit 4 Interactive Multimedia Concepts
- Unit 5 Digital Sound
- Unit 6 Digital Video

The qualification is designed to be accessible to you even if you are entirely new to using iMedia software applications.

The qualification maps to the National Occupational Standards for Interactive Media created by Skillset.

AIMS OF THE QUALIFICATION

The qualification aims to:

- develop your knowledge of a range of different software applications and your ability to use different applications effectively to complete tasks
- develop your ability to manage information and data in a variety of applications
- develop your ability to plan and prioritise tasks effectively
- develop your skills and knowledge in contexts that are directly relevant to employment situations
- encourage progression by assisting in the development of skills and knowledge that you will need to undertake further study.

STRUCTURE OF THE QUALIFICATION

This qualification is made up of eight units:

UNIT STATUS	UNIT TITLE
Mandatory unit	Unit 1 Digital Graphics
Optional units	Unit 2 Web Authoring Unit 3 Digital Animation Unit 4 Interactive Multimedia Concepts Unit 5 Digital Sound Unit 6 Digital Video Unit 7 2D Game Engines Unit 8 Game Design

All units are equally weighted and you may work towards the units in any order.

GUIDED LEARNING HOURS

On average, provided you have the stated recommended prior learning suggested by OCR, it should take around 30 **guided learning hours** per unit to acquire the knowledge, skills and understanding necessary to pass that unit. However, this figure is for guidance only and may vary depending on individual candidates and mode of learning.

Key terms

Guided learning hours
The recommended number of hours of tutor-led study.

RECOMMENDED PRIOR LEARNING

You may find it helpful to have achieved units from the Level 1 Certificate/ Diploma iMedia Users (Scheme Code 06460). The Level 1 qualification aims to:

- recognise your understanding of the digital media environment
- evaluate your level of organisation and planning when dealing with customer requirements
- provide evidence of the essential knowledge, skills and understanding needed by a competent user in a digital role within your chosen sector.

The Level 1 qualification includes the following units:

UNIT STATUS	UNIT TITLE
Mandatory unit	Unit 1 Exploring the Digital World of Media
Optional units	Unit 2 Introduction to Web Page Production Unit 3 Creating an Animated Object Unit 4 Introduction to Digital Imaging Unit 5 Digital Sound and Video Unit 6 Interactive Media Presentations Unit 7 Design and Test Computer Games

These units allow progression to the Level 2 qualification.

There are no formal entry requirements for the Level 2 iMedia User units. However, it is expected that you will be able to:

- show evidence of creativity
- demonstrate basic IT literacy and show an interest in developing your skills further
- demonstrate skills and knowledge at or above Level 1 in the Key Skills areas of Communication and Working with Others.

CANDIDATE PROFILE

You should already possess foundation skills (at Level 1 or equivalent) and wish to further develop your skills and ability. This qualification is suitable if you are in full-time education and wish to gain access to the Media industry. It is also suitable if you are in employment and wish to develop skills in one or more specialist areas in order to meet the requirements of your workplace situation and job role; and if you are following part-time courses for skill development or recreational purposes.

This qualification is suitable if you are working in, or preparing for, roles/work activities such as the following:

web design; graphic art; multimedia production; flash animation; 3D animation; sound design and editing; special effects; video production; logo/titles design; desktop publishing; games design; storyboarding.

ASSESSMENT

Assessment of each unit takes the form of practical activities which are assessed by your tutor and are then externally moderated by an OCR Examiner-Moderator. The assignment may be an OCR-set assignment or one which has been devised in your centre.

In order to achieve a pass in a unit, you must demonstrate skills in each one of the assessment objectives. You must provide evidence to show that you have achieved every assessment objective.

OCR provides sample assignments for all units, which can be used as practice – these can be downloaded from the OCR website. Live assignments which can be used for the assessment are issued by OCR every academic year.

EVIDENCE

You will be required to complete OCR-provided forms identifying where and how the assessment objectives have been met. Additionally, you will be required to provide copies of the work you have produced as part of your tasks.

An Evidence Checklist is available for each unit. These checklists must be used by you and your tutor to record achievement of assessment objectives. It is essential that you reference the submitted evidence to show how the evidence meets the **assessment objectives**.

Key terms

Assessment objective
The assessment objectives for each unit identify skills, understanding and knowledge that you will need to demonstrate in order to achieve the unit.

All evidence produced will be submitted to an e-portfolio for assessment.

CERTIFICATION

You will be awarded an OCR Level 2 Certificate for iMedia Users when you have successfully achieved the mandatory unit (Unit 1) plus **two** optional units.

You will be awarded an OCR Level 2 Diploma for iMedia Users when you have successfully achieved the mandatory unit (Unit 1) plus **four** optional units.

Units you have achieved will be listed on your certificate.

Units will be graded only pass or fail.

If you achieve fewer than the number of units required for a full qualification you will be awarded a unit certificate for each unit achieved.

PROGRESSION

If you are successful in achieving the OCR Level 2 Certificate/Diploma for iMedia Users you will be able to progress directly to the OCR Level 3 Certificate/Diploma for iMedia Users.

If you wish to extend your skills at Level 2 you will be able to progress to different optional units.

KNOWLEDGE, SKILLS AND UNDERSTANDING

The knowledge, skills and understanding identified in each unit sets out the underpinning knowledge and understanding that you will need in order to undertake the assessment for the unit and to meet the requirements of the assessment objectives. It is anticipated that you will learn all of the skills, knowledge and understanding requirements fully prior to entering for an assessment.

QUALIFICATION ACCREDITATION NUMBERS

Certificate	100/5678/6
Diploma	100/5679/8

ABOUT THIS CHAPTER

This chapter includes an overview of the book and covers the two **assessment objectives** which are common to all units, i.e. 3a and 3b in Units 1 to 5 and 2a and 4e in Unit 6. In the iMedia level 2 units, assessment objective 3a (2a in Unit 6) covers **planning** the work, and assessment objective 3b (4e in Unit 6) covers **reviewing** the work. These two assessment objectives and their corresponding knowledge, skills and understanding are covered in this chapter. Please note that these assessment objectives are NOT covered again in the individual unit chapters.

You should read this chapter before you start any of the units. Once you have read this chapter, start working through your chosen unit chapter. You will be instructed to refer back to the common skills covered in this chapter for planning and reviewing.

Key terms

Assessment objective
The assessment objectives for each unit identify skills, understanding and knowledge that you will need to demonstrate in order to achieve the unit.

E-PORTFOLIO

All your evidence for a unit will be submitted to OCR via an **e-portfolio**. Therefore, if any of your evidence is in hard-copy format, you will need to scan these hard copies and save them in electronic format so that they can be uploaded to your e-portfolio.

E-portfolio *For more information and a tutorial on the OCR iMedia e-portfolio, and to download student and centre e-portfolio iMedia user guides, visit the OCR website on http://www.ocr.org.uk Follow the link to* **e-assessment → e-portfolio.**

FILE ORGANISATION AND FILE NAMING

File organisation

Before you begin, you are advised to create a main folder for your iMedia work, within which you should create sub-folders for each iMedia unit. You may create a unit sub-folder as you begin a unit or create a sub-folder for every unit that you are working towards (if you know which units these are).

Within a unit sub-folder, you could create folders for the ***practice tasks*** that you will complete in this book, a folder for any ***research*** you may carry out and a folder for your ***source files***. The source files folder could contain sub-folders for the different types of source files, e.g. ***images***, ***clip art***, ***animations***, ***sounds***, ***video clips***. You may use original, edited or created files from one unit in any other unit.

You must remember to back up your work frequently.

A list of accepted file types is provided in the OCR iMedia Student Guide.

File naming

You should save all files with logical names that reflect the content of the file. In some iMedia units, you need to show evidence of using certain skills (e.g. manipulating images). You will find it helpful to save the original file and each version of the edited file using a filename that will help you identify the progression or the skill used. For example, **harbour_original**, **harbour_cropped**, **harbour_scaled**.

Avoid spaces in filenames, use hyphens or underscores instead.

Avoid punctuation characters in filenames – this is because some characters such as \ / : * ? " < > | are reserved by the operating system's shell.

File management

▸▸ HOW TO ... Create a folder in your user area

- **File** menu → **New** → **Folder** → delete the text **New Folder** and enter an appropriate folder name → press **Enter**.

or

- Right-click → a menu is displayed → select **New** → **Folder** → enter a suitable folder name → press **Enter**.

▸▸ HOW TO ... Create a subfolder

- Double-click to open an existing folder → repeat the steps for 'How to create a folder' above.

▸▸ HOW TO ... Copy a folder

- Click on the folder to select it → **Edit** menu → **Copy** → **Edit** menu → **Paste**.

▸▸ HOW TO ... Rename a file or folder

- Click on the file or folder to select it → **File** menu → **Rename** → delete the existing name and enter the new name → press **Enter**.

▶▶ HOW TO … Produce a screen print

1 Open the folder containing the files you wish to screen print.

2 From the Standard buttons toolbar, click the drop-down arrow to the right of **Views** and select an option (refer to Figure 1.4):

- To display miniatures of your original images, select **Thumbnails**.
- To display the file Size and Type, select **Details**. The Details option will also show the **Date Picture Taken** for any digital images.

3 To capture only the active window, press the **Alt** + **PrtSc** (Print Screen) keys (*or* to capture the entire screen press the **Print Screen** key only).

4 Open a new Word document.

5 Right-click → **Paste** *or* **Edit** menu → **Paste**.

6 Remember to enter your name in the screen print document.

7 To print the screen print document, click the **Print** icon .

Figure 1.4
Selecting a view

▶▶ HOW TO … Set a file or folder to read-only

Right-click on the file folder → a menu is displayed → select **Properties** → place a tick in the box for **Read-only** → **Apply** → **OK**.

Backing up files

To avoid accidentally deleting, overwriting or corrupting your files, once you have organised them, you should create a back-up copy on another network area or removable medium.

▶▶ HOW TO … Back up work on to a CD-R or CD-RW

1 Using a computer that has a CDR drive, insert a blank, writable CD into the CD drive → open the **My Computer** window → select the folders you want to copy to the CD (to select more than one folder, hold down the **Ctrl** key).

2 In the **My Computer** window, below **File and Folder Tasks** → select **Copy this folder** → in the **Copy Items** dialogue box, select the CD drive → select **Copy**.

3 In the **My Computer** window, double-click the CD drive → below **Files Ready to be Written to the CD** select the folder(s) you want to write to CD → below **CD Writing Tasks**, select **Write these files to CD** → Windows displays the **CD Writing Wizard**.

4 Follow the instructions in the wizard.

▶▶ HOW TO … Back up a folder onto a memory stick

- Insert the memory stick into a USB port → right-click on the folder name → **Send To** → **Removable Disk**.

PLANNING YOUR WORK

In all the level 2 units you will be required to plan your work to a specific brief. For example, in Unit 1 you will need to 'plan the image editing to a specific brief'; in Unit 2 you will need to 'plan the website to a specific brief' and so on.

As part of your planning you also need to show 'ways of identifying a client's requirements' and you need to 'use a variety of planning methods', e.g. conceptualise, visualise, storyboard. These terms are explained on pages xx to xxi of this chapter.

Once you have completed your project, you will need to review it against an **assignment brief**.

AOs (Assessment objective 3a for Units 1 to 5, Assessment objective 2a for Unit 6)

Key terms

Brief/Assignment brief For an OCR assessment, you will be given several tasks as well as an 'assignment brief'. This brief is a scenario outlining the background and requirements of a fictitious company or person (the 'client', see key term below). The brief is intended to 'set the scene' for the tasks you need to do.

Client In business, a client is any person or company who pays another person or company for goods or services e.g. a client would pay a lawyer a fee for legal advice. In an OCR assignment you will be asked to produce work for a 'client'. This is a fictitious person for whom you need to do a particular job.

Planning your activities

Before you begin working on your product, you must spend some time planning it and producing documentation to show this planning process. This is very important as it will help to ensure that you meet the requirements of the **client**. You will need to complete the planning sections of the Planning and Reviewing Form.

It is essential that you keep a record of how and when you intend to complete each task given in the assignment because it is easy to fall behind with your work. You may record your planning ideas in a variety of ways, for example:

- Planning and Review Form
- Word-processed document
- Presentation e.g. PowerPoint presentation
- Audio recording
- Video recording

▶▶ HOW TO ... Research your topic

Reading
There are many ways in which you can conduct research into a topic for an assignment. Researching a topic will help you to generate your own ideas. You could carry out some research which would involve reading documents such as a daily newspaper, a magazine, books, journals or articles available on the Internet.

Interview
If you know someone who has the information you need, you could conduct an interview. Interviews can be formal, where you will ask clearly defined questions, or informal, where your questioning will be led by the responses you received from the interviewee. If you are conducting a formal interview you will need to prepare your questions in advance making sure that they are presented in a logical manner so that you ask everything you need to about one topic before moving on

Continued ...

to the next. It may not always be appropriate to write down the answers. In such cases you may find that an audio recording device would be a good idea.

Observations/visits
Observations and visits can be a good method of obtaining information. You can collect information for a project when you make a visit to anywhere that is appropriate, e.g. a shopping centre, a museum, an exhibition, a park, a bowling alley. Before visiting the site, plan the questions that you are looking for answers to, and think about how you will record, store and retrieve the information. It is not always appropriate to write notes as you go along, so you may need to write a report immediately afterwards. Alternatively you may decide to draw sketches, record sounds or notes onto a recording device, or take pictures using a digital camera or your mobile phone.

Ask people you know
Don't forget that while you are researching your topic, you can also ask friends, classmates, parents, librarians and tutors to help with information. Asking questions is a sign that you are trying to learn.

▶▶ HOW TO ... Generate ideas

When you are given an assignment, you may be asked to generate your own ideas to complete the tasks. There are many techniques that are used to help you to generate ideas. When writing an essay, you need to organise your thoughts so that the ideas are presented in a logical order. However, when thinking about iMedia products, you need to be more creative, and creative thinking can be untidy, i.e. it may not follow any logical sequence.

It is important to be relaxed before starting an idea-generating activity. If this is a group activity, your tutor may try to get the group to think more freely by completing some exercises, such as drawing some shapes on the whiteboard and asking the group what they could be.

Working in a group could help your ideas to flow, as other people's comments may trigger useful thoughts.

Thought shower
A thought shower is a **lateral thinking** process which can be done on your own or with a group of people. The idea of a thought shower is to jot down or record thoughts about a subject as you think of them. During the process you should record all ideas; don't cut out those you do not like or select the best ones or put them in any particular order – this can be done at the end when you can't think of any more new ideas.

Key terms

Lateral thinking
A method of solving problems that involves using the imagination to think of associations that are not immediately obvious, as opposed to step-by-step reasoning.

Continued ...

Listing
Listing is a tool that can be used when you know what your topic is. It allows you to see connections between your ideas. Using a blank piece of paper or computer screen, write your topic at the top and then using single words or phrases, list everything that comes into your mind about the topic. When you have finished, look at the list and group items that belong together. Try to give each group a name.

Spidergrams
Spidergrams are an easy way to show a central topic and then show ideas about that topic. You begin in the centre with a word or phrase that describes your main idea or subject and then you branch out with each sub-theme.

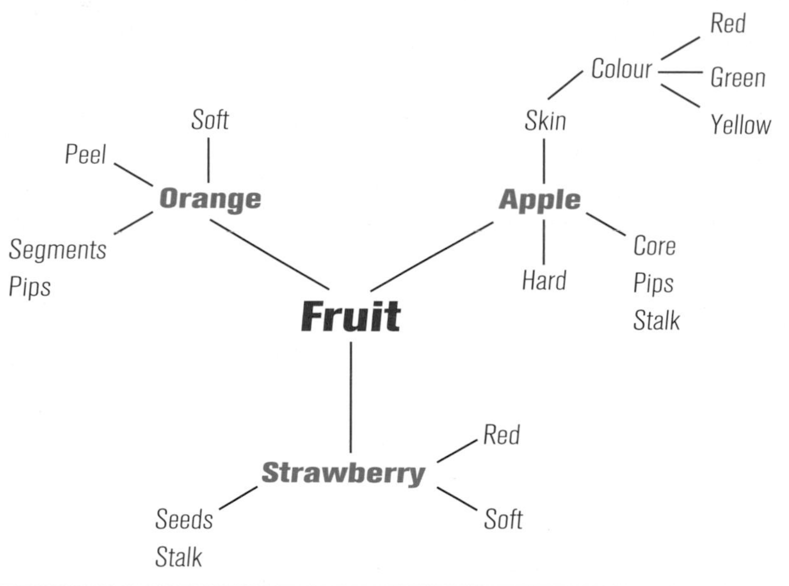

Instead of using words in your spidergram, you could draw pictures or include sketches.

There are several advantages of using spidergrams to show your ideas for a project.

- The main theme (idea) is clear
- Links between ideas can be shown easily
- Creating a structure can generate more ideas
- New ideas can be added in any area

No single strategy will work for everyone; experiment with different techniques and use one that you find that will work best for you.

Hardware, software and source files

You should find out the following and record details about each point e.g. in your Planning and Review Form:

- What hardware you will use and why it is necessary (e.g. digital camera for Unit 1, sound recorder for Unit 5, video camera for Unit 6, speakers and sound card for various units)
- What software program(s) you will use and explain why you have chosen it
- Identify your source files (your assets) and record how you will obtain these, e.g. will you create them yourself or source them from the Internet. If they are not being created by you, you must keep a record of where they are from and acknowledge any copyright.

Source files (assets)

Start each project logically by creating an organised folder structure.

When sourcing/organising the components you are going to use, you should check the requirements in your assignment brief. For example, in Unit 1, how many images you will need to edit; in Unit 2, how many web pages you need to create and what components you need to use (e.g. sound, video); in Unit 3, the length of the animation; in Unit 4, the duration of the multimedia product; in Units 5 and 6, the duration of the sound and video clips.

You may use the same files for more than one unit. For example, you could use the images you took/edited in Unit 1 in your web pages for Unit 2 and/or in your animation for Unit 3 and/or in your multimedia product for Unit 4.

Depending on which unit you are working towards, find out if your 'client' (who can be your tutor) can provide you with any source files or suggest where you could get these from, e.g. CD or DVD photo libraries and/or video libraries, Internet sites.

Find out what file formats are appropriate for the software you will be using to create the product.

Spend some time finding and selecting appropriate files – if they are not appropriate for the client brief or software to be used, you will need to find more suitable files later on, so it is important to be certain that your files are appropriate during your planning stage. Once you have sourced your assets, copy the required files to your working area and organise them into folders.

Remember to keep back-up copies of all your electronic files.

Key terms

Source files/assets
Your source files are the files (e.g. images, animations, text, sound clips, video clips) that you will collect or create to use for a particular task. These source files are often referred to as assets.

Referencing sources

Ensure that any files you download are either free from copyright or that you have obtained permission to use the file. You must always keep a record of all the files you use and reference your source. This could be by copying and pasting the URLs of files obtained from the Internet into a word-processed table.

Key dates

Make a note of all key dates. You can record these in the Planning and Review Form or you could devise a calendar listing all key dates and activities. This could be created a table in a word-processed document which you can then upload to the e-portfolio when you are ready to submit your work.

An example of some key milestones is shown below.

1 Produce concept by: [enter date]
2 Produce visualisation by: [enter date]
3 Source files to be collected by: [enter date]
4 Storyboard to be completed by: [enter date]
5 Begin creating product on: [enter date]
6 Finish creating product on: [enter date]
7 Review product by: [enter date]

You could also record:

- the date you were given the assignment brief
- dates, times and locations of all meetings that you have with your 'client'
- the estimated completion date for each task
- any interim or review dates with the 'client'
- the deadline date for submission of your work.

In the form, the question 'What assets will you produce and how will you edit them? (Identify appropriate hardware and software)' will vary from unit to unit.

Ways of identifying client requirements

When you first begin any assignment, you must read the assignment brief and task instructions carefully. In most assignments, you will be instructed to identify the client's requirements. This information should be extracted from the assignment brief.

Make sure you understand the 'client's' requirements, i.e. what you need to do. You may have a discussion with your tutor acting as the client. Whilst working on a project and after completion, you must refer to the brief and instructions again and have discussions with your 'client' as and when you need to.

You should present a brief overview of what the client has asked you to do. In addition, clearly identify the aim and audience of the product you are going to create. Your description of the aim of your product should make it clear what the purpose of your product is. The purpose is your expected outcome, i.e. the overall objective.

Your target audience could be narrow (e.g. 14 to 16 year olds) or wide (e.g. anyone interested in sport) or could be a combination of more than one category. The intended target audience will influence the choice of content (assets) you use in your product.

Preparing for a meeting with the 'client'

1. Read the assignment brief carefully.
2. Make a note of the questions that you need to ask your client.
3. Arrange a mutually convenient meeting time with your client.
4. Prepare yourself for the meeting, ensure you take with you:
   - the assignment brief
   - your list of questions
   - your Planning and Review Form
   - a notepad and pen/pencil and/or audio recording device
   - any resources you may already have:
     Examples for Unit 1: digital camera, digital images.
5. At the meeting, ensure you record details of the following:
   - all client's answers to your questions
   - all suggestions made by your client
   - all instructions given.
6. At the meeting, ask your client if they are able to provide you with any resources.
   Examples: Unit 1, digital camera; Unit 6, video recorder etc.

Understanding the terms conceptualise, visualise, storyboard

In all units, you will be expected to present the **concept** for your project, **visualise** it, then produce a graphical plan, e.g. **storyboard** and/or site map.

Conceptualise

When you are instructed to conceptualise your project, you simply need to think about it, and form an idea of what you are going to do. You could start by looking at other similar projects, e.g. if you are creating a website, you could start by looking at other websites to see how these have been created. This could provide you with ideas. Your initial ideas should be recorded in the form of a brief overview of what the product will be and the style in which it will be produced (e.g. humorous, factual etc.). Try to be as precise as possible about the idea you are trying to convey.

Visualise

Visualising involves sketching your ideas. It is a graphical presentation of your information, translating the words from concept into images – in no particular order.

Visualising your initial concept enables you to develop those ideas and to see if they will work. The sketches do not have to be perfect. Try doodling as you might do if you were talking to someone on the telephone. This method of planning allows you to play around with several different ideas until you find one you are happy with.

Storyboard

The **storyboard** is collating your visualisations into the order in which they will appear in the finished product.

Creating a storyboard

A storyboard shows a visual overview of the plan for your product and can show when automated actions are going to happen, e.g. animations, sound, video. As the name implies, a storyboard tells a story of the product as it will be viewed – it shows the main events that will occur. There are different types of storyboard, e.g. text only storyboard, simple linear storyboard, graphical storyboard and hand-drawn storyboard. Graphical storyboards are widely used in film production.

Designing a storyboard for your project will make it easier for you when you start to create the project. It should save time because it will give you a useful guide for what items you will need to use at each stage. The storyboard should show what objects (images, sounds, videos, animations, text) will be displayed on each screen or change of event. It should also show the approximate

TIP!

A useful test to find out if your storyboard is clear and identifies all assets and features is to see if someone else would be able to use your storyboard to create the product you are planning. Remember your ideas must be recorded; they should not be in your head!

positioning of items on a page/screen/frame and the sequence of each scene/event/page in your product.

If appropriate to the type of product being created, the storyboard should also show how pages/screens will be linked.

It should include sufficient detail for someone else to see what the final product will look like when finished. A simple rule is that if an asset is going to be included in your product, it should be shown on the storyboard. There should not be much difference between the content and features shown on the storyboard and the content and features of the completed product.

Your storyboard can be hand-drawn or produced on the computer. You could use a template provided by your tutor. If you are creating your own, create about six to eight text boxes on a page. You could then print the page and sketch the content that will be displayed on each page or screen or do so using a computer.

Don't worry if you are not good at drawing – your storyboard is not going to be published, it is simply a sketch to show the placement of items on the different pages/screens of your product. Don't spend too much time producing an artistic storyboard – just draw suitable shapes to represent items on each page/screen.

Consider the following points when creating your storyboard:

- The number of pages/frames/slides/screens or you could show the main sections instead of every page
- Navigation: use arrows to show how the pages/screens will be linked
- Orientation or page/screen size
- Overview of the content on each page/frame/slide/screen including multimedia elements
- If appropriate to the product, show effects, transitions, timings
- Indicate colours to be used for backgrounds, text, etc
- Include housestyle details e.g. font styles, font sizes, alignment, etc if appropriate.

REVIEWING YOUR WORK

AOs (Assessment objective 3b for Units 1 to 5, Assessment objective 4e for Unit 6)

For each unit you complete you will be required to review your work against the original brief.

You will need to identify how the product meets the original brief and if it does not, state why it did not. To help you, you should obtain appropriate feedback on your work. This could be from your tutor acting as the client or from your peers who may have tested the product for you.

You will need to comment on the quality of the finished product. Recording comments and observations you may have received from your tutor and peers could be helpful in suggesting improvements to the finished product.

Some general questions you could ask to help you review your product include the following:

- Have I met the objectives of the original brief?
- Is the final product effective?
- How could the final product be improved?
- Is the information organised in an appropriate manner?
- Do the assets used convey the right message?
- Is the product fit for purpose?

You will need to identify at least two **parameters** and/or **constraints** that influenced your choices with regard to the assets you used in the product and how you manipulated them.

Key terms

Parameter A parameter is a variable that determines the choices available to you. For example, in a project on fruit, a parameter might be to only include **red** fruit e.g. red apples, strawberries, raspberries, in which case, bananas and oranges could not be included.

Constraint A constraint is a boundary or restriction on the amount of freedom you have to solve a problem. For example, you may be constrained to only including one sound on your website, or a photograph may only be 3cm high.

Example of parameters and constraints for Unit 1

- Your choice of photograph to edit could have been influenced by the composition of the photograph not providing good evidence for one of the rules of photography. However, by cropping the photograph, you were able to show a good example of the rule of thirds.
- You should give reasons for using different file formats when saving your finished product. For example, in Unit 1 where a particular file format was chosen because it was more suitable for distribution on the web, or where a particular file format was chosen as it provided better quality for printing.
- You should also comment on compression techniques that you have used in completing the task. For example, where compression significantly reduces the size of the file but could cause loss of quality.

EVIDENCE

You will carry out a series of tasks based on a given assignment brief (also referred to as a client brief). The evidence that you gather for each task should be saved for your portfolio of evidence.

You will need to:

- provide copies of the work you produce as part of the tasks
- complete forms provided by OCR to show how you have planned and reviewed the final project
- complete an Evidence Checklist to identify where and how the assessment objectives have been met
- cross-reference the copies of your work to show how the evidence meets the assessment objectives
- ensure that you/your tutor scan all hard-copy evidence so that it can be uploaded to your e-portfolio.

Examples of the type of evidence that you could provide for each unit are explained in the individual chapter for each unit.

THE EVIDENCE CHECKLIST

The aim of the Evidence Checklist is to help your tutor/assessor to identify that you have covered all the assessment objectives for the unit. In order for you to achieve a unit, you must show evidence of achievement of all the criteria listed in the Evidence Checklist. This checklist :

- is provided in the e-portfolio site to be completed electronically
- is provided by OCR in an OCR-set assignment
- may be designed by your tutor.

Whichever format you use, you must reference your work to show where you have covered each assessment objective.

An Evidence Checklist for each unit is provided within the OCR iMedia e-Portfolio site. You will need to complete this checklist when uploading your work to the e-Portfolio site.

Examples of software that could be used for Units 1 to 6

Unit 1
Adobe Photoshop
Adobe Photoshop Elements
Macromedia Fireworks
CorelDRAW
Jasc Paint Shop Pro
Serif PhotoPlus

Unit 2
Macromedia Dreamweaver
Microsoft FrontPage
Notepad
Adobe GoLive

Unit 3
Macromedia Flash
Adobe ImageReady
Serif ImpactPlus

Unit 4
Macromedia Flash
Microsoft PowerPoint
Macromedia Director MX 2005
Macromedia Dreamweaver
Macromedia Authorware
Matchware Mediator 8

Unit 5
Audacity
Adobe Audition
Sony Sound Forge 7
Serif MoviePlus

Unit 6
Adobe Premiere Elements
Apple Final Cut Pro
Adobe Premiere
Serif MoviePlus

Microsoft Windows Movie Maker

For a more detailed list of websites for software providers, refer to the OCR iMedia microsite on **www.imedia.ocr.org.uk/**

UNIT 1
DIGITAL GRAPHICS

INTRODUCTION

This practical unit is designed to provide you with an understanding of the types and uses of digital graphics. You will develop skills in using digital image manipulation software to edit digital images and save these in different formats. This unit is mandatory for the Certificate or Diploma.

LEARNING OUTCOMES

After studying this unit you will be able to:

- use a digital camera to obtain images and transfer these electronically
- use the basic editing tools and features of a digital image manipulation program
- edit a digital graphic for a particular purpose.

RESOURCE TOOLKIT

Hardware
- Computer
- Digital camera

Software
- Adobe Photoshop

Other
- Planning and Review Form
- Digital camera images
- Evidence Checklist

Optional
- Books on photographic techniques
- Photography magazines
- Access to the Internet to research different types of digital cameras and photographic techniques
- Objects to photograph (e.g. people, landscapes, buildings)
- Scanner
- Word-processing application (e.g. Microsoft Word)

ABOUT THIS UNIT

For this unit you will need access to a digital camera. You will need to be familiar with the camera parts and the basic rules of photography.

You will need to plan and record what images you will obtain based on the needs of your client as detailed in an assignment brief. You will look at ways of identifying your client's requirements and use planning methods appropriate for your brief.

You will obtain appropriate digital images, transfer these to your computer, organise and rename the images, and select which images you will edit. You will then use the editing tools and features of a digital image manipulation program to edit, retouch and repair your digital photographs. You will need to save images in different file formats.

Finally you will review the quality of your edited images against the original assignment brief and assess if the edited images meet your client's requirements.

The Student Review activities and Practical Tasks in this chapter will allow you to develop your understanding of the requirements for an OCR assessment and practise the skills required for the unit 1 syllabus. The images you take and edit in this chapter **CANNOT** be submitted for assessment purposes.

Digital image files have not been provided with this book because you will need to source and manipulate your own images for an OCR assessment.

You may use your original and/or edited images for other units.

ASSESSMENT FOR UNIT 1

Your assessment work should be submitted to OCR via e-portfolio. You should therefore save all original and edited images and all screen prints in electronic format. Any hard-copy evidence should be scanned and saved electronically.

Evidence

You will need to provide:

- *evidence of planning your project. This could be included in, or be in addition to, the Planning and Review Form*
- *Planning and Review Form*
- *a diary (e.g. digital diary) or log of your activities for the given assignment*
- *evidence of original images taken using a digital camera (a minimum of six images)*
- *screen print(s) to show evidence of downloading original images from a camera and renaming these images*
- *evidence of editing images with a brief description of editing techniques used on each image*
- *edited images saved in appropriate file formats*
- *Evidence Checklist (OCR template).*

TIP!

For the assessment, you must ensure that you show evidence of progression from one task to the next. For example, the images you edit must be selected from the ones you originally took.

Refer also to 'Evidence' on pages ix and xxii.

Copyright

You must ensure you comply with copyright law when working with images. Note that images from the Internet are not necessarily in the public domain and may be subject to copyright. If you are using any images downloaded from the Internet you must either obtain permission or reference your sources.

Note: There are many ways of performing the skills covered in this book. The guidelines in this book explain one way only. The HOW TO guidelines provided have proven to be easily understood by learners.

SOFTWARE

This chapter is written specifically for Adobe Photoshop CS but it may also be used with other versions of Photoshop or Photoshop Elements. However, please note that some screenshots, methods and features may not be available and/or will not match other versions exactly.

ABOUT THIS CHAPTER

This chapter for Unit 1 is divided into three sections. You must work through the sections in sequence.

- In Section 1 you will learn about different types of digital graphics, how they may be used, some basic rules of photography and the basic parts of a digital camera. You will learn how to save your digital images, and create and rename files and folders. You will learn about different file formats and file extensions. You will learn about the types of software applications that are available for manipulating images and their capabilities.

AOs 1a, 1b, 2a

- In Section 2 you will become familiar with the Photoshop interface and toolbox tools, use the selection tools and work with layers. You will learn about image and canvas size, resolution and how to correct mistakes. You will learn how to open, edit, retouch and repair graphics using the functions in Photoshop.

AOs 2a, 2b

- In Section 3 you will learn how to save images in different file formats.

AO 2c

Assessment objectives 3a (plan the image editing to a specific brief) and 3b (review the edited image against the original brief) and the corresponding knowledge, skills and understanding criteria are covered in the 'Common Skills' chapter.

Refer to 'Planning your work' and 'Reviewing your work' sections on pages xiv and xxi of the 'Common Skills' chapter.

ASSESSMENT OBJECTIVES

The following assessment objectives will be covered in this section:

1a Obtain source digital image files

1b Save the digital images

2a Open a bitmap image manipulation software application

The following knowledge, skills and understanding criteria corresponding to assessment objectives 1a, 1b and 2a will also be covered:

- *Types of digital graphic*
- *Understand where, when and how digital graphics are used*
- *Basic rules of photography*
- *Component parts of a digital camera*
- *Different types of file formats and common file extensions*
- *Different types of software manipulation application*
- *Properties and capabilities of image manipulation software applications*

1a: For an OCR assessment, you will need to take a minimum of six digital photographs, choose four of these and then manipulate at least one of your four images.

TYPES OF DIGITAL GRAPHIC

There are two main categories of computer graphics: **bitmap** and **vector**. Raster images are the technical name for bitmap images. You will need to understand the difference between the two categories.

Refer to page 10 for more detail on these file formats.

Bitmap image

A bitmap is a map of dots or bits (hence the name). A bitmap image is made of pixels (dots) that are arranged and coloured differently to form an image or pattern such as a photograph. Each pixel has its own colour value. A bitmap might contain millions of colours. Bitmap images are dependent on resolution. When you zoom into a bitmap effect, the individual pixels that make up the image can be seen more clearly (refer to Figure 1.1). When you edit a bitmap image, you are manipulating the pixels in the image. Common bitmap file types include **bmp** (the raw bitmap format), **jpg/jpeg**, **gif**, **pict**, **png**, **pcx**, **tiff** and **psd**.

a

b

Figure 1.1 A bitmap image: a) at 100% b) zoomed in to 1500%

Key terms

Bitmap *A collection of pixels. Bitmaps make it possible to represent almost any combination of colours. Bitmaps lose some of their quality when they are reduced or enlarged.*

Vector *An image based on mathematical formulae measurements that represent lines and curves. A vector graphic can be reduced or enlarged without losing any detail.*

Vector graphics

Vector graphics are made up of lines and curves defined by mathematical formulae and measurements called vectors. Vector graphics are often used for simple graphics that need to be easily reproduced and resized. Examples include company logos, illustrations, text and clip art. Vector graphics are not dependent on resolution and keep their crispness when altered. They can be increased or decreased in size, moved or have their colour changed without losing any quality or detail (refer to Figure 1.2). A vector graphic might contain only a few colours. Vector graphics can be easier to work with because they lack the complexity of a bitmap image. Common vector format include **ai** (Adobe Illustrator), **wmf** (Windows Metafile), **cdr** (CorelDRAW), **cmx** (Corel Presentation Exchange), **cgm** (Computer Graphics Metafile) and **dxf** (AutoCAD).

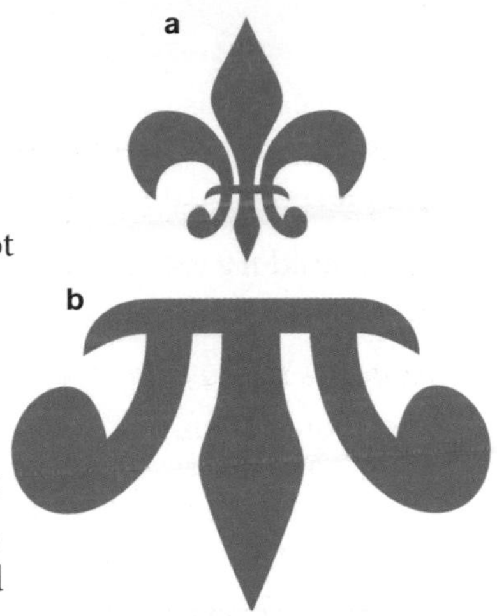

Figure 1.2 The same vector graphic in different views: a) at 100% b) zoomed in to 500%

WHERE, WHEN AND HOW DIGITAL GRAPHICS ARE USED

Refer to 'Different file formats and file extensions' on page 10, and 'Saving images in different file formats' on page 44.

Digital graphics can be used for many different purposes. Images can be published in books, magazines, on the World Wide Web or inserted on web pages. If you are intending to publish images on the Internet, you will need to save the image in a file format that can be read by most browsers (e.g. **gif**, **jpg**).

Student review 1.1 – Identify types of digital graphics

Assessment objective 1a

1 *What is another name for a raster image?*
2 *Which image file format is made up of dots called pixels?*
3 *Which type of digital graphic (bitmap or vector) may contain only a few colours?*
4 *Which image file format is better for producing a company logo that will need to resized and reproduced easily?*
5 *Which image file format will display jagged edges when enlarged?*
6 *Give three examples of bitmap file types.*
7 *List two examples of vector graphic file types.*

BASIC RULES OF PHOTOGRAPHY

There are no defined or agreed 'rules of photography'. You should become familiar with how to use your digital camera and practise taking as many photographs as you can. Some basic guidelines are explained in this book; these are by no means comprehensive or definitive.

TIP!

To see how rules of photography have been applied, visit the website for the National Museum of Photography: **www.nationalmediamuseum.org.uk/photography/**

Modern cameras can focus for you, work out exposure and select a suitable shutter speed or aperture as well as many other functions; however, they cannot compose the picture for you.

You should try your hand at different types of photography:

Pictorial	e.g. landscape and nature photography
Portrait	e.g. people and animals
Photojournalism	e.g. press photography (compelling storytelling)
Abstract	e.g. extreme close ups of detail of something

Composition

An important point to consider when taking photographs is **composition**. Below are *some* basic principles of composition:

- Look at the **forms** in your image. A good photo is a good arrangement of form. In a portrait, the form could be the features in a woman's face whereas in a landscape, the forms are the landscape, trees, rocks, hills etc.
- **Colour** – you need to consider what colours go together. Colours can harmonise, contrast dramatically or clash violently.
- **Contrast** – your photos should have a good balance between different colours. Even black and white photos should have a good contrast of black, white and grey.
- **Motion** – avoid having movement in or outside your image. It will direct the eye away from the main focus in the image.
- **Leading lines** – use these to draw the viewer's eye to the intended subject. A leading line can be almost anything, e.g. a road, building, tree, river or shadow. You will not find strong leading lines around every subject, but if present, take advantage of them. Lines in a picture should lead into the picture and should lead your eye toward the main subject.
- **Orientation**: **landscape/portrait** – before you take a picture, think about whether it would better taken with the camera held horizontally (landscape) or vertically (portrait). For example, a vertical shot of a tall building emphasises its height. A horizontal shot of a landscape can give a feeling of space and breadth.

Rule of thirds

The rule of thirds is probably the most recognised rule and has been used for centuries by artists and photographers. Imaginary lines are drawn dividing the frame into three vertical and three horizontal sections making a total of nine rectangles (refer to Figure 1.3).

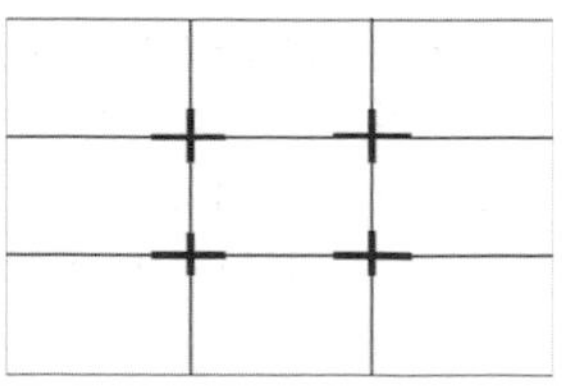

Figure 1.3 The rule of thirds

Where these lines intersect is an ideal spot to place important elements of your composition, e.g. an individual or a point of interest. The subject is given more emphasis than if it is in the middle of the photo. The intersection points are also useful if there is more than one main subject in a photo. Features and objects can also be placed along the imaginary lines.

COMPONENT PARTS OF A DIGITAL CAMERA

You should become familiar with your digital camera and how to make the most of its features to take effective photographs. Below are some brief explanations of the basic parts of digital cameras. Please note that cameras, like computers, are constantly being updated.

Shutter and aperture

A digital camera **shutter** is a device which opens and closes to control the time of a photographic exposure.

The shutter opening time affects the image exposure and how motion is portrayed in it. Most digital cameras have an automatic setting to determine the appropriate shutter speed; some will have the option to set shutter speed manually for greater artistic control.

Shutter speed is calculated in relation to **aperture**. The aperture is the size of the lens opening which regulates how much light passes through the lens to strike the image sensor. Aperture is measured in f-stops: a higher number represents a smaller amount of light.

The shutter and aperture settings are used together to determine the amount of light that strikes the image sensor.

> **Key terms**
>
> **Aperture** The size of the lens opening. The aperture controls the amount of light that passes through the lens. The smaller the aperture, the slower the shutter speed required.

Flash

Most digital cameras have an automatic flash setting which can be set to trigger automatically in poor light conditions, and some have additional settings that allow greater control over the flash. Automatic flash settings should be used carefully as problems can occur with digital flash photography. The most common problem is red eye, where the subject's pupils appear red in the resulting photo. These problems can be overcome by selecting the correct flash mode, for example:

- **Automatic mode** triggers the flash automatically if there is too little light for a good exposure.
- **Red-eye reduction** fires a short burst prior to exposing a photo, causing a subject's pupils to contract. This reduces the reflection in the eyes before the photograph is taken.
- **Forced** or **Fill-in flash** keeps the flash on in situations when additional illumination is needed, e.g. when the main source of light or a particularly bright light is behind a subject or shadows prevent details from showing.

Liquid crystal display screen

The liquid crystal display (LCD) screen is the screen on the back of a digital camera that the photographer may use to compose images. The LCD is also used to preview images immediately after they are taken and to review captured images stored in the camera's memory card. It can be also be used to view camera settings and menus. Because the LCD consumes a lot of battery power, in order to save power it can be set to shut off or standby automatically after a set time period.

Memory card

A digital camera memory card is a small electronic device that stores image files. In some models, images are stored in the camera's own internal memory. Memory cards vary in storage size from 16 MB (megabytes) to 4 GB (gigabytes). The larger the memory card storage capacity, the more images of a given size/quality it can hold. Once you have taken photographs, you can delete them from the memory card, before or after transferring them to your computer, to free up space on your memory card.

Assignment brief

Cove Photography Club – Booklet
You have recently become a member of a photography club. The club organiser is in the process of producing a booklet for new members. In it, he would like to include some guidelines for new photographers showing the parts of a digital camera and giving some tips for taking photographs.

At the last photography club meeting, all the members were split into groups. Each group will be required to present their photographs at the club's quarterly meetings. The next meeting will take place in three months' time. The group that submits the best retouched photograph will win a free digital camera. Each stage of the editing and retouching will need to be shown with a brief explanation of the editing technique used and why. Each group member has been assigned the task of taking photographs, which they will need to repair and retouch individually. The group will then agree which member's photograph will be presented at the club meeting. Each member must present their edited photo to their group in two months' time.

Every member must take at least six photographs:

- Three well-composed, digital photographs: one of a landscape, one of a building and one of an individual. These three photographs must be composed or framed creatively following the basic rules of photography.
- Three photographs which will require retouching and repairing. These photos can be of any appropriate but not offensive subject (e.g. streets, buildings, places of interest).
- At least one photo must be in portrait orientation and at least one in landscape orientation.

PRACTICAL TASK 1.1 **Demonstrate an understanding of basic parts of a camera and basic rules of photography**

Assessment objective 1a

1 Refer to the 'Cove Photography Club – Booklet' assignment brief.

2 Produce a simple guide about the basic rules of photography that could be included in a booklet about photography.

3 In your guide, include some information about digital cameras that new members should consider, for example, shutter speeds and using flash.

4 You may present your guide as a bulleted list or short paragraphs with subheadings.

SAVING DIGITAL IMAGES

Once you have taken your digital images, you must download them from your digital camera into a folder on your computer. To connect your digital camera to your computer and download the images, you should refer to your digital camera user manual. Windows XP usually detects any new hardware so you may be able to take advantage of its 'plug and play' capability.

Once you have downloaded your images to your computer, you should save the required images into a folder, then rename each image using an appropriate filename to reflect the image content. Digital camera images will usually be a **jpg/jpeg** file format so you will not need to change the file format at this stage.

TIP!

Copy the folder containing the original downloaded images before renaming any photos so that you have back-up copies of your originals.

Refer to 'File organisation and file naming' on page xi in the 'Common Skills' chapter.

PRACTICAL TASK 1.2 **Plan project**

Assessment objective 3a

1 Refer to the 'Planning your work' and 'Reviewing your work' sections in the 'Common Skills' chapter.

2 Obtain a copy of a Planning and Review Form (ask your tutor for a copy).

3 Refer to the Assignment Brief for the 'Cove Photography Club – Booklet' on page 8.

4 Using the suggested planning techniques, plan when (date, time etc.) and where (locations) you will take the images required for the photography club.

5 As part of your planning, you may have a discussion with your tutor.

6 In your plan, identify how you will source your images.

7 Note down all relevant dates and any interim dates that you need to meet to complete tasks.

Different file formats and file extensions

Table 1.1 explains some common file extensions for image files, what they mean and when each file format would be used. Table 1.2 explains other file formats you may come across.

FILE EXTENSION	DEFINITION	CHARACTERISTIC
bmp	**b**it**m**a**p**	Produces large file sizes. Used for print-quality images. Not suitable for the web.
eps	**e**ncapsulated **p**ost**s**cript file	Used to proof or print company logos, photographs and drawn graphics. Not suitable for the web.
gif	**g**raphics **i**nterchange **f**ormat	Common format – can be used in most programs. Supports transparency and is frequently used for web graphics and screen presentations. Not suitable for photographs. A **gif** file has a bit depth of 8, which means it can support only 256 colours. **gif** images are compressed using **lossless** compression – no part of the original image is deleted during compression so there is no loss of quality as the result of compression.
jpg or **jpeg**	**j**oint **p**hotographic **e**xperts **g**roup	Common format – can be used in most programs. User can control the quality and file size. Ideal format for photographs, images intended for the web and screen presentations. A **jpg** file has a bit depth of 24, which means it can support up to 16 million colours. **jpg** images are compressed using **lossy** compression – a technique that permanently eliminates some tonal information.
pict	**pict**ure file format	A file format used on Apple Macintosh computers. **pict** files can contain both vector and bitmap images, as well as text.
png	**p**ortable **n**etwork **g**raphics	A compressed file format similar to a **jpg** format. Enables compression of images without any loss of quality, including high-resolution images.
psd	**p**hoto**s**hop **d**atafile	For use within Photoshop only. Can store layers which can be edited at a later date but can also be used for 'flattened' files. Produces large file sizes.
tiff or **tif**	**t**agged **i**mage **f**ile **f**ormat	Usually produces large, high-quality files but can save down to very low quality/size. Can store layers and is good for storing/archiving images. Can be used in most print applications. Not suitable for the web.

Table 1.1 Common image file types and their uses

FILE EXTENSION	DEFINITION	CHARACTERISTIC
htm or **html**	**h**yper**t**ext **m**arkup **l**anguage	A web page containing hypertext. HTML is a mark-up language designed for the creation of web pages and other information viewable in a web browser.
pdf	**p**ortable **d**ocument **f**ormat	A file format that can be read with Adobe Acrobat. The fonts, images, graphics and layout of any source file are preserved regardless of the application and platform used to create it.
txt	**t**e**xt** file	A text file saved in a format that can be read by most systems and a wide range of applications. Only the text is preserved; all formatting will be lost.

Table 1.2 Other file formats

PRACTICAL TASK 1.3 *Take digital photographs, transfer images to computer, save and rename images, plan image editing*

Assessment objectives 1a, 1b

1. Refer to the Assignment Brief for the 'Cove Photography Club – Booklet' on page 8.
2. Take the three required well-composed photographs of a landscape, a building and an individual. Ensure that you compose or frame these photographs creatively using your digital camera viewfinder – your photographs should show evidence that you have considered the basic rules of photography (e.g. rule of thirds, composition, framing).
3. In addition, take the three required photographs of your choice, which will require retouching and repairing.
4. Transfer your six images to your computer – save them into a folder with an appropriate folder name. Ensure that your images are saved in an appropriate file format. (Note: if your images are already in an appropriate format, e.g. **jpg/jpeg**, then you do not need to change the file format at this stage.)
5. Copy the folder containing your six original images and rename the copied folder using a suitable folder name.
6. Rename each of the images in the copied folder using filenames that reflect the content of each image.
7. Produce screen print evidence showing thumbnails of the original folder contents, of the copied folder and thumbnails of the renamed images. Produce another screen print showing the image details (Size and Type).
8. On your Planning and Review Form, write down the names of the three images you are going to edit and what changes and improvements need to be made for each one. To plan the editing, you may have a discussion with your tutor.

TYPES OF IMAGE MANIPULATION SOFTWARE APPLICATIONS

There is a wide variety of professional as well as free, downloadable image manipulation programs. Some programs are bitmap image manipulation programs (e.g. Microsoft Paint, Adobe Photoshop, Corel Photo-Paint and Jasc Paint Shop Pro), while others are vector-based drawing applications (e.g. Adobe Illustrator, CorelDRAW and Macromedia Freehand).

Some applications (e.g. Adobe Photoshop) are capable of handling both bitmaps and vector images. Although Photoshop will allow you to draw and export vector shapes, it is primarily a bitmap package and cannot open all vector-based images, e.g. **wmf** files.

Photoshop is a powerful, industry-standard application that can be used to create, edit and manipulate images to a professional standard. It has a wide range of image-editing, drawing and text tools that enable you to produce sophisticated graphics for the World Wide Web and for printing. ImageReady, a program included with Photoshop, has a powerful set of web tools for optimising and previewing images, creating rollovers and animations.

Student review 1.2 – Identify software applications

Assessment objective 2a

1. *List the names of three bitmap image manipulation programs.*
2. *List the names of three vector-based drawing applications.*
3. *Name one image file format that cannot be opened in Adobe Photoshop.*

SECTION 2 • Manipulate graphics

ASSESSMENT OBJECTIVES

The following assessment objective will be covered in this section:

2a Open a bitmap image manipulation software application

2b Use the functions of the application interface to open, edit, retouch and repair the graphic

The following knowledge, skills and understanding criteria corresponding to assessment objectives 2a and 2b will also be covered:

- *Properties and capabilities of image manipulation software applications (Photoshop)*
- *Functions of Photoshop*
- *Editing tools and features*
- *Methods of retouching and repairing graphics*
- *Selection tools*
- *Layers*
- *Text*

STARTING PHOTOSHOP

Photoshop settings

Unlike most other computer programs, Photoshop retains the settings used the last time the program was running (e.g. background colour, tolerance, mode and options). You may restore the default settings before you begin a session if you wish, so that previous settings do not affect your image editing.

▸▸ HOW TO ... Restore the Photoshop settings (optional)

The default settings can be restored whilst starting Photoshop through the Start menu, not by using a desktop or taskbar shortcut.

1 Start → All Programs → click on **Adobe Photoshop CS** then immediately hold down the **Ctrl**, **Alt** and **Shift** keys at the same time as the program is loading.

2 A dialogue box will be displayed (refer to Figure 1.5) → **Yes**.

3 Another dialogue box may be displayed (refer to Figure 1.6) → **No**.

4 Photoshop will open with all windows and options restored to the default settings.

5 The **Welcome Screen** dialogue box may display, click **Close**.

Figure 1.4 Starting Photoshop

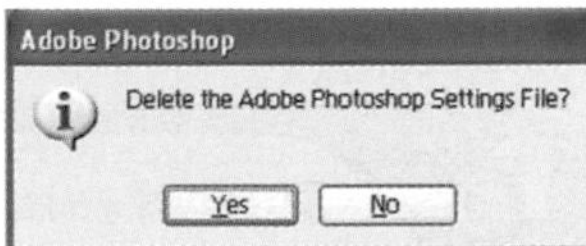

Figure 1.5 Resetting Photoshop settings

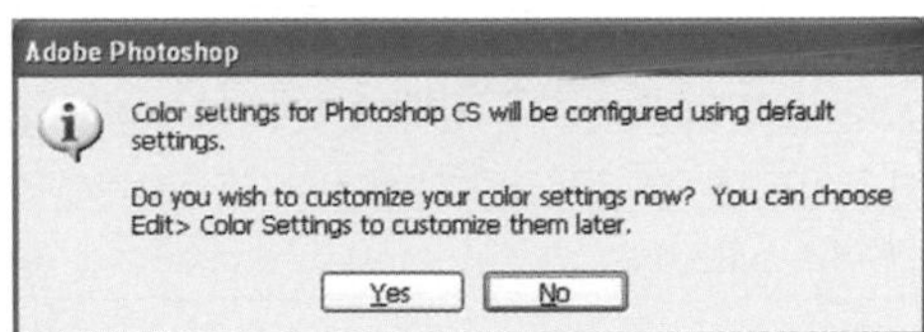

Figure 1.6 Restoring default colour settings

UNDERSTANDING THE PHOTOSHOP SCREEN

Figure 1.7 The Photoshop screen

PART OF WINDOW	DESCRIPTION
Program title bar	Displays the name of the program.
Menu bar	A list of options.
Options bar	Displays options that relate to the tool that is currently selected from the Toolbox. The options displayed will change when the tool is changed.
Toggle File Browser	An icon which, when clicked, displays the File Browser. The File Browser lets you view, sort and process images; create new folders; rename, move and delete files; and rotate images. It also allows you to view individual file information and data imported from your digital camera.
Palette well	An area where palettes not currently being displayed can be stored. Also referred to as the docking area.
Image title bar	Displays the title of the open image. If the image is maximised, the title appears after the program title bar: Adobe Photoshop - [view.jpg @ 34.3% (RGB/8)]
Toolbox	Displays a variety of image manipulation tools. A tool tip is displayed when the pointer is hovered over a tool. Some tools have a **black triangle** in the bottom right corner – this indicates the presence of related hidden tools.
Active image area	Displays open images.
Status bar	Displays information about an open image, e.g. the file size, the zoom percentage.
Navigator palette	A window that displays a miniature of the current image and allows you to zoom in and out of the image.
Color palette	A window that allows you to select colours and patterns.
History palette	A window that displays each action performed and allows you to undo actions.
Layers palette	A window that displays the individual layers (items) in an image or artwork. A layer works as in a collage – one effect is built upon another to create a final image.

Table 1.3 Parts of the Photoshop window

▶▶ HOW TO ... Open an image in Photoshop

- **File** menu → **Open** → the **Open** dialogue box is displayed → click the drop-down arrow to the right of **Look in** and double-click to open the folder containing the images → select the required image → click **Open**.

▶▶ HOW TO ... View images on screen

1 To see the entire image: **View** menu → **Fit on Screen**.

2 To display an image at 100%: **View** menu → **Actual Pixels**.

3 To see the print size: **View** menu → **Print Size**.

TIP!

*In the **Files of type** box, ensure **All Formats** is selected.*

TIP!

*Click on **Toggle File Browser** for an alternative method of opening images.*

To zoom in **Ctrl** and +
To zoom out **Ctrl** and –

THE PHOTOSHOP TOOLBOX

The Photoshop Toolbox, also referred to as the Tools window, has a variety of tools that allow you to manipulate artwork and images (e.g. select areas in an image, move items) and has a range of painting and editing tools (e.g. Clone Stamp, Blur).

A tooltip is displayed when you hover the mouse pointer over a tool. Not all the tools are visible at any one time; some are hidden from view. A tool that has a tiny black triangle at the bottom right corner has other related hidden tools. To display the hidden tools, right-click within the tool then left-click to select another tool.

Figure 1.8 shows the tools available in the Photoshop Toolbox.

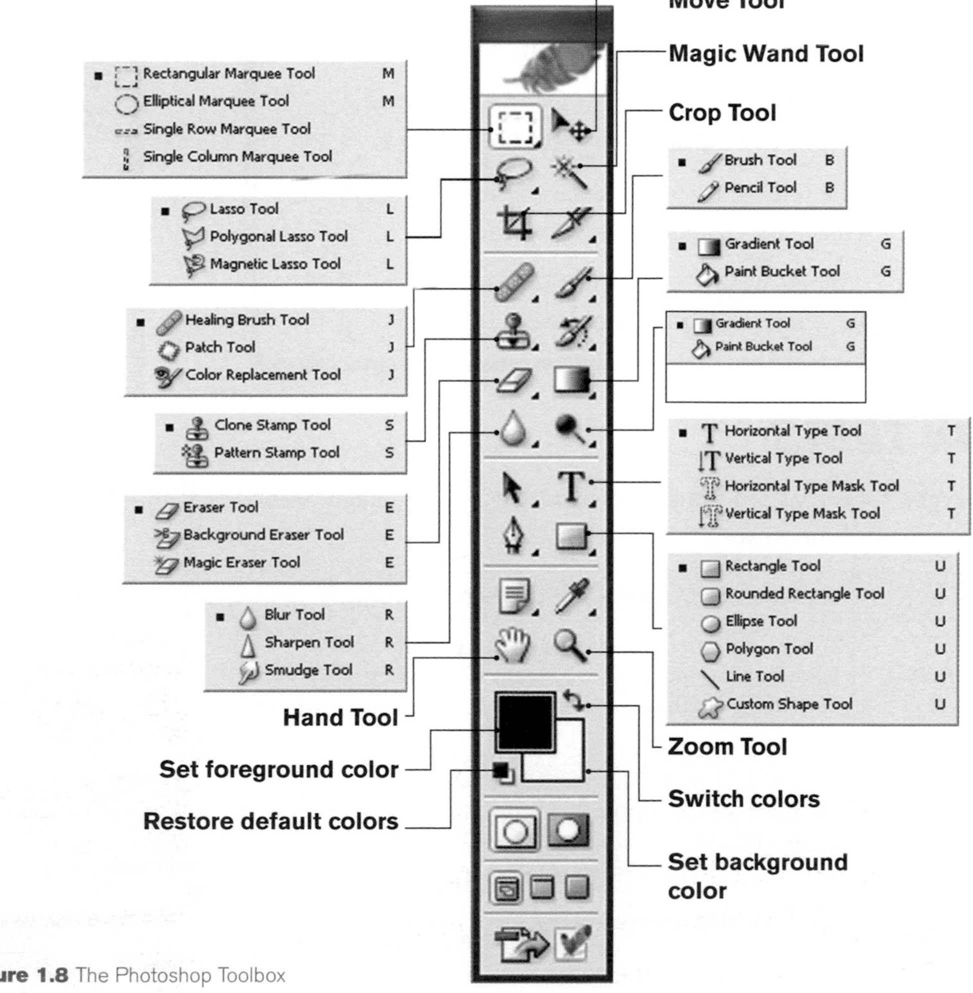

Figure 1.8 The Photoshop Toolbox

PRACTICAL TASK 1.4 **Open and view image in Photoshop, become familiar with the program interface**

Assessment objectives 2a, 2b

1 Launch Photoshop, resetting the default settings.
2 From within Photoshop, open one of your renamed digital images, from the folder containing your copied images.
3 View your image's print size, actual pixels, then fit it on screen. Zoom in to different parts of the image, then fit the image on screen.
4 Referring to your computer screen and Table 1.3 'Parts of the Photoshop window' on page 14, identify all the parts of the Photoshop window listed in the table.
5 Write down the names of three tools from the Toolbox that do not have any hidden tools.
6 Write down the names of five tools that do have hidden tools.
7 Practise displaying the hidden tools and selecting some of these tools so that they replace the default tools in the Toolbox.
8 Write down three options available with the **Horizontal Type Tool** that are not available when the **Brush Tool** is selected.

To prepare you for an OCR assessment, you should manipulate your own digital photographs. However, if you do not yet have access to images and wish to practise working with images to become familiar with the editing tools and features, you could use copies of the sample images available within the Photoshop program files folder: File menu → **Open** → **My Computer** → **Local Disk (C:)** → **Program Files** → **Adobe** → **Adobe Photoshop CS** → **Samples.**
Alternatively, you could use the sample images available in the My Pictures folder on your computer.

SELECTION TOOLS

Photoshop has several tools that can be used to select parts of an image. Some of these selection tools and their uses are shown in Table 1.4:

ICON	TOOL	DESCRIPTION AND HOW TO USE THE TOOL	EXAMPLE
	Rectangular Marquee Tool	Used to make square or rectangular shaped selections. Click and drag the mouse diagonally from the top left to the bottom right of the area to be selected.	
	Elliptical Marquee Tool	Used to make oval or circular shaped selections. Click and drag the mouse diagonally from the top left to the bottom right of the area to be selected.	
	Magic Wand Tool	Used to select similarly coloured pixels. Click anywhere in the area containing the pixels (colours) to be selected. In the example on the right, all the black pixels have been selected with one click.	
	Lasso Tool	Used to draw irregular shaped areas within an image to create a selection. Hold down the left mouse button and drag to draw out a freehand shape. To draw a straight border around a selection, hold down the Alt key and click at the beginning and end points.	

ICON	TOOL	DESCRIPTION AND HOW TO USE THE TOOL	EXAMPLE
	Polygonal Lasso Tool	Also used to draw irregular shaped areas within an image to create a selection. It is faster to use and requires less mouse dexterity than the Lasso Tool. Click the mouse to create points around the object. A line is then drawn between consecutive points.	
	Magnetic Lasso Tool	This is the smartest of the lasso tools. It is used to trace around irregular shaped areas and is useful for selecting objects with complex edges set against high contrast backgrounds. Click the mouse at intervals around the object. The tool attaches itself to any defined edges of the shape, creating anchor points. To close the selection, click back on the first anchor point.	

Table 1.4 Photoshop selection tools

Working with selections

Use the following options when using any of the selection tools in Table 1.4:

- To select more than one part of an image, or to add to a selected area: click the **Add to selection** button on the Options bar (refer to Figure 1.9), then use a selection tool to make new selections or to add to your selected area.
- To deselect all or part of a selected area: click the **Subtract from selection** button on the Options bar (refer to Figure 1.9), then use a selection tool to remove a selection.
- To deselect all selected areas: **Select** menu → **Deselect** or **Ctrl** + D.

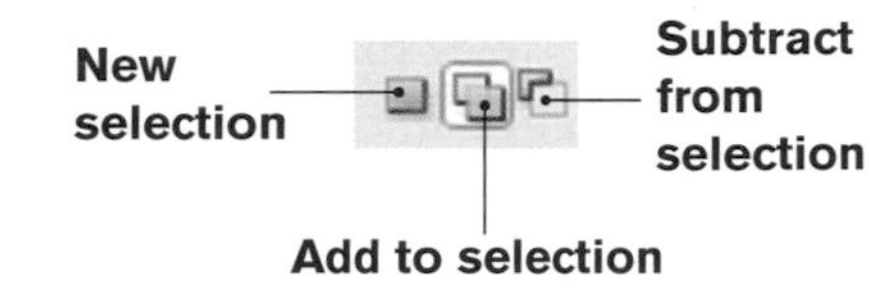

Figure 1.9 The Options bar

PRACTICAL TASK 1.5 Use selection tools

Assessment objective 2b

1. Open an image that has a clearly contrasting background.
2. Use the **Rectangular Marquee Tool** to create selections in the image.
3. Repeat this using the **Elliptical Marquee Tool**.
4. Select the **Lasso Tool**. Use it like you would use a pen to make a selection in the image.
5. Repeat this using the **Polygonal Lasso Tool**, then the **Magnetic Lasso Tool**.
6. Did you find the **Magnetic Lasso Tool** the easiest to use of the three lasso tools?
7. Deselect all marquees, and use the **Magic Wand Tool** to select pixels of the same colour within the image.
8. Close all open files.

WORKING WITH LAYERS

A layer works as a collage – one effect is laid upon another to create a final image. Using layers is very effective because you can radically change the content of one layer, without disturbing any of the others. You can work with any layer, usually one layer at a time.

Think of layers as sheets of acetate or clear plastic. When laid on top of one another, all the individual layers make up an entire image – each layer contains a part of the whole image. You can change the composition of an image by changing the order and attributes of the layers. Special features such as adjustment layers, fill layers and layer styles let you create sophisticated effects.

▶▶ HOW TO ... Select a layer

- Click on the layer name in the Layers palette. An active layer displays an icon representing a paintbrush to the left of the layer thumbnail in the Layers palette (refer to Figure 1.10). The tooltip displays 'Indicates painting on layer or layer mask'.

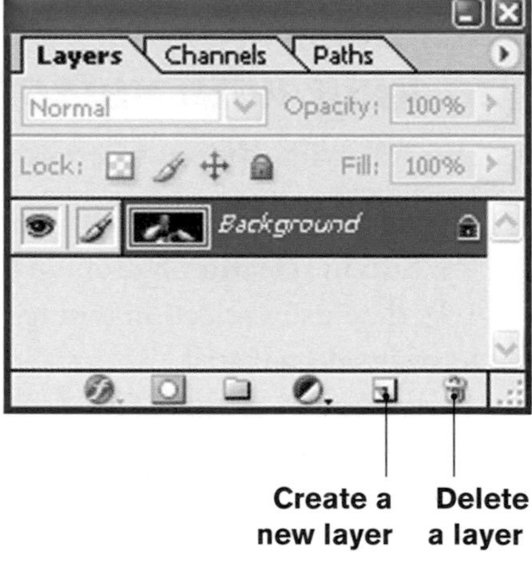

Figure 1.10 The Layers palette

▶▶ HOW TO ... Hide/display a layer

- To display a layer, ensure the **Indicates layer visibility** (an eye symbol) is displayed.
- To remove the visibility of a layer, click on the eye symbol.
- To restore the layer visibility, click in the empty box.

▶▶ HOW TO ... Insert a new layer

- **Layer** menu → **New** → **Layer** → enter a suitable name in the dialogue box that opens (optional) → **OK** *or*
- Click on the **Create a new layer** icon at the bottom of the Layers palette (refer to Figure 1.10).

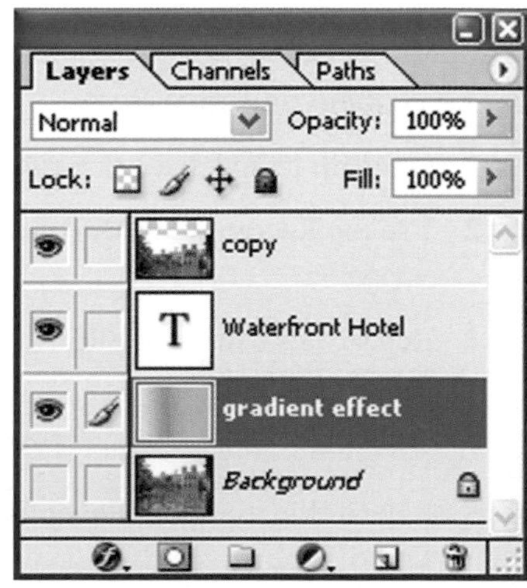

Figure 1.11 Layers palette with new layers

▶▶ HOW TO ... Make a layer active

- Click on the layer name in the Layers palette.

HOW TO ... Duplicate a layer

- Right-click on the layer → **Duplicate Layer** → **OK** *or*
- Drag the layer to the **Create a new layer** icon at the bottom of the Layers palette.

HOW TO ... Rename a layer

- Double-click on the layer name in the Layers palette → enter the new name.

HOW TO ... Re-order layers

- In the Layers palette, click and drag the layer to just below or just above the required position.

HOW TO ... Delete a layer

- Select the layer, **Layer** menu → **Delete** → **Layer** → click **Yes** in the dialogue box that opens *or*
- Drag the layer to the **Delete layer** icon at the bottom of the Layers palette.

HOW TO ... Move an item on a layer

- Select the required layer, select the Move Tool → click and drag to move the item or hold down the Ctrl key and tap the arrow (cursor) key on the keyboard.

TIP!

Use ruler guides to position items more precisely.

To display rulers: **View** *menu→* **Rulers***.*

To position a ruler guide on the image: move the pointer to the ruler area → click and drag the guide to the required position.

To move a ruler guide: select the **Move Tool***, click and drag the guide.*

PRACTICAL TASK 1.6 Work with layers

Assessment objective 2b

1 Open the image of a building that you took in Practical task 1.3.
2 Insert a new layer and hide the original layer (Background layer).
3 Duplicate the background layer then rename the copied layer.
4 Display horizontal and vertical ruler guides in the approximate centre of your image.
5 Move the image on the copied layer to align with a horizontal ruler guide.
6 Change the order of the layers so that the copied layer is the top layer.
7 Delete the blank layer created at step 2.
8 Save the image in **psd** format.

To save in Photoshop format, refer to page 45.

IMAGE SIZE AND RESOLUTION

When you first open an image in Photoshop, you should check the original image size and resolution. It is also a good idea to retain the original image and work on a copy.

TIP!

To copy an original image: **Image → Duplicate.**

To display more than one image on screen: **Window → Arrange → Tile.**

▸▸ HOW TO ... Check an image size and/or resolution

- **Image** menu → **Image Size** (refer to Figure 1.12).

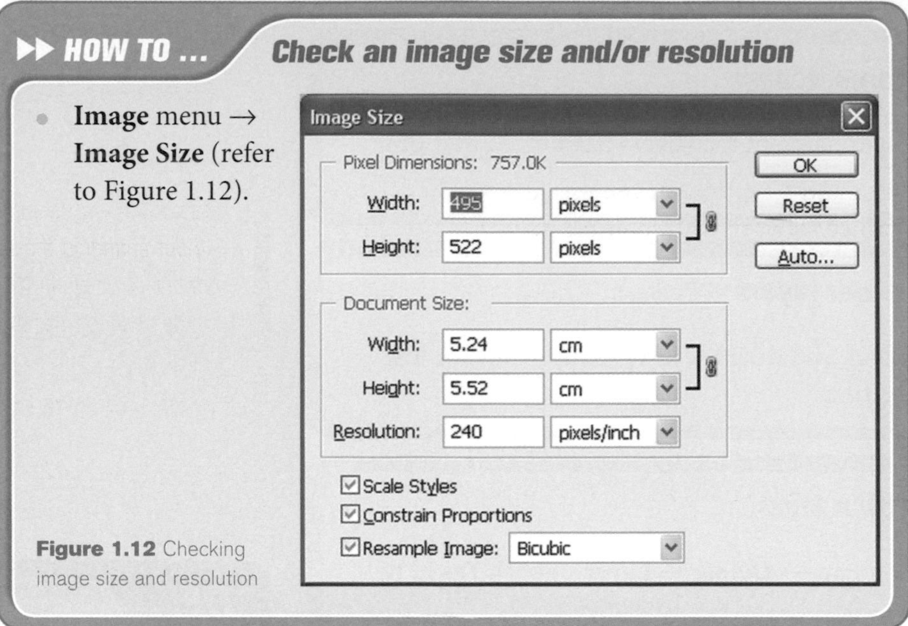

Figure 1.12 Checking image size and resolution

▸▸ HOW TO ... Amend the image size

- In the **Image Size** dialogue box, ensure that there is a tick for **Constrain Proportions** → below **Document Size**, click the drop-down arrow and select the required unit of measurement (e.g. **cm** or **pixels**) → enter either the new width or height (Photoshop will automatically adjust the other dimension proportionally) → **OK**.

Key terms

Resampling refers to changing the pixel dimensions of an image. When you reduce the image resolution (down sample), information is deleted from the image. When you increase the resolution (resample up), you increase the number of pixels and new pixels are added.

What is resolution?

The resolution of an image is determined by the number of pixels per centimetre or pixels per inch (ppi) in the image. The number of pixels along the height and width of an image are called the pixel dimensions of the image. An image with a high resolution contains more, and therefore smaller, pixels than an image of the same size with a lower resolution. Higher-resolution images can reproduce more detail and more subtle colour changes than lower-resolution images because the pixels are packed more tightly (the density of the pixels is greater). High-quality images often look good in any print size.

▶▶ HOW TO ... Amend the resolution of an image

- **Image menu** → **Image Size** → below **Document Size**, delete the existing value for **Resolution** → enter the new resolution → **OK**.

TIP!

To change only the resolution and adjust the total number of pixels in the image proportionately, select **Resample Image** in the **Image Size** dialogue box.

To amend the print dimensions and resolution without changing the total number of pixels in the image, deselect **Resample Image**.

CANVAS SIZE

When you open an image in Photoshop, the image size and the canvas size are the same. You can alter the canvas size to add work space around an image. For example, you might want to add a caption for the image or insert other images on your canvas to produce artwork with multiple items on the canvas.

▶▶ HOW TO ... Amend the canvas size

1 **Image** menu → **Canvas Size**.

2 Either enter the new dimensions in the **Width** and **Height** boxes or select **Relative** and enter the amount by which you want to increase or decrease the size of the canvas.

3 To position the current image in the canvas, click a square in the **Anchor** section (refer to Figure 1.13).

4 To select a canvas colour, click in the colour square to the right of **Canvas extension color** → the **Color Picker** dialogue box is displayed → select a colour or use the **Eyedropper Tool**  to select a colour from the image → **OK**.

5 Click **OK** to close the **Canvas Size** dialogue box.

The Eyedropper Tool is used to select a colour from within the image.

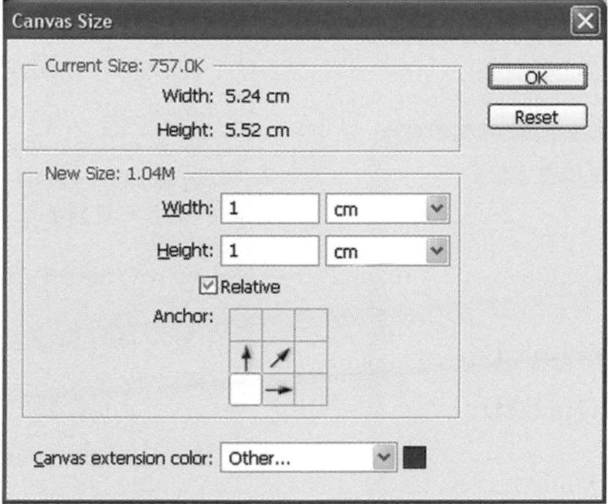

Figure 1.13 Amending the canvas size

Figure 1.14 Canvas added to the top and right of the image; canvas colour selected from within image

MISTAKES

It is considered good practice to work on a copy of an image instead of the original. This allows you to compare your amended image with the original whilst editing. It also allows you to go back to the original and start again with a new copy. You may also want to undo actions because you don't like the effect or because you have made mistakes. The commands listed in Table 1.5 will help you to rectify errors or undo actions. You can also use the History palette to undo actions.

ACTION	COMMAND
To revert to the last saved version	**File** menu → **Revert** *or* press **F12**
To undo the last action	**Edit** menu → **Undo** *or* **Ctrl + Z**
To undo one step at a time	**Ctrl, Alt + Z**
To redo the last action	**Edit** menu→ **Redo** *or* **Ctrl + Y**

Table 1.5 Commands to undo actions

The History palette

Each time you edit an image, a record of the edit is added to the History palette (refer to Figure 1.15) . You can then delete any edit and those that were applied after it, regardless of when you made that change. (This has an advantage over some other 'undo' commands which undo each previous action in sequence, one at a time.) For example, if you select, crop, clone stamp, use the healing brush, change the resolution, each of these edits is listed in the History palette. If you delete the clone stamp edit, all the other edits performed after it will also be deleted.

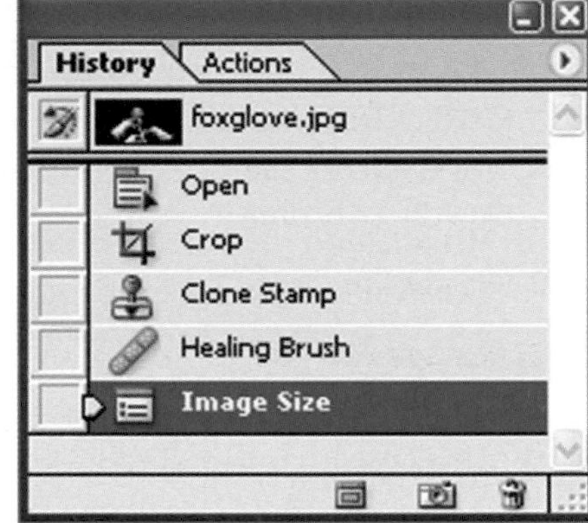

Figure 1.15 The History palette

You can also select any of the edits and the image will revert to how it looked when that edit was first applied and you can then continue to work from that stage.

PRACTICAL TASK 1.7 Amend image size, resolution and canvas size

Assessment objective 2b

1 Open the image of a landscape that you took in Practical task 1.3.

2 Resize the image, maintaining proportion, to half its original size. Resample the image and reduce the resolution.

3 Add a canvas, of any appropriate measurement, to the top and right of the image, using a canvas colour appropriate for your image.

4 Save this amended image in a **jpg** format in a medium file size, using a different filename to the original.

Refer to pages 45 and 47 for 'How to save in jpg format'.

CROPPING IMAGES

Cropping is the process of removing portions of an image, e.g. to create focus.

▶▶ HOW TO ... Crop an image

1 Select the **Crop Tool** .
2 To crop an image without resampling, ensure that all the text boxes in the Options bar are empty. To resample during cropping, enter a height, width and/or resolution in the Options bar.
3 Click and drag the mouse diagonally (from top left to bottom right) to draw a marquee around the area to be retained.
4 Press the **Enter** key or click on **Commit** on the Options bar.

TIP!

To amend the marquee: click and drag a square handle.

To move the marquee: position the mouse within the marquee and drag.

To rotate the marquee: position the mouse outside the marquee and drag.

▶▶ HOW TO ... Straighten an image while cropping

1 Increase the size of the image window so that you have some space around the photo. (Maximise the image window.)
2 Select the **Crop Tool** .
3 Ensure that the **Width**, **Height** and **Resolution** boxes in the Options bar are blank.
4 To straighten or rotate the image, drag the cropping rectangle over the entire photo.
5 Move the pointer outside the cropping rectangle to get the rotate arrow and drag – the cropping rectangle rotates, but the image remains stationary until you crop it.
6 Press **Enter** or click on **Commit** .

TIP!

Select the ***Move Tool***

when you have finished using the other tools to avoid making any accidental changes or selections to an image. Think of the ***Move Tool*** *as the safety tool.*

TRANSFORMING IMAGES

To transform an item means to change the form of the item, i.e. to change its size or shape. The following transformations can be applied to an image or a shape on a layer: **scale**, **rotate**, **skew**, **distort**, apply **perspective**. Text can be scaled, rotated or skewed.

Key terms

Scale *to enlarge or reduce an item vertically, horizontally or in both directions*
Rotate *to change the direction of an item*
Skew *to slant an item vertically or horizontally*
Distort *to stretch an item in all directions*
Perspective *to change the shape of an item*

▶▶ HOW TO ... Apply transformations to an item on a layer

1 Select the layer containing the item you want to transform.

2 **Edit** menu → **Transform** (or **Transform Path** if the layer contains a shape) → select the required option: **Scale** *or* **Rotate** *or* **Skew** *or* **Distort** *or* **Perspective**.

3 A frame with handles called a **bounding box** is displayed around the item on the layer.

To resize (scale):

- ❑ Drag a handle on the bounding box (refer to Figure 1.16).
- ❑ To scale proportionally, click the **Maintain aspect ratio** symbol on the Options bar or press the **Shift** key and drag a corner handle.

Figure 1.16 Resizing an image

To rotate:

- ❑ Move the pointer outside the bounding box and drag.
- ❑ To constrain the rotation to 15-degree increments, press the **Shift** key as you drag.

To skew:

- ❑ Drag a side handle to slant the bounding box.

To distort:

- ❑ Drag a corner handle to stretch the bounding box.

To apply perspective:

- ❑ Drag a corner handle to apply perspective to the bounding box.

4 Press the **Enter** key to confirm the transformation or click on the **Move Tool** → a dialogue box is displayed prompting you to confirm the transformation → select **Apply**.

TIP!

*You can switch to a different type of transformation by selecting another option from the **Edit → Transform** menu, e.g. choose **Scale**, drag a handle to scale, then choose **Distort**, drag a handle to distort and press **Enter** to apply both transformations.*

RETOUCHING IMAGES

One of the most common uses of Photoshop is to retouch images. You can make many changes to images, e.g. remove scratches on old photographs, remove wrinkles and blemishes, change shades of colour, change tonality and where shadows fall in an image.

Images can be retouched using a number of different methods, for example:

- using the options from the menus (e.g. Hue/saturation)
- by adding adjustment layers (e.g. the Color Balance adjustment layer)
- by using the retouching tools from the Toolbox (e.g. the smudge, focus or toning tools)
- by using a combination of different options.

When manipulating images an important skill to develop is the ability to manipulate images without leaving any evidence of the manipulation. It is a good idea to work on a copy of an image instead of the original.

To retouch images using the toolbox tools, refer to 'Methods of retouching and repairing graphics' on page 35. Retouching images using the menus is covered in this section.

Refer to 'Applying colour and tonal adjustments using adjustment layers' on page 28.

Hue and saturation

The **Hue/Saturation** command lets you adjust the hue, saturation and brightness of a specific colour component or all the colours in an image/selection. These adjustments can be made to make the image/selection look sharper, to make part of an image stand out more or to change an image/selection to appear greyscale. You can adjust the hue/saturation on the image itself, on a layer or by using an adjustment layer.

Key terms

Hue is the colour reflected by or transmitted through an object. It is the actual colour apparent to the human eye. When adjustments are made to the hue, all the pixels in the image are shifted around the colour wheel to a different location.

Saturation is the strength or purity of the colour. Saturation represents the amount of grey in proportion to the hue. When adjustments are made to the saturation, the amount of grey in a colour is altered.

HOW TO ... Adjust the hue and saturation

1. To adjust part of an image, select the area using a marquee tool *or* to apply the adjustment to the entire image or item on a layer, select the image or layer.
2. To adjust the original image: **Image** menu → **Adjustments** → **Hue/Saturation** *or* to modify the image using an adjustment layer: **Layer** menu → **New Adjustment Layer** → **Hue/Saturation**.
3. A **Hue/Saturation** dialogue box is displayed.
4. To adjust all the colours, ensure **Master** is displayed to the right of **Edit** in the dialogue box and drag each of the sliders in turn until the colours appear as you want.
5. To adjust only a particular colour in the image, click the drop-down arrow to the right of **Edit** and select one of the preset colours (red, green or blue), then drag each of the sliders in turn.
6. Click **OK** to confirm the adjustments.

TIP!

The two colour bars in the **Hue/Saturation** dialogue box represent the colours in their order on the colour wheel. The upper colour bar shows the colour before the adjustment; the lower bar shows how the adjustment affects all of the hues.

Brightness and contrast

This option allows you to make simple adjustments to the tonal range of an image. It allows you to make the same adjustment to every pixel in the image. If an image appears too dark or washed out, you probably need to adjust the brightness and contrast.

▶▶ HOW TO ... Adjust the brightness and contrast

1 Refer to step 1 in 'How to adjust the hue and saturation'.

2 To adjust the original image: **Image** menu → **Adjustments** → **Brightness/Contrast** *or* to modify the image using an adjustment layer: **Layer** menu → **New Adjustment Layer** → **Brightness/ Contrast**.

3 A **Brightness/Contrast** dialogue box is displayed.

4 Drag the **Brightness** and/or **Contrast** sliders → **OK**.

PRACTICAL TASK 1.8 Crop, transform, adjust hue/ saturation and brightness/contrast

Assessment objectives 2b, 2c

Using a copy of one or more of your digital photographs, make the following changes:

1 Crop an image ensuring you straighten while cropping.

2 Reduce the image size by scaling proportionately, then rotate the scaled image.

3 Apply the following transformations consecutively: skew, distort and apply perspective.

4 Duplicate the layer containing the image and amend the hue and saturation on the duplicated layer.

5 Insert an adjustment layer as the top layer to alter the brightness and contrast of all the layers beneath the adjustment layer.

6 Save the amended image in **tiff** format preserving all the layers.

Refer to page 46 for 'How to save in tiff format'.

WORKING WITH COLOUR

Colours are defined using **colour models**. These determine how colours look on-screen and when printed. Photoshop bases its colour modes on the colour models that are useful for images used in publishing. You can work with a variety of colour modes, e.g. indexed colour, lab colour, multichannel as well as the two most common colour models, CMYK (Figure 1.17) and RGB (Figure 1.18).

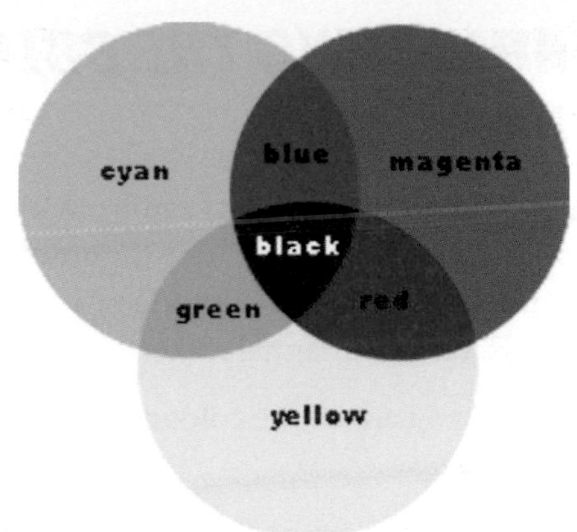

Figure 1.17 The CMYK colour model

Colours on a computer screen are displayed using combinations of **r**ed, **g**reen and **b**lue values (the **RGB colour model**), while colours on a printout are created using a combination of four ink colours – **c**yan, **m**agenta, **y**ellow and blac**k** (the **CMYK colour model**). In CMYK mode, each pixel is assigned a percentage value for each of the process colour inks.

RGB images use a combination of red, green and blue colours, or channels, to reproduce colours on-screen. An intensity value is assigned to each pixel, ranging from 0 to 255 for each of the red, green and blue components in an image. A blue value of 255 with a zero value for red and green produces a bright blue colour. Similarly, a red value of 255 with zero values for blue and green produces a bright red colour. Equal values of 85 for all three components produces a grey shade, whereas values of 255 for the three colours produces white, and zero values for all three colours produces black. Other colours are created when the colours are mixed, e.g. mixing red and green makes yellow, mixing blue and green makes cyan.

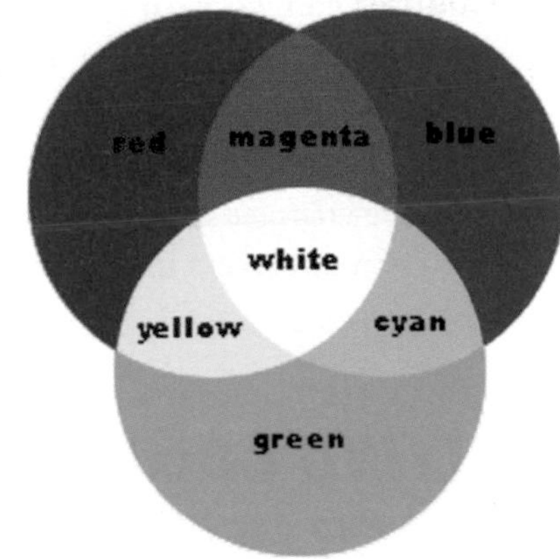

Figure 1.18 The RGB colour model

In Photoshop, you are advised to work in RGB colour mode as this colour model offers more options. If you need to print your image, after you have completed manipulating it, you can retain the RGB colour or convert it to CMYK colour. When an image is converted to CMYK, any colours from the RGB palette that are not available in the CMYK palette will be converted into their nearest printable equivalents.

HOW TO ... Convert the image mode

- **Image** menu → **Mode** → select an option (e.g. **RGB color** or **Grayscale**).

TIP!

*A **gif** image may open in **Indexed Color** mode in Photoshop. To manipulate it, convert it to **RGB color**.*

Student review 1.3 – Colour models

Assessment objective 2b

1 What do RGB and CMYK stand for?
2 What colour model are you advised to work in whilst editing your images in Photoshop?
3 What colour is produced when the red, green and blue values are set to 255 in the RGB colour model?
4 What values should be set for the red, green and blue components to achieve a shade of grey in the RGB colour model?
5 In the RGB colour model, what colour is produced when red and green are mixed?

ADJUSTING THE COLOUR AND TONE IN IMAGES

A variety of adjustments can be made to an image to enhance, repair and correct the colour and tone (lightness, darkness and contrast) in the image. Photoshop offers a multitude of adjustment options, e.g. colour balance, levels, curves, channel mixer.

Before you adjust the colour and/or tone, note the following tips for adjusting images:

- When you adjust the colour or tone, some image information is discarded. To preserve the image as much as possible, convert the image mode to 16-bit (**Image** → **Mode** → **16bits/Channel**).
- Ensure that you work on a copy of your image in case you need to return to the original (**Image** menu → **Duplicate**).
- Retouch and repair the image first (e.g. remove scratches, blemishes) before making colour adjustments.
- To observe changes as you make them use the Histogram palette.
- Use adjustment layers instead of applying an adjustment directly to the image layer.

TIP!

To use an adjustment layer: ***Layer*** *menu →* ***New Adjustment Layer*** *→ select an option.*

To apply a change to the image or layer directly: ***Image*** *menu →* ***Adjustments*** *→ select an option.*

Refer to 'Histogram palette' on page 32.

APPLYING COLOUR AND TONAL ADJUSTMENTS USING ADJUSTMENT LAYERS

Adjustments can be made directly on an image or layer, or by using adjustment layers. The advantage of using adjustment layers is that you can experiment with colour and tonal adjustments to an image without permanently modifying the pixels in the image. The colour and tonal changes reside within the adjustment layer, which acts as a veil through which the underlying image layers appear. An adjustment layer affects all the layers below it. This means that you can change multiple layers by making a single adjustment, rather than making the adjustment to each layer separately. If you change your mind you can simply delete the adjustment layer. You can insert as many adjustment layers as you wish. Adjustment layers can be displayed or not by selecting the **Indicates layer visibility** icon in the Layers palette.

TIP!

To make adjustments to multiple layers, select the top layer in the Layers palette so that the adjustment layer resides above all existing layers.

Adjusting the levels

The **Levels Adjustment Layer** allows you correct the tonal range and colour balance of an image by adjusting intensity levels of the image's shadows, midtones and highlights. The **Levels** histogram displays a visual guide of the image's key tones.

HOW TO ... Use the Levels command

1 **Layer** menu → **New Adjustment Layer** → **Levels** → **OK**.

2 A **Levels** dialogue box is displayed → click the drop-down arrow to the right of **Channel** to adjust tones for a specific colour channel or select **RGB**.

3 To adjust the shadows and highlights, drag the black and/or white **Input Levels** sliders → **OK**

You can also adjust the levels without using an adjustment layer: **Image** menu → **Adjustments** → **Levels.**

Adjusting the curves

The **Curves Adjustment Layer** lets you adjust the entire tonal range of an image similarly to the Levels command. In addition to allowing you to change the shadows, midtones and highlights, this command also allows you to adjust any point along a 0–255 scale. This enables you to make precise adjustments to individual colour channels in an image. It takes a while to master this – but you can achieve quite dramatic results by experimenting!

You can also adjust the curves without using an adjustment layer: **Image** menu → **Adjustments** → **Curves.**

HOW TO ... Use the Curves command

1 **Layer** menu → **New Adjustment Layer** → **Curves** → **OK**.

2 A **Curves** dialogue box is displayed → click the drop-down arrow to the right of **Channel** to adjust the colour balance for a specific colour channel or select **RGB** (refer to Figure 1.19).

3 To add a point on the curve click on the curve, or to adjust the shape of the curve, click and drag a point on the curve → **OK**.

TIP!

Changing the shape of the curve in the **Curves** dialogue box alters the tonality and colour of an image. Bowing the curve upward lightens an image, bowing the curve downward darkens it.

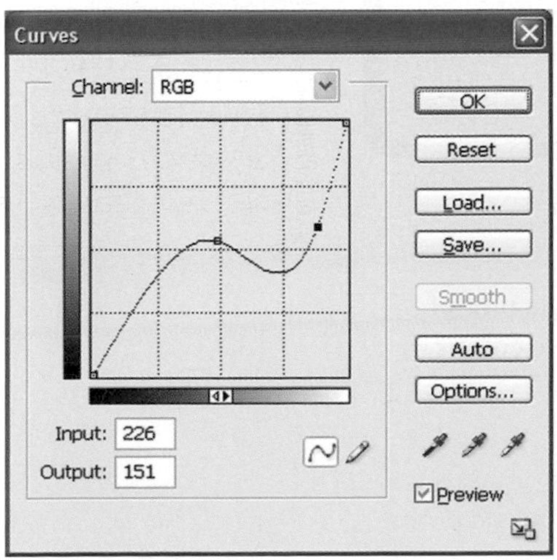

Figure 1.19 The Curves dialogue box

Figure 1.20 Image adjusted using the Curves command

Adjusting the colour balance

The **Color Balance** command changes the overall mixture of colours in an image allowing you to apply generalised colour correction.

▶▶ HOW TO ... Adjust the colour balance

1 **Layer** menu → **New Adjustment Layer** → **Color Balance** → **OK**.

2 A **Color Balance** dialogue box is displayed.

3 To select the tonal range on which you want to focus the changes, select the button for **Shadows**, **Midtones** or **Highlights** (refer to Figure 1.21).

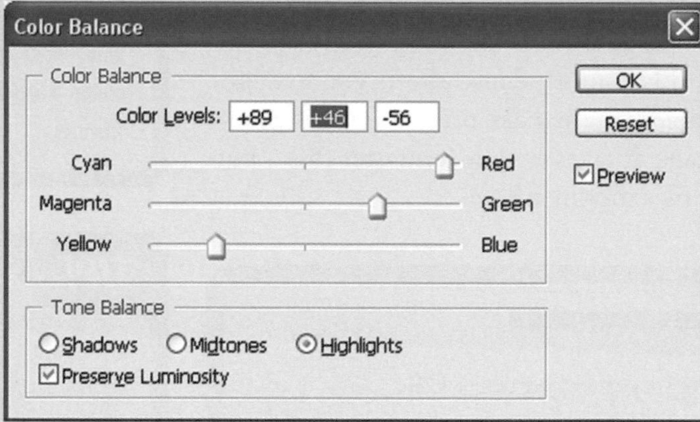

Figure 1.21 The Color Balance dialogue box

4 To maintain the tonal balance in the image, select **Preserve Luminosity**.

5 Drag a slider toward a colour you want to increase in the image; drag a slider away from a colour you want to decrease.

6 If required, select the button to adjust another tonal range, e.g. if you have already adjusted the Shadows, you could adjust the Highlights → **OK**.

You can also adjust the colour balance without using an adjustment layer: ***Image*** *menu →* ***Adjustments*** *→* ***Color Balance.***

The Channel Mixer

The **Channel Mixer** allows you to modify a colour channel using a mix of the current colour channels thereby allowing you to make creative colour adjustments.

▶▶ HOW TO … Use the Channel Mixer

1 **Layer** menu → **New Adjustment Layer** → **Channel Mixer** → **OK**.

2 A **Channel Mixer** dialogue box is displayed → click the drop-down arrow to the right of **Output Channel** and select the colour that you wish to adjust from the list (refer to Figure 1.22).

Figure 1.22 Modifying colour channels

3 Below **Source Channels**, drag any slider to the right or left to increase or decrease a colour.

4 Drag the slider for the **Constant** option. This option adjusts the greyscale value of the output channel: negative values add more black; positive values add more white.

5 To change the image to greyscale, select **Monochrome**, then adjust the **Source Channels** and **Constant** value → **OK**.

You can also adjust the colour channels without using an adjustment layer: ***Image*** *menu →* ***Adjustments*** *→* ***Channel Mixer.***

Student review 1.4 – Amending image colours

Assessment objective 2b

1 *What is the advantage of using adjustment layers?*
2 *True or false: an adjustment layer allows you to make changes to multiple layers beneath it.*
3 *Name five types of adjustment layers.*
4 *Which adjustment layer should be selected if you want to apply generalised colour correction?*
5 *Which adjustment layer allows you to change the image's shadows, midtones and highlights?*
6 *Which adjustment layer allows you to make precise adjustments to individual colour channels in an image?*
7 *Which adjustment layer would you use to make creative colour adjustments?*

Histogram palette

The Histogram palette offers many options for viewing tonal and colour information about an image.

▶▶ HOW TO ... Display the Histogram palette

1 **Window** menu → **Histogram** *or* click the Histogram tab in the Navigator palette.

2 The Histogram palette opens in Compact View with no controls or statistics.

3 To display detail about the colour information in an image click the arrow (refer to Figure 1.23) → a menu is displayed → select **Expanded View** or **All Channels View**.

4 Click the drop-down arrow to the right of **Channel** and select an individual colour channel to display a histogram of the image's individual channels.

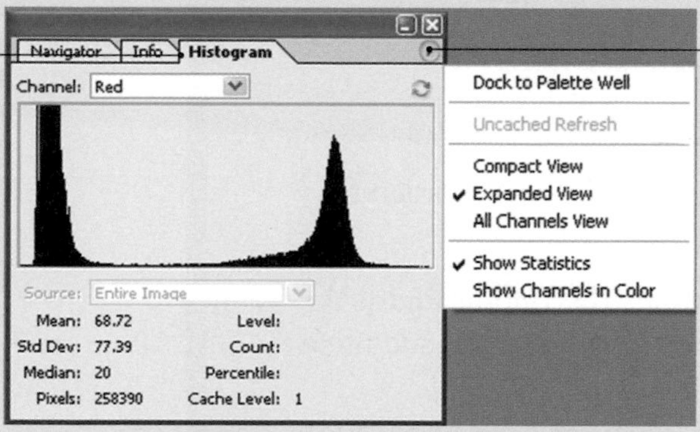

Figure 1.23 Using the Histogram

TIP!

When applying image adjustments, the Histogram palette will display a preview of how the adjustment will affect the histogram.

Shadow/highlight correction

This adjustment is useful for correcting photographs with silhouetted images due to strong backlighting or for correcting items that have been slightly washed out because they were too close to the camera flash. It is also useful for brightening up areas of shadow in an image. The **Shadow/Highlight** option lightens or darkens parts of an image based on the surrounding pixels enabling separate controls of the shadows and the highlights.

▶▶ HOW TO ... Correct shadows and highlights

1 To work on a specific area in an image, select the area using a marquee tool or apply the adjustment to the entire image or item on a layer.

2 **Image** menu → **Adjustments** → **Shadow/Highlight**.

Continued ...

3 A **Shadow/Highlight** dialogue box is displayed.

4 To adjust the amount of lighting, drag the slider for **Shadows** and/or **Highlights**.

5 For finer control, select **Show More Options** to make additional shadow or highlight adjustments → **OK**.

PRACTICAL TASK 1.9 Apply colour corrections, edit and retouch images

Assessment objectives 2b, 2c

You will apply a variety of colour adjustments to onc of your digital images – this should be an image that you will submit for the 'Cove Photography Club – Booklet'. Refer to the assignment brief on page 8.

1 Open one of your images to be edited in Photoshop and display the Histogram palette.

2 Using the repair and retouching techniques you have learned and practised, repair and retouch the image that you intend to show your group. Produce screen print evidence of each editing stage.

3 Save the repaired image using a different filename.

4 Insert a new adjustment layer for levels and amend the levels for the red channel. Then adjust the channels in turn for the green and blue channels. Produce screen print evidence of adjusting each colour channel.

5 On the same image, insert a new adjustment layer for curves and adjust the RGB colour channels. Produce screen print evidence of this adjustment.

6 On the same image, insert a new adjustment layer for the colour balance. In turn, adjust the shadows, midtones and highlights. Produce screen print evidence of each adjustment.

7 On the same image, insert a new adjustment layer for the channel mixer and select the monochrome option. Adjust the colours to create an effective greyscale photograph. Produce screen print evidence of this adjustment.

8 Apply shadow/highlight correction to the image.

9 Produce a screen print of the Layers palette to show clearly each adjustment layer.

10 Save the amended image in a suitable file format that will preserve the layers.

If you prefer, you may adjust the levels, curves, colour balance and channel mixer without adding an adjustment layer – you could make these adjustments through the ***Image*** *menu (Image menu →* ***Adjustments****).*

FILTERS

Filters can be used to apply special effects, or to make modifications to an entire image or an object on a layer. Filters cannot be applied to bitmap or indexed-colour images. To apply filters to these images, you have to change the **Mode** to **RGB Color**.

To apply a single filter only, select the **Filter** menu and choose a category from the list. As filters can also be applied cumulatively, you will use the Filter Gallery. This allows you to see how each filter affects your image.

▶▶ HOW TO ... Apply filters

1. To apply a filter to an entire layer, select the layer *or* to apply a filter to an area of an image or layer, use a marquee tool to select that area.
2. **Filter** menu → **Filter Gallery** → A dialogue box is displayed and a filter from one of the categories may be applied automatically.
3. To view your image in full in the dialogue box, click the arrow at the bottom left of the dialogue box (refer to Figure 1.24) and select **Fit in View** or **Fit on Screen.**
4. Click the triangle ▷ next to a category to see thumbnails of all the filters in that category. Then click on a thumbnail to select that filter.
5. In the right-hand side of the dialogue box, set options for the filter.
6. Click the inverted triangle ▽ to hide the thumbnails for a category.
7. To apply additional filters, click the **New Effect Layer** button and repeat step 4.
8. To remove the visibility of a filter, click the eye symbol.
9. When you are satisfied with the result, click **OK.**

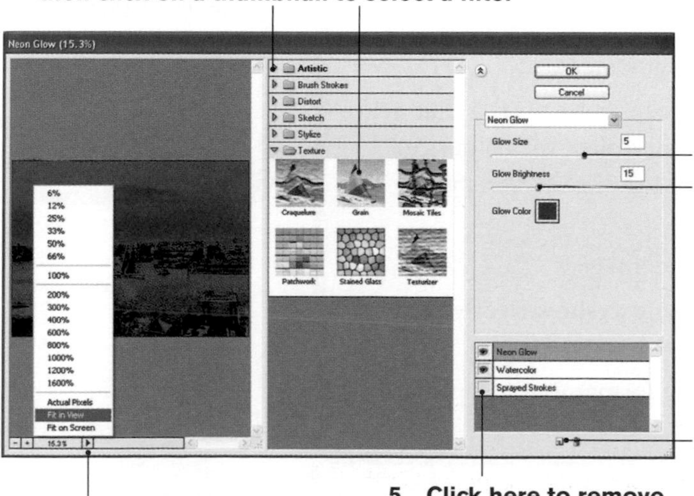

Figure 1.24 Applying filters

Blending mode

The blending mode controls how pixels in the image are affected by a particular painting or editing tool. When using some of the image manipulation tools from the Toolbox, you can set the blending mode from the Options bar by clicking on the drop-down arrow to the right of the default blending mode **Normal** (refer to Figure 1.25). A list of blending options is displayed. The blending mode selected determines how the blend colour (the blend option being applied with the painting or editing tool) mixes with the original colour in the image. You should experiment with different blending modes to see the effect.

Figure 1.25 Blending options

METHODS OF RETOUCHING AND REPAIRING GRAPHICS

As stated in the section 'Retouching images' on pages 24 and 25, images can be retouched using the menu options, by inserting adjustment layers, by using the toolbox tools or by using a combination of methods.

Note that some toolbox tools (e.g. **Blur**, **Sharpen**, **Smudge**, **Dodge**, **Burn** and **Sponge Tools**) cannot be used with bitmap or indexed-colour images. To retouch these images, you should convert the image **Mode** to **RGB Color** first. (Note that in Photoshop, **gif** images usually open in indexed-colour mode.)

Tools preset

When you are working with some painting or editing tools, e.g. cloning tools, eraser tools and the toning or focus tools, you can change how the preset brushes are displayed. You can add or append brushes from a number of different categories. Refer to the section below 'How to amend the preset tools' if you want to amend the default brush options when you are using the **Clone Stamp**, **Healing Brush**, **Smudge**, **Blur**, **Sharpen**, **Dodge**, **Burn** and **Sponge Tools**.

▸▸ HOW TO ... Amend the preset tools

1 Select the tool from the Toolbox.

2 From the Options bar, click the drop-down arrow to the right of **Brush**.

3 Click on the right arrow to display a menu and choose a display option, e.g. Small Thumbnail, Stroke Thumbnail (refer to Figure 1.26).

4 To load another category of brushes, click on a category name to select it. A dialogue box will display prompting you to **Replace** or **Append** the new category: click **OK** to replace the existing brushes or **Append** to add the new category to the existing brushes.

Continued ...

5 To return to the default brushes, choose **Reset Brushes** from the menu (Figure 1.26).

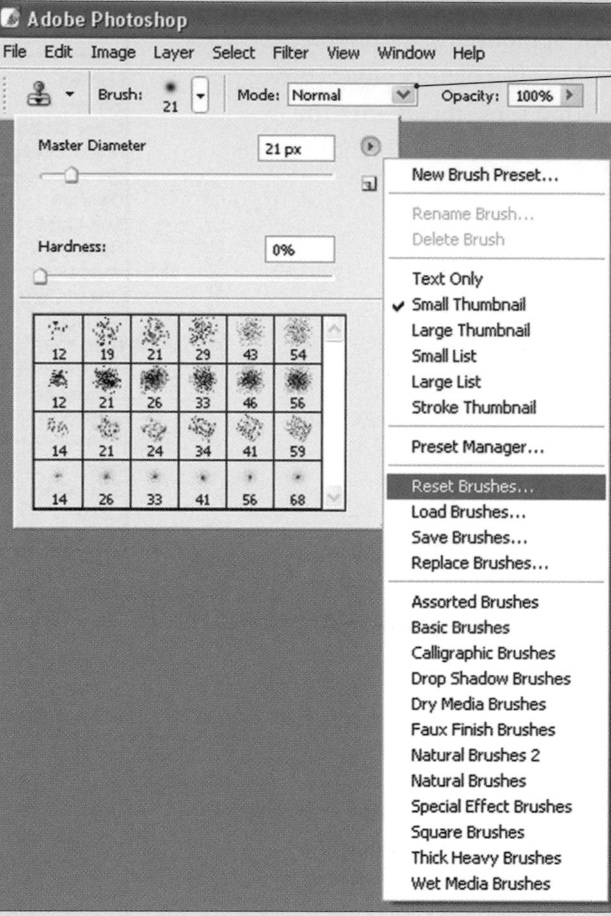

Figure 1.26 Setting the Brush options

Student review 1.5 – Image mode and blending

Assessment objective 2b

1 *Note five different blending modes that could be selected when using the image manipulation tools.*

2 *Which image mode can the* ***Blur, Sharpen, Smudge*** *and* ***Dodge Tools*** *not be used with?*

3 *Name five tools for which the default brush options can be changed.*

4 *List five views (e.g. text only) for displaying different brush styles when the* ***Blur Tool*** *is selected.*

5 *What option should be selected to reset the default brushes?*

The Clone Stamp Tool

The **Clone Stamp Tool** takes a sample of an image, which you can then apply over another part of the image or over another image. You can also clone part of one layer over another layer. You can fix blemishes and flaws in an image and even copy entire objects. Each stroke of the tool paints on more of the sample. Imperfections can be corrected, causing them to disappear into the surrounding image, e.g. a lamp post can be removed from an image to improve the view of a building.

The Healing Brush Tool

The **Healing Brush Tool** works in a similar way to the **Clone Stamp Tool** but is even better. It copies pixels from the area you select and then clones those pixels to another area whilst matching the texture, lighting, transparency and shading of the sampled pixels to the source pixels. As a result, the repaired area blends into the rest of the image very well.

▶▶ HOW TO ... Use the Clone Stamp or Healing Brush Tools

1 Select the **Clone Stamp Tool** or the **Healing Brush Tool**.

2 From the Options bar:

- ❏ select a brush size and set the required brush options
- ❏ select the blending mode (refer to 'Blending mode' on page 35)
- ❏ if using the **Clone Stamp Tool**, set the **Opacity** and **Flow**
- ❏ to sample data from all visible layers, select **Use All Layers** in the Options bar *or* to sample only from the active layer deselect this option.

3 Position the mouse over the area of the image to be copied (cloned), hold down the **Alt** key and click once. You have taken a sample.

4 Click repeatedly or drag over the area of the image you want to correct. (You may need to experiment!)

Figure 1.27 Image a) before cloning and healing b) after cloning and healing

Key terms

Opacity specifies the maximum amount of paint coverage to be applied – the higher the opacity, the greater the coverage.

Flow specifies how quickly paint is applied – a low setting produces a lighter stroke.

*When using the **Clone Stamp Tool**, select **Aligned** in the Options bar. This allows you to reuse the most current sampling point, no matter how many times you stop and resume painting.*

TIP!

Figures 1.27a and 1.27b show an example of an image before/after the intrusive parasol has been removed using the **Clone Stamp** and **Healing Brush Tools**.

The Patch Tool

The **Patch Tool** is useful for repairing large flaws in images or flaws that are difficult to correct using other tools. Correcting each flaw using the **Clone Stamp Tool** or **Healing Brush Tool** can be time-consuming. Instead the **Patch Tool** could be used to select an unflawed area of an image and then copy that over the flaws.

▶▶ HOW TO ... Correct patches and flaws using the Patch Tool

1 Select the **Patch Tool** .
2 In the Options bar ensure **Source** is selected.
3 Draw a marquee around the the area containing the flaw.
4 Select **Destination** in the Options bar.
5 Draw a border around a flawless area. The border should be approximately the same size as the source area.
6 Position the mouse within the marqee and drag the flawless area to the flawed area.
7 Deselect the marquee (**Select → Deselect** *or* **Ctrl + D**) if necessary.

Figures 1.28a and 1.28b show how the **Patch Tool** has been used to replace a patch of grass and the shaded area with paving.

Figure 1.28 Image a) before using the Patch Tool b) after using the Patch Tool

PRACTICAL TASK 1.10 Retouch and repair images

Assessment objective 2b

You will need to retouch and repair one of your digital images – this should be an image that you will submit for the 'Cove Photography Club – Booklet'. Refer to the assignment brief on page 8. You may continue to work with an image that you have already applied some editing to.

1 Apply one or more filters to the original image or to a layer containing an image. Produce evidence of the filter(s) applied.

2 Use the **Clone Stamp** and **Healing Brush Tools** to alter part of the image. Produce screen print evidence showing a 'before and after' of the repair.

3 Use the **Patch Tool** to repair part of the image. Produce screen print evidence of this repair.

4 Save the image in **jpg** format using an appropriate file size.

The Smudge Tool

The **Smudge Tool** simulates the actions of dragging a finger through wet paint. The tool picks up colour where the stroke begins and pushes it in the direction you drag.

HOW TO ... Smudge an image

1 Select the **Smudge Tool**.

2 From the Options bar:

- select a brush size and set the required brush options
- select a blending mode and strength (refer to 'Blending mode' on page 35)
- to use colour data from all visible layers, select **Use All Layers**; if this is deselected, the smudge tool uses colours from only the active layer
- select **Finger Painting** to smudge using the foreground colour at the beginning of each stroke; if this is deselected, the **Smudge Tool** uses the colour under the pointer at the beginning of each stroke.

3 Drag within the image to smudge the colour.

The focus tools

The focus tools consist of the **Blur Tool** and the **Sharpen Tool**. The **Blur Tool** softens hard edges or areas in an image to reduce detail. The **Sharpen Tool** focuses soft edges to increase clarity or focus. If you want to make a particular part of an image stand out, you could blur all the other objects in the image. You could sharpen part of an image so that it stands out from the rest in addition to or instead of blurring it.

▶▶ HOW TO ... Blur or sharpen an image

1 Select the **Blur Tool** or the **Sharpen Tool**.

2 From the Options bar:

- ❑ select a brush size and set the required brush options
- ❑ select a blending mode and strength (refer to 'Blending mode' on page 35)
- ❑ to blur or sharpen using data from all visible layers select **Use All Layers**; if this is deselected, the tool uses data from only the active layer.

3 Drag over the part of the image you want to blur or sharpen.

TIP!

Use the **Sharpen Tool** with caution as it can quickly make your image appear grainy.

Figure 1.29a shows the original image. Figure 1.29b shows the effect of using the **Blur Tool** at the bottom of the image – this causes the viewer's attention to be drawn to the peppers in the bowl. It also shows the effect of using **Sharpen Tool** on the peppers in the bowl.

Figure 1.29 Image a) before blurring and sharpening b) after blurring and sharpening

The toning tools

The toning tools consist of the **Dodge Tool** and the **Burn Tool**. These tools are based on a traditional photographer's technique for regulating exposure on specific areas of a print. Photographers hold back light to lighten an area on the print (dodging) or increase the exposure to darken areas on a print (burning). The **Dodge Tool** is used to lighten areas of an image. It is a great tool for removing excessive shadows or to emphasise an object within an image. The **Burn Tool** is used to darken areas of an image and is a good tool to use if an image has areas that are over-exposed or if you want to de-emphasise objects.

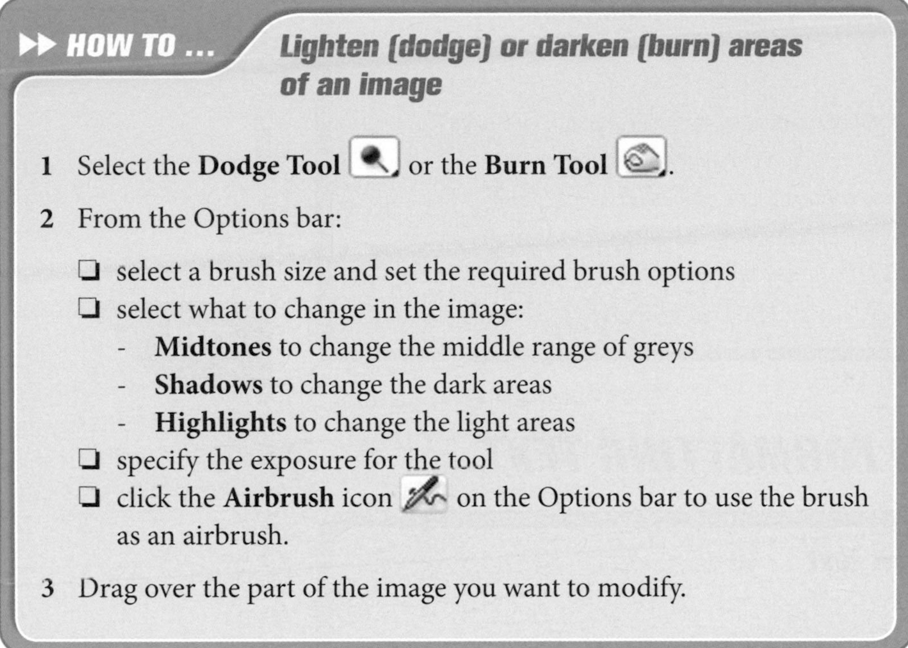

HOW TO ... Lighten (dodge) or darken (burn) areas of an image

1 Select the **Dodge Tool** or the **Burn Tool**.

2 From the Options bar:

- select a brush size and set the required brush options
- select what to change in the image:
  - **Midtones** to change the middle range of greys
  - **Shadows** to change the dark areas
  - **Highlights** to change the light areas
- specify the exposure for the tool
- click the **Airbrush** icon on the Options bar to use the brush as an airbrush.

3 Drag over the part of the image you want to modify.

The Sponge Tool

The **Sponge Tool** subtly changes the colour saturation of an area. When an area of an image is saturated with the **Sponge Tool**, the colours become darker. When an area is desaturated, the colours become more subtle.

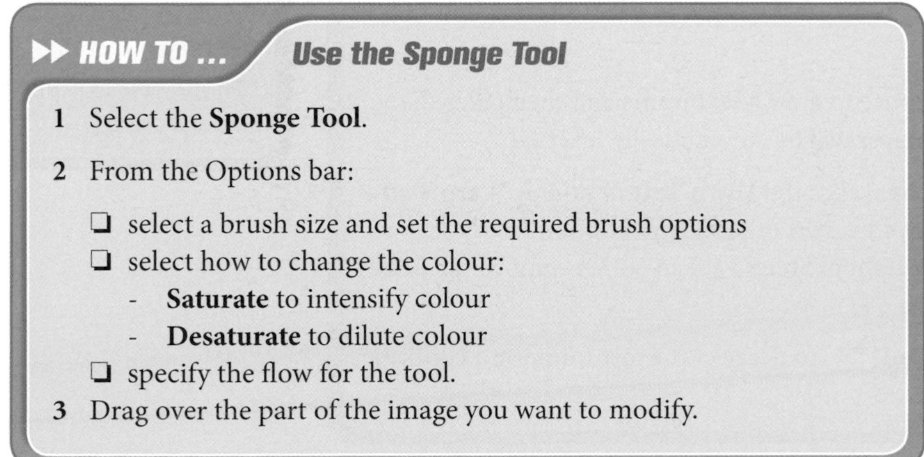

HOW TO ... Use the Sponge Tool

1 Select the **Sponge Tool**.

2 From the Options bar:

- select a brush size and set the required brush options
- select how to change the colour:
  - **Saturate** to intensify colour
  - **Desaturate** to dilute colour
- specify the flow for the tool.

3 Drag over the part of the image you want to modify.

Student review 1.6 – Identify retouching tools

Assessment objective 2b

1 Which tool is best for softening hard edges in an image?
2 Which tool should be used for darkening areas (increasing exposure) on an image?
3 Which tool gives a similar effect to dragging a finger through wet paint?
4 Which tool focuses soft edges to increase clarity or focus?
5 Which tool is useful for removing excessive shadows?
6 Which tool will change the colour saturation subtly?
7 Which tool should be used in an image where you want to de-emphasise an object that is over-exposed?

INSERTING AND FORMATTING TEXT

HOW TO ... Insert text

1 From Toolbox, select the **Horizontal Type Tool** T or the **Vertical Type Tool** ↓T.

2 Select the required options (font style, size, emphasis) from the Options bar by clicking on the drop-down arrow to the right of the **Set the font family** box, **Set the font size** box etc. (refer to Figure 1.30).

3 Select the font colour by clicking in the **Set the text color** box. A **Custom Picker** dialogue box is displayed → select a text colour → **OK.**

4 Click and drag the mouse to draw a text frame and then enter the required text. A new layer will be automatically inserted.

5 To change the text shape, click the **Warp Text** option. A **Warp Text** dialogue box is displayed → select the required option from the drop-down list to the right of **Style** → set any other options for **Bend** and **Distortion** → **OK.**

6 Click on the **Move Tool** to deselect the text frame and confirm the text.

TIP!

To insert two layers of text in the same style, create and format text on the first layer, then duplicate the layer, move the text and edit it.

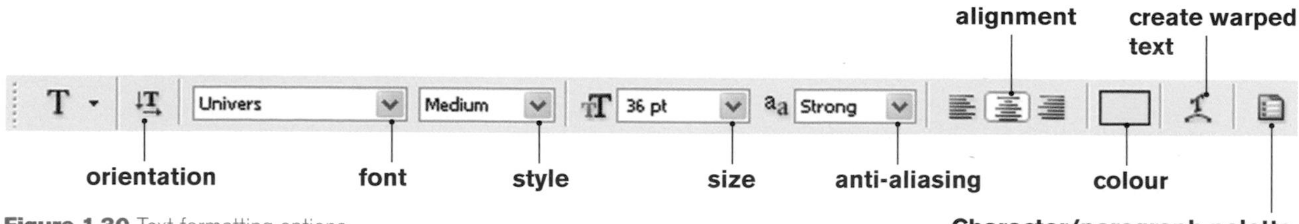

Figure 1.30 Text formatting options

▶▶ HOW TO ... Format text after it has been entered

You will usually need to highlight the required text on the layer first.

1 Select the **Horizontal Type Tool** [T] or **Vertical Type Tool** [↓T].

2 Click within the text. The text frame is displayed.

3 Click and drag to highlight the text.

4 Select the required options from the Options bar.

TIP!

To select a line of text, triple-click within the text.

To select a block of text, click four times in quick succession.

Layer Blending

You can apply a variety of blending options to any item (text, shape or image) on a layer.

▶▶ HOW TO ... Apply blending to layers

1 Select the required layer.

2 **Layer** menu → **Layer Style** → **Blending Options** → a **Blending Options** dialogue box is displayed.

3 Ensure you click on the option required, e.g. **Drop Shadow** – do not click in the box but click on the words instead; this displays the options associated with a particular blending option in the middle section of the dialogue box (refer to Figure 1.31).

4 Select the required options from the middle pane.

5 Repeat step 3 to apply another blend. You can apply as many blends to a layer as you wish → **OK**.

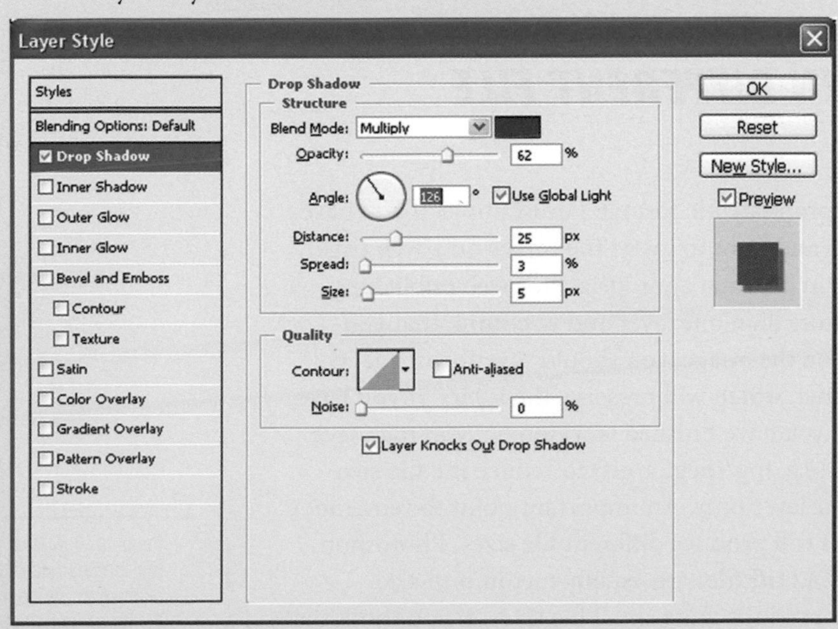

Figure 1.31 Blending options

PRACTICAL TASK 1.11 Retouch images

Assessment objective 2b

Refer to the assignment brief on page 8. You will apply fine retouching to one of the images that you have already retouched in Practical tasks 1.9 or 1.10. This will be the image that you will select as your contribution to the next photography club meeting.

1 Open one of your digital images that you have repaired.
2 Use two appropriate retouching tools (e.g. **Smudge**, **Blur**, **Sharpen**) to apply fine retouching to your image. Produce screen print evidence of each amendment.
3 Use a toning tool (**Dodge** or **Burn**) or the **Sponge Tool** to retouch an appropriate area of the image.
4 Save the image in an appropriate file format.

SECTION 3 • Save digital graphics

The following assessment objective will be covered in this section:

2c Save and close the image in an appropriate format for print and the web

The following knowledge, skills and understanding criteria corresponding to assessment objective 2c will also be covered:

- *How to save as different file formats*
- *Common file extensions*

SAVING IMAGES IN DIFFERENT FILE FORMATS

Images must be saved in the appropriate file format. For example, if you have finished manipulating an image and want to insert the image on a web page, you will need to save the image in a format appropriate for web publishing. If you have an image that has more than one layer and you think that you may want to continue working on the image, you should save the image in Photoshop (**psd**) or **tiff** file format, which will preserve the layers. If you have an image containing layers that you have finished working on, you may save that image in other file formats (e.g. **jpg/jpeg** or **gif**) to reduce the file size. Note that these formats have one layer only. An important point to remember is saving in different file formats will produce different file sizes. Photoshop files are usually large, **jpg/jpeg** and **tiff** files are usually medium in size whereas **gif** files usually tend to produce quite small file sizes. If you think that you may need to continue editing the image, you are advised to keep a copy of the image with layers (in **psd** or **tiff** format).

Refer to 'Different file formats and file extensions' on page 10 for an explanation of file formats and file extensions.

▶▶ HOW TO ... Save an image

1 **File** menu → **Save As** → the **Save As** dialogue box is displayed.

2 Click the drop-down arrow to the right of **Save in** and open the folder where the file is to be saved.

3 Enter a suitable filename in the box to the right of **File name**.

4 Click the drop-down arrow to the right of **Format** → a list of file types is displayed (refer to Figure 1.32).

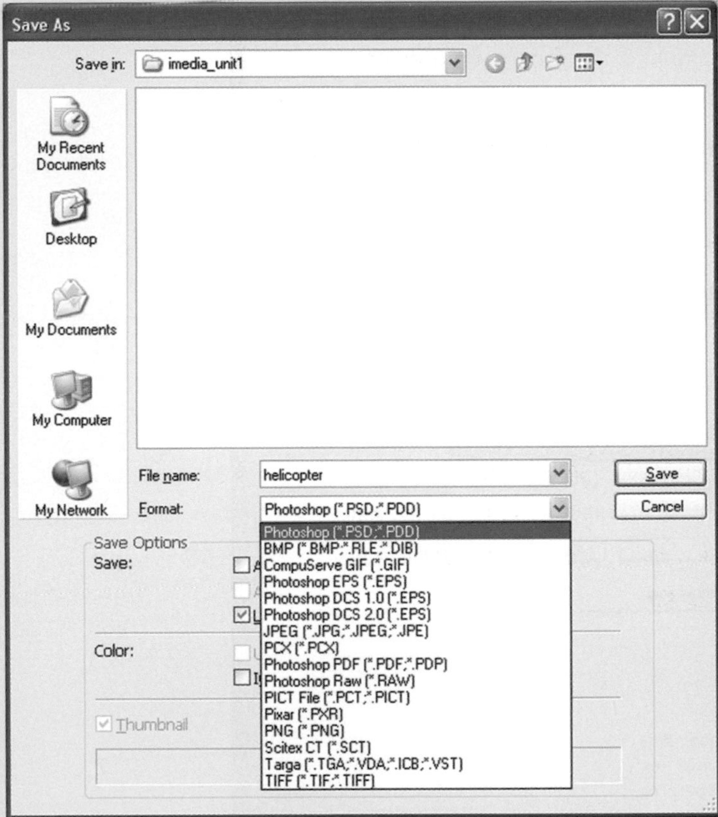

Figure 1.32 Saving in Photoshop format

To save in a specific format, refer to the relevant section below.

▶▶ HOW TO ... Save in Photoshop format

Follow steps 1 to 4 above.

5 In the **Save As** dialogue box, from the drop-down list to the right of **Format**, select **Photoshop** (*.PSD,*.PDD).

6 In the **Save Options** section, ensure that the **Layers** check box is ticked.

7 Click **Save** → a **Photoshop Format Options** dialogue box will display → click **OK**.

▶▶ HOW TO ... Save in tiff format

Follow steps 1 to 4 on page 45.

5 In the **Save As** dialogue box, from the drop-down list to the right of **Format**, select **TIFF (*.TIF,*.TIFF)**.

6 In the **Save Options** section, tick or uncheck the **Layers** box as required for your image.

7 Click **Save** → a **Tiff Options** dialogue box is displayed.

8 Select the options you want under **Image Compression** and **Layer Compression** → click **OK**.

9 If you had selected the check box for **Layers**, a dialogue box is displayed informing you that including layers will increase file size (refer to Figure 1.33).

10 Click **OK**.

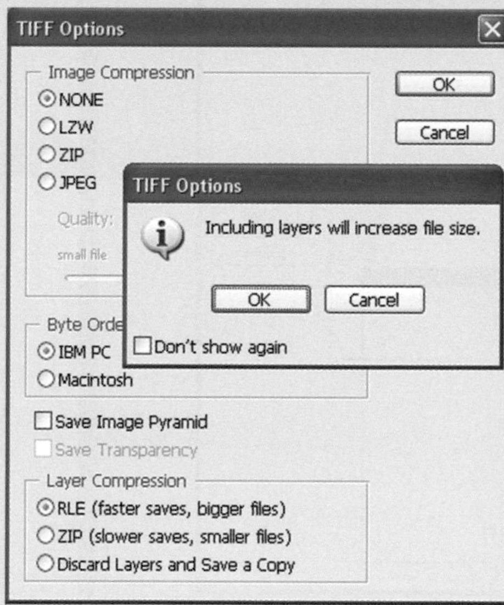

Figure 1.33 Saving in tiff format

▶▶ HOW TO ... Save in jpg (jpeg) format

Follow steps 1 to 4 on page 45.

5 In the **Save As** dialogue box, from the drop-down list to the right of **Format**, select **JPEG (*.JPG,*.JPEG,*.JPE)**.

6 Click **Save** → a **JPEG Options** dialogue box is displayed.

7 If you wish to change the file size, click the drop-down arrow to the right of the size displayed (e.g. **Medium**) and select the required file size (refer to Figure 1.34). Note: if you reduce the file size, you will be reducing the resolution.

8 Click **OK**.

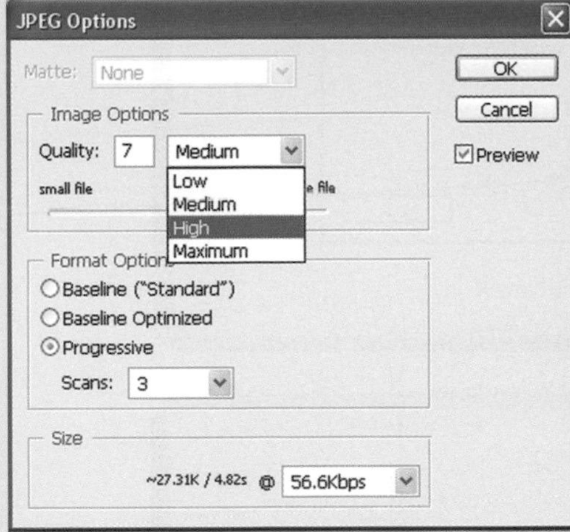

Figure 1.34 Saving in jpg/jpeg format

▶▶ HOW TO ... Save in gif format

Follow steps 1 to 4 on page 45.

5 In the **Save As** dialogue box, from the drop-down list to the right of **Format**, select **CompuServe GIF (*.GIF)**.

6 Click **Save** → an **Indexed Color** dialogue box is displayed → click **OK**.

7 A **GIF Options** dialogue box is displayed → click **OK**.

TIP!

When you save an image with layers as a **gif** or **jpg** file, you may be prompted to **Flatten Layers** → click **Yes**.

Photoshop will preserve transparent areas in the image when you save in **gif** format. However, you may choose to export your image as a **gif** image instead as described on the next page.

▸▸ HOW TO ... Export an image as a gif image

1 **Help** menu → **Export Transparent Image** → an **Export Transparent Image Wizard** dialogue box is displayed .

2 Select an option → **Next** (refer to Figure 1.35).

3 Select **Print** or **Online** → **Next.**

4 Follow steps 5 to 7 under 'How to save in gif format'.

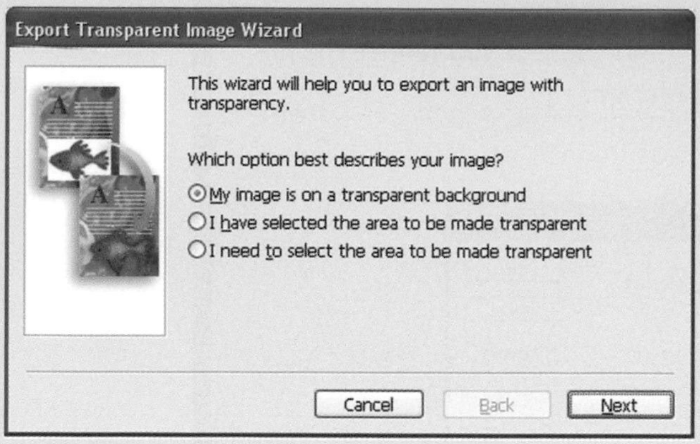

Export Transparent Image Wizard

This wizard will help you to export an image with transparency.

Which option best describes your image?

- ⦿ My image is on a transparent background
- ○ I have selected the area to be made transparent
- ○ I need to select the area to be made transparent

Cancel | Back | Next

Figure 1.35 Exporting an image with a transparent background

PRACTICAL TASK 1.12 Save images

Assessment objectives 2b, 2c

1 Open one of your original images from the folder containing the copied images.

2 Save this image in a **gif** file format.

3 Insert a new text layer and enter appropriate text.

4 Warp the text and apply two blending options.

5 Save the image in **tiff** format.

Optimisation

Optimisation is the process by which an image is saved in a specific file format, at a set storage size and within colour parameters (constraints). The goal of optimisation is to find a balance between preserving the image's quality as much as possible and compressing it enough so that it loads onto a web page quickly.

HOW TO ... Optimise an image and save for the web

To select optimisation options and preview optimised images you can use the **Save for Web** option.

1 **File** menu → **Save for Web**.

2 To select a display option, select a tab at the top of the image area (refer to Figure 1.36).

3 Click the drop-down arrow to the right of **Preset** and select an optimisation setting.

4 A medium number will produce a medium file size and selecting **Dithered** ensures that colours appear smooth, e.g. **GIF 64 dithered**.

5 Click **Save** → a **Save Optimized As** dialogue box is displayed → enter a suitable filename and select the correct storage location → click **Save**.

Figure 1.36 Optimising an image for the web

PRACTICAL TASK 1.13 Optimise image and save for the web

Assessment objective 2c

1 Open the image saved in Practical task 1.11 – this is the image that you will submit for the next club meeting.

2 Optimise this image and save the optimised image in a format suitable for the web.

PRACTICAL TASK 1.14 Review work against original brief

Assessment objective 3b

1 Refer to 'Reviewing your work' on page xxi of the 'Common Skills' chapter.

2 Collate all your evidence (images, diary, screen prints, notes, storyboard, Planning and Review form, feedback notes).

3 Refer to the Assignment Brief for the 'Cove Photography Club – Booklet' on page 8.

4 Review your evidence and your edited images against the assignment brief. You may have a discussion with your tutor.

5 Ensure that you have carried out all the tasks required in the assignment brief.

6 Obtain a copy of an Evidence Checklist (ask your tutor for a copy).

7 Complete the Evidence Checklist.

8 Identify at least two constraints that influenced your project, e.g. image manipulation, file format, compression. Note these in your Planning and Review Form or in a separate document.

9 Back up all your files to a removable medium.

You should now have all the skills, knowledge and understanding required to complete an OCR iMedia sample or live assessment for this unit.

UNIT 2
WEB AUTHORING

INTRODUCTION

This practical unit is designed to give you an understanding of the capabilities of web authoring and the skills involved in building a website. You will develop an understanding of the requirements and capabilities of web authoring and the necessary resources. You will learn how to use appropriate software to create, add content to and publish a website.

LEARNING OUTCOMES

After studying this unit you will be able to:

- understand the requirements and capabilities of web authoring
- understand the range of ways of accessing web pages and connecting to the Internet
- create a website structure
- use the tools and features of a web authoring program to add content to a website
- manage and upload a website.

RESOURCE TOOLKIT

Hardware
- Computer

Software
- Macromedia Dreamweaver
- Web browser program (e.g. Internet Explorer)

Other
- Planning and Review Form
- Text and images (images from other units, e.g. Unit 1, may be used)
- Evidence Checklist

Optional
- Multimedia elements, e.g. sound clips, video clips, animations
- Digital camera
- Web space to upload website (e.g. your centre server)
- Books on HTML basics
- Existing text files (for creating web pages)
- Word-Processing application (e.g. Microsoft Word)

For this unit you will need images (e.g. photographs, clip art, animated images) and text to create your web pages. You may use images you have already sourced and/or edited in other units.

You will need to plan the website to a specific assignment brief and record all stages of your planning. The assignment brief will describe a client's needs. You will look at ways of identifying your client's requirements and will use planning methods appropriate for your brief and appropriate to planning and creating websites.

You will create a template for your website and use the template to create web pages for your site. You will create folders for your website and file all your source files (also referred to your assets) in these folders. You will add content to each of your web pages using a range of skills, e.g. creating lists and tables, inserting images, creating image maps and creating internal and external hyperlinks. After completion, you will test the website.

Finally, you will review the finished website against the original assignment brief and obtain appropriate feedback (e.g. from peers or your tutor). You will need to identify any constraints that influence your choice and file format of the elements (images, text) included in your website. You will decide if the website meets your client's requirements.

The Student Review activities and Practical Tasks in this chapter will allow you to develop your understanding of the requirements for an OCR assessment and practise the skills required for the Unit 2 syllabus. The website you create in this chapter **CANNOT** be submitted for assessment purposes.

If you are in a centre that does not permit access to the Internet, this does not exclude you from doing this unit. The web pages will be created in Dreamweaver and can be tested by viewing the HTML code VERY carefully to see if the links would work. Alternatively, once you have created your website, you could save it on a removable medium or on a network drive accessible by your tutor, and ask your tutor to check that all the links work.

Source files

Text and image files have not been provided with this book because in an OCR assessment you will need to source your own files. You may use files from other units, e.g. images from Unit 1, animations from Unit 3, sound files from Unit 5, and video clips from Unit 6.

You are not required to create your own files; your tutor may provide you with files in generic format (e.g. images may be in gif, jpg, tiff, bmp or other common formats, text files should be in txt format etc.). Any files that you use which you have not created yourself should be referenced.

Copyright

The Internet can be a valuable resource for images and text for your website; however, you must remember that copyright applies to work published on the Internet. If you wish to use images or text from another website you must check to ensure the author has given permission for the content to be used or seek permission from the author to use it.

TIP!

You should keep a record of the files you have sourced, of copyright permissions obtained or a reference of the URLs if copyright was not sought or needed. Your record could be a format as follows:

FILENAME AND FILE TYPE	SOURCE	DATE COLLECTED	REFERENCE (E.G. URL, COPYRIGHT DETAILS)	INTENDED USE

ASSESSMENT FOR UNIT 2

Your assessment work should be submitted to OCR via e-portfolio. You should therefore save all evidence in electronic format. Any hard copy evidence should be scanned and saved electronically.

Evidence

You will need to provide:

- *evidence of planning your project. This could be included in, or in addition to, the Planning and Review Form*
- *Planning and Review Form*
- *a diary (e.g. digital diary) or log of your activities for the given assignment*
- *storyboard*
- *site map*
- *saved web pages in the website folder. Web pages must be saved in **htm** or **html** format*
- *reports when checking for broken links and browser compatibility (e.g. reports shown in Dreamweaver)*
- *Evidence Checklist (OCR template).*

Refer also to 'Evidence' on pages ix and xxii.

SOFTWARE

This chapter is written for Macromedia Dreamweaver version 8 from the Studio 8 suite (education version). It can also be used with Dreamweaver MX 2004 although some screenshots and methods will not exactly match this version. Dreamweaver is an industry-standard web-authoring editor.

Please note that you are not required to create templates and web pages by writing HTML code. The template and web pages can be created in an editor (e.g. Dreamweaver). However, you will need a basic understanding of writing, checking and viewing HTML code. This is covered in this chapter.

ABOUT THIS CHAPTER

This chapter for Unit 2 is divided into three sections. You must work through the sections in sequence.

- Section 1 will cover some practical skills and some theory. You will learn how to create, name and rename folders and plan a website using a storyboard and a site map. This section will also cover the knowledge you require about ways of accessing web pages and connecting to the Internet; the role of Internet Service Providers; and the purpose and benefits of websites. You will learn to use a text editor to write basic HTML code and a web browser to view the HTML tags. You will plan a website for a client, create a site map, define the house style, and source and organise the files required for this website.

AOs 1a, 1b, 1c, 3a

- In Section 2 you will learn how to use Dreamweaver. You will use site management tools to create a website. You will learn to create and format a template, insert and format tables, meta tags, images and hyperlinks; create cascading style sheets and editable regions.

AOs 1a, 1b, 1c, 1d, 1e, 2a

- In Section 3 you will use your template to create web pages, enter and insert text, create lists, insert multimedia elements and image maps. You will learn to preview your web pages and test your website for broken links and browser compatibility. You will learn about prototype testing, stepwise refinement, how to correct problems in your website and upload a website.

AOs 1c, 1d, 1e, 2a, 2b, 3b

Assessment objectives 3a (plan the website to a specific brief) and 3b (review the website against the original brief) and the corresponding knowledge, skills and understanding criteria are covered in the 'Common Skills' chapter. Refer to 'Planning your work' and 'Reviewing your work'. In addition to the planning skills covered in the 'Common Skills' chapter, producing a site map, which forms part of Assessment objective 3a, is also covered in this chapter.

Refer to 'Planning your work' and 'Reviewing your work' sections on pages xiv and xxi of the 'Common Skills' chapter.

SECTION 1 • Write HTML code, plan a website

The following assessment objectives will be covered in this section:

1a Define a website

1b Examine, write and view HTML tags

1c Create a basic web page

3a Plan the website to a specific brief

Note: most of objective 3a is covered in the 'Common Skills' chapter.

The following knowledge, skills and understanding criteria corresponding to assessment objectives 1a, 1b and 1c will be covered:

- *Ways of connecting to the Internet and accessing web pages*
- *The role of Internet service providers and the purpose and benefits of a website*
- *How to use a web browser*
- *How to create, name and rename folders*
- *Basic html tags*
- *Methods of using a text editor*
- *Methods of viewing tags in a browser*
- *Components of a web page*
- *Ways of enhancing web pages*

Note: in this section you will learn to create a basic web page by writing HTML code in Notepad. In Section 2, you will create a template and web pages in Dreamweaver.

Note: the criteria 'ways of identifying client requirements' and other planning methods, i.e. visualise, conceptualise, storyboards are covered in the 'Common Skills' chapter.

FILE NAMING CONVENTION FOR WEBSITES

You must be particularly careful when creating the folder structure for your website, and when saving and naming files. Follow the guidelines below when naming files and folders for a website:

- Use lower case.
- Do not use spaces in file or folder names.
- Use only one word for the name, combine words into one if necessary (e.g. **covehotel** instead of **cove hotel**).
- Use short words – this makes the URL simpler.
- Use a dash instead of an underscore if a filename is long.

Refer also to 'File organisation and file naming' on page xi of the 'Common Skills' chapter.

Underscores are accepted convention and used frequently in naming files and folders. However, for websites, these should be avoided as an underscore is difficult to identify in a URL; an underscore is generally obscured when the link is underlined.

CREATING FOLDERS

Folder structure

You must create a main folder for your website, within which you should have at least one subfolder for the image files; all other files can be stored in the website folder. Alternatively, if you have many files, you could create subfolders for different file types, e.g. one subfolder for text files, and one for multimedia elements (e.g. sounds, videos).

You must choose appropriate, descriptive names for your folders. Use logical names that will enable you, and others, to know where to look for certain types of files. You should also back up your source files onto a removable medium.

You must create a subfolder named **images** inside your main website folder. You must save all images and animations in this subfolder.

Note that for the Level 2 iMedia syllabus, you are not required to insert sounds, videos or animations in your website. However, this is a useful skill and helps to enhance websites, therefore you may use these elements in your website if you wish.

To find sound files, try www.findsounds.com
To find sound and video clips, try www.archive.org

PRACTICAL TASK 2.1 Set up website folder structure and organise files

Assessment objective 1a

1 Create a folder named **covesite**

2 In this folder create four subfolders named **images**, **sounds**, **videos** and **text**

3 Find or create three images of digital cameras (from the Internet or elsewhere) and save them using appropriate filenames into the **images** subfolder.

4 Find or create two animated **gif** or **swf** files about digital cameras and save them into the **images** subfolder.

5 Find or create at least one sound of a camera clicking. Ensure the format is **wav**, **midi** or **mp3** and save the file using a suitable filename into the **sounds** subfolder.

6 Find or create at least one video clip about digital or video cameras. Ensure the format is **mov** and save it using a suitable filename into the **videos** subfolder.

7 Find or create two text files about digital cameras and save the text files in **txt** format into the **text** subfolder.

8 Produce screen print(s) of your folders and subfolders showing the Details view.

9 Back up the **covesite** folder onto a removable medium.

Check your website folder structure carefully before moving on. File management is particularly important for websites. You must ensure your website folder structure is set up correctly and that all files are saved into the correct folders and are appropriately named.

WAYS OF CONNECTING TO THE INTERNET AND ACCESSING WEB PAGES

There are many different ways of connecting to the Internet to access web pages, email and other data using a computer, mobile phone or interactive television. You will also need an **Internet service provider (ISP).**

Key terms

ISP **I**nternet **S**ervice **P**rovider A company that provides access to the Internet and generally offers other services such as web hosting.

Internet service providers

ISPs use a range of the following technologies to enable connection to the Internet: dial-up, cable modem, **ISDN**, **ADSL**, Broadband wireless access and **Ethernet**.

Key terms

ISDN **I**ntegrated **S**ervices **D**igital **N**etwork is a telephone network system that allows digital transmission of data and voice over ordinary telephone wires.

ADSL **A**symmetric **D**igital **S**ubscriber **L**ine is a data communications technology that enables fast data transmission.

Ethernet A large, diverse family of computer networking technologies for local area networks (LANs).

Modem

The word **modem** is derived from the words **modulator-demodulator**. Modems allow terminals to connect to computers over telephone lines. A modem is used to send digital data over a phone line. The sending modem **modulates** the data into a signal that is compatible with the phone line, and the receiving modem **demodulates** the signal back into digital data. Wireless modems convert digital data into radio signals and back.

Broadband

The word **broadband** comes from the words 'broad bandwidth'. Broadband is a type of data transmission in which a single medium (wire) can simultaneously carry several channels including voice, data and video. It is also a term for different types of high-speed, high-bandwidth connections to the Internet. Broadband connections allow users to be connected to the Internet at all times, usually for a fixed charge.

Wireless networking

Nowadays, many people use wireless networking, called **WiFi** (**Wi**reless **Fi**delity), to interconnect their computers at home. Wireless 'hotspots' are also provided in places where lots of people congregate (stations, airports, hotels and conference centres). WiFi is easy to set up, inexpensive and unobtrusive. It allows you to access the Internet from almost anywhere, at any time, without using wires.

WiFi is also referred to as 802.11 networking. The 802.11 numbering comes from the Institute of Electrical and Electronics Engineers who set standards for technological protocols. They use a numbering system to classify these standards.

A wireless network uses radio waves. A computer's wireless adaptor translates data into a radio signal and transmits it using an antenna. A wireless router receives the signal and decodes it. It sends the information to the Internet using a physical, wired connection. The process also works in reverse, i.e. the router receives information from the Internet, translates it into a radio signal and sends it to the computer's wireless adaptor.

Refer to 'Understanding network and Internet connections' on pages 161 and 162.

Bluetooth

Bluetooth is a radio technology that makes it possible to transmit signals over short distances between computers and hand-held devices without the use of wires. It allows communication between wireless devices such as mobile phones, **PDAs (personal digital assistants)** and hand-held computers, as well as wireless-enabled laptop or desktop computers and peripherals. A Bluetooth-enabled wireless device is capable of making phone calls, synchronising data with desktop computers, sending and receiving faxes, and printing documents.

Key terms

PDA ***P**ersonal **D**igital **A**ssistant* A hand-held device that combines computing, telephone, fax and networking features. A PDA can function as a cell phone, fax sender, and personal organiser. PDAs also are called palmtops, hand-held computers and pocket computers.

PURPOSE AND BENEFITS OF A WEBSITE

The World Wide Web is an excellent channel for marketing a business, product or service to potential clients anywhere in the world, and at any time of the day or night, every day of the year. Your website can act as a virtual shop front for your business, product or service. It offers a convenient and cost-effective way of providing up-to-date information about your business. Information can be updated cheaply and easily. You avoid the time, cost and stress of producing and sending promotional material by post and the cost of redundant material.

A website has the benefits of allowing you to trade online and gather contact details and information about visitors to your site. You can conduct market research easily, have targeted marketing campaigns and build customer relations through personalised service.

Your website visitors will judge the standard of your site so you must ensure it is professional, informative and easy to navigate.

Data protection

If you gather data about individuals or businesses you must ensure that you comply with the Data Protection Act. You must store this data securely and use it only for the purposes for which it was supplied. You must not keep this data for longer than is necessary.

WAYS OF ENHANCING WEB PAGES

The look of web pages can be enhanced by using different font types, colours and alignment for text, and different formatting for the background of the web page.

Formatting instructions that tell an Internet browser how to display the information on a web page are referred to as **tags**. The body tag will contain the information about the formatting of the background to the page, the text, links and **visited links**. When you set these properties, Dreamweaver will automatically generate the body tag for you.

Key terms

Visited link colour The text colour when a link has already been clicked. By setting a visited link colour, visitors to your site can quickly identify whether or not they have used the link previously.

Colours can be set by using a specific set of colour names understood by web browsers or by using the hexadecimal code.

You may set a background colour or use an image as a background. The image will fill the entire background of the web page and the background colour will not be visible. However, even if you use an image as a background, you should still set a background colour because some users select the option not to download images in their browser so that pages load faster.

Student review 2.1 – Understand ways of accessing websites and benefits of websites

Assessment objective 1a

1 *What is the term modem derived from?*

2 *What do the following stand for: ISDN, ADSL, ISP, PDA?*

3 Name five technologies that enable connection to the Internet.

4 What type of connection allows users to be connected to the Internet at all times for a fixed charge?

5 *What allows terminals to connect to computers over phone lines?*

6 *What is 802.11 networking more commonly known as?*

7 *What is the main feature of broad bandwidth?*

8 *What type of network uses radio waves?*

9 *What type of technology transmits signals over short distances between computers without the use of wires?*

10 *Which Act should you comply with if you gather personal data about individuals?*

11 *What is a formatting instruction that tells an Internet browser how to display information on a web page?*

EXAMINE, WRITE AND VIEW HTML TAGS

Every web page has two aspects: the display you see on-screen and the underlying **HTML** code. Web pages can be created in two ways:

1 Writing HTML code in a text editor such as Notepad or WordPad. This is sometimes referred to as 'hand-coding' or 'coding'. The formatted result of the coding can be viewed a web browser.

2 Using a web page editing application, referred to as an 'editor', 'web page editor' or 'web-authoring' application. Examples of frequently used editing applications are Macromedia Dreamweaver and Microsoft FrontPage. If you use an editing application, you can create effective websites without writing or understanding the underlying HTML code. The program will automatically generate the underlying HTML code.

Key terms

HTML **H**yper**T**ext **M**arkup **L**anguage is a language that is read and interpreted by a web browser. Markup tags inform the web browser how to display the page.

Some editing applications are referred to as WYSIYWG editors – what you see on screen when you are creating the web page is what you get on screen when the web page is viewed in the browser.
(WYSIYWG What You See Is What You Get)

Examples of web browsers are Internet Explorer, Netscape, Firefox, Mozilla, Opera and Safari.

HTML is based on the use of **tags**. Tags are key words or phrases enclosed in angle brackets **< >**. The words or phrases describe how text and images should be displayed and how links are created.

This section will cover the basics of writing basic HTML tags. In Section 2 you will learn to create web pages using Dreamweaver.

BASIC RULES FOR WRITING HTML

- Each tag must be enclosed in angled brackets, e.g. **<h1>**
- Most tags come in pairs: the opening tag and the closing tag. The closing tag starts with a forward slash **/**
- Example of a pair of tags for a heading with the heading text displayed between the tags:
  <h1>Enter your text here**</h1>**
- Every HTML document starts with the opening tag
  <html> and ends with the closing tag **</html>**
- Although you can use upper or lower case letters for codes and colours, present day HTML convention is to use lower case for all code.
- Web browsers ignore:
  - ❑ spaces after an opening tag or before a closing tag
  - ❑ new lines around tags
  - ❑ tabs
  - ❑ carriage returns (using the Enter key).

HEAD AND BODY TAGS

An HTML document is usually divided into two parts: the **head** and the **body**:

- The head part contains the title and any other annotations (e.g. **meta tags**). Items contained in the head tags *will not* be displayed on the web page.
- The body part contains all the items that will be displayed on the web page. All items enclosed between the opening and closing body tags *will* be displayed on the web page.

Head tags

Every web page should have a title. In web pages the title is not the heading that viewers see on the web page itself. A web page title displays on the title bar of the browser. When you bookmark a page, the title is used as the default bookmark.

TIP!

You can view the HTML code of any web page on the World Wide Web by clicking the **View** menu → **Source**.

Key terms

Tags Key words or phrases enclosed in angle brackets < >.

To open a Notepad page, click the Start button → All Programs → Accessories → Notepad.

Opening and closing head tags:
<head>
</head>

Opening and closing body tags:
<body>
</body>

Key terms

Meta tags Key words that provide information about a web page.

HTML code for a web page title:
<title> your text **</title>**

Body tags

The body section contains the heading to be displayed on the web page and all formatting instructions.

Examples of coding for heading sizes:

<h1>your text</h1>
<h2>your text</h2>
<h3>your text</h3>
<h4>your text</h4>
<h5>your text</h5>
<h6>your text</h6>

Headings

Headings can be defined in six sizes, ranging from 1 to 6.

FORMATTING

To display specific font formatting use the following tags.

Font size

<font size ="12**">**Enter your text here**</font>**
You would enter the actual size you want.

Font type

<font face="Arial**">**Enter your text here**</font>**
You would enter the actual font name you want.

Emphasis

Bold: **<b>**your text**</b>** *or* **<strong>**your text**</strong>**
Italic: **<i>**your text**</i>** *or* **<emphasis>**your text**</emphasis>**

Alignment

To align a paragraph, enter the following code at the beginning of the paragraph. All text after this tag will be aligned as specified.

<p align="center"> *or* **<p align="right">**

To change the alignment, enter another instruction as above at the end of the text.

The default alignment for headings and body text is left. If you want left alignment, there is no need to create an ***align*** *tag.*

To centre a heading

<h1 align="center">your text**</h1>**
You would enter the heading size (h1, h2, etc) you want.

In HTML code, the word **center** MUST be in American spelling.

Background and text colours

<body bgcolor="#ff0000**" text="#**0000ff**">**
You would enter the code for the colours you want.

Font colour for a specific line or section

<font color="#800080">

TIP!

Colour can also be entered by using the word, e.g.

<body bgcolor="red**">**

In HTML code, the word **color** MUST be in American spelling and the code itself should be preceded with a hash **#** symbol.

Paragraphs

To break blocks of text into paragraphs or to start a new line, use one of these tags:

**
** creates a line break. **
** does not have a closing tag.
<p> marks the start of a new paragraph and creates a blank linespace above it.
<p> can be used on its own or with a closing **</p>** tag.

Hexadecimal code for key colours

000000	black
ffffff	white
ff0000	bright red
800000	dark red
00ff00	bright green
008000	dark green
0000ff	bright blue
000080	dark blue
808080	grey
ffff00	yellow

Images

<img src="xxx.gif"> *or* **<img src="xxx.jpg">**
Instead of **xxx**, *you would enter the image filename.*

When inserting images, you must enter the image **name** followed by a full stop and the **file extension**, e.g. **bike.gif** or **bike.jpg**

HYPERLINKS

All links begin with **<a href=** and end with **</a>**

Internal link linking text to a page in your website

<a href="index.htm">your text**</a>**
You would enter the required web page name followed by the file extension.

External link linking an image to another web page/website

An external link must be preceded by http:// and must NOT have any spaces in the link.

<a href="http://www.ocr.org.uk**"><img src="**xxx.jpg**"></a></p>**
You would enter the URL address and image name followed by the file extension you want.

Email link linking text

An email link must be preceded by mailto: and must NOT have any spaces in the link.

<a href="mailto:r.patel@jhc.ac.uk**">Contact us</a></p>**
You would enter the email address you want.

PRACTICAL TASK 2.2 Write, examine, view html code and view web page in browser

Assessment objective 1b

In this task you will create a new web page about yourself – you will enter HTML code in a Notepad document. You will save the page then view it in a browser.

1 Create a new folder named **site1**

2 Find two images: one of yourself and one other and save these using suitable filenames into the **site1** folder. (Note for this task you do not need to create an images subfolder.) Ensure the image dimensions are quite small. Resize the images in **Paint** if necessary (**Image → Stretch/Skew**). Save these images in the **site1** folder.

3 You need a web page named **index.htm**. Open your browser and save your home page, or any search engine page into the **site1** folder using the filename **index.htm**. Ensure the file type is **webpage, complete (*.htm,*.html)**.

4 Create a new document in Notepad and enter the HTML code shown below.

5 All essential code that you must enter is displayed below in **bright blue**.

6 All text that you should key in is shown in red.

7 You should substitute text in *green italics* with the name and file extension of the images you have sourced.

8 You should enter your own suitable text where shown in *black* and *italics*.

9 Enter your own email address where instructed after **mailto:**

```
<html>
<head>
<title>My Web Page</title>
</head>

<body> <body bgcolor ="#c0c0c0"> <link="#ff0000">
<p align ="center"> <img src="xxx.gif"></p>

<p align ="center"> <b> <font face="times new roman"
size="7"
color="#ff0000">Enter a heading here</font> </b> </p>

<i><font face="arial" size="5">
<b>Enter a subheading here</b> </font> </i> </p>

<p align="left">Enter a paragraph of text here.</p>
<p align="left">Enter a second paragraph of text here.</p>
```

Continued

Continued ...

```
<a href="index.htm">Back to homepage</a></p>

<a href="mailto:your own email address">Contact me</a> </p>

<a href="http://www.ocr.org.uk"> <img src="xxx.jpg"> </a>
</p>

<p align="left"> <font face="Arial" size="2">
Created by Enter your name here</font> </p>

</body>
</html>
```

10 Save the page into the **site1** folder using the filename **mypage.htm** Ensure the file type is **Text Documents** (*.**txt**).

11 Open the **site1** folder, then double-click on the **mypage.htm** page to open the web page in your browser. View your web page and click on each link to test the links.

If everything does not display correctly on your web page, close the browser. Open the page in Notepad – check the code carefully, edit it, resave the page and open it again in the browser.

Assignment brief

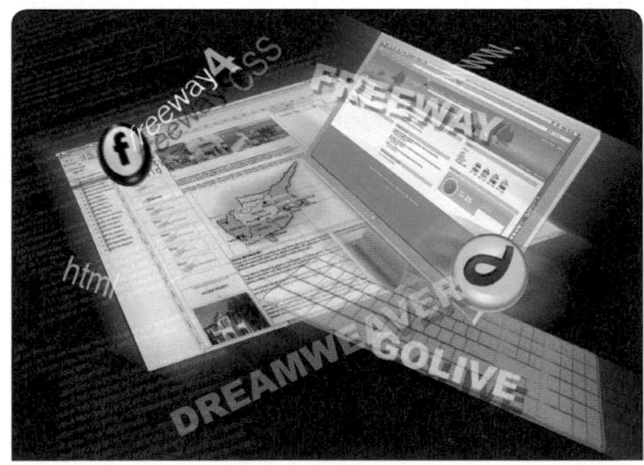

Cove Photography Club – Website
You are a member of a photography club. The organisers have recently produced a booklet with guidelines and tips for new photographers – this has been well received. The Chairman would like to reach a wider audience and has approached you to help plan, design and create a small website for the club.

He would like to include information about the club and its activities, joining details, an online application form, facts about different digital camera types, advice about buying digital cameras and details of a quarterly competition. The Chairman thinks a site of about six to eight pages may be appropriate and has asked you for your comments. He is able to provide you with images used in the production of the booklet and has given you permission to source your own suitable, copyright-free images. He has also given you permission to use any of the text from the magazine.

He would like you to present your planning documents and ideas for the site at the next club meeting. You will then be given the go-ahead to create the website.

PLANNING YOUR WEBSITE

In an OCR assignment, you must use the provided Planning and Review Form to make notes of your planning. To become familiar with using the correct forms, it is a good idea to use this form for your practice work as well. You can use other planning documents as well. For a website, a **site map** is very useful in helping you to plan the site. An assignment may also require you to use a Storyboard – this is covered in the 'Common Skills' chapter.

Refer to 'Planning your work' and 'Reviewing your work' sections on pages xiv and xxi of the 'Common Skills' chapter.

When creating your planning documents, you must refer to the given assignment brief frequently. You may be required to write a **proposal** for a website. If so, you could include details of why the website is needed, the purpose it will serve, who it is intended for, the plan for website, how it will be produced and tested, what resources will be needed and how long it will take to produce.

Key terms

Proposal A written document with ideas for the planned website. The proposal may include sketches such as a site map and/or storyboard.

Site map

Site maps can be textual but are more commonly visual models. The site map makes it easier for a user to find information on a site without having to navigate through the site's many pages. A site map is also often created when planning a website.

Key terms

Site map An overview of the entire structure of a website, like a table of contents. It shows users the pages, the scope of the site and how it can be navigated.

Before you create a website it is a good idea to create a site map. This will keep you focused on what to include on each page. It will also help when you create links to pages because the page names will have already been decided.

An example of a site map to plan a website is shown in Figure 2.1. The arrows indicate how each page will link to the other pages in the site.

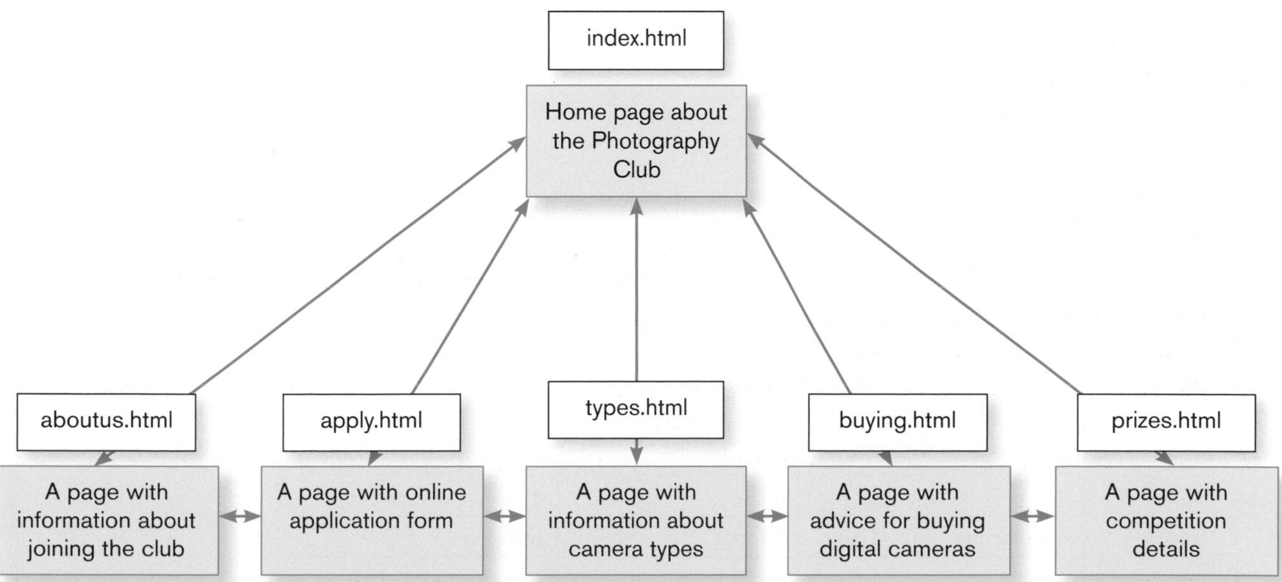

Figure 2.1 Example of a site map

House style

It is common practice to produce **house style** guidelines for a website. The guidelines can be presented in many different ways, e.g. as a single sheet in the form of a list or using tables or tabs.

Before you create your house style sheet, refer to your assignment brief. The house style must be appropriate for the target audience stated in the brief. Your house style sheet could include:

- font type
- font sizes
- background, text and link colours
- background image and other images or logos
- image sizes
- the overall layout and spacing
- file formats for the pages in your site.

An example of a house style sheet is shown in Figure 2.2.

Key terms

House style A set of guidelines or conventions (rules) that organisations use to create and maintain a consistent look for the documents produced by anyone in that organisation.

Cove Photography Club Website House Style Guidelines

Meta tags:

keywords	camera, digital, megapixel, resolution
author	(Web page creator's name)
description	(to describe the content of each web page)

Page properties:

background image	grainy.gif
background colour	#cccccc
text colour	#336699
link colour	#000099
visited link colour	#990099

Table:

columns	1	cell spacing	2	cell width column 1	72 pixels
rows	6	cell padding	2	cell height column 1	100 pixels
width	750 pixels	border	0	align	centre
Split cells in rows 2, 3, 4 to create two columns.					

Navigation table, in column 1. Image attributes and links:

Image width=70 pixels, height=98 pixels, border=0

row	2	3	4
image	dchome.jpg	res.jpg	info.jpg
alt text	camera types	about resolution	request a fact sheet
link to	index.htm	guide.htm	fsform.htm

Figure 2.2 Example of a house style sheet

PRACTICAL TASK 2.3 Identify client's requirements, produce planning documents, organise source files

Assessment objectives 1a, 3a

1. Refer to the 'Planning your work' and 'Reviewing your work' sections on pages xiv and xxi in the 'Common Skills' chapter.
2. Obtain a copy of a Planning and Review Form (ask your tutor for a copy).
3. Refer to the Assignment Brief for the 'Cove Photography Club – Website' on page 64.
4. Identify the 'client' and their requirements. You may have a discussion with your tutor, acting as the client.
5. Produce a brief proposal for a website for the club. The proposal should state the hardware and software that you will need to create the website.
6. Explain how and from where you will source text and image files for your client's website.
7. To help the client visualise the proposed website, create a site map for the proposed site. The site map must show the total number of pages planned, the web page names, and a brief overview of the page content. The site map must include a minimum of six pages and should show how the pages will be linked.
8. Produce a house style sheet for the site (do not copy the example shown!).
9. Source all the files that you will need to create the client's website. All downloaded material must be referenced.
10. Ensure all the file types are appropriate: text files should be saved in **txt** format; images in **gif**, **jpg/jpeg** or **png** format; sounds in **wav**, **mp3** or **midi** format; video clips in **swf** or **mov** format.
11. Create suitable folders and subfolders for the website and organise all files. Open and check all files.

SECTION 2 • Create a template, a cascading style sheet and insert hyperlinks

The following assessment objectives will be covered in this section:

1a Define a website
1b Examine and view HTML tags
1c Create a basic web page
1d Use templates
1e Use site management tools to manage files
2a Add content to a website

The following knowledge, skills and understanding criteria corresponding to assessment objectives 1b, 1c, 1d, 1e and 2a will also be covered:

- *Methods of viewing tags in a browser*
- *Components of a web page*
- *Ways of enhancing web pages*
- *Reasons for using templates*
- *Ways of using templates to build websites more efficiently*
- *Site management tools*
- *Appropriate naming conventions*
- *Tools and features*

Note that for the Level 2 iMedia syllabus, you are not required to use cascading style sheets. However, this is a useful skill and will help you to use consistent styles on all pages in your website.

For an OCR assessment, you will need to:

- ***create a minimum of six web pages for AO 1c***
- ***use at least one template for AO 1d***
- ***create a minimum of one hyperlink on each web page, including a minimum of one external hyperlink in the website, for AO 2a.***

Before you start creating your website, make absolutely sure that you have created your folder structure in your working area, that you have all the files you will need and that you have organised and checked all files.

STARTING DREAMWEAVER

Dreamweaver is a web-authoring program which allows you to see how a page will look on screen as you create it.

▸▸ HOW TO ... Start Dreamweaver

1 Click on **Start → All Programs → Macromedia → Macromedia Dreamweaver 8** *or*
if you have shortcut icons on the Desktop 

or Taskbar , click on the shortcut icon.

2 First-time users will see a **Workspace Setup** dialogue box, giving you two options for the workspace. Keep the default option for **Designer → OK**.

3 A Macromedia Dreamweaver 8 **Start Page** will be displayed (refer to Figure 2.3).

Continued ...

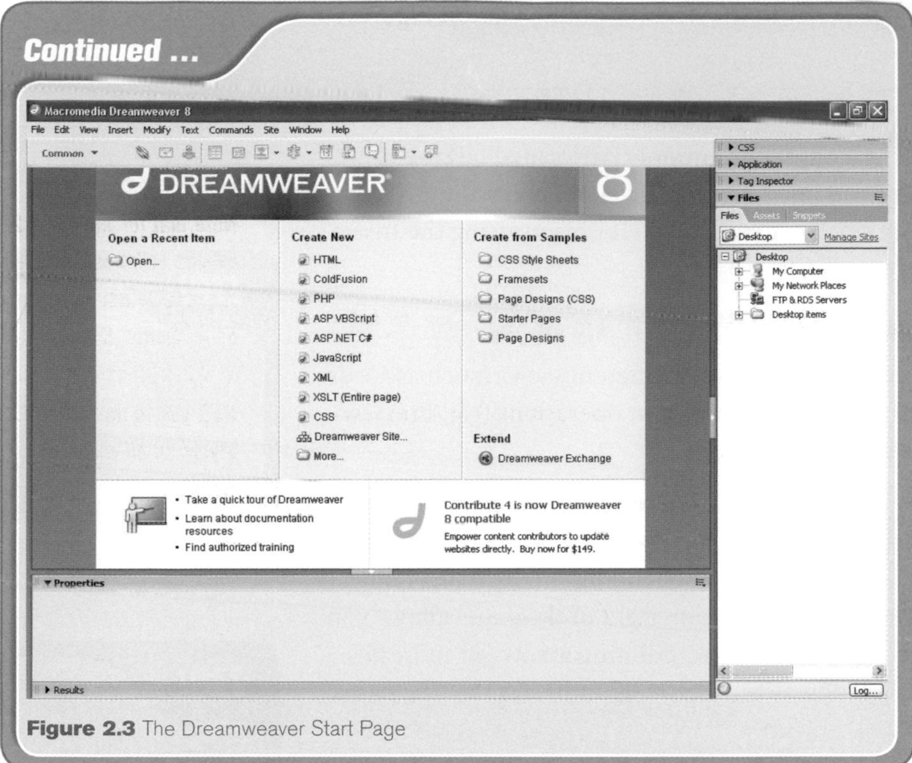

Figure 2.3 The Dreamweaver Start Page

TIP!

You can change the workspace options at any time: **Edit ⟶ Preferences ⟶** select the required options. In the **General** tab, set the spelling dictionary to **English (British)**.

UNDERSTANDING THE DREAMWEAVER SCREEN

To understand the Dreamweaver screen, it will help if you open a new web page. From the centre pane of the Start Page (Figure 2.3), below **Create New**, select **HTML** Create New HTML. You should see a blank page as in Figure 2.4.

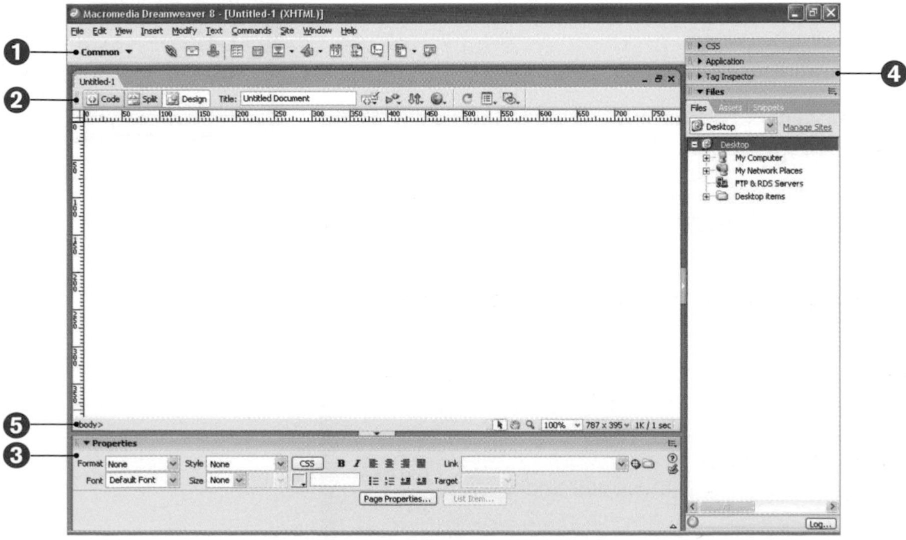

Figure 2.4 The Dreamweaver screen

The numbers in the following list refer to the features pointed out in Figure 2.4.

❶ 

The **Insert toolbar** contains icons for commonly performed tasks, e.g. inserting hyperlinks, tables and images. Hover over an icon with the mouse pointer to see a tool tip. You can also insert objects using the Insert menu instead of the Insert toolbar.

❷ 

The **Document toolbar** contains buttons for different views (such as Code view and Design view), as well as some common operations (e.g. Preview in browser) and various viewing options.

❸ The **Properties panel**, also referred to as the **Property inspector**, allows you to see and change various properties for a selected object or block of text. Different properties will be displayed depending on the type of object selected on the page. The arrow at the bottom right of the panel allows you to expand or contract the panel. An upward pointing arrow △ indicates that the panel is expanded. A downward arrow ▽ indicates that the panel is contracted.

❹ Panel groups are sets of related panels grouped together under one heading. For example, in Figure 2.4 the **Files** group is displayed – within this group are the **Files**, **Assets** and **Snippets** tabs. A down arrow, e.g. **▼ Files** indicates the panel is expanded, and an arrow to the right, e.g. ▶ CSS indicates the panel is contracted.

- To hide or expand a panel, click the vertical or horizontal arrow at the edge of it ▼.
- To display a panel, click the **Window** menu and select the panel name.

❺ The **tag selector** <body> in the status bar at the bottom of the Document window shows the HTML tag for the current selection. Click a tag to select it and all its contents.

TIP!

When working on your web pages you will find it easier to work in Design View.

TIP!

*To hide all panels: **Window** menu → **Hide Panels** or press **F4** to display and hide panels.*

TIP!

*To see the underlying HTML code: click the **Show Code View** button Code at any time, even when you create a new page.*

Student review 2.2 – Understand the Dreamweaver screen

You will find it useful to spend a few minutes becoming familiar with the Dreamweaver window.

1. *Use your mouse to hover over various different icons. Click the arrows to expand and contract different panels.*
2. *Click the **Show Code view** button Code – notice that there is already some underlying HTML code even though there is no content on the page.*
3. *Click the **Split** button (the tool tip displays as **Show Code and Design views**) and enter some text on the web pages (not in the **Code view**!). Notice where the text is placed in the **Code view**.*

Student review 2.2 – continued

4 Click in the **Title** text box in the Document toolbar, delete the text 'Untitled Document' and enter a title. Notice where the title is placed in the Code view. You may need to scroll up.

5 Highlight some text on the web page and practise using different formatting options in the **Properties** panel. As you do this, notice the changes on the web page view and the Code view.

6 Click the **Show Design view** Design button.

7 Click the cross at the top right of the web page (not the red cross at the top of the screen!).

8 A dialogue box will be displayed, asking if you want to save the page. Click **No**.

USING SITE MANAGEMENT TOOLS TO SET UP A WEBSITE AND MANAGE FILES

To create web pages in Dreamweaver, the first thing you need to do is set up a new website.

HOW TO ... Set up a new website

1 **Site** menu → **New Site** → a **Site Definition for Unnamed Site 1** dialogue box is displayed → select the **Basic** tab → below **What would you like to name your site?**, delete the existing text and enter a suitable website name (notice the dialogue box title change as you enter a site name, refer to Figure 2.5) → do not enter anything in the box below → click **Next**.

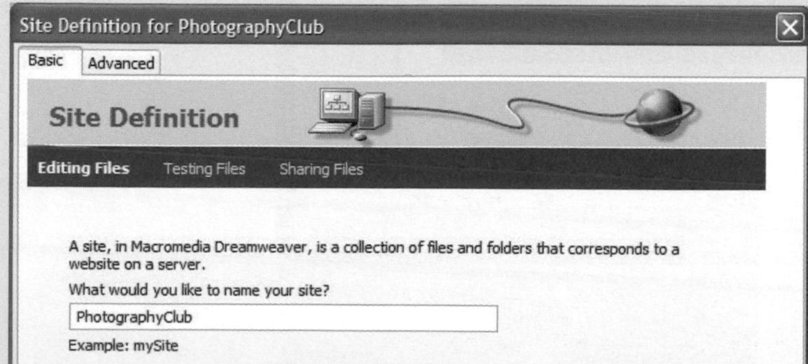

Figure 2.5 Step 1 of Defining a new site

2 A second dialogue box for **Editing Files, Part 2** is displayed → click the button for **No, I do not want to use a server technology** (refer to Figure 2.6) → click **Next**.

At step 2, the button for **Yes, I want to use a server technology** is selected if you are creating web pages dynamically from the contents of a database.

Continued ...

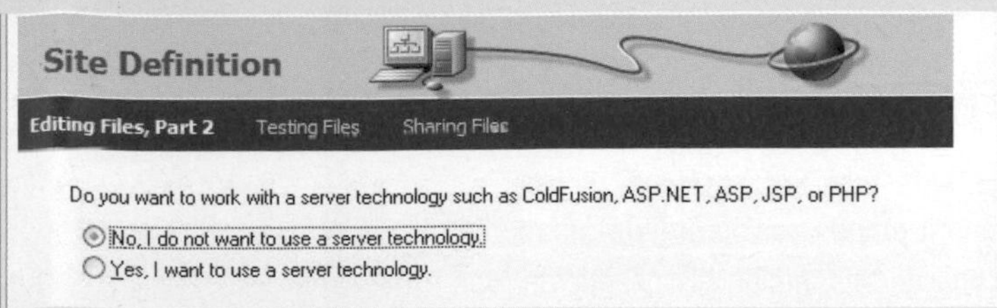

Figure 2.6 Step 2 of Defining a new site

3 An **Editing Files, Part 3** dialogue box is displayed → select the option for **Edit local copies on my machine, then upload to server when ready** → below this click the icon representing a folder and select the location in your user area where you want to save the website (refer to Figure 2.7) → click **Next**.

*Note: If you have already created a folder for your website, select this folder → click **Open** then **Select** → click **Next**.*

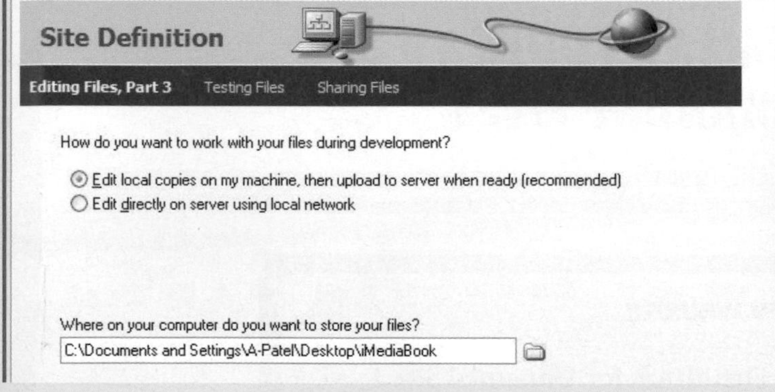

Figure 2.7 Step 3 of Defining a new site

4 Click the drop-down arrow below **How do you connect to your remote server?** and select **None** (refer to Figure 2.8) → click **Next**.

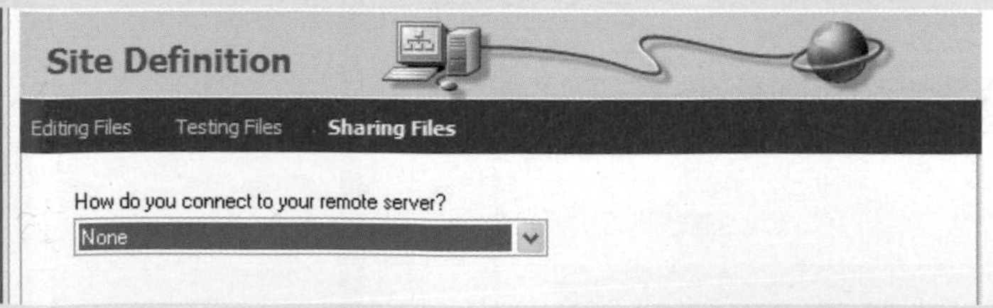

Figure 2.8 Step 4 of Defining a new site

TIP!

At step 3, select the location for your website carefully. Dreamweaver looks for the website folder in that location every time you start the program. If the website folder has been moved, you will need to define the website every time you start Dreamweaver.

Continued ...

5 A summary dialogue box is displayed (Figure 2.9) → click **Done**.

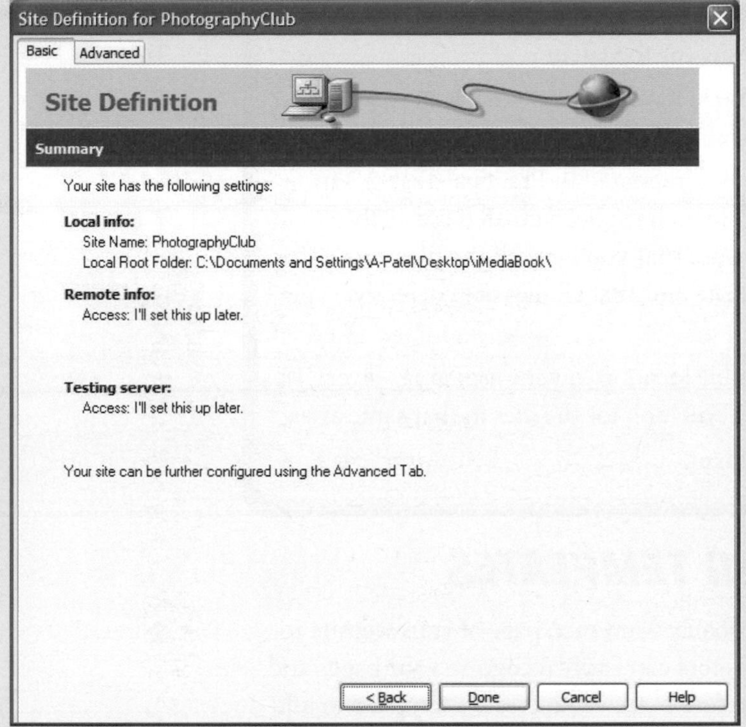

Figure 2.9 The summary of a new site

6 Check the **Files** panel to ensure that you have all the source files you need for your website. Click the plus symbol to view a folder contents.

Dreamweaver will maintain a link to the folder in your working area. It is important that you do not move or delete this folder because the link will then be lost. In a centre, you may not be using the same computer for every session. If so, at the beginning of a new session, you should re-establish the link by defining the site again.

TIP!

To delete a site, click the ***Site*** *menu →* ***Manage Sites*** *→ a* ***Manage Sites*** *dialogue box is displayed → select the site → click* ***Remove*** *→ a dialogue box is displayed prompting you to confirm the deletion → click* ***Yes*** *→ close the* ***Manage Sites*** *dialogue box.*

TIP!

To delete a file from within the site, select the file and press the ***Delete*** *key. The file will also be deleted from the folder in your user area.*

TIP!

To undo an action, press the ***Ctrl + Z*** *keys or* ***Edit*** *menu →* ***Undo****.*

PRACTICAL TASK 2.4 **Check folders and set up site**

Assessment objectives 1a, 1e

1 In your planning documents, identify what hardware and software you will use to create the website for the client.
2 Identify how and from where you have sourced your text, image files and other filed for your website.
3 In your user area, open your folder created in Practical Task 2.3 in Section 1. Check that all subfolders have been created correctly. Open and check all files to ensure that you have all the files you need, that all files are appropriate and that all files are correctly saved in subfolders.
4 Ensure that the folder is a suitable location in your user area – every time you start Dreamweaver, it will look for the files in that same area.
5 Set up a new site in Dreamweaver.

REASONS FOR USING TEMPLATES

When creating a website, you will probably want each page of your website to have a uniform appearance so that visitors can easily recognise your pages and can navigate your site easily. It is therefore practical to create a template to add uniformity to your website. The template will not be uploaded when/if the website is uploaded; it simply provides you with a model on which to build each of the pages.

Key terms

Meta tag A special HTML tag that provides information about the web page. Meta tags are not displayed on the web page. They contain information about the page (description), which keywords represent the page content, etc.

Basic page layout features such as font types, sizes, colours, alignment and meta tags can be set on the template. When a new web page is created, a copy of the template can be opened and the new content simply inserted. Using a master page ensures that the layout and standard content (for example a navigation table containing the links to other pages or a copyright notice) will remain consistent and will save time as the common elements will not need to be re-inserted on each new page.

Another advantage of using a template is the ease of updating existing web pages in the site. If you change your mind about a feature after creating a few pages, e.g. you want to change the font type, you can change it once on the template page and all pages in your site will be automatically updated.

TEMPLATES IN DREAMWEAVER

Dreamweaver automatically locks most regions of a template. As the template author, you need to define which regions of the template will be editable – to do so you need to insert editable regions. When the template is used to create web pages, changes can only be made to these editable regions, all other locked regions cannot be changed. 'How to create editable regions in a template' and 'How to insert a repeating region in a template' are covered on pages 88 and 89.

▶▶ HOW TO ... Create and save a new template

1 **File** menu → **New** → a **New Document** dialogue box is displayed. Ensure the **General** tab is selected. In the left pane below **Category**, select **Template page**. In the middle pane below **Template page**, select **HTML template** (refer to Figure 2.10) → click **Create**.

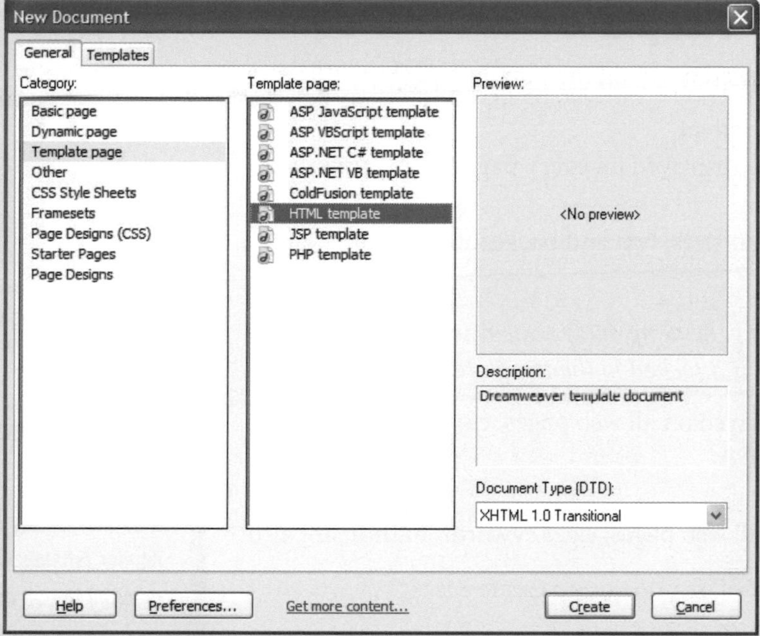

Figure 2.10 Creating a new template

2 To save the template: **File** menu → **Save** (or **Save As Template**) → a dialogue box is displayed telling you that **This template doesn't have any editable regions** (Figure 2.11) → click **OK** → a **Save As Template** dialogue box is displayed, enter a suitable filename (refer to Figure 2.12) → click **Save.** Notice that a **Templates** folder is automatically created in the **Files** panel, within it is your new template (Figure 2.13).

*Note: In Dreamweaver, a template is saved with a **.dwt** file extension (dreamweaver template).*

TIP!

At step 1, you can also select **Basic page** below **Category**.

TIP!

When you save a new template you have created, it is good practice to avoid absolute links (refer to the section 'Understanding relative and absolute links' on page 86).

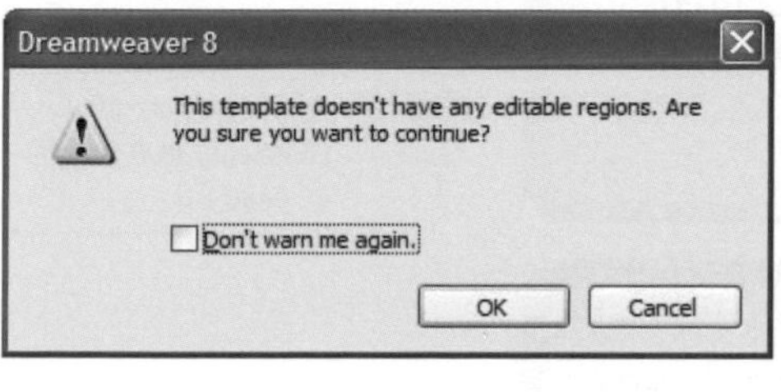

Figure 2.11 Warning displayed when saving a new template

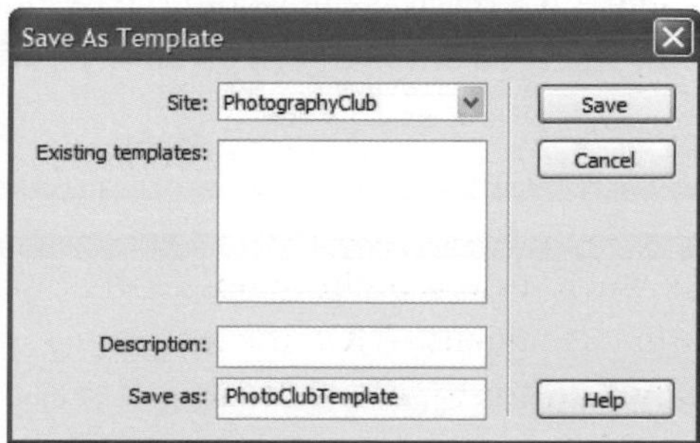

Figure 2.12 Saving a template

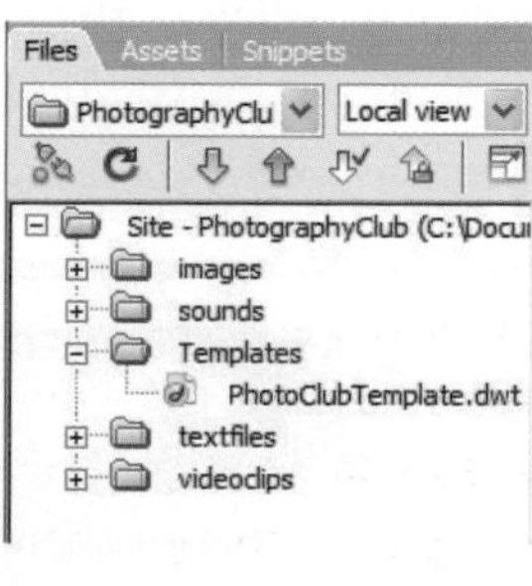

Figure 2.13 A template saved in the Files panel

Student review 2.3 – Templates

Assessment objective 1d

1 Describe the advantages of using a template for a website.
2 Explain how a template can be used to build a website efficiently.

What to add on your template

The following items should be inserted or set on the template page:

- Tables or frames to align page content.
- Standard content that should be displayed on every page for example, a copyright notice.
- Formatting of the font types, font sizes, text and background colours, link colours.

  Note: Formatting of text styles (e.g. heading, body text) is usually defined in a cascading style sheet (css) which is attached to the template page.

- Hyperlinks that should be displayed on all web pages, e.g. a navigation bar/table and/or navigation buttons.
- Repeating regions.
- Meta tags that are common to all web pages, e.g. keywords, author, are also frequently added to a template page.

Refer to 'Cascading style sheets' on page 83.

Note that for the Level 2 iMedia syllabus you are not required to use meta tags

Formatting a template

HOW TO ... Format text, links and background colours

1 Ensure your saved template page is open → **Modify** menu → **Page Properties** → a **Page Properties** dialogue box is displayed (refer to Figure 2.14).

2 With **Appearance** selected below **Category**, set the **Text color** and **Background color** in turn:

- click on the down arrow → a colour palette is displayed → select a colour – the mouse pointer changes to an eye-dropper when you move over the colour swatch *or*
- click in the box, enter a # (hash) symbol and the hexadecimal code (if you know the code or have been given specific colour codes).

You must refer to your planning documentation when formatting the template and adding standard content. Ensure that you stick to your plan, storyboard, site map and house style guidelines.

Refer to 'Ways of enhancing web pages' on page 58.

TIP!

Colours selected from the colour palette are web safe, i.e. they will look the same on all browsers. Codes entered or colours selected from the ***Color Picker*** *may not be web safe.*

Continued ...

3 If you want to use the same font type for all text, click the drop-down arrow to the right of **Page font** and select an option. Otherwise, you can set different font types for the different text styles (e.g. heading, body text) when you create your style sheet.

4 To display a background image on all web pages → click the **Browse** button to the right of **Background image** → browse to the **images** subfolder in your website folder → select the image.

5 Below **Category**, select **Links** and set the link colours, e.g. **Link colour**, **Visited links**, **Active links** (refer to Figure 2.15).

6 Check all the settings → click **OK**.

TIP!

Entering a title for the template is not necessary as the template is not displayed in the browser.

TIP!

Click the ***Show Code View*** *button*  *to see the HTML code that has been generated for the formatting you have set on the template.*

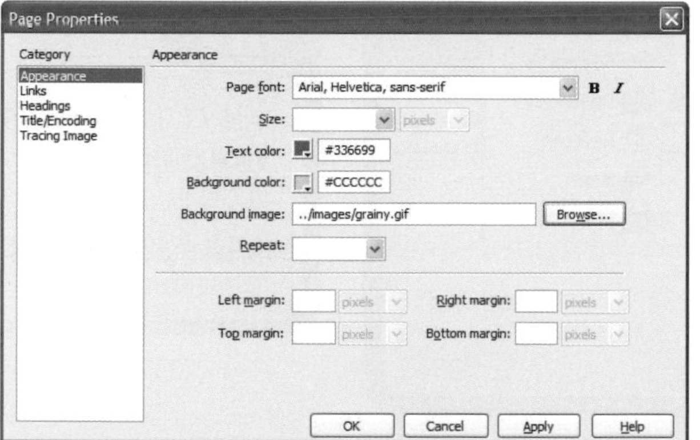

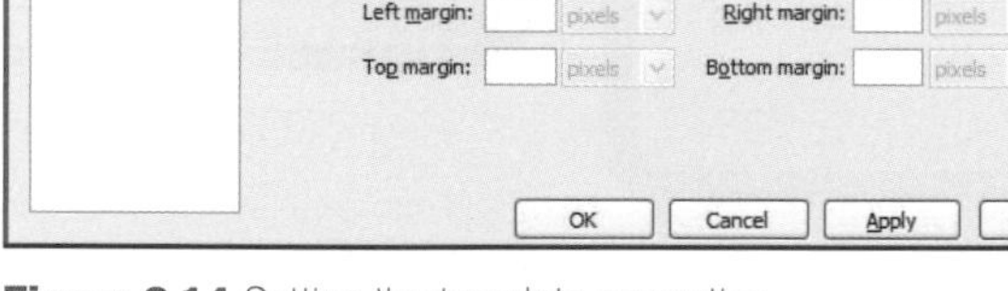

Figure 2.14 Setting the template properties

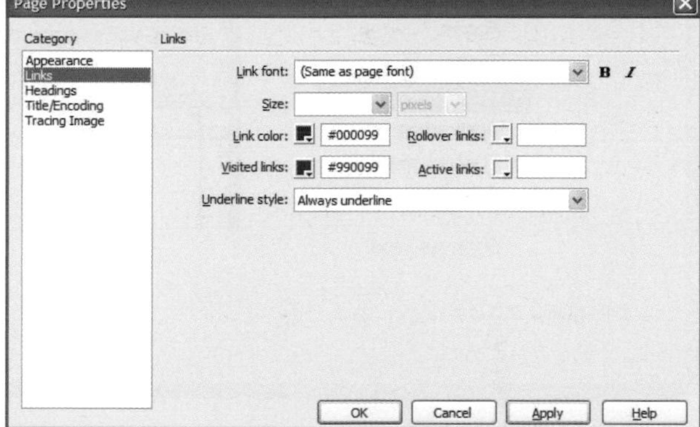

Figure 2.15 Setting the link colours

META TAGS

A meta tag is an HTML code used to describe different aspects of a website. Meta tags are not displayed on a web page, but give additional information about the page. Commonly used meta tags are keywords, author, title and description.

- **Keywords**: Enter the words that you think are important on your web page. If the keywords are also on the web page, some search engines will use these keywords to return search results when people search the Internet. An increasing number of search engines ignore keywords.
- **Author**: Entering the name of the person who created the web page in the author meta tag enables them to be identified.
- **Title**: Information entered in the title meta tag is displayed in the Title bar of the web page when the page is viewed in a browser. The title is used as the default bookmark.
- **Description**: Some search engines use this information to display a summary of the content of the web page when search results are displayed.

i

The title and description should be entered for each web page – these should be unique for each web page.

▸▸ HOW TO ... Create meta tags

1 From the Insert toolbar, click the drop-down arrow to the right of **Common** → select **HTML** (refer to Figure 2.16).

2 From the HTML toolbar, click the drop-down arrow to the right of the **Head: Meta** icon  and select an option.

- To enter the author name, select **Meta** from the list → a **Meta** dialogue box is displayed → **Name** is displayed in the Attribute box, do not change this → in the **Value** box enter the word **author** → enter your own name in the **Content** box → **OK**.
- To enter keywords, select **Keywords** from the list → a **Keywords** dialogue box is displayed → enter your keywords selectively, separating each word with a comma → **OK**.

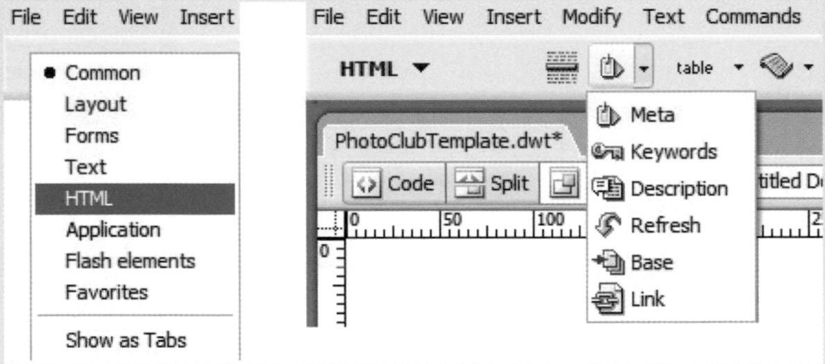

Figure 2.16 Adding meta tags

When you create each new web page, enter a description following steps 1 and 2, selecting ***Description*** *from the list. Refer to the information box on page 92 for how to enter a title.*

TIP!

Click on the **Show Code View** button Code to see the HTML code that has been generated for the meta tags.

PRACTICAL TASK 2.5 Create and format a template, insert meta tags, view html tags

Assessment objectives 1b, 1c, 1d

1 Create a new template and save it using a suitable name.

2 Format the page properties (background colour/image, text colour, link colours and page font).

3 Enter your own name and suitable keywords in the author and keywords meta tags (optional).

4 Check the HTML code for your template.

5 Save the updated template (**File** menu → **Save**).

USING TABLES TO ALIGN PAGE CONTENT

Tables are often used to organise the contents of a web page; their main use on web pages is as a layout tool. The width of the whole web page can be set so that the contents display in full regardless of the browser or the screen size and/or resolution used to view the web page. Rows and columns can be used to divide the page into sections.

Many sites use a width of 800 pixels which will allow the web page to fit on most screens without needing to scroll across. Some sites, for example, www.payne-gallway.co.uk use a narrower width of 600 pixels so that people with narrower screens can view the page.

Frames

Instead of using tables, frames can be used to divide a browser window into multiple regions, each of which can display a different HTML page independent of what is being displayed in the rest of the browser window. In the most common use of frames, one frame displays a page containing navigation controls, while another frame displays a page with content. Using frames is beyond the requirements of this syllabus.

Table properties

Table dimensions (size) can be set in pixels or as a percentage. Although the height of a table can be specified, it is more common to set only the width. This is because the content of each table cell will determine the height.

Defining the width in pixels will display the table on-screen to the exact width specified. If the screen used to view the website has a resolution less than the size of the table, or if the window has been resized, scroll bars will appear enabling visitors to view the information that is not visible by scrolling across or down.

Defining the width as a percentage will display the table to the percentage of the available space. If the size of the window is reduced, the table (and contents) will be reduced in size so that the entire table will still be displayed.

Pixels or percent

*To set an **absolute** (fixed) size for the table, select **pixels.***

*To size the table **relative** to the size of the browser window, select **percent.***

TIP!

*Defining the width in pixels sets the **minimum** width for the table or cell. If the content of the table cell is greater than the number of pixels specified, the table or cell will expand to accommodate the table or cell content.*

TIP!

Tables can be created on the template or on individual web pages.

INSERTING AND FORMATTING TABLES

▶▶ HOW TO ... Insert a new table and set table properties

1 Before you begin, ensure **Common** is selected from the **Insert** toolbar and check the cursor is flashing at the top left of the page.

2 On the **Common** toolbar, click the **Table** icon → a **Table** dialogue box is displayed (refer to Figure 2.17) → in the appropriate boxes, enter the required values for **Rows, Columns, Table width**

***Cell padding** sets padding (space) inside the cell. Setting cell padding prevents the cell content from touching the cell borders.*

Continued ...

(select **pixels** or **percent** as required), **Border thickness**, **Cell padding** and **Cell spacing**.

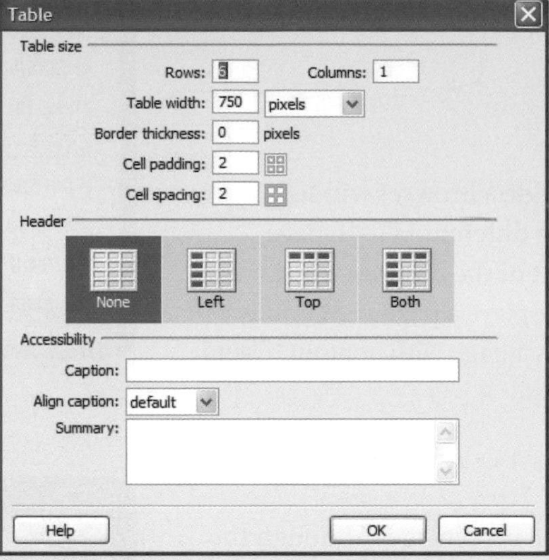

Figure 2.17 Setting table properties

> ⓘ **Cell borders** create a visible border between cells. If you do not want a visible border the **Border thickness** must be set to 0 (zero).

> **TIP!**
> The default table alignment is left. To change the alignment select the **table** tag <table>, click the drop-down to the right of **Align** in the **Properties** panel, and select an option.

Selecting table elements to display properties

▶▶ HOW TO ... Select table elements

- Use the **Tag selector**: click in the table → look at the bottom left of the page above the **Properties** panel → the **table tags** display in an area called the **Tag selector** <body> <table> <tr> <td> .
- Clicking on a tag will select the object in the table containing the cursor as follows:
  - <table> will select the entire **table**.
  - <tr> will select the row (tr stands for **table row**).
  - <td> will select the table cell (td stands for **table data**).

> **TIP!**
> To resize a table or cell, select the appropriate tag, and change the properties in the **Properties** panel as required.

▶▶ HOW TO ... Insert or delete rows and columns at the end of a table

- To add or delete the bottom row or right-hand column, select the Table tag <table> and change the number of rows or columns in the **Properties** panel.

> **TIP!**
> To insert a new row at the bottom of the table quickly, click in the last cell and press the **Tab** key.

▶▶ HOW TO ... Add a row or column within a table

- Position the cursor in the required cell → right-click to display a menu → **Table** → **Insert Row** or **Insert Column**.

A new row is inserted above the cell containing the cursor. A new column is inserted to the left of the cell containing the cursor.

▶▶ HOW TO ... Delete a row or column

- Position the cursor in the required cell → right-click to display a menu → **Table** → **Delete Row** or **Delete Column**.

TIP!

*Save your updated web page file often: **File** → **Save** → the dialogue box about the template not having editable regions will be displayed → **OK** → **Save**.*

▶▶ HOW TO ... Merge cells

- Highlight the required cells → right-click to display a menu → **Table** → **Merge Cells** *or* click the **Merges selected cells using spans** icon in the **Properties** panel.

▶▶ HOW TO ... Split cells

- Position the cursor in the required cell → right-click to display a menu → **Table** → **Split Cell** or click the **Splits cells into rows or columns** icon in the **Properties** panel.

▶▶ HOW TO ... Set cell properties (width, height, alignment)

- Highlight the required cells (do not select the entire table) → set the required options in the **Properties** panel (refer to Figure 2.18).
- To set the properties of one cell, click in the cell → set the required options in the **Properties** panel:
  - To set the horizontal alignment, click the drop-down arrow to the right of **Horz** and select an option (e.g. **Center** or **Right**).
  - To set the vertical alignment, click the drop-down arrow to the right of **Vert** and select an option.
  - To enter a width, click in the box for **W** and enter a number.
  - To enter a height, click in the box for **H** and enter a number.

  *Note: to set the cell width or height in pixels, you only need to enter a number as the default is pixels, **but** if you want to set the cell width or height to a percentage of the table width/height, you **MUST** enter a % symbol after the number.*

TIP!

*The default horizontal cell alignment is **Left** and default vertical alignment is **Middle**. If these are the options you want, you don't need to change the alignment in the **Properties** panel.*

TIP!

W is width; H is height.

Continued ...

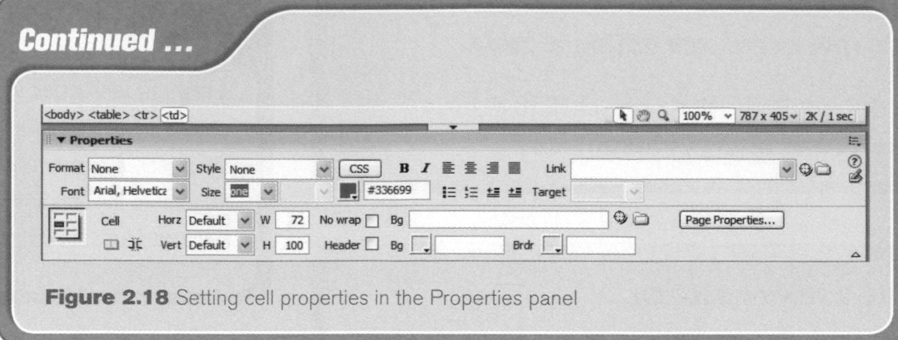

Figure 2.18 Setting cell properties in the Properties panel

▶▶ HOW TO ... Insert a nested table

- Click in the required table cell → click the **Table** button  on the **Common** toolbar → a **Table** dialogue box is displayed → set the required options.

PRACTICAL TASK 2.6 Create and format a table

Assessment objective 2a

1 You need to create a table in your template. Before you do, plan the table width, decide how many rows and columns you will create, how you will split, merge and align cells and what you will include in the table.

2 In your Planning and Review Form, draw a sketch of the table – include brief notes to indicate what you will include in it. Below are some examples of sketches. You must also indicate the table width.

3 In your saved template, create a table as shown on your plan. Split and merge cells as required. Set the cell properties as appropriate.

LINK IMAGE	LINK IMAGE	LINK IMAGE
Heading area		
Body text area		
Link image		
Copyright notice		

TIP!

Click the **Show Code View** button Code to see the HTML code that has been generated for the table you have created.

Key terms

Nested table A table within an existing table cell. If you use a table to set the layout of a page, and you want to use another table to arrange the information, you can insert a nested table.

i

When you make any change to a template or web page, an asterisk * appears to the right of the filename. This asterisk indicates that the latest changes to the page have not been saved.

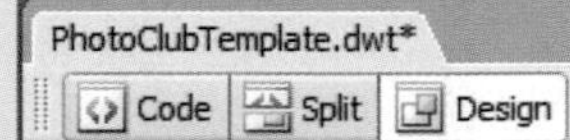

Once you have saved the page, the asterisk disappears.

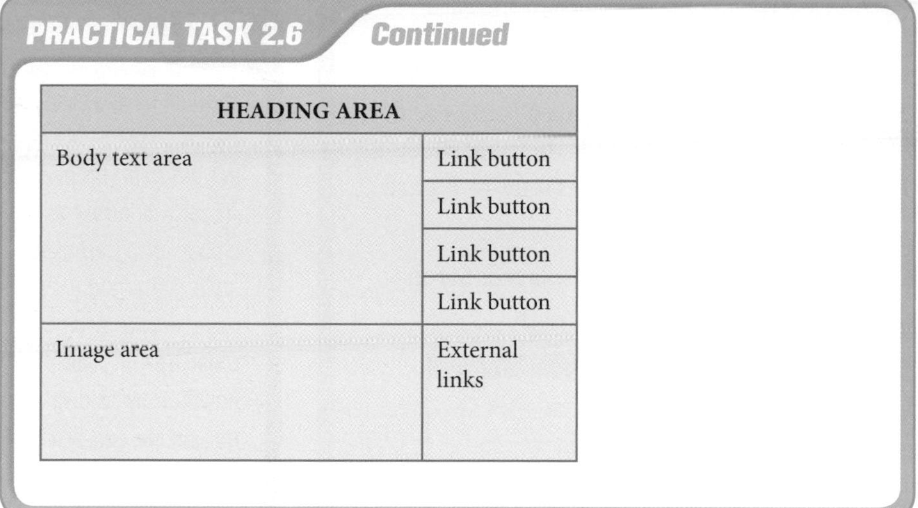

PRACTICAL TASK 2.6 Continued

HEADING AREA	
Body text area	Link button
	Link button
	Link button
	Link button
Image area	External links

CASCADING STYLE SHEETS

Cascading Style Sheets (CSS) are a collection of formatting rules which control the appearance of content in a web page. The style sheet tells the web browser how to display different aspects of the web page. Styles can be applied to paragraphs of text, table cells, images and other HTML elements.

Some advantages of using a cascading style sheet are:

- The amount of code on every web page is reduced making the page faster to load.
- Styles can be applied easily and consistently to different pages.
- If you want to change a style on several pages, and you are using an external style sheet, you only need to do so once. All pages linked to that CSS are updated to reflect the edits.

There are different types of cascading style sheet (e.g. external and embedded), and different ways of creating them. As most web designers use external style sheets and to ensure ease of use, you will create an external CSS and attach it to the template.

Key terms

Cascading Style Sheets (CSS) *A set of formatting rules which control the appearance of content in a web page.*

HOW TO ... Create a new CSS style

1. **Text** menu → **CSS Styles** → New → the **New CSS Rule** dialogue box is displayed.
2. In the **Name** box, enter a full stop followed by the name for the style (e.g. **.heading**, **.subheading**, **.body**, **.table**) (refer to Figure 2.19) → ensure the **Selector Type** is **Class** → to the right of **Define In:** select the button for **New Style Sheet File** → **OK**.

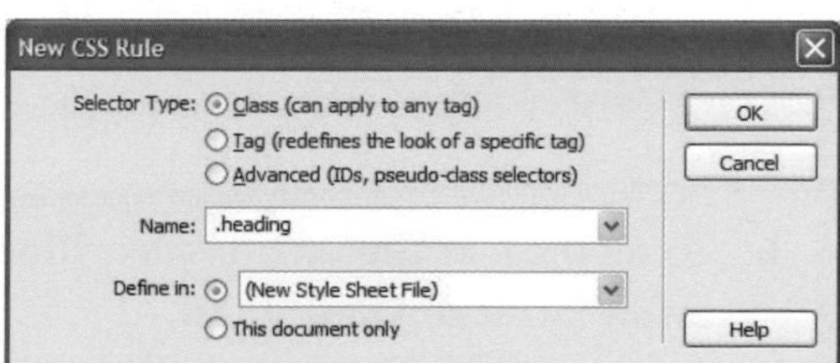

Figure 2. 19 Creating a new CSS style

Continued ...

3 The **Save Style Sheet File As** dialogue box is displayed (only the first time you create a style) → enter a suitable name for the style sheet → ensure that you **Save in** your website folder → **Save** (refer to Figure 2.20).

4 The **CSS Rule Definition for ...** dialogue box is displayed. Set the properties for that style (refer to Figures 2.21 and 2.22).

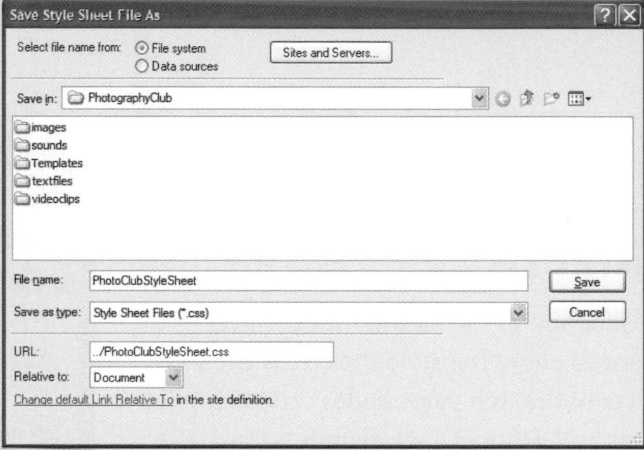

Figure 2.20 Saving a CSS style sheet

5 With **Type** selected below **Category**, click the drop-down arrow beside each option and set the **Font** type, **Size** (make sure you set the measurement to **points** not the default which is pixels), **Style** (e.g. normal, italic), **Weight** (e.g. bold).

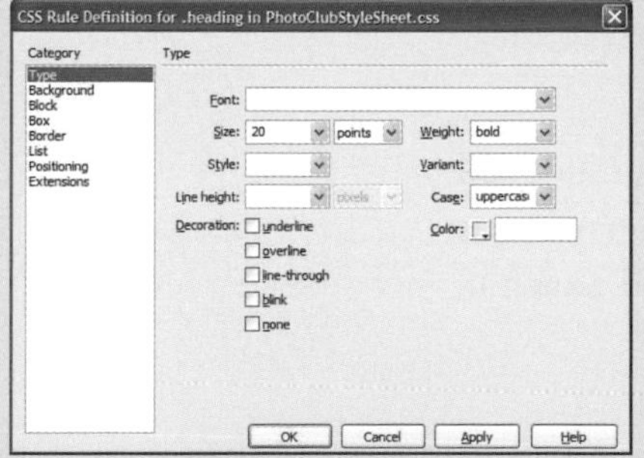

Figure 2.21 Setting the font properties for a style

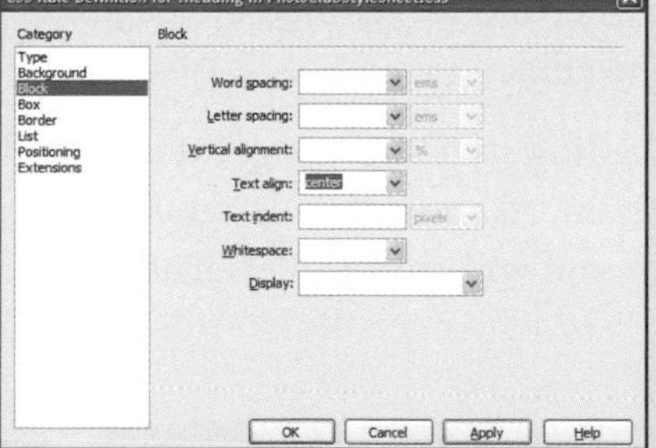

Figure 2.22 Setting the alignment

6 To set the text alignment, select **Block** then click the drop-down arrow for **Text Align** → **OK**.

7 Repeat steps 1–6 to set each new style (e.g. subheading, body, etc).

TIP!

You will have already set the text colour when you set the Page Properties. To set a different text colour for a particular style, either enter the hexadecimal code in the **Color** box or click the down arrow to display the palette and select a colour.

TIP!

To set a font size not displayed on the list, enter the size in the box.

TIP!

Click the **Show Code View** button Code to see the HTML code that has been generated for the CSS styles you have created.

APPLYING STYLES

You should apply your defined styles to appropriate parts of the page – you can apply styles to table cells even if you don't have any text in the cells yet. The advantage of applying the styles on your template is that when you insert text later on individual web pages, the style will be applied automatically.

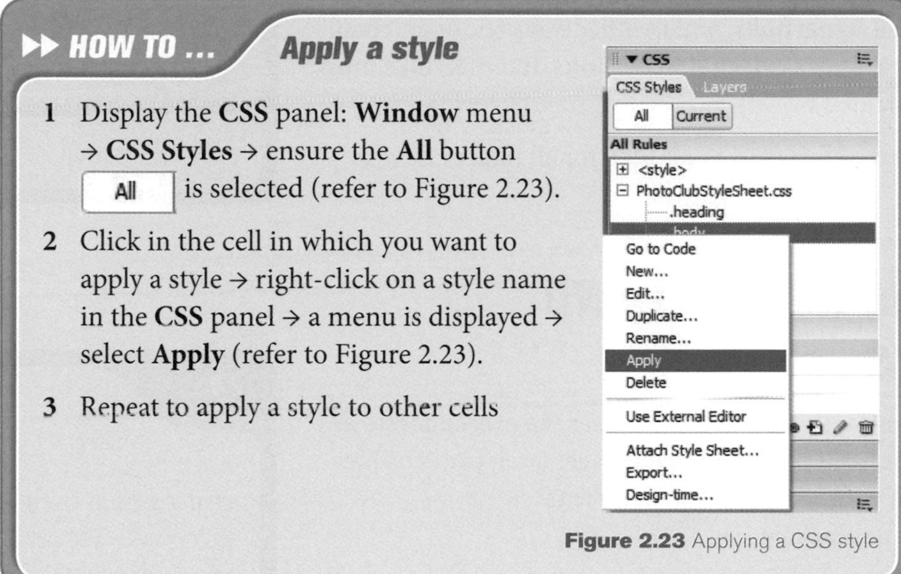

HOW TO ... Apply a style

1 Display the **CSS** panel: **Window** menu → **CSS Styles** → ensure the **All** button [All] is selected (refer to Figure 2.23).

2 Click in the cell in which you want to apply a style → right-click on a style name in the **CSS** panel → a menu is displayed → select **Apply** (refer to Figure 2.23).

3 Repeat to apply a style to other cells

Figure 2.23 Applying a CSS style

*The default line spacing is single. To set other line spacing, with the **Type** Category selected → click the arrow for **Line height** → select **(value)**, enter the required line spacing value in the box → change the measurement to **%**.*
e.g. 1.5 line spacing is 150%

Line height: 150 %.

PRACTICAL TASK 2.7 Create and apply styles

Assessment objectives 1c, 1d

1 Create a style sheet for your website and save it as a **css** file using a suitable filename within your site folder.

2 Create at least three different, suitable styles (e.g. heading, subheads, body).

3 Set suitable font types, sizes, alignment, linespacing etc. for each style.

4 Apply the styles to the appropriate parts of your template.

CREATING A NAVIGATION BAR OR TABLE

A navigation bar, also referred to as a navigation table, is often created on a template page – it will then be visible on every web page that is based on the template. A navigation bar is normally displayed in a row at the top or bottom of a page or in a column on the left or right of a page.

A navigation bar contains images and/or text that are linked to pages in the website, referred to as **internal hyperlinks**, and to other websites, or an email address or a document, referred to as **external hyperlinks**. Internal links must be relative, not absolute (explained below).

You should set **alternative text**, referred to as **alt text**, for all images in your site.

Key terms

Alternative text (alt text) displays when the mouse pointer is hovered over an image. It enables people using a screen reader, or those who have images turned off (to speed up download time), to still understand the content of the website.

UNDERSTANDING RELATIVE AND ABSOLUTE LINKS

An absolute link is an instruction to tell the web browser the *exact* address at which to find the web page or file. Links to **external** pages (web pages or files that are not contained within your website), for example to http://www.ocr.org.uk, must be absolute.

A relative link is an instruction to tell the web browser to find the file from within the website structure. If the website is moved to a different location, the link will still work because it is relative to the actual website and is not affected by where the website is located.

If you do not use the correct type of link the web browser will not be able to find the web page or image and it will not be displayed.

▶▶ HOW TO ... Insert images and animations on templates or web pages and set image properties

In Dreamweaver, images and animations can be inserted easily by dragging the image from the **Files** panel. To insert an image or animated image in between, above or below text, press the **Enter** key to create a blank paragraph first. To insert an image beside text, click at the start of the line of text.

- Before you begin, ensure the template or web page has been saved (to avoid absolute links), and is open.

1 In the **Files** panel, open the **images** folder.

2 Drag the image from the **Files** panel to the required position in the web page → an **Image Tag Accessibility Attributes** dialogue box is displayed (Figure 2.24)→ enter your alt text → do not enter anything in the **Long description** box → **OK**.

Continued ...

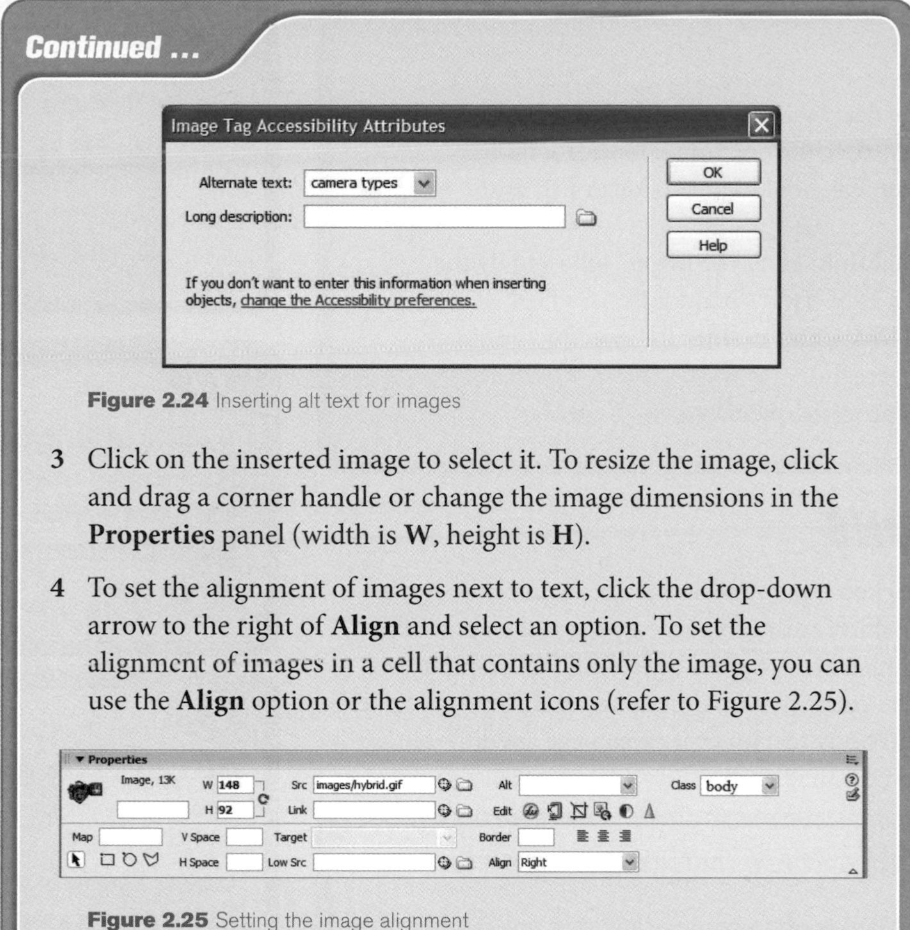

Figure 2.24 Inserting alt text for images

3 Click on the inserted image to select it. To resize the image, click and drag a corner handle or change the image dimensions in the **Properties** panel (width is **W**, height is **H**).

4 To set the alignment of images next to text, click the drop-down arrow to the right of **Align** and select an option. To set the alignment of images in a cell that contains only the image, you can use the **Align** option or the alignment icons (refer to Figure 2.25).

▼ Properties | Image, 13K | W 148 | H 92 | Src images/hybrid.gif | Link | Alt | Edit | Class body | Map | V Space | H Space | Target | Low Src | Border | Align Right

Figure 2.25 Setting the image alignment

If you use the alignment icons to align images next to paragraphs or a heading, the alignment of the text will also change!

When you insert an image onto a template the link will be displayed as follows in the Properties panel:

Src ../images/info.jpg .

Don't be concerned; this is not an absolute link. Images inserted on individual web pages, will not display the ... (dots) before the images subfolder name as shown in Figure 2.25.

TIP!

*You can reduce the download time of higher resolution images by resampling the images in Dreamweaver. To resample, reduce the image size in Dreamweaver first, then click the **Resample** button in the **Properties** panel.*

INSERTING HYPERLINKS

▶▶ HOW TO ... Insert hyperlinks

- Click on an image to select it or highlight the required text → in the **Properties** panel, click in the **Link** box:
  - **to create an internal link**: enter the name of the web page to be linked to, followed by **.htm** or **.html**

    Link index.html

TIP!

*If the web page or document to be linked to already exists in your website, you can create the link quickly by dragging the **Point to File** icon from the **Properties** panel to the web page name in the **Site** panel.*

Continued ...

- **to create a link to a file**: make sure the file is contained within your website folder, enter the document **name** followed by the **file extension**, e.g. bookingform.doc or prices.xls
  Link prices.xls
- **to create an external link**: enter the **http://** followed by the website address, e.g. http://www.ocr.org.uk
- **to create an email link**: enter **mailto:** followed by the email address (with no spaces)
  e.g. mailto:r.patel@progress-media.co.uk

EDITABLE REGIONS

An editable region is an unlocked region in a template, i.e. a section a user can edit. You need to define which areas of your template you want to allow changes to be made in and which areas should be locked. For example, the navigation/bar table should be consistent on every page, so it is common for it to be locked. The heading and body text on every web page are different, so it is common for these areas to be editable.

▶▶ HOW TO ... Create editable regions in a template

1. Select the content that you want to make editable or position the cursor in the required position (e.g. in a table cell).
2. **Insert** menu → **Template Objects** → **Editable Region** *or* from the Common bar, click the drop-down arrow to the right of the **Templates** button → select **Editable Region.**
3. The **New Editable Region** dialogue box is displayed → in the **Name** box, enter a unique name for the region → **OK.**
4. A tab at the top-left corner of the region shows the name of the editable region and the region is enclosed in a box.

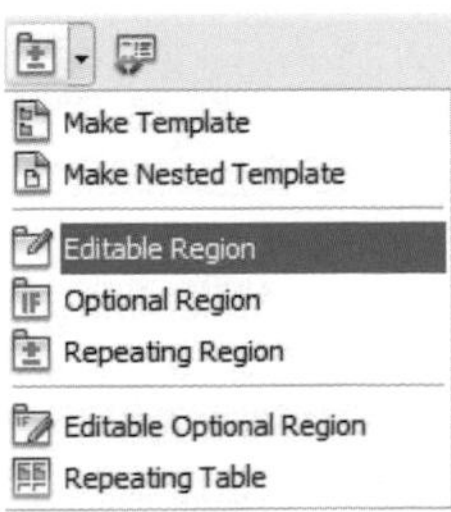

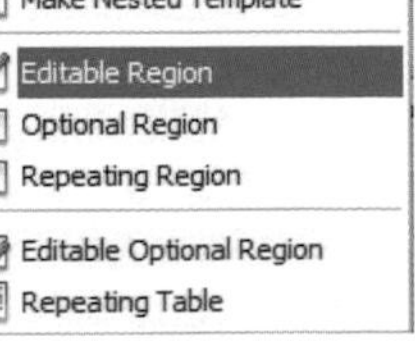

Figure 2.26 Creating an editable region

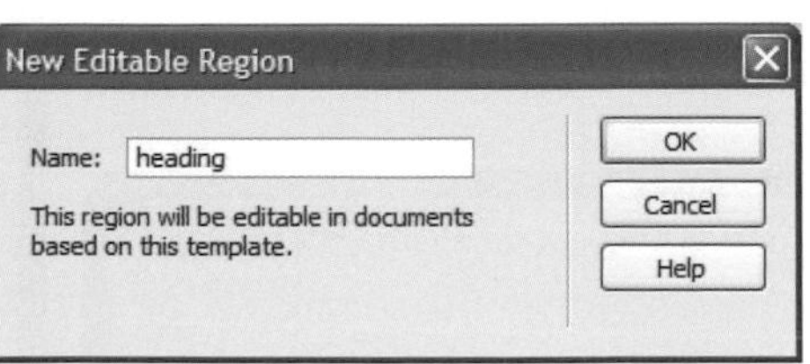

Figure 2.27 Naming an editable region

Figure 2.28 An editable region

TIP!

Click the **Show Code View** button Code to see the HTML code that has been generated for the links you have created.

To insert a special character (e.g. a copyright symbol): Insert menu → HTML → Special Characters → select an option.

Before inserting editable regions ensure you are working on a saved template. If you insert an editable region in a web page, Dreamweaver will warn you that the page will automatically be saved as a template.

TIP!

Do not use special characters in the name of an editable region or a repeating region.

TIP!

To remove an editable region, click the editable region name (top-left of region) → **Modify** menu → **Templates** → **Remove Template Markup**.

REPEATING REGIONS

A repeating region is a section that is set to repeat. It is a section of a template that can be duplicated as often as needed in a template-based page. Repeating regions are often used with tables (e.g. you can set a table to repeat) but can also be used for other page elements.

▶▶ HOW TO ... Insert a repeating region in a template

1 Position the cursor where you want to insert the repeating region.

2 **Insert** menu → **Template Objects** → **Repeating Region** *or* from the Common toolbar, click the drop-down arrow to the right of the **Templates** button → select **Repeating Region**.

3 The **New Repeating Region** dialogue box is displayed → in the **Name** box, enter a suitable name for the template region → **OK**.

4 A repeating region should be made an editable region if needed.

Each repeating region must have a unique name.

PRACTICAL TASK 2.8 Insert images on a template, set image attributes, create hyperlinks and create editable regions

Assessment objectives 1b, 2a

1 Create a navigation bar on your template and insert suitable text and/or images in the navigation bar.

2 Insert at least one image on your template and set suitable alt text. Set the image attributes (width, height, alignment).

3 Create at least one internal, one external and one email link on your template page.

4 Insert editable regions on your template using appropriate region names.

5 If appropriate, insert repeating region(s).

6 Check the HTML code for your template page.

The following assessment objectives will be covered in this section:

1c Create a basic web page

1d Use templates

1e Use site management tools to manage files

2a Add content to a website

2b Apply basic design principles

The following knowledge, skills and understanding criteria corresponding to assessment objectives 1c, 1d, 1e, 2a and 2b will also be covered:

- *Components of a web page*
- *Ways of enhancing web pages*
- *Ways of using templates to build websites more efficiently*
- *Appropriate naming conventions*
- *Tools and features (list formats, image maps)*
- *Basic design principles*

CREATING WEB PAGES BASED ON A TEMPLATE

Once you have created your template, you will find it easy to create web pages. Although new web pages which are not based on the template can be created, you are advised to base all the web pages in your site on the template page. If you decide to make changes to your template, Dreamweaver will ask if you want to update all pages too.

> ⚠ You can only insert content in the editable regions of your template.

Web page names

You should ensure that you save all web pages using appropriate filenames. It is common practice to name the home page of a website as index.html or home.html. Other pages should be saved with names that reflect the content, e.g. if the page contains a form for ordering items, it can be called form.html or order.html.

> **TIP!**
>
> When saving your web pages, use meaningful names that reflect the content. Avoid using meaningless web page names such as **new_page.html**, **untitled1.html** or **webpage1.html**.

▶▶ HOW TO ... Create and save a new web page based on a template

1 **File** menu → **New** → the **New Document** dialogue box is displayed → select the **Templates** tab → below **Templates for** select your site → below **Site ...** → select the template name (refer to Figure 2.29) → **Create**.

Continued ...

2 Save the web page now to avoid the possibility of absolute links later → **File** menu → **Save As** → the **Save As** dialogue box is displayed → make sure you save the web page in your website folder not in the Templates folder → enter a suitable name for your web page (refer to Figure 2.30) → **Save.**

TIP!

When saving a web page, you can use the file extension **.htm** or **.html**. If you don't enter a file extension, Dreamweaver will insert an **.html** extension automatically.

Although **.htm** extensions are fine, a few browsers don't recognise it, so you are advised to use **.html.**

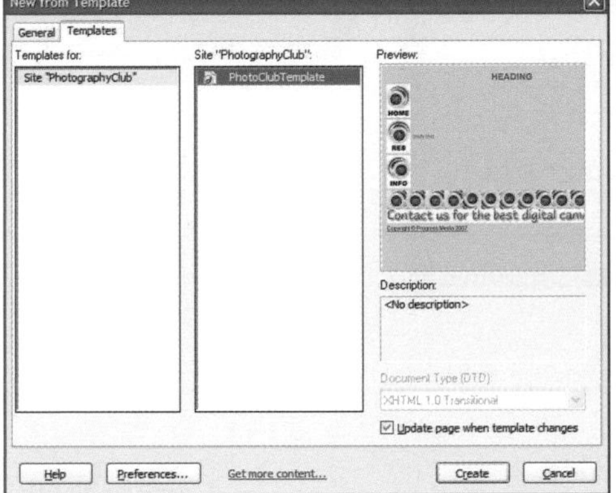

Figure 2.29 Creating a web page based on a template

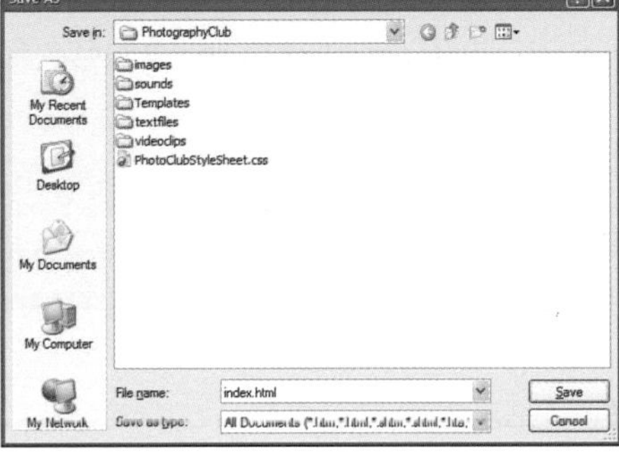

Figure 2.30 Saving a new web page

To avoid problems when formatting text on the web page, it is a good idea to ensure that the linespacing and hard returns are correct in the text file before importing. From your working area, open the text file in Microsoft Word, use the Show/Hide tool to check the hard returns and paragraph spacing. Make any changes as needed and resave the file – the text file in your website folder will also be updated.

To insert images and hyperlinks into the editable regions of individual web pages, refer to 'How to insert images. . .', on page 86, and 'How to insert hyperlinks' on page 87 in Section 2 of this chapter.

▶▶ HOW TO ... Enter text

- Click in an editable region → enter the required text → the CSS style will be applied automatically if you had applied a style to that editable region.
- To create a paragraph break with a **</p>** tag, press **Enter**.
- To create a soft return with a **</br>** tag, press **Shift** + **Enter**.

▶▶ HOW TO ... Insert text from an existing text file

- Before you begin, ensure the text file is in your website folder.

1. Double-click on the file in the **Files** panel to open it → highlight all the text: **Edit** menu → **Select All** *or* press **Ctrl + A** → copy the text: **Edit** → **Copy** *or* **Ctrl** + C.
2. Select the tab for your web page and paste the text: **Edit** → **Paste** *or* **Ctrl** + V.
3. The text will be automatically formatted in the style set for that region.
4. Apply additional formatting if needed by highlighting the text and selecting the options from the **Properties** panel.

Enter a title for your web page by clicking in the Title box on the Document toolbar.

To enter a Description, refer to 'How to create meta tags' on page 78.

LIST FORMATS

In HTML, numbered lists are called **ordered lists** and are enclosed in **<ol> </ol>** tags. Bulleted lists are called **unordered lists** and are enclosed in **<ul> </ul>** tags. Dreamweaver creates a list item for each paragraph ending in a **</p>** tag. You should therefore ensure that the spacing in your text is correct before applying numbers or bullets.

▶▶ HOW TO ... Create a bulleted list

- Position the cursor where you want to start a list → **Text** menu → **List** → **Unordered List** *or* click the **Unordered List** button in the **Properties** panel.
- To format existing text into a list, highlight the text first.

▶▶ HOW TO ... Create a numbered list

- Position the cursor where you want to start a list → **Text** menu → **List** → **Ordered List** *or* click the **Ordered List** button in the Properties panel.

INSERTING MULTIMEDIA ELEMENTS

You can embed video or audio clips into your web pages, or create a link to an audio file. Linking to an audio file is a simple and effective way to add sound to a web page. This method allows visitors to choose whether they want to listen to the file. You are advised to use this method instead of embedding the sound file in a page.

A media object could be a sound or video clip, or any of the items shown in Figure 2.31.

▶▶ HOW TO ... Insert a media object in a page

1 You can insert Flash **swf** files, QuickTime **mov** or Shockwave movie clips into Dreamweaver. However, **avi** files are not supported.

2 Check your video file type and follow step 4 or step 5 below depending on the file type.

3 Position your cursor where you want to insert the object.

If you are inserting a Flash or Shockwave object:

4 From the **Common** toolbar, click the drop-down arrow to the right of the **Media** icon and select the type of object you want to insert *or* **Insert** menu → **Media** → select the type of media object you want from the list (e.g. Flash Video, Shockwave) → follow the steps in the **Select File** dialogue box → **OK**. A Flash file will be represented by a Flash icon on the page.

If the media object is *not* a Flash or Shockwave object:

5 **Insert** menu → **Media** → **Plugin** → *or* select **Plugin** from the list to the right of the **Media** icon on the **Common** toolbar (refer to Figure 2.31). Follow the instructions in the **Select File** dialogue box (refer to Figure 2.32). Once inserted, the file will be represented by a 'puzzle' icon on the page.

6 Select the media object icon on the page and set the properties (e.g. width and height) in the **Properties** panel.

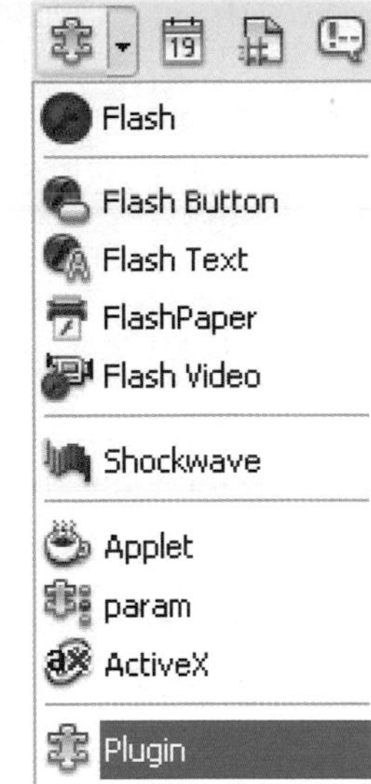

Figure 2.31 Inserting a media object

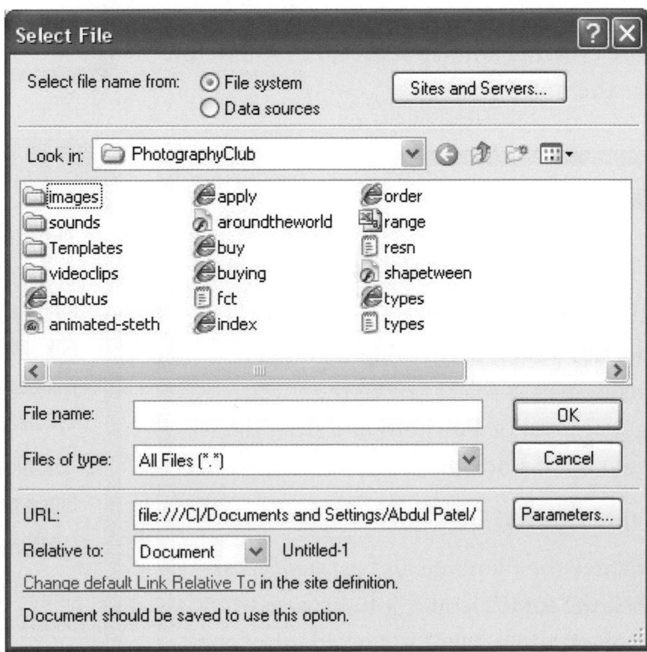

Figure 2.32 The Select File dialogue box

▶▶ HOW TO ... Create a link to an audio file

1 Ensure your sound file(s) are in one of these file formats: **wav**, **midi**, **mp3**.

2 Select the text or image you want to use as the audio link.

3 In the **Properties** panel, click the **Point to file** icon and drag it to the sound file in the **Files** panel *or* click the folder icon to browse for the audio file.

TIP!

Ensure the media object is in your website folder first.

When you open web pages containing media objects in your web browser, you may receive the message shown below. To allow blocked content, right-click on the message and select ***Allow Blocked Content*** *from the menu.*

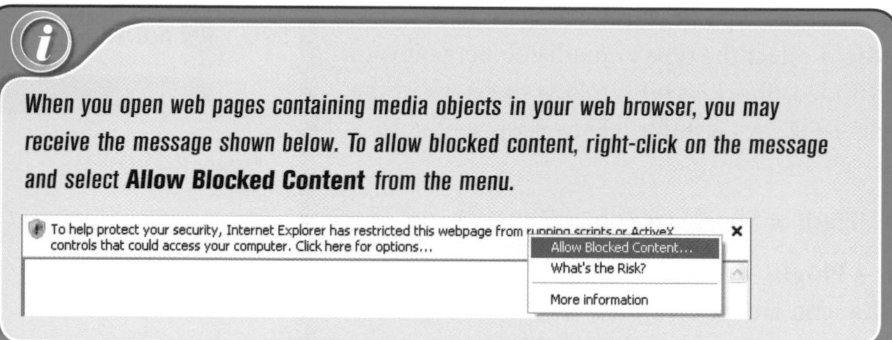

IMAGE MAPS

An image map is an image that has been divided into regions, or hotspots. When a user clicks on a hotspot, an action occurs, for example, a new file opens.

When you insert an image map, you are creating a hotspot area, i.e. you define a link that will open when a user clicks the hotspot area.

You can create multiple hotspot areas but they are part of the same image map.

▶▶ HOW TO ... Create an image map

- Before you begin, ensure the image has been inserted and that the link to the image is relative, not absolute.

1 Select the image → in the **Properties** panel, in the **Map** text box, enter a unique name for the image map → select one of the three **Hotspot Tool** shapes (Rectangular, Oval or Polygon) and drag the mouse pointer over the image to create a hotspot.

2 Click the **Pointer Hotspot Tool** to deselect the Hotspot shape tool.

3 In the **Properties** panel, either enter the filename and extension, *or*, to the right of the **Link** box, click the folder icon to browse to and select the file to be opened when the hotspot is clicked, *or*, if the file is within your website, use the **Point to File** icon to create a link to the file.

Target options:

_self *loads the linked file into the same window as the link. This is the default – if you don't select an option, it will default to self.*

_blank *loads the linked file into a new browser window.*

_parent *loads the linked file into the parent window that contains the link.*

_top *loads the linked file into the full browser window.*

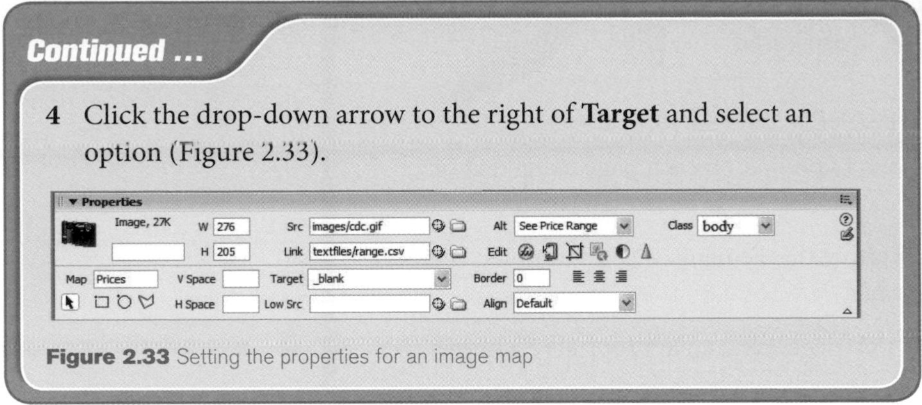

Continued ...

4 Click the drop-down arrow to the right of **Target** and select an option (Figure 2.33).

Figure 2.33 Setting the properties for an image map

PREVIEWING A WEB PAGE IN THE BROWSER

When you have finished creating a web page, you should check it in the browser to ensure that all the elements are displayed correctly and that all the links work.

To test an email link, you will need to have an email program (e.g. Microsoft Outlook) and an email account set up on the computer you are using, otherwise check the link carefully in Code view. When an email link is tested, a blank email message opens with the email address entered in the email link, in the **To:** line.

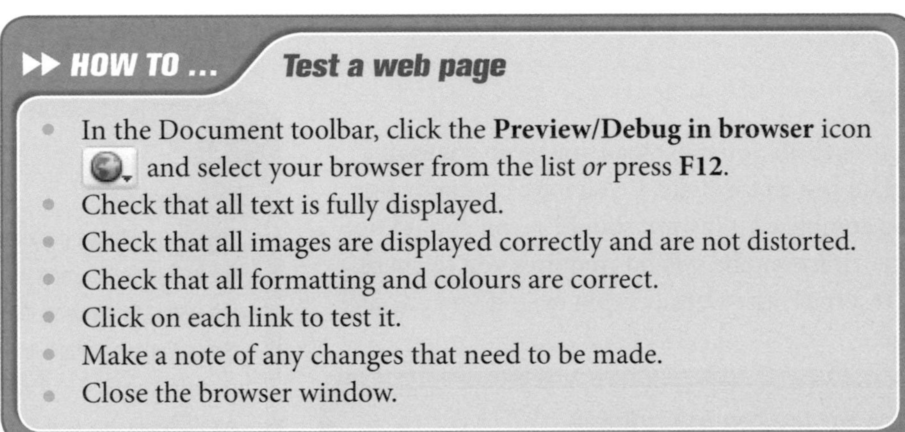

HOW TO ... Test a web page

- In the Document toolbar, click the **Preview/Debug in browser** icon and select your browser from the list *or* press **F12**.
- Check that all text is fully displayed.
- Check that all images are displayed correctly and are not distorted.
- Check that all formatting and colours are correct.
- Click on each link to test it.
- Make a note of any changes that need to be made.
- Close the browser window.

PRACTICAL TASK 2.9 Create web pages

Assessment objectives 1c, 1d, 2a, 2b

In this task you will be creating the web pages for your site using the template and your source files. You must create each page carefully and check each page before creating the next.

1 Create a minimum of six web pages based on your template.

2 Apply the styles from your cascading style sheet to the appropriate parts of the text.

3 Format the text on all pages as appropriate, ensure you use a bulleted or numbered list on at least one page.

PRACTICAL TASK 2.9 *continued*

4 Create at least one image map on a web page.
5 Create a minimum of one hyperlink on each page using text or images as the link.
6 If appropriate, insert multimedia elements, e.g. a sound file, a video clip and/or an animation.
7 Ensure you save every web page using an appropriate filename.

APPLY BASIC DESIGN PRINCIPLES

For this part of the syllabus, you will need to show evidence that you have created your website according to your client's needs, that you have sought user feedback, and tested links and browser compatibility. You will also need to understand prototype testing and stepwise refinement.

To ensure your website meets your client's needs, you must ensure that the site covers the requirements stated in the assignment brief. Your tutor may act as your client, so you could ask them for feedback.

Testing hyperlinks

To test the functionality of your website you must load your web pages in a browser and click on each link to test all the links. If you have checked your template and each page as you completed it (as you should!), you should not find any problems at this stage. However, the syllabus requires you to check for broken links so you must test the entire website again even if you are sure that you have tested each page.

Continued ... **Check for broken hyperlinks**

1 To check links in the entire site: **Site** menu → **Check Links Sitewide**.
2 To check links in a single web page, open the page. **File** menu → **Check Page** → **Check Links**.
3 The **Broken Links** report will be displayed in the **Results** panel at the bottom of the screen (refer to Figure 2.34). The **Link Checker** tab will be automatically selected.

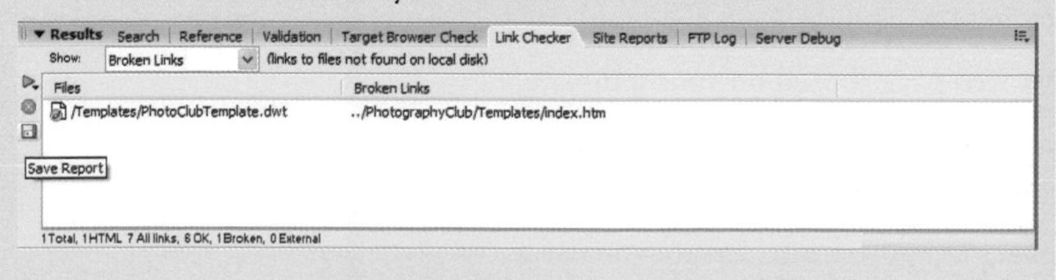

Figure 2.34 A broken links test report

Evidence
To show evidence of testing for broken links, save the report by clicking the **Save Report** button in the **Results** panel → a **Save As** dialogue box is displayed → enter a suitable filename for the report → **Save**.

You must correct any errors found as a result of testing for broken links, then carry out the test again.

Continued ...

4 Ideally you should find no broken links. The summary at the bottom of the **Results** panel should show no broken links:

1 Total, 1 HTML 11 All links, 8 OK, 0 Broken, 3 External

Checking for browser compatibility

You may need to decide what browsers your audience are likely to use. You should then avoid using tags that are not supported by those browsers. For example, some older browsers do not support CSS styles.

When you test whether browsers are compatible, Dreamweaver checks to see if the code in your web page is not supported by your target browser; this check does not change your web page in any way. The check gives information about **errors**, **warnings** and **informational messages**.

▶▶ HOW TO ... Test for browser compatibility

1 On the **Document** toolbar, click the drop-down arrow to the right of the **No Browser Check Errors** icon on the right of the title (refer to Figure 2.35) → a menu is displayed → select **Settings**.

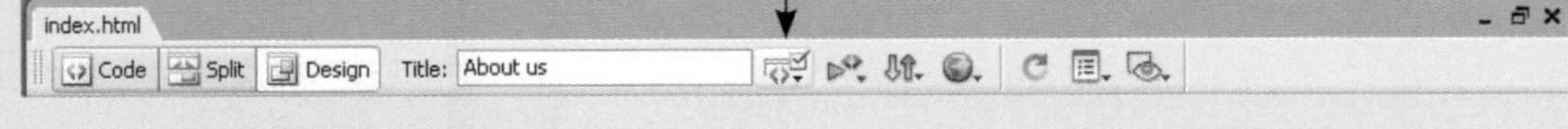

Figure 2.35 Location of No Browser Check Errors icon

2 The **Target Browsers** dialogue box is displayed (refer to Figure 2.36) → select the checkbox for each browser you want to check → to the right of each browser type, click the drop-down and select a minimum version to check against → **OK**.

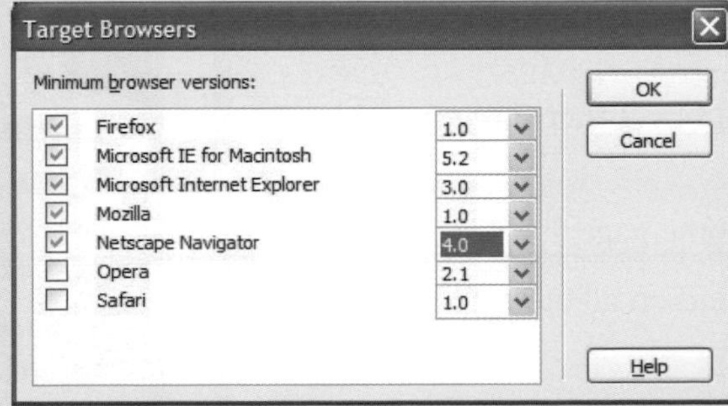

Figure 2.36 Target Browsers dialogue box

3 To check the entire site or several web pages, ensure that **Local view** is selected in the **Files** panel, select your website folder *or* hold down the **Ctrl** key and select multiple web pages.

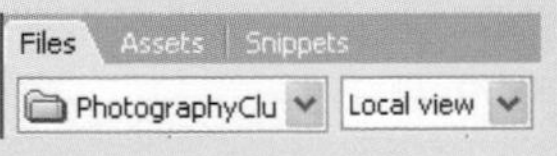

*An **error** indicates code that may cause a serious problem in a particular browser, e.g. causing parts of a page to disappear.*

*A **warning** indicates a piece of code that will not be displayed correctly in a particular browser but will not cause any serious display problems.*

*An **informational message** indicates code that isn't supported in a particular browser but that has no visible effect.*

You can run a target browser check on a web page, on a folder, or on an entire site. It is a good idea to carry out this check when you finish creating your template, and then again when you finish creating your website.

Continued ...

4 Click the drop-down arrow to the right of the **No Browser Check Errors** icon in the Document toolbar, and select **Check Browser Support**.

5 To view the results of a browser check, click the drop-down arrow to the right of the **No Browser Check Errors** icon in the Document toolbar, select **Show All Errors**. The **Results** panel will show errors with a red exclamation mark icon, warnings with a yellow exclamation mark icon, and informational messages with a word balloon icon (refer to Figure 2.37).

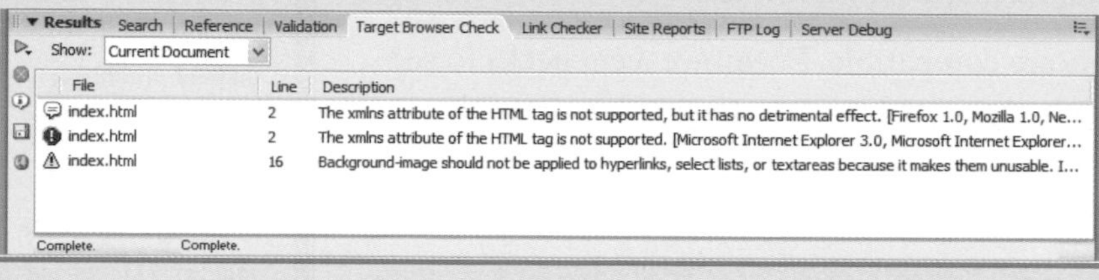

Figure 2.37 A Browser Compatibility test report

TIP!

A quick way to check for compatibility of one particular browser is: **File** menu → **Check Page** → **Check Target Browsers** → select a browser from the list → **Check**.

PRACTICAL TASK 2.10 Test links and browser compatibility

Assessment objective 2b

1. Carry out a test for broken links on all web pages in your website.
2. Save the broken links report. If there are no problems found, take a screen print as evidence.
3. Carry out a test for browser compatibility – try to include as many browsers as you can. Take a screen print to show which browsers you are testing compatibility for.
4. Run the browser compatibility test.
5. Save the browser compatibility test report. If there are no problems found, take a screen print as evidence.
6. Close Dreamweaver and open your home page in a web browser.
7. Test all the links on your home page and on all other pages in your browser.
8. Make a note of any links that need to be corrected.
9. If you need to correct any links, open your site in Dreamweaver, open the web page, delete the link and create it again. Repeat for all links that need correcting.
10. Test the links again.

You must correct any errors found as a result of testing for browser compatibility, and then carry out the test again.

Evidence

To show evidence of testing for browser compatibility, save the report by clicking the **Save Report** button in **Results** panel → a **Save As** dialogue box is displayed → enter a suitable filename for the report → **Save**.

PROTOTYPE TESTING

Prototype testing helps you to find out, at an early stage in the development of your website, whether it meets your client's needs and expectations. The testing method involves target-group test users carrying out specific tasks on the prototype of your website.

The purpose of this testing is to collect feedback at a point in the development process when changes would be relatively cheap and easy to implement.

The benefits of prototype testing are that your product is evaluated on the basis of test results. The intermediate results are shown to the client. Changes can be made before the website is fully completed saving time and cost in the longer term.

Key terms

Prototype A pre-release version of an end product used for testing purposes. It is used to demonstrate a concept quickly, check feasibility, and/or gain feedback.

How to apply prototype testing to your website

Even though you may not be producing a professional website for a 'real' client, it is still a good idea to apply the principle of prototype testing to your site. You should ask at least one test user, e.g. a colleague or classmate, their opinion of the product you have created. You should show them the assignment brief to get their opinion on whether your website meets the needs of your client. Remember prototype testing is done before the website is fully completed, so you should get it tested in the earlier stages, e.g. after you have created the template and one or two web pages based on the template.

STEPWISE REFINEMENT

In a professional context, stepwise refinement is the technique of writing software where you gradually add error checking and functionality. It is also referred as 'top-down programming'. This is a software development technique that imposes a hierarchical structure on the design of the program. It starts out by defining the solution at the highest level of functionality and breaking it down further and further into small routines that can be easily documented and coded.

Student review 2.4 – Understand basic design principles

Assessment objective 2b

1 Describe how and when you would apply prototype testing to your website. Explain who your test users would be, how you would arrange for testing and how you would document feedback.

2 Explain how you would apply the principle of stepwise refinement to your site.

CORRECTING PROBLEMS

If, as a result of your testing, or as a result of feedback from your client or test users, you need to make any amendments to your web pages, you will need to open each web page, one at a time, in Dreamweaver. Although it is possible to amend the code from a web browser, it is easy to make mistakes in the code, so you are advised to edit the pages from the Design view.

TIP!

To edit a web page or template, ensure the file is not set to read-only.

*You should only rename web pages if absolutely necessary. When you amend a web page ensure you save the amended web page in the **same** place, using the **same** filename and the **same** file extension as the original file. If you save the web page with a different name, any links to that page from other pages in your website will either load the original file, or if you have deleted it, will display an error message saying that the page cannot be displayed.*

▶▶ HOW TO ... Edit a hyperlink on a web page

- Select the linked image or click within the linked text → in the **Properties** panel, delete the old link and enter the correct link accurately.

▶▶ HOW TO ... Rename a web page

- Refer to the Warning opposite!
- In the **Files** panel, right-click on the page name → a menu is displayed → select **Edit** → **Rename** → enter the new name and the file extension → **Enter**.

▶▶ HOW TO ... Edit a template

- Open the template in Dreamweaver → make the changes needed, e.g. edit any hyperlinks as described above or make any regions editable as described on page 88 → save the updated template → a dialogue box will be displayed (Figure 2.38)→ click **Update**.

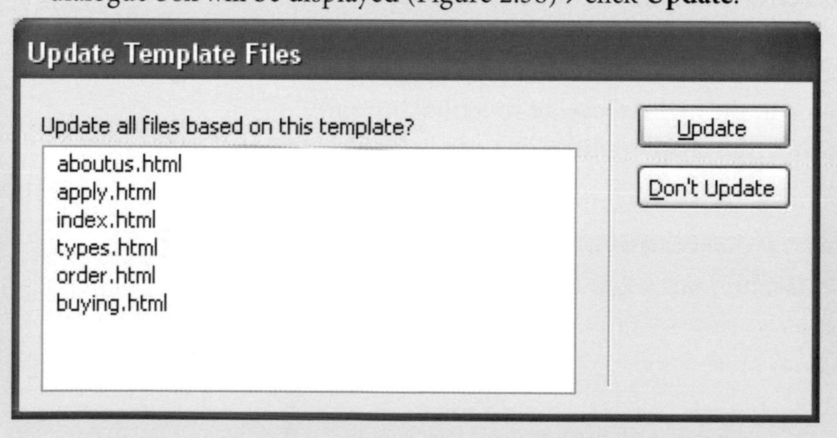

Figure 2.38 Prompt to update web pages based on a template

UPLOADING A WEBSITE

A website can be published to an Intranet (a private network inside an organisation that is only for internal use) or on the World Wide Web.

To publish your website on the Internet you must have a **web host**, who will provide space on their web server for you to **upload** your website. You will need a file exchange program, such as **FTP**, **SFTP** or **SCP** to transfer your files to the web host's server. Once your website has been uploaded, web browsers can view your pages using **HTTP**. Web addresses usually begin with HTTP so that they can be recognised as pages suitable for viewing over the World Wide Web.

Many Internet Service Providers (ISPs) offer free web space to their subscribers. A number of hosts offer free space in return for placing advertising on your site whereas other web hosts may charge fees to host your site. The web host will generally provide you with instructions on how to upload your website to their server and how to maintain your website.

▶▶ HOW TO ... Upload your website

The method you use to upload your website may vary depending on which file exchange program you use. If you are using an FTP program you could upload your website as follows.

1 Connect to the Internet and open an FTP program.

2 Enter the **host name** of your website, enter your **user name** and **password**.

3 Connect to the site.

4 Highlight the files you would like on your website.

5 Click on the option to transfer them to your website.

PRACTICAL TASK 2.11 Upload website

Learning Outcome 3

For an OCR assignment, it is not mandatory that you upload your website to the World Wide Web. However, if you have the facilities and wish to do so, you may upload your site.

1 Check your website folder structure carefully. Delete any unnecessary files.

2 Ask your client for feedback for your completed website.

3 Ensure you have tested and corrected all links.

4 If you have a web server and a file exchange program, upload your website to the World Wide Web.

5 Test the site once you have uploaded it or ask your client for feedback.

Key terms

Web host A web host provides server space, web services and file maintenance for websites controlled by individuals or companies who do not have their own web servers.

Key terms

Upload To transfer file(s) from a user's computer to a remote computer (usually a web server).

Key terms

FTP **F**ile **T**ransfer **P**rotocol
SFTP **S**SH **F**ile **T**ransfer **P**rotocol
SCP **S**ecure **C**opy **P**rotocol

Each of the above is a set of rules that gives instructions on how to transfer files from one device to another.

Key terms

HTTP **H**yper**t**ext **T**ransfer **P**rotocol is a set of rules that a web browser uses to connect and receive data from web servers.

PRACTICAL TASK 2.12 Review work against original brief

Assessment objective 3b

1. Refer to the 'Reviewing your work' section, on page xxi of the Common Skills chapter.
2. Collate all your evidence (e.g. saved files, scanned copies of any printouts, screen prints, proposal, Storyboard, site map, planning notes, feedback from test users etc.).
3. Refer to the Assignment Brief for the 'Cove Photography Club – Website' on page 64.
4. Review all your evidence, your template and web pages against the assignment brief. You may have a discussion with your tutor.
5. Ensure that you have carried out all the tasks required in the assignment brief.
6. Obtain a copy of an Evidence Checklist (ask your tutor for a copy).
7. Complete the Evidence Checklist.
8. Identify at least two constraints that influenced your project, e.g. image manipulation, file format, compression. Note these in your Planning and Review Form or in a separate document.
9. Comment on the quality of the finished website and its fitness for purpose.
10. Explain how the website fulfils the original client brief.
11. Back up all your files on to a removable medium.

You should now have all the skills, knowledge and understanding required to complete an OCR iMedia sample or live assessment for this unit.

UNIT 3

DIGITAL ANIMATION

INTRODUCTION

This practical unit is designed to give you an understanding of digital and non-digital animation and the skills required for the creation of different types of digital animation. You will develop an understanding of what animation is, how it is produced, and when, where and why it is used. You will develop skills in using a digital animation program to create different types of animation that will be suitable for integration into digital pages, and in exporting animation files in a variety of formats.

LEARNING OUTCOMES

After studying this unit you will be able to:

- understand what animation is and identify where, when and why it is used
- understand what digital animation is and identify where, when and why it is used
- understand and use the tools and features of a digital animation program which allow the creation of animated sequences suitable for use in multimedia productions
- create digital animation sequences.

RESOURCE TOOLKIT

Hardware

- Computer

Software

- Macromedia Flash (including Flash Player)

Other

- Planning and Review Form
- Images to create animation
- Paper to draw non-digital animations
- Pencil, rubber, hole punch, string
- Evidence Checklist

Optional

- Digital camera
- Books or magazines on the history and types of animation
- Web browser program (e.g. Internet Explorer) to test animations
- Printer (with paper and ink), to print planning documents including Storyboard etc.

For this unit you will need to have an understanding of the different types of non-digital animation, e.g. flipbook, cell animation, time-lapse photography and cut out animation.

For an OCR assessment, you will need to plan your animations according to a specific assignment brief that will be provided, and record all stages of your planning. The assignment brief will describe a client's needs. You will look at ways of identifying your client's requirements and use planning methods appropriate to the given brief and appropriate to creating animations.

You will need to show that you have used the tools and features of a digital animation program to create animated sequences which can be used in multimedia productions, e.g. websites and presentations. You can do this by providing 'before and after' screen prints with a brief description of the tools used. You will understand and use symbols, instances and libraries. When you have completed your animation, you will need to export it in a file format suitable for inclusion in other products, e.g. web pages.

Finally you will review your completed animation(s) against the original assignment brief and obtain appropriate feedback (e.g. from peers or your tutor). You will need to identify any parameters and constraints that influenced your choices when creating your animations.

The Student Review activities and Practical Tasks in this chapter will allow you to develop your understanding of the requirements for an OCR assessment and practise the skills required for the Unit 3 syllabus. The animations you create in this chapter **CANNOT** be submitted for assessment purposes.

ASSESSMENT FOR UNIT 3

Your assessment work should be submitted to OCR via e-portfolio. You should therefore save all evidence in electronic format. Any hard-copy evidence should be scanned and saved electronically.

For an OCR assessment, you may be required to create a digital and a non-digital animation.

For the non-digital animation, you may use a digital camera to take still shots or you may sketch the images yourself.

Source files

Images and buttons have not been provided with this book because in an OCR assessment you will need to source the required files.

You are not required to create your own files, your tutor may provide you with suitable files or you may use any appropriate images and buttons from within Flash. You may use files from other units, e.g. images from Unit 1. If you use any files from the Internet or other sources, you must reference all your sources.

Refer to pages 52 and 53 for guidelines on observing copyright and referencing your sources.

Evidence

You will need to provide:

- evidence of planning your project, this could be included in, or in addition to, the Planning and Review Form
- Planning and Review Form
- a diary (e.g. digital diary) or a log of your activities for the given assignment
- storyboard showing plans for all animations
- saved electronic files of all digital animations (your Flash animations may be saved in **swf**, **html** or **gif** format)
- saved electronic files or scanned hard copies of non-digital animations
- evidence to show that you have used the drawing and selection tools specified in the syllabus, e.g. 'before and after' screen prints.
- Evidence Checklist.

Refer also to 'Evidence' on pages ix and xxii.

SOFTWARE

This chapter is written specifically for Macromedia Flash version 8 from the Studio 8 suite (education version). It can also be used with Flash MX 2004 although some screenshots and methods will not match exactly. Flash is an industry-standard software program which allows you to create animations from scratch as well as import and animate graphic content created in other packages.

ABOUT THIS CHAPTER

This chapter for Unit 3 is divided into three sections. You must work through the sections in sequence.

- In Section 1 you will learn about different types of early animation methods.
- In Section 2 you will learn how to use the tools and features of Flash. You will learn how to work with Flash documents, layers and text. You will create, modify and select shapes and objects.
- In Section 3 you will learn how to use libraries and how to create symbols and instances. You will use the skills gained in Section 2 to create different types of digital animations, i.e. frame-by-frame and tweened animation. You will save your animations in suitable file formats.

AO 1a

AOs 1c, 2a, 2c, 2d

AOs 1b, 2b, 2e

Assessment objectives 3a (plan the animation to a specific brief) and 3b (review the animation against the original brief) and the corresponding knowledge, skills and understanding criteria are covered in the 'Common Skills' chapter.

Refer to 'Planning your work' and 'Reviewing your work' sections on pages xiv and xxi of the 'Common Skills' chapter.

SECTION 1 • Create graphical animation

The following assessment objective will be covered in this section:

1a Create simple graphical animation

The following knowledge, skills and understanding criteria corresponding to assessment objective 1a will be covered:

- *Types of animation*
- *Methods of creating graphical animation*
- *Physical hand-drawing skills, including transfer of images sketched on paper, life drawing*

For an OCR assessment, you will need to create two animations: a non-digital animation lasting between 12 and 14 seconds, and a digital animation lasting between 20 and 30 seconds.

TYPES OF ANIMATION

Animation is the process of bringing still images to life. Many different types of animation are used today. In the early days of animation at the beginning of the twentieth century, each page of an animation was drawn by hand. Animations were 2D (two dimensional). 3D animation, including clay animation, later became popular, followed by the most popular type of animation nowadays – computer animation.

You should also carry out some research into the history of, and ways of creating, different types of non-digital animation.

FLIPBOOK ANIMATION

A **flipbook** is an old and simple form of animation consisting of a sequence of hand-drawings or photographs that change gradually from one page to the next. When the pages are turned quickly (flipped) by a viewer, the images appear to animate, creating the illusion of movement.

This illusion is an optical illusion phenomenon known as the **persistence of vision**. The human eye retains an image for about one-twelfth of a second. If consecutive images are shown quickly, the eye blends the images together, creating the illusion of movement. A flipbook animation is usually quite short and has a single theme which is best conveyed as a short animated movie clip.

Flipbook animation techniques were used traditionally for teaching animation techniques – this practice is still used today. An idea can be tested quickly using the flipbook technique. Creating a flipbook can be a useful technique when planning to create a digital animation.

A flipbook is not always a separate book. It is sometimes included as an additional feature in a magazine (e.g. on page corners) or in children's books.

Creating a flipbook animation

You will need:

- a pad of plain paper
- pencils and a rubber
- a hole puncher
- string.

A flipbook is sometimes referred to as a flick book.

Preparation

Ensure all the pages are lined up and in one pile. Use a hole puncher to punch holes in the same place on all sheets – if you are using reminder notes you will not have to do this.

TIP!

Faster movement sequences require fewer drawings. Slower movements need more drawings.

Planning

1 On scrap paper, work out the sequence you want to show.

2 Decide how the movement will start and how it will end, and how you want the drawing to move.

3 Sketch the first and last pictures of the sequence.

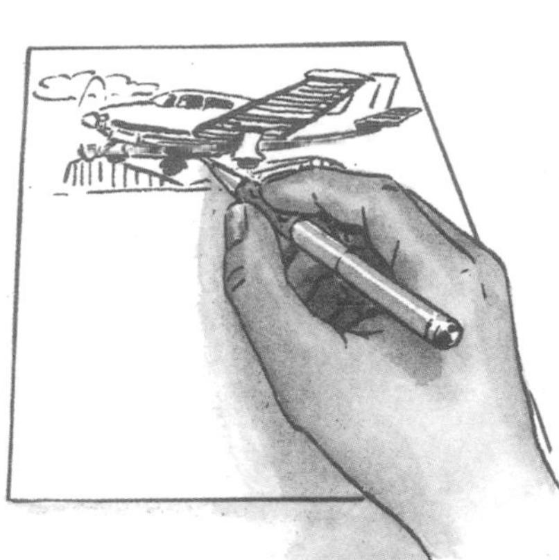

The paper should be thin enough to allow you to see through the pages.

Pages should not be lined, and should not have any holes.

The paper should not be too large – A5 is probably the biggest you should use.

Square paper works well. You can even use a pad of reminder notes – say 75 mm × 75 mm.

HOW TO ... Draw a flipbook animation

1 Once you have planned the animation, you can start illustrating. Note: You will be working from the bottom page of the pad toward the top page. Each drawing will move from the bottom drawing to the top.

2 Using a pencil, draw the sketch on the *last* page.

3 On the blank page on top of your first drawing, trace or redraw most of the first image. You must change part of the drawing slightly – this will give the illusion of movement when the pages are flipped through.

4 On the next blank page on top of the second drawing, trace or redraw the image changing it slightly.

5 On the next blank page on top of the most recent drawing, trace or redraw the image changing it slightly again.

Continued ...

6 Repeat step 5 until the movement sequence is complete.

7 Add colour to your drawings if you wish.

8 Thread the string through the holes to make the paper into a booklet – with reminder notes you won't need to do this.

9 Hold the book with one hand and flip through its pages with the thumb of the other hand. Your drawings should come to life!

Starting your drawing on the last page makes it easier for you to see what you have already drawn and allows you to line up the next frame of the movement sequence.

CELL ANIMATION

Cell animation came about later in the twentieth century. It was invented in 1915 and used as the standard technique for studio animation. In cell animation drawings are traced or copied on to transparent acetate sheets called **cells**.

Cells are transparent **cell**uloid acetate sheets that can be drawn and painted on. Because the sheets are transparent, several cells (acetates) can be placed on top of each other, allowing different 'scenes' to be drawn on each sheet. The transparent cells (acetates) allow the background to be seen underneath the object so the background only has to be created once. Using cell sheets reduces the amount of drawing for the animator because they only need to draw the movement of one part of the object instead of having to redraw the whole object on every sheet (as in flipbook animation).

The sheets are laid over a static background drawing or photograph. They are then photographed one-by-one using an animation camera. These are specially adapted cameras, designed for frame-by-frame shooting of animation. They consist of a camera body with lens and film magazines, a stand that allows the camera to be raised and lowered, and a table, usually with lighting above and underneath it. The drawings on acetate to be photographed are placed on the table. The Looney Tunes and Merrie Melodies cartoons released by Warner Bros between the 1930s and 1950s are examples of traditional cell animation.

Nowadays, cell animation is used less frequently because the process can be done more quickly and economically using a computer. Also, animation cameras have been replaced with scanners and video cameras. However, the main steps used in the traditional cell animation process, i.e. concept, storyboard, layout and backgrounds, character animation filming and sound plus text, are still used today.

Cell animation is also spelt as **cel animation.** *Cells can also be spelt* ***cels.***

Cell animation is used for cartoons and special effects, for example distortions, colour effects applied to graphics, photographs or films.

A form of cell animation is still used in modern-day digital animation. Single frames are created using a computer graphics program (e.g. Photoshop, Flash). The animator can then composite the images, and save the frames as a movie file or output to video.

TIME-LAPSE PHOTOGRAPHY

Time lapse is where a camera takes a sequence of images of a subject that changes imperceptibly slowly, with an interval of time between each image. Depending on the subject being photographed, the interval can vary from a few seconds, to a day, several days, a month or even years. When the images are replayed consecutively they are played at normal speed over a shorter time, therefore time appears to be moving faster and is said to be '**lapsing**'. The effect is that a smooth impression of motion is created. The technique can also be used to slow down action.

Key terms

Wait time is the period when the camera is not exposing frames.

Time-lapse photography is used to photograph a process where any change would normally appear subtle to the human eye, for example, flowers opening, trees growing, clouds moving, a bird's egg hatching, a building construction.

In time-lapse photography moving pictures are taken at any rate slower than the standard 24 frames per second (fps). 24 fps is the standard setting used currently in the movie industry. A difficult, but important point to decide in time-lapse photography is the **wait time**, i.e. how long to turn off the camera between frames. The wait time can range from seconds to minutes or even days.

Example of working out exposure time

To make a 12-hour cloud sequence into a one-minute animation:

1 minute at 24 fps = 60 × 24 = 1440 frames

12 hours = 12 × 60 × 60 = 43 200 seconds

43 200 ÷ 1440 = 30

Therefore, exposure should be every 30 seconds.

To determine the time between exposures, you will need to know how long the event you want to record will actually take (if this is possible!). You then need to decide how long your finished sequence on film will last. The wait time between each exposure is calculated as follows: Total filming time divided by the total number of frames.

However, if you don't know how long the sequence will last, you will find it difficult to determine the correct wait time. You will need to estimate the wait time. Remember though, that when you play your time-lapse sequence, the motion should appear fluid and smooth. There should be only a small amount of movement between each frame for the sequence to appear smooth and realistic.

CUT OUT ANIMATION

Cut out animation is one of the oldest forms of animation. In cut out animation, characters, backgrounds and props are drawn or photographed, then cut from materials such as paper, stiff card, fabric and photographs. These movable, cut out parts, sometimes referred to as puppets, are moved in small steps. A photograph is taken at each stage using a cine camera, to create an illusion of an action. This is easier than having to draw every single frame of the animation as in flipbook animation.

Before the introduction of computer animation, this was considered one of the easiest forms of animation to create. Nowadays, cut out style animation is still produced on computers using programs such as Adobe Premier. Scanned images or vector graphics are used instead of the cut out parts. The South Park television series is an example of using cut out animation.

Student review 3.1 – Types of non-digital animation

Assessment objective 1a

1. In what type of animation are materials cut from paper, stiff card or fabric?
2. In what type of animation are images taken at intervals?
3. What are the main steps in the traditional cell animation process?
4. In what type of animation are transparent acetate sheets used?
5. In what time of animation does time appear to be moving faster when the images are played back?
6. What type of animation would be suitable for showing the stages of a daffodil flowering?
7. What time of animation reduces the amount of drawing for an animator?
8. What type of animation is used to draw a sequence of images that change gradually from one page to the next?

Assignment brief

Cove Photography Club – Animation

The club have recently launched their website. Although feedback about the site has been positive, the club organiser would like to include animations and interactivity on the site. He would also like the website to be educational and informative as there many young members.

All new initiatives are presented at club meetings. You have been asked to research the four main non-digital animation techniques and create a simple non-digital animation which you will present at the next club meeting.

Following your presentation of the non-digital animation, you will need to create a digital animation that will be included on the club's website. The long-term plan is to include several animations and banners on the website. You have been asked to create one animation from the following list:

- An animation about a safari planned for nature photographers
- An animation showing the location of the club and how to get there (e.g. a virtual map)
- An animation showing a club meeting or social event

PRACTICAL TASK 3.1 Identify client's requirements, produce planning documents, research and create a non-digital animation

Assessment objectives 3a, 1a

1. Refer to the 'Planning your work' and 'Reviewing your work' sections on pages xiv and xxi in the 'Common Skills' chapter.
2. Obtain a copy of a Planning and Review Form (ask your tutor for a copy).
3. Refer to the 'Cove Photography Club – Animation' assignment brief on page 110.
4. Identify the 'client' and their requirements. You may have a discussion with your tutor acting as the client.
5. Note down all relevant dates in your Planning and Review Form.
6. Visualise the concept of your non-digital animation, and create *two* storyboards. One for the non-digital animation and one for the digital animation.
7. Carry out some research and write a brief description (approximately 50 words each) about the four main types of early animation techniques, i.e. flipbook, cell animation, cut out animation and time-lapse photography.
8. Using one of the types of non-digital animation techniques, create the non-digital animation as specified in the assignment brief. Approximately 12 frames should be sufficient.
9. Present this animation to your 'client'.

SECTION 2 • Use tools and features of a digital animation program

The following assessment objectives will be covered in this section:

1c Use the digital animation interface

2a Use the tools panel and the options panel associated with each tool

2c Use drawing

2d Use selection

The following knowledge, skills and understanding criteria corresponding to assessment objectives 1c, 2a, 2c and 2d will be covered:

- *Interface functions*
- *Tools*
- *Drawing capabilities*
- *Selection tools*

STARTING FLASH

Flash is a program that allows you to create exciting animations and presentations.

▶▶ HOW TO ... Start Flash

1 Click on **Start → All Programs → Macromedia → Macromedia Flash 8** *or* if you have shortcut icons on the Desktop   or Taskbar click on the shortcut icon.

2 A Macromedia Flash 8 **Start Page** will be displayed. This contains several options for creating documents (Figure 3.1).

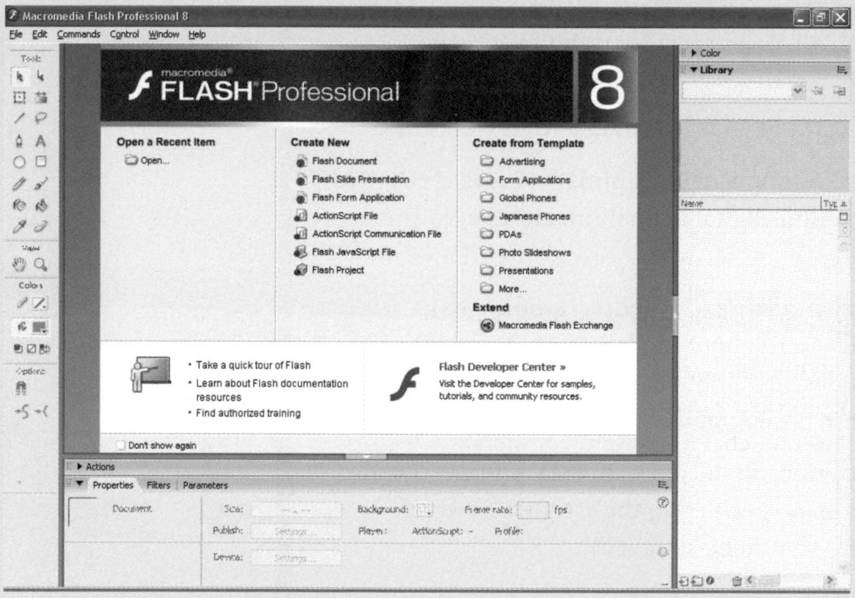

Figure 3.1 The Flash Start Page

3 Below **Create New**, select **Flash Document**  . If the Start Page is not displayed, click the **File** menu → **New → Flash Document.**

4 The Flash screen will be displayed (refer to Figure 3.2).

Once you have created file(s) in Flash, below **Open a Recent item** on the Start Page will be a list of files. To open a file quickly, select the **Open...** folder.

On the right of the Start Page, below **Create from Template**, is a list of existing templates that you could use.

TIP!

*If you don't see the Start Page, it may be that the previous user has selected the check box for **Don't show again**. To display the Start Page every time, select the **Edit** menu → **Preferences** → a **Preferences** dialogue box is displayed → with the **General** category selected, click the drop-down arrow to the right of **On launch** and select **Show Start Page**.*

UNDERSTANDING THE FLASH SCREEN

The numbers in the following list refer to the features pointed out in Figure 3.2.

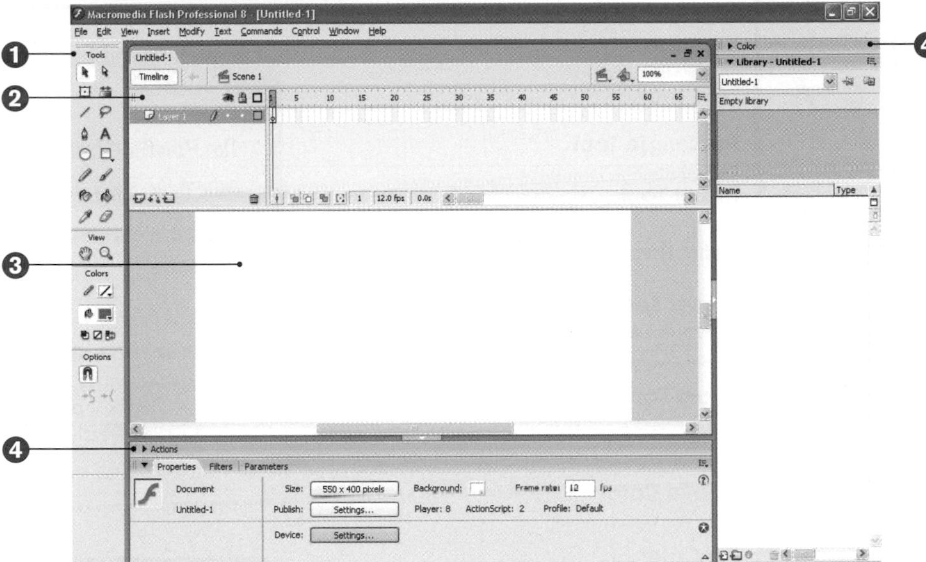

Figure 3.2 The Flash screen

❶ The **Toolbox**, also referred to as the **Tools panel**, contains a selection of tools that can be used for drawing, making selections, entering text and manipulating items. A tool tip is displayed when you hover the mouse pointer over a tool. To select a tool, click on it. Some tools have options that control how the tool works. These options will be displayed at the bottom of the Toolbox when you select the tool.

The Toolbox, Timeline and panels can be undocked by clicking and dragging the gripper at the edge or top of its window. You are advised to keep the items docked as in Figure 3.2.

The toolbox in Flash is similar to the toolbox in other graphics packages (e.g. Photoshop, Fireworks).

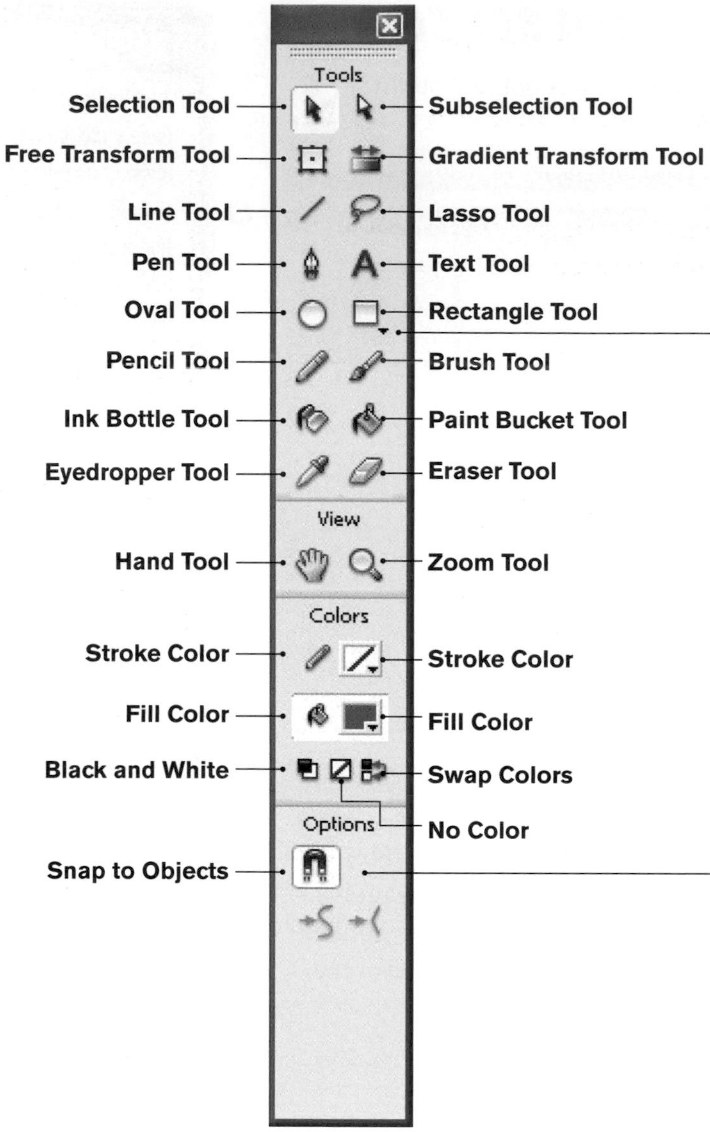

Tools
Selection Tool
Subselection Tool
Free Transform Tool
Gradient Transform Tool
Line Tool
Lasso Tool
Pen Tool
Text Tool
Oval Tool
Rectangle Tool
Pencil Tool
Brush Tool
Ink Bottle Tool
Paint Bucket Tool
Eyedropper Tool
Eraser Tool
View
Hand Tool
Zoom Tool
Colors
Stroke Color
Stroke Color
Fill Color
Fill Color
Black and White
Swap Colors
Options
No Color
Snap to Objects

Figure 3.3 The Flash Toolbox, also referred to as the Tools Panel

*The **PolyStar** Tool is hidden behind the **Rectangle Tool**.*

Rectangle Tool
PolyStar Tool

*The options displayed in the **Options** section of the Toolbox will vary depending on which tool is currently selected in the Toolbox.*

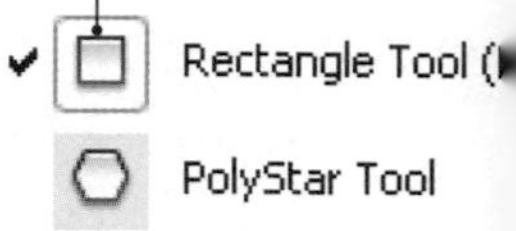

❷ The **Timeline** organises and controls the content over time in layers and frames – it controls what happens in an animation and when. The Timeline consists of layers, frames and the playhead.

Refer to 'Working with layers' on page 117.

Timeline
Layer 1
5
10
15
20
25
30
35
40
45
50
55
1
12.0 fps
0.0s

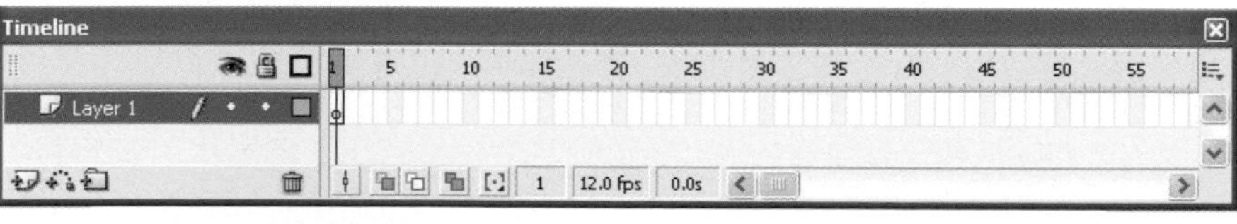

- **Layers** [Layer 1] are listed on the left side of the Timeline.
- **Frames** are displayed in a row to the right of the layer name. Each frame is numbered – the numbers are displayed in the Timeline header in increments of 5. By default, each frame lasts half a second. Each layer has its own Timeline – the frames for each layer are displayed to the right of that layer.

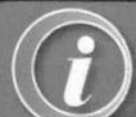

*A **Frame** is a snapshot of an animation. It is like a page in a flip book.*

- The **Timeline header** 5 10 15 at the top of the Timeline indicates the frame numbers.
- The **playhead** 1 indicates the current frame displayed on the Stage. As an animation plays, the playhead moves from left to right through the Timeline.
- The **Timeline status** at the bottom of the Timeline indicates the selected frame number, the current frame rate, and the elapsed time to the current frame. 1 12.0 fps 0.0s

3 The **Stage** is the rectangular white area where content (images, imported graphics, text boxes, buttons, video clips etc.) is placed. You can zoom in and out to change the view of the Stage as you work. Anything visible on the Stage will be displayed when the Flash movie is played, e.g. in a web browser window. The grey area around the Stage is the Work Area.

4 **Panels** are displayed at the bottom and to the right of the screen. Panels can be opened, closed, maximised and minimised just like windows in Microsoft programs. A down arrow e.g. ▼ Properties indicates the panel is expanded, and an arrow to the right e.g. ▶ Actions indicates the panel is contracted.

When creating animations, you will frequently be using the **Properties** panel as well as the **Library** panel.

The **Properties panel**, also referred to as the **Property inspector**, provides information about the document you are working on. If an object on the Stage is selected, it displays the attributes for the object and allows you to modify the properties quickly without having to access menus.

TIP!

To see the Stage more clearly, minimise the panels at the bottom and to the right of the screen. To hide or expand a panel, click the vertical or horizontal arrow at the edge of it.

TIP!

*To zoom in or change the view of the Stage, use the **Zoom Tool** in the Toolbox or click the drop-down arrow at the top right of the Document window and select a magnification option.*

Fit in Window
Fit in Window
Show Frame
Show All
25%
50%
100%
200%
400%
800%

TIP!

*To hide all panels: **Window** menu → **Hide Panels** or press **F4** to hide and unhide panels.*

*To display a panel, click the **Window** menu and select the panel.*

Student review 3.2 – Understand the Flash screen

Assessment objective 1c

You will find it useful to spend a few minutes becoming familiar with the Flash window.

1. *Use your mouse to hover over various different icons in the Toolbox and on the Flash screen.*
2. *Click the arrows to expand and contract different panels.*
3. *Close all panels and open them again (**Window** → **Hide Panels** or press **F4**).*
4. *Using the **Window** menu, close the **Properties** panel and open it again. Use the arrow at the very bottom right of the panel to expand ▽ and contract △ this panel.*

Student review 3.2 – Continued

5 Close and re-open the Toolbox: note in the **Window** menu, this is listed as **Tools**.

6 Select different tools from the Toolbox – notice how the options at the bottom of the Toolbox changes depending on which tool you select.

7 Use the **Zoom Tool** in the Toolbox to zoom in. When you select the **Zoom Tool**, notice the zoom **Enlarge** and **Reduce** icons displayed in the **Options** section of the Toolbox.

8 Use the drop-down arrow at the top right of the Document window to change the magnification size of the stage on screen.

9 Click the **New Layer** icon to insert new layers in the Timeline.

10 Click in different frames in the Timeline.

11 Click the cross at the top right of the page (not the red cross at the top of the screen!).

12 A dialogue box will be displayed asking if you want to save the page, click **No**.

In Flash, you create scenes on the Stage by arranging objects such as text and graphics. The scenes run in frames on the Timeline. You animate the objects using the Timeline. You then play the movie on the Stage or in a browser. Finally you export the movie in a suitable file format (e.g. html, swf or gif).

TIP!

To undo previous actions: **Edit** menu → **Undo** or **Ctrl + Z**.

To select all objects: **Edit** menu → **Select All** or **Ctrl + A**.

WORKING WITH FLASH DOCUMENTS

A Flash document is called a **movie**. When you save a Flash file, it is saved with a **fla** file extension. **fla** files can only be opened and edited in Flash.

▸▸ HOW TO ... Create a new document

- **File** menu → **New** → from the **General** tab, select **Flash Document**. Set the document properties.

To set the frame rate and document size, refer to 'Frame rate' and 'Document size' on page 138.

▸▸ HOW TO ... Open an existing document

- **File** menu → **Open** → the **Open** dialogue box is displayed → navigate to the file → click **Open**.

▸▸ HOW TO ... Save a new document

- **File** menu → **Save** → navigate to your user area → enter a suitable filename → **Save**. Your file will be saved as an editable Flash document in **fla** format.

TIP!

If you use **Save As**, instead of **Save** to save an existing document (keeping the same filename), Flash arranges the new information into the file creating a smaller file.

If you use **Save**, Flash adds the new information to the existing file, creating a larger file.

In 'Saving an animation in a format suitable for the web' on page 151, you will learn to save animations in different file formats suitable for publication on the web.

▶▶ HOW TO ... Save an existing document

- **File** menu → **Save As** → navigate to your user area → **Save**.

Save and Compact should be used to permanently remove items deleted by the **Undo** command. For example, if you have inserted an image and then deleted it using **Undo**, the file size still includes the image size (in case you want to use **Redo**).

WORKING WITH LAYERS

Flash organises objects in two ways: the position of the object on the Stage and the stacking order of the objects. Layers are used as a way of organising the stacking order of the objects. Layers are like transparent sheets stacked on top of each other on the Stage. Each layer has its own Timeline. You can draw, import or edit objects on a layer without affecting the objects on other layers.

A new Flash document contains only one layer, but new layers can be easily inserted. Adding new layers does not increase the file size of your published file, the objects you place on layers increases the file size. The pencil icon indicates the active layer.

An asterisk * is displayed after the document name in the title bar if the document contains any unsaved changes shapes* . When you save the document, the asterisk is removed.

- To **insert** a new layer: click the **Insert Layer** icon at the bottom left of the Timeline.
- To **display** all layers, click and drag the bottom pane of the Timeline window further down.
- To **move** a layer: click and drag it to the new position.
- To **rename** a layer: double-click the layer name, delete the existing name and enter the new name.
- To **hide** a layer temporarily: click the round, black dot in the required layer, *below* the **Show/Hide All Layers** icon, represented by an eye symbol . A cross will indicate that it is hidden.
- To **delete** a layer: drag it to the Delete Layer icon below the first layer.
- To **lock** a layer (to prevent editing on that layer or deleting the layer): click the black dot *below* the **Lock/Unlock All Layers** icon.
- To **hide or lock all layers**: select the relevant icon *above* the layers.

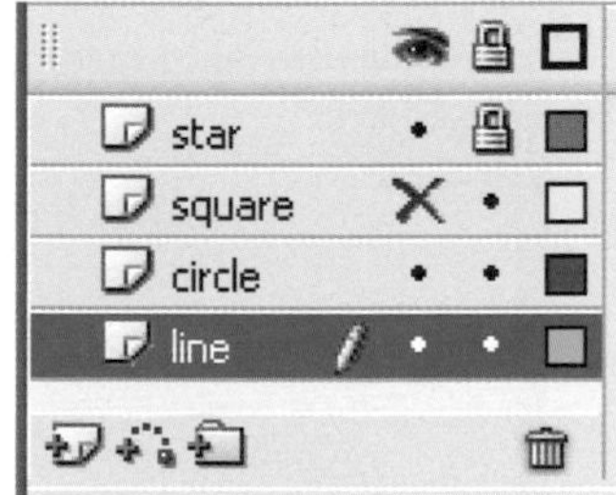

Figure 3.4 Layers section of Timeline

Figure 3.4 shows the **Layers** section of the Timeline. The layer named **line** is the active layer, the layer named **square** is hidden and the layer named **star** is locked.

THE TOOLS PANEL AND THE ASSOCIATED OPTIONS

This section will cover the frequently used tools in Flash. You will need to know how to use these tools before you begin creating animations.

Creating vector graphics using the drawing tools

When you draw in Flash, you are creating vector graphics. The **Line Tool**, **Oval Tool** and **Rectangle Tools** are used to draw basic geometric shapes.

The **Line Tool** is used to draw straight lines in any direction.

The **Oval Tool** is used to draw ovals and circles.

The **Rectangle Tool** is used to create rectangles and squares, both with sharp or rounded corners.

The **PolyStar Tool** (hidden behind the Rectangle Tool) is used to draw polygons and stars.

TIP!

*To help you position items, display Rulers (**View** menu → **Rulers**) and/or Grid Guides (**View** menu → **Grid** → **Show Grid**).*

The grid and ruler guides are only visible on-screen; they will not display in your completed animation.

To align items precisely, click and drag horizontal and/or vertical ruler guides from the ruler to the Stage.

*To automatically align items with each other or with the grid or ruler guides, use one of the snapping options: **View** menu → **Snapping** → select the required option(s).*

Student review 3.3 – Understanding the save options and drawing tools

Assessment objectives 2a, 2c, 2e

1. When should the **Save and Compact** option be used?
2. Which option from the **File** menu should be used to save an existing document?
3. When is an asterisk displayed to the right of the filename?
4. Which shape tool should be used to draw a 12-point star?
5. What is a vector graphic? Give five examples of vector graphics.
6. Which two tools should be used to draw a rectangle with rounded corners?
7. What options should be used to align a shape to a specific position on the Stage?

Key terms

Vector graphics consist of lines, curves and shapes defined mathematically. They are not dependent on resolution so can be resized without losing clarity. Vector graphics download faster than bitmap images.

To draw rounded corners for a rectangle or square, select the **Set Corner Radius button** at the bottom of the Options bar → a **Rectangle Settings** dialogue box is displayed → enter a value, the higher the number, the more rounded the corners → **OK**, then draw the rectangle. **Or** when drawing the rectangle, press the up or down arrow keys while dragging to adjust the radius of rounded corners.

TIP!

Anything you draw on the Stage will be seen by others when the animation is played.

Anything drawn in the grey work area is 'off the stage' and will not be seen in your completed animation.

TIP!

*To undo an action: **Edit** menu → **Undo**.*

▸▸ HOW TO … Draw shapes (create vector graphics)

1 Select the **Line Tool, Oval Tool, Rectangle Tool** or **PolyStar Tool**.

2 The options applicable to the selected tool will be displayed in the **Properties** panel (Figure 3.5).

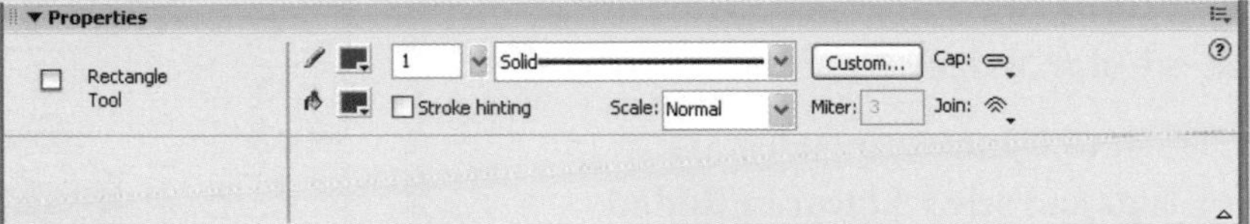

Figure 3.5 The properties for a shape

3 Click the drop-down arrow to the **Stroke Color** option → the **Color Picker** window is displayed (refer to Figure 3.6) → move your mouse over any colour square, an **Eyedropper** symbol is displayed → select a colour by clicking in a square.

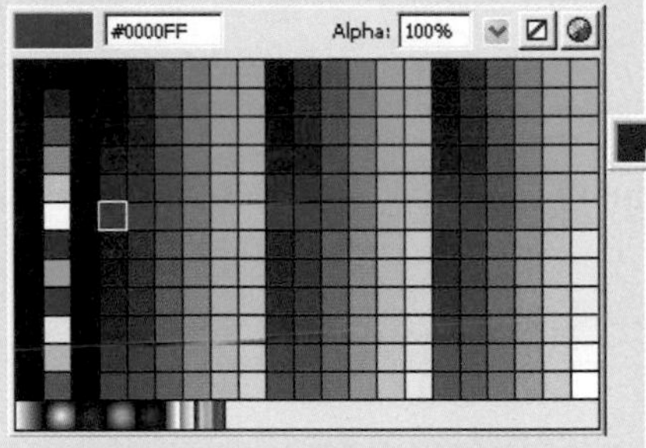

Figure 3.6 The Color Picker window

4 Select a **Stroke height** by clicking the arrow or entering a number in the box.

5 Select a **Stroke style** by clicking the arrow and selecting an option (refer to Figure 3.7).

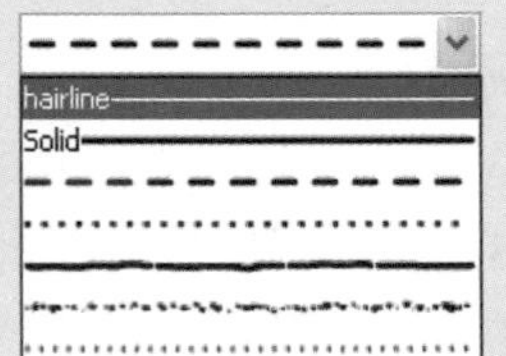

Figure 3.7 Stroke style options

6 To select the fill colour for a shape, click the drop-down arrow to the right of **Fill Color** and select a colour.

7 To draw a circle, hold down the **Shift** key whilst drawing with the **Oval Tool**. To draw a square, hold down the **Shift** key whilst drawing with the **Rectangle Tool**.

8 To draw a star, select the **PolyStar Tool** → make sure the **Properties** panel is expanded → click the **Options** button [Options...] in the **Properties** panel → a **Tool Settings** dialogue box is displayed (Figure 3.8) → click the drop-down arrow to the right of **Style** and select **star** → enter the required **Number of Sides** (i.e. the number of points you want for the star) → set the **Star point size**: the lower the number, the narrower the points from the centre.

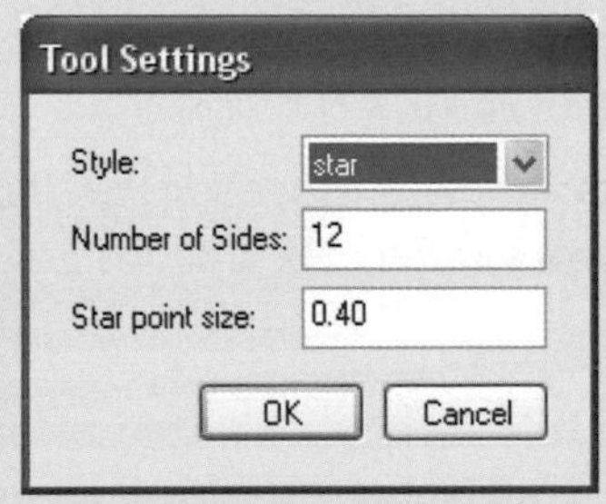

Figure 3.8 Setting the tool options before drawing a star

9 Click and drag the mouse pointer on the Stage to draw the shape.

If the **Line Tool** is selected, only the **Stroke Color** option is displayed. The stroke colour is the line colour. **Fill Color** does not apply to this tool.

The stroke colour is the outline colour of the shape. If you don't want an outline colour, click the **No Color** button in the **Color Picker** window.

TIP!

Lines and shapes can also be modified after they have been created. Fills and strokes for shapes are treated as separate objects – they can be selected separately to move or modify them.

TIP!

When selecting a stroke or fill colour, you can move your cursor (the dropper) to clone (copy) any colour on the screen.

The star on the left of Figure 3.9 has with no stroke colour, 12 sides (points) and a point size of 0.40. The star on the right of Figure 3.9 has a blue stroke colour, 7 sides (points) and a point size of 0.60.

Figure 3.9 Drawing a star

▶▶ HOW TO ... Fill a shape with a gradient

1 Follow steps 1 to 3 on page 119, ensure the **Color Mixer** panel is displayed (**Window** menu → **Color Mixer**).

2 In the **Color Mixer** panel (refer to Figure 3.10), select the drop-down arrow to the right of **Type** and select **Linear** or **Radial**.

3 Double-click the gradient swatch button at the bottom right, below the six letter hexadecimal code → a **Color Picker** window is displayed → select a colour.

4 Double-click the gradient swatch on the left and select a colour. To adjust the gradient, click and drag the left and/or right gradient swatches further inwards.

5 Draw the shape.

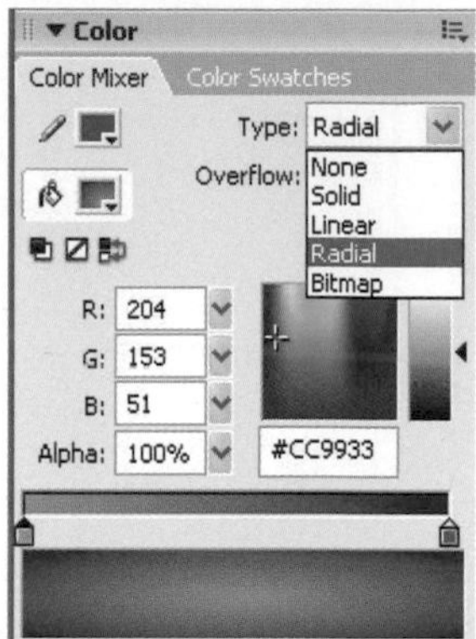

Figure 3.10 Filling with gradients

Adjusting the opacity

The opacity of an object can be adjusted by changing the **Alpha** value in the **Color Mixer** panel. **Alpha** sets the opacity for a solid or gradient fill. An alpha value of 0% creates a transparent fill and an alpha value of 100% creates an opaque fill.

Shapes are created on the Stage level on which objects are a collection of lines/strokes and fills which can be moved independently. Converting an object to Overlay level converts it to a single graphic which is easier to manipulate. Make sure you are happy with the shape, colours etc. before you convert it to a single object.

*To convert an object from Stage level to Overlay level, either group it (select the objects, then press **Ctrl + G**) or convert it into a symbol (refer to Section 3 of this chapter).*

TIP!

*The **History** panel allows you to undo multiple edits.*

***Window** menu → **Other Panels** → **History** or press **Ctrl + F10**.*

Click on the vertical bar at the left of the window; a slider arrow is displayed. Drag the slider to select the actions to be undone.

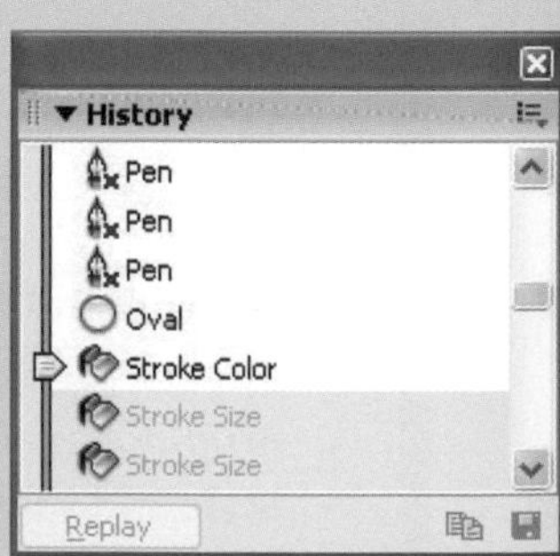

PRACTICAL TASK 3.2 Create layers, draw geometric shapes

Assessment objectives 1c, 2a, 2c, 2d, 2e

1 Create a new document and display the rulers and grid guides.

2 Select the **Snap to Grid** option only; deselect all other snapping options.

PRACTICAL TASK 3.2 Continued

3 Create a new layer and rename it **line**. Draw a straight horizontal black solid line, with a stroke height of 3, to span the full width of the Stage towards the bottom of the Stage.

4 Create a new layer and rename it **circle**. On this layer, towards the top left of the Stage, draw a yellow circle with a dashed line stroke in red (stroke height 2).

5 Create a new layer and rename it **square**. On this layer, towards the top right of the Stage, draw a square with rounded corners, radius 12, and a dotted line stroke in blue (stroke height 5). Fill the square with a radial gradient mixing any two colours.

6 Fit the view on screen.

7 Create a new layer and rename it **star**. In the middle of the Stage, draw a 15-point star to fill most of the Stage. Use a 0.40 point size and a hairline stroke style. Use a stroke colour and fill colour/gradient of your choice. Set the opacity to 50%.

SELECTING OBJECTS

To manipulate objects, you need to know how to select them – objects in Flash don't always behave as you would expect! You must practise using the various selection tools to help you understand and work with selections.

You can select objects using the **Selection Tool**, **Subselection Tool** and **Lasso Tool**.

▶▶ HOW TO ... Select objects

1 To select a single object, use the **Selection Tool** to click once on the object → a square or rectangular bounding box is displayed around the object, as shown in the top image of Figure 3.11.

2 To select multiple objects on the Stage, use the **Selection Tool** to draw a frame around all the objects: click and drag diagonally from top left to bottom right *or* bottom right to top left → square or rectangular bounding boxes are displayed around the different objects, as shown in the middle image of Figure 3.11.

3 To select part of an object, e.g. to select only the outline of a circle, use the **Subselection Tool** to click once on the object → square handles are displayed on the object, as shown in the bottom image of Figure 3.11.

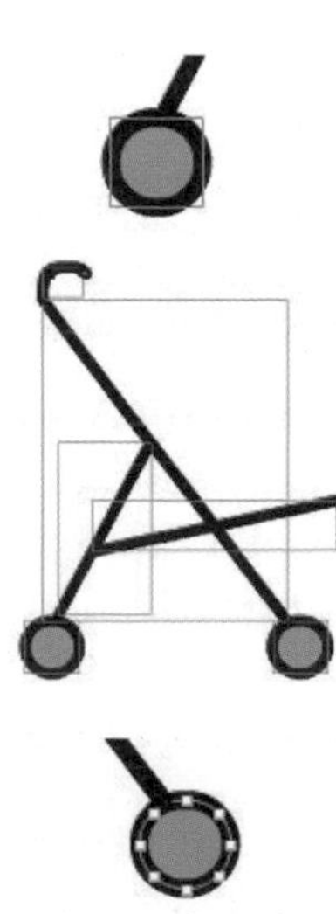

Figure 3.11
Different selections

Continued ...

4 To select objects by drawing a freehand outline, use the **Lasso Tool** → click and hold down the left mouse button to draw around the area → square or rectangular bounding boxes are displayed around the selected objects. *Note: unlike the Lasso Tool in Photoshop, the selection is not displayed as an irregular shape.*

5 To draw a straight-edged selection area, use the **Lasso Tool** and select the **Polygon Mode**  from the **Options** section of the Toolbox.

*To modify a shape, use the **Selection Tool**. Ensure the entire object is not selected (no rectangular selection box). Move the mouse pointer to the outside edge of the shape until a curve is displayed just below the pointer. Click and drag an edge to bend the shape.*

*If you double-click a grouped object, you enter the editing mode. You can check if you are in editing mode by looking above the Timeline, next to **Scene 1** (refer to Figure 3.12). To return to the Stage, click **Scene 1** or click the blue arrow (to the left of Scene 1) to go back to the Stage.*

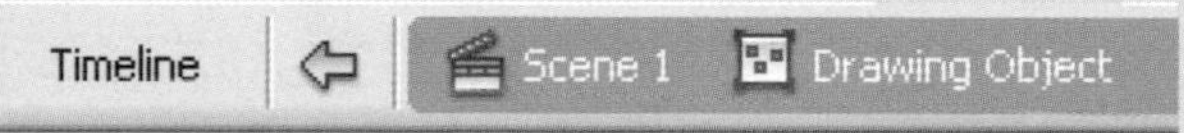

Figure 3.12 Timeline bar

*If you are in editing mode and you select an object, the selection will be displayed as dots. Figure 3.13 shows the object selected on the Stage using the **Selection Tool** (left), the fill colour selected in editing mode (middle) and the stroke colour selected in editing mode (right).*

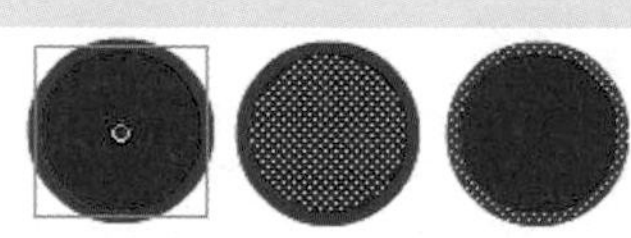

Figure 3.13 Different selections

TIP!

You can manipulate a shape's stroke and fill separately, or if you group it, you can manipulate is as a single graphic. Similarly, you can group then manipulate multiple objects. To group: use the **Selection Tool** to select the entire object or multiple objects → **Modify** menu → **Group** (or press **Ctrl + G**). Double-click the group to go to the editing mode.

CHANGING STROKES WITH THE INK BOTTLE TOOL

The **Ink Bottle Tool** can be used to change the stroke colour, width, line styles and shape outlines. Using the **Ink Bottle Tool** makes it quicker and easier to change the stroke properties of multiple objects at the same time instead of selecting and modifying individual lines.

▶▶ HOW TO ... Use the Ink Bottle tool

1 Select the **Ink Bottle tool** from the Toolbox.

2 From the **Properties** panel, select a **Stroke color**, **Stroke height** and **Stroke style**.

3 Click an object on the Stage to apply the stroke modifications.

4 The stars at the bottom of Figure 3.14 show a changed stroke colour and style.

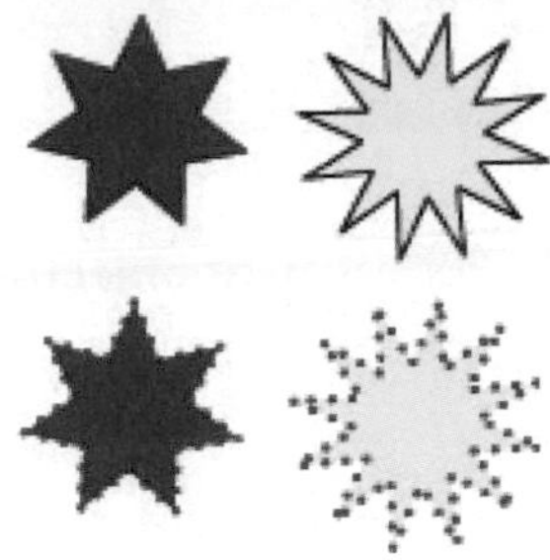

Figure 3.14 Changing strokes

ERASING

You can erase strokes and fills using the **Eraser Tool**. You can quickly erase everything on the Stage, erase individual stroke segments or filled areas or erase by dragging.

From the **Options** section of the Toolbox, you can select a round or square eraser in a variety of different sizes.

TIP!

To quickly delete everything on the Stage, double-click the ***Eraser Tool*** *in the Toolbox (do not double-click on the Stage).*

▶▶ HOW TO ... Use the Eraser Tool

1 Select the **Eraser Tool** .

2 To erase stroke segments or filled areas, select the **Faucet** modifier from the **Options** section of the Toolbox.

3 Click the stroke segment or filled area that you want to delete → the stroke or fill will be deleted (Figure 3.15).

4 To erase by dragging, make sure the **Faucet** modifier is *not* selected. Select the **Eraser Mode** modifier from the **Options** section and select an erasing mode (refer to Figure 3.16):

- **Erase Normal** erases strokes and fills on the same layer.
- **Erase Fills** erases only fills.
- **Erase Lines** erases only strokes.
- **Erase Selected Fills** erases only fills that are selected fills.
- **Erase Inside** erases only the fill on which you begin the eraser stroke. If you start erasing from an empty point, nothing is erased.

5 To change the eraser shape, select the **Eraser Shape** modifier from the **Options** section and select an eraser shape and size.

6 Drag the eraser on the Stage.

Figure 3.15 Fill erased from star shape

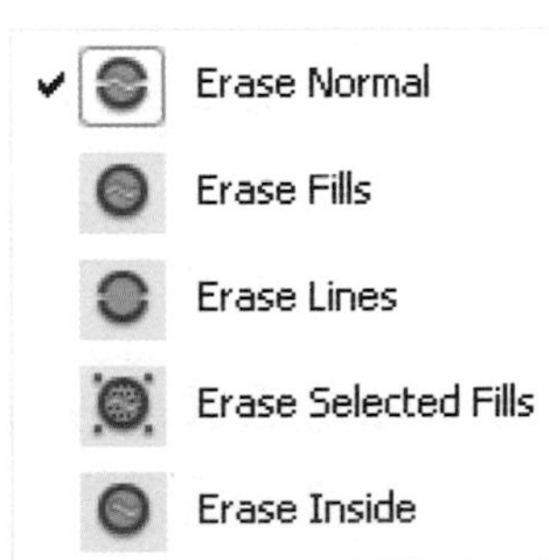

Figure 3.16 Erasing options

PRACTICAL TASK 3.3 **Use selection tools, work with layers, modify strokes and erase objects**

Assessment objectives 1c, 2a, 2d, 2e

1 Open your saved document **shapes**

2 Use the **Ink Bottle Tool** to change the stroke colour of the three shapes (circle, square and star) to black, with a solid stroke style and stroke height of **3**.

3 Use the **Eraser Tool** and **Faucet** modifier to erase the fill for the star.

4 Save the document using the new filename **shapes2**

5 Use the **Selection Tool** to select only the stroke for the circle and change the stroke style to dotted, and the colour to pink.

6 Hide the **star** layer. Group the square. Use the **Selection Tool** to move the square to the bottom right corner of the Stage.

7 Hide the **star** layer. Use the **Eraser Tool**, with the **Erase Lines** option to erase the middle third of the line.

8 Use the **Subselection Tool** to select the right-hand side of the line and move it to be in the centre of the circle. Resize the line to fit in the circle.

9 Move the **line** layer to be above the **circle** layer. Display all layers.

10 Save the document using the filename **shapes3**

For an OCR assessment, you must provide evidence that you have used at least five tools, including tools with drawing capabilities. To do so, you could provide 'before and after' screen prints with a brief description about the tool(s) used.

DRAWING AND PAINTING FREEHAND LINES AND SHAPES

The **Pencil Tool** is used to draw freehand lines and shapes as if drawing with a real pencil. The **Brush Tool** is used to create brush-like strokes as if painting with a brush. You can create special effects, including calligraphic effects.

▶▶ HOW TO ... Draw using the Pencil Tool

1 Select the **Pencil Tool** . The related options are displayed at the bottom of the Toolbox (Figure 3.17):
- Select **Straighten** to draw straight lines and to convert roughly drawn shapes into common geometric shapes.
- Select **Smooth** to draw smooth curved lines.
- Select **Ink** to draw freehand lines.

2 From the **Properties** panel, select the required options (**Stroke color**, **Stroke height** and **Stroke style**).

3 Click in the Stage and drag to draw.

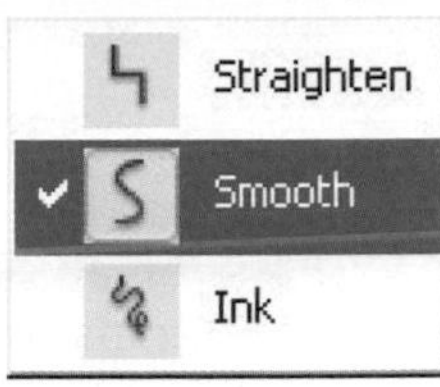

Figure 3.17 Pencil Tool options

TIP!

Hold down the ***Shift*** key to constrain lines to vertical or horizontal directions when using the ***Pencil Tool*** or ***Brush Tool***.

▶▶ HOW TO ... Paint using the Brush Tool

1 Select the **Brush Tool**.

2 From the **Properties** panel, select a **Fill Color**.

3 From the **Options** section of the Toolbox, click the **Brush Mode** modifier and select a painting mode (refer to Figure 3.18):
- **Paint Normal** paints over lines and fills on the same layer.
- **Paint Fills** paints fills and empty areas, leaving lines unaffected.
- **Paint Behind** paints in blank areas of the Stage on the same layer, leaving lines and fills unaffected.
- **Paint Selection** applies a new fill to the selection when you select a fill in the **Fill** box of the **Properties** panel. (This is the same as selecting a filled area and applying a new fill.)
- **Paint Inside** paints the fill in which you start a brush stroke. It does not allow you to paint outside any lines.

4 Below **Options** in the Toolbox, select a brush size and brush shape .

5 Drag the brush on the Stage. Hold down the **Shift** key and drag to constrain brush strokes to horizontal and vertical directions.

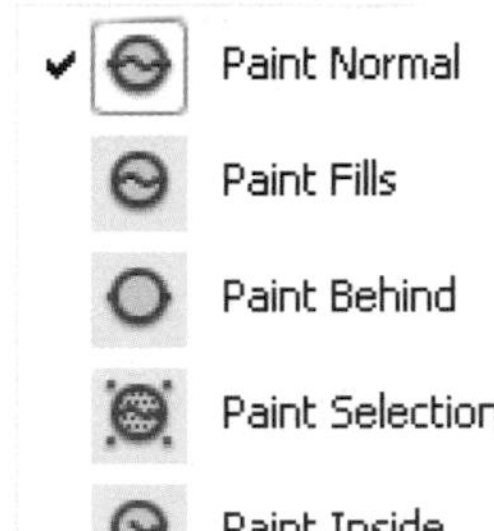

Figure 3.18 Brush options

TRANSFORMING OBJECTS

The **Free Transform Tool** allows you to scale (resize), stretch, rotate and skew lines and shapes. You can transform graphic objects, as well as groups, text blocks and instances.

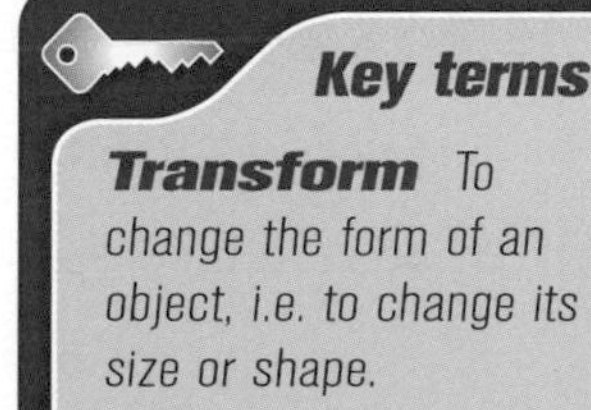

Key terms

Transform *To change the form of an object, i.e. to change its size or shape.*

▶▶ HOW TO ... Transform objects

1 Select the **Free Transform Tool** .
- To transform multiple objects at the same time, click and drag to draw a marquee around the objects.
- To transform a single object, click once on the object.

2 A frame with black square handles and a round centre point is displayed around the object(s).

3 To scale a selection, position your mouse over a corner handle → a double-headed arrow is displayed → click and drag the handle. To maintain proportion, hold down the Shift key. To stretch a selection, click and drag a side handle (note this will distort the original shape).

4 To rotate a selection, position your mouse over a corner handle → a circular arrow is displayed → click and drag to rotate.

5 To skew a selection, position your mouse pointer on the outline → the pointer changes to or → click and drag to distort the shape.

6 You can also use any of the four options with this tool from the **Options** section of the Toolbox.

Figure 3.19 shows the original selection and Figure 3.20 shows the selection resized proportionally and then rotated.

Figure 3.19 Original object

Figure 3.20 Transformed object

FILLING EMPTY AREAS AND CHANGING FILL COLOURS

The **Paint Bucket Tool** allows you to fill empty areas and change the colour of painted areas. You can paint with solid colours, gradient fills and bitmap fills.

*Select a **Close** option if you want Flash to fill a shape that has gaps. However, if the gaps are too large, you should close them yourself first before filling.*

▶▶ HOW TO ... Use the Paint Bucket Tool to fill an area

1 Select the **Paint Bucket Tool** from the Toolbox.

2 Select a fill colour and style from the **Properties** panel.

3 From the **Options** section of the Toolbox, select the **Gap Size** modifier and select a gap size option (refer to Figure 3.21).

4 Click the shape or area that you want to fill.

Figure 3.21 Fill options

TRANSFORMING GRADIENT AND BITMAP FILLS

You can use **Gradient Transform Tool** to transform a gradient or bitmap fill by adjusting the size, direction or centre of the fill.

▶▶ HOW TO ... Use the Gradient Transform Tool

1 Select the **Gradient Transform Tool** → click an area filled with a gradient or bitmap fill.

2 If you want to apply a gradient transform to a shape with a solid colour, change the solid colour to a **Linear** or **Radial** gradient first, then use the **Gradient Transform Tool** to transform the gradient (refer to Figure 3.22).

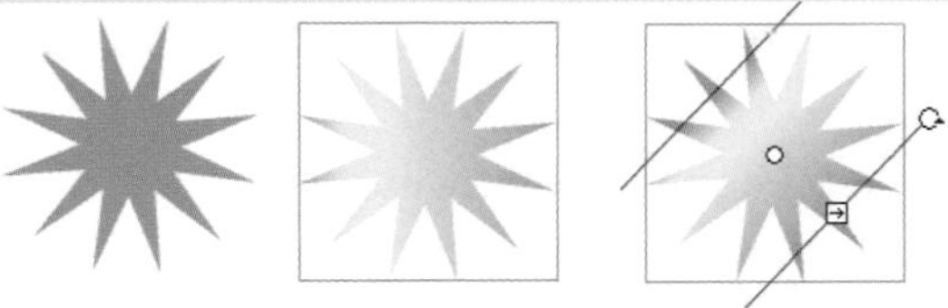

Figure 3.22 Using Gradient Transform

3 A bounding box with editing handles is displayed around the object. If you position your mouse pointer over any handle, it changes to indicate the function of the handle:

- To reposition the centre point of the filled area, drag the centre point.
- To change the width, drag the square handle on the side of the bounding box.
- To change the height, drag the square handle at the bottom of the bounding box.
- To rotate, drag the circular rotation handle at the corner.
- To scale, drag the square handle at the centre of the bounding box.

The top image in Figure 3.23 shows a shape selected using the Gradient Transform Tool; the bottom image shows the changed fill and size.

USING THE PEN TOOL

The **Pen Tool** is used to draw straight lines or smooth flowing curves in a vector format. To create the lines or curves, you set **anchor points** by clicking with the mouse. To adjust the direction of curves you need to move the handles.

The Fill Transform Tool included in the OCR syllabus, is available in Flash MX 2004. This tool has been replaced by the ***Gradient Transform Tool*** *in Flash version 8.*

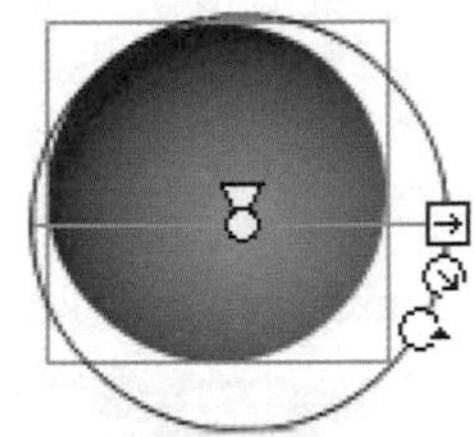

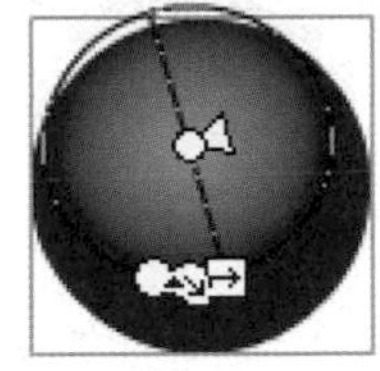

Figure 3.23 Using Gradient Transform

Key terms

Anchor point *A location (point) on a vector line or curve which determines the direction and length of the line.*

▶▶ HOW TO ... Draw straight lines

1. Select the **Pen Tool** . In the **Properties** panel, select the **Stroke color** and **Stroke style**.
2. Position the mouse pointer on the Stage where you want the straight line to begin and click to define the first anchor point.
3. Click again where you want the first segment of the straight line to end. Continue clicking to create additional straight segments.
4. To complete the path as an open shape, double-click the last point.
5. To close a path, position the **Pen Tool** over the first anchor point → a small circle is displayed next to the pen tip when it is positioned correctly → click to close the path.

TIP!

To constrain lines to 45-degree angles, hold down the ***Shift*** *key whilst using the* ***Pen Tool*** *or other drawing tools.*

▶▶ HOW TO ... Draw curved lines

Using the **Pen Tool** to draw curved lines will require some practice and patience! To become familiar with using this tool, try drawing the letter C. You will need five points: start, top, middle back, bottom and finish. Each point will be joined by a curve. Don't try and get it exactly right first time – you can edit the points and curves later.

1. Position the **Pen Tool** at the start and click. An anchor point is displayed.
2. Position your mouse at the top of the C, click and hold the mouse button down. A curve is drawn with two handles. Move the mouse to swing the curve to approximately the right shape.
3. Move to the other points and repeat step 2.
4. When you have drawn the C, click back on the **Pen Tool** in the Toolbox to end the shape.
5. To edit the shape, use the **Subselection Tool** in the Toolbox:
   - To move a point, click *exactly* on the anchor point and drag (or nudge it with the arrow keys) to a new position.
   - To alter the curve, click on the anchor point and drag (or nudge with the arrow keys) the end of the handle to swing the curve to a better position.
   - To convert a curve point to a corner, click with the **Pen Tool**.
   - To convert a corner to a curve, click with the **Subselection Tool** and hold down the **Alt** key while dragging the handles.
   - To add a point, click with the **Pen Tool** between two existing anchors.
   - To delete a point, click with the **Subselection Tool** and press the **Delete** key.

COPYING STROKES AND FILLS

The **Eyedropper Tool** can be used to select colours from existing objects and to copy fill and stroke properties from one object and immediately apply them to another object.

▶▶ HOW TO ... Use the Eyedropper Tool to copy and apply stroke or fill properties

1. Select the **Eyedropper Tool** → click the stroke or filled area whose properties you want to copy.
2. When you click a stroke, the tool automatically changes to the **Ink Bottle Tool**. When you click a filled area, the tool automatically changes to the **Paint Bucket Tool** with a lock symbol.
3. Click another stroke or filled area to paste the copied properties.

PRACTICAL TASK 3.4 Using drawing, painting and selection tools

Assessment objectives 1c, 2a, 2c, 2d, 2e

1. Create a new document. Use a combination of the pencil, brush and oval tools to draw two custom shapes, one resembling a disabled sign as shown in Figure 3.19, and one resembling a pushchair as shown in the centre of Figure 3.11.
2. Save the document using a suitable filename.
3. Open the document **shapes3**
4. Hide all layers except the layer named **star**
5. Transform the star shape maintaining proportion so that it is approximately half its original size.
6. Display the layer named **square** and rotate the square to look like a diamond shape. Save the document using the filename **shapes4** and close it.
7. Open your saved document **shapes**
8. Hide all layers except the **star** layer. Use the **Gradient Transform Tool** to change the gradient fill so that only the centre of the star has a gradient fill (Figure 3.24 shows an example). Hide the **star** layer and display all other layers.
9. Use the **Eyedropper Tool** to copy the fill from the circle and paste it on the square so that it has the same fill.
10. Save the document using the filename **shapes6**

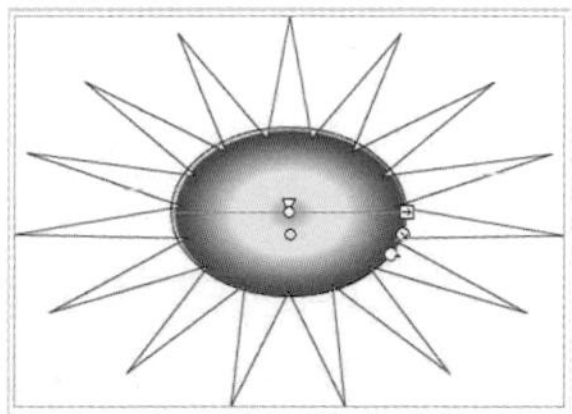

Figure 3.24 An example of a gradient fill

INSERTING TEXT

You can add three types of text in Flash: static, dynamic and input.

You can enter text horizontally or vertically. Horizontal (left to right) is the default. Text is usually added in variable or static text blocks. You can also add text using text fields but this requires use of action scripts which is beyond the requirements of this syllabus. Text in a text block can be formatted, edited and moved. Text properties such as emphasis, colour, size, alignment, text direction, character spacing, borders and hyperlinks can be set in the **Properties** panel.

Static text is used when you want to add decorative text or text that does not need to change.

Dynamic text displays continually updating text, such as sports scores.

Input text fields allow users to enter text in forms or surveys.

▶▶ HOW TO ... Add text

1 Insert and rename a new layer if needed.
2 Select the **Text Tool** A .
3 Select the text properties in the **Properties** panel, e.g. font type, size, colour, emphasis, alignment.
4 To create text in a single line, click on the Stage where you want the text to start and enter your text.
5 To create a text block with a fixed width (for horizontal text) or fixed height (for vertical text), click and drag to draw a text frame on the Stage and enter the required text.

Flash displays a handle on the corner of a text block to identify the type of text (refer to Figure 3.25):

- A round handle is displayed at the top right corner for static horizontal text that extends.
- A square handle is displayed at the top right corner for static horizontal text with a defined width.
- A round handle is displayed at the bottom right corner for dynamic or input text that extends.
- For dynamic or input text with a defined height and width, a square handle displays at the bottom right corner.

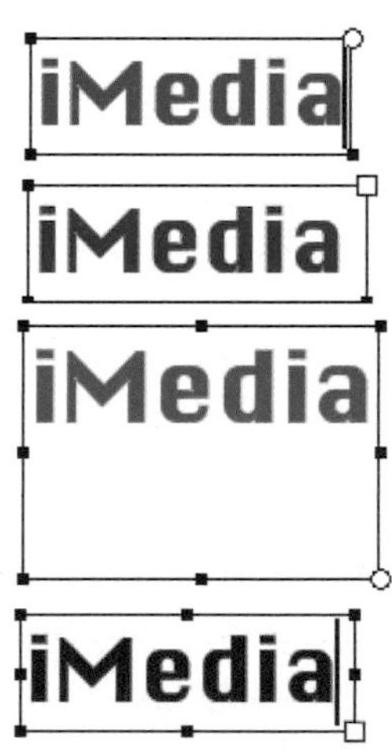

Figure 3.25 Entering text

Refer to 'Animating text' on page 147.

PRACTICAL TASK 3.5 Insert and format text

Assessment objective 2a

1 Create a new document. Using a new layer for each text block, enter and format text on each layer. Ensure you use static, dynamic and input text.
2 Select different text options (e.g. font type, font size, text colour, bold, italic, text alignment) in the **Properties** panel for each layer.
3 Save the document using the filename **text**. You will use this document to practise animating text in Section 3.

TIP!

Use the **Free Transform Tool** to scale, rotate and skew your text.

SECTION 3 • Libraries, symbols, instances and create digital animations

The following assessment objectives will be covered in this section:

1b Use animation features

1c Use the digital animation interface

2b Use symbols, instances and the library

2e Save in a format suitable for inclusion in a web page

The following knowledge, skills and understanding criteria corresponding to assessment objectives 1b, 1c, 2b and 2e will be covered:

- *Frame by frame animation*
- *Tweened animation*
- *Digital devices and programs used to create animation*
- *How digital animation is used*
- *Interface functions*
- *Symbols*
- *Instances*
- *Document library*
- *Different types of file format*
- *Common file extensions*

To create animations in Flash, you need to understand libraries, symbols and instances and their properties.

LIBRARIES

The **Library** panel is where symbols and imported files, including bitmap graphics, sound files and video clips, are stored and can be organised into folders and sorted by type (Figure 3.26). The **Library** panel also displays how often an item has been used in a document. Items stored in the library are referred to as **assets**. Each document has its own library, referred to as the **Document Library**.

Figure 3.26 Symbols in a Document Library

Working with common libraries

Flash has sample common libraries which you can use to add buttons or sounds to your documents. You can also create your own custom libraries, which you can then use in any document.

Refer to Figure 4.16 on page 180 for more detail about the Library panel.

▶▶ HOW TO ... Use an item from a common library

1 Select the **Window** menu → **Common Libraries** → select a category from the submenu → the library will be displayed on screen.

2 Click on the folder icon to open a folder (Figure 3.27).

3 Drag an item from the common library into the library for the current document *or* drag it to the Stage and it will be automatically added to the current document's library.

Figure 3.27 Common Library items

IMPORTING ASSETS

You can import a variety of assets into Flash, such as images, sounds and video clips, which you can then use in your animations.

- Image file formats that can be imported into Flash include: **bmp**, **gif**, **tiff**, **png**, **jpg/jpeg**, **al** and **psd**.
- Sound file formats that can be imported into Flash include: **mp3**, **aiff**, **au** and **wav**.
- Video file formats that can be imported into Flash include: **mov**, **avi**, **dv** and **mpeg/mpg**.

All imported assets are stored in the document's library. This also holds symbols that you create in Flash. You can import assets to the library or to the Stage. Any assets imported to the Stage will be automatically stored in the document's library.

Key terms

Assets In the context of this qualification are the source files (images, sounds, videos etc.) that you have created or collected.

▶▶ HOW TO ... Import images

1 **File** menu → **Import** > select **Import to Library** or **Import to Stage**. The **Import to Library** dialogue box is displayed (if you select **Import to Stage**, the dialogue box will be titled **Import**).

2 Browse to the folder in your user area containing the file.

3 To display the library panel: **Window** menu → **Library**.

To import video clips: **File** → **Import** → **Import Video** → then follow the **Import Video** wizard instructions.

Sounds are imported in the same way as images.

Refer to 'Importing video' on page 186.

PRACTICAL TASK 3.6 Import assets into library

Assessment objectives 2c, 2e

1 Refer to the assignment brief 'Cove Photography Club – Animation' on page 110. Create a new document and look at the resources available in Flash's common libraries. Identify any items within the common libraries that you may be able to use in your animation.

PRACTICAL TASK 3.6 Continued

2 You may wish to copy any items from the common library to the library in your own document. (This will save you time later instead of finding the item again from the common library.)

3 Save your document using the filename **clubanim**

4 Source the assets that you will need to create the animation required by the 'client'.

5 Import your assets into the Document Library.

6 Save the document retaining the filename.

SYMBOLS AND INSTANCES

A **symbol** is a graphic, button or movie clip. Symbols can be created using shapes that you have created yourself or using imported images or video clips. You can create a symbol once and can then reuse it as many times as you want in any document. Any symbol that you create automatically becomes part of the **library** for the current document.

Refer to 'Libraries' on page 131.

You can also create font symbols. However, that is beyond the requirements of this syllabus.

Types of symbols

You can create three main types of symbols.

- **Graphic symbols** are used for static images and to create reusable pieces of animation. They have their own separate Timeline. Graphic symbols cannot contain button symbols or sounds and cannot be made interactive.
- **Button symbols** are used to create interactive buttons that respond to mouse clicks, rollovers or other actions. A button symbol contains four frames, one for each state of the button, i.e. up, down, over and hit.
- **Movie clip symbols** are used to create reusable pieces of animation. They allow you to create independent animations within the main movie Timeline. If the main movie stops playing, the movie clip symbol's animation does not necessarily stop.

The advantage of using symbols is that file size is reduced considerably. For example, you could convert a background image into a symbol and reuse it several times. Using symbols can also speed playback because a symbol needs to be downloaded to the player (e.g. Flash Player) only once. Saving several instances of a symbol requires less storage space than saving multiple copies of the contents of the symbol.

The two main differences between instances and symbols are that an instance does not add to the file size significantly and instances automatically change when the parent symbol is updated.

An **instance** is a *copy* of a symbol located on the Stage or nested inside another symbol. An instance can be different from its symbol in terms of colour, size and function. When a symbol is edited, all its instances are automatically updated. If effects are applied to an instance, only that instance is updated.

▶▶ HOW TO … Convert an image to a graphic symbol

1 Drag the image from the library to the Stage.

2 Use the **Selection Tool** to drag around the image or click once to select the image → **Modify** menu → **Convert to Symbol** → in the **Convert to Symbol** dialogue box (Figure 3.28) name the symbol. For **Type**, select **Graphic** → **OK**.

Figure 3.28 Creating a symbol

3 The graphic on the Stage is now an instance of the graphic symbol in the Library.

4 The **Properties** panel displays the properties for the graphic symbol instance (Figure 3.29).

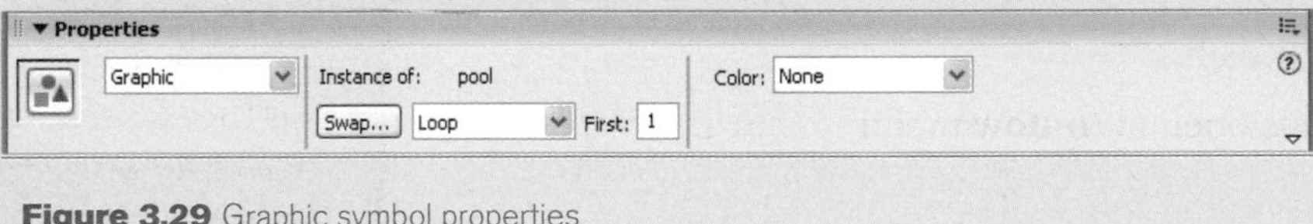

Figure 3.29 Graphic symbol properties

▶▶ HOW TO … Convert a shape to a button symbol

1 Use the **Selection Tool** to draw a marquee around the whole shape (do not click to select the shape).

2 **Modify** menu → **Convert to Symbol** *or* press **F8** → a **Convert to Symbol** dialogue box is displayed → enter a name for the symbol → select **Button** for the **Type** → **OK**.

3 The **Properties** panel displays the properties for the button symbol instance.

▶▶ HOW TO … Create a movie clip symbol

1 Use the **Selection Tool** to select the object → **Modify** menu → **Convert to Symbol** → in the **Convert to Symbol** dialogue box, enter a name → select **Movie clip** as the **Type**.

2 Select the registration point in the **Registration** grid → **OK**.

TIP!

To rename a symbol, right-click on the symbol name in the **Library** panel → select **Rename** from the menu → enter a new name → press **Enter**.

The black square in the Registration grid of the Convert to Symbol dialogue boxes indicates where, within the symbol, the registration point is located. A registration point is the axis around which the symbol rotates, and the point along which the symbol aligns.

Refer to pages 189 to 191 for more information about working with buttons.

Refer to 'Using symbols in more than one movie' on pages 187–188.

Continued ...

3 The image on the Stage is now an instance of the movie clip symbol in the library.

4 Your created symbols will automatically be displayed in the Library of the document.

A movie clip symbol is similar to a document within a document. You can add movie clips within other movie clips and add buttons to create nested movie clips.

CREATING INSTANCES

After you create a symbol, you can create instances of that symbol anywhere in your document, as well as inside other symbols.

Flash names movie clip and button instances with default names when they are created, but you can change the names in the **Properties** panel.

Key terms

Keyframe A frame in which you define a change in an animation.

▸▸ HOW TO ... Create a new instance of a symbol

1 Select a layer in the Timeline (because Flash places instances in keyframes on the current layer).

2 Ensure the **Library** panel is open (**Window** menu → **Library**).

3 Drag the symbol from the library to the Stage.

TIP!

If you do not select a keyframe when creating instances, Flash will add the instance to the first keyframe to the left of the current frame.

▸▸ HOW TO ... Name an instance

Note: you cannot give a custom name to a graphic symbol.

1 Select the instance on the Stage using the Selection Tool.

2 Flash recognises particular code hints for instances. When naming a movie clip instance, always give the instance a suffix of **_mc**. e.g. **swimming_mc**
When naming a button instance, use the **_btn** suffix e.g. **pool_btn**
When naming a text field instance, use the **_txt** suffix.

3 Enter a name for the instance in the **Instance Name** [<Instance Name>] text box on the left side of the **Properties** panel.

TIP!

*If you create an instance of a graphic symbol, click **Insert → Timeline → Frame** to add the quantity of frames that will contain the graphic symbol.*

Modifying instances and symbols

Once you have created a symbol, you can create instances of the symbol as many times as you want. The properties of one instance (e.g. colour, size, rotation, blending options) can be modified without altering other instances.

If you modify the original symbol, the modified instance acquires the edited symbol properties and retains its own modified properties.

▶▶ HOW TO ... Copy and modify an instance of a symbol

1 Use the **Selection Tool** to select the instance on the Stage.

2 To copy an instance, hold down the **Alt** key and drag it.

3 Ensure the copy remains selected and that the **Properties** panel is expanded.

4 From the **Properties** panel, click the drop-down arrows for **Color**, **Blend** etc. to select the new properties for the copied instance (refer to Figure 3.30).

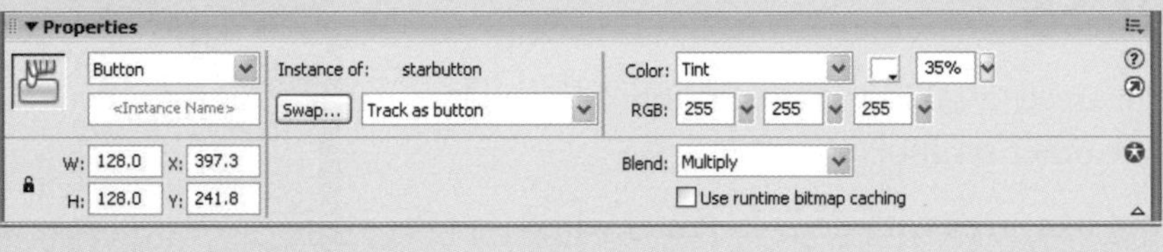

Figure 3.30 Setting the properties for an Instance

For an OCR assessment, you must show evidence of using at least one symbol.

▶▶ HOW TO ... Modify a symbol

1 Double-click on a symbol to enter the symbol-editing mode.

2 Above the Timeline, next to **Scene 1**, the name of the symbol is displayed to indicate that you are in symbol-editing mode.

3 Use the appropriate tools in the Toolbox or select the required options in the **Properties** panel to modify the symbol. For example, to change the size or rotation, use the **Free Transform Tool**; to change the gradient fill, use the **Gradient Transform Tool**.

4 To exit the symbol-editing mode, click **Scene 1** above the Timeline.

TIP!

Remember any changes made to a symbol will be applied to all instances of that symbol.

PRACTICAL TASK 3.7 Create and modify symbols and instances

Assessment objectives 1c, 2b

1 Open your saved document **clubanim**

2 On a new layer, create at least two shapes that will be appropriate for the animation that you will create for your client. Fill one with a gradient and one with a solid fill.

3 Convert the shapes to button symbols.

4 Convert at least two of your own imported graphics to symbols.

5 Convert any imported video clips to movie clip symbols.

6 On a new layer, create an instance for at least one symbol.

7 Open each one of your library items on the Stage and modify each one as needed (e.g. size, rotation, colour, opacity).

8 Save your updated document retaining the filename.

HOW DIGITAL ANIMATION IS USED

For an OCR assessment, you will need to create a digital animation lasting between 20 to 30 seconds. This could include use of shape tweening, motion tweening and frame-by-frame animation as well as animated text.

Animation is used in a variety of ways in a range of multimedia products, for example, on websites; on interactive and educational CD-ROMs and DVD-ROMs; in advertisements on the web, television, on billboards, multiplex screens; in presentations and during demonstrations.

Using animated instead of static images is an effective, visually captivating way of:

- introducing information
- attracting attention
- adding interest
- drawing focus
- giving visual reminders/prompts
- adding impact
- conveying a message
- demonstrating a skill
- illustrating a process or sequence
- presenting a simulation or 'mock-up'
- supporting narration
- developing a theme
- enhancing a learning aid.

Used wisely, animation can liven up any multimedia product.

Animations in Flash

You can work with several different types of frames in the Timeline: keyframes, static frames, tweened frames and placeholder frames.

An animation is created in Flash by adding content to the Timeline. When the playhead moves across the Timeline, the individual frames play, making the static images appear to be moving. The animation is created when the frames are played in quick succession (similar to a flipbook).

Understanding keyframes

A keyframe is a frame where you define changes in the animation. In a frame-by-frame animation, every frame is a keyframe. In a tweened animation (see below), you define keyframes at significant points in the animation – and Flash creates the contents of frames in between.

TWEENED ANIMATION

Simple animations can be created in Flash using a process known as **tweening**. Tweening is short for 'in between' and refers to filling in the frames between two keyframes so that a graphic displayed in the first keyframe changes into the graphic displayed in the second keyframe. In tweened animation, you define keyframes at significant points in the animation and let Flash create the contents of frames in between. You should create keyframes only at those points where something changes.

In the Timeline, a keyframe with content in it is represented by a solid, black circle, and an empty keyframe is represented by an empty circle before the frame. **Tweened animation** is an effective way to create movement and changes over time. In tweened animation, Flash stores only the values for the changes between frames, keeping the file size small.

To create tweened animation, you create a starting frame and an ending frame. Then Flash creates the animation for the frames in between – it varies the object's size, rotation, colour and other properties between the starting and ending frames to create the appearance of movement.

You can create two types of tweening in Flash: **motion tweening** and **shape tweening**.

- **Motion tweening** operates on *grouped objects* or *symbols*. In motion tweening you define the properties (e.g. position, size, rotation) for an instance, group or text block at one point in time and you change these properties at another point in time.
- **Shape tweening** is used with objects that are *not symbols* and are *ungrouped*. In shape tweening, you create a shape at one point in time, and then you change that shape or create another shape at another point in time. Flash estimates the shapes for the frames in between and creates the animation.

Shape tweening can be applied to groups, instances or bitmap images if the elements are broken apart first. To apply shape tweening to text, the text must be broken apart to convert the text to objects.

The main difference between motion tweening and shape tweening is that in motion tweening the object remains the same shape and size, it simply moves from one location to another. In shape tweening, the object transforms (morphs) as it moves from one position to another.

Frame rate

The frame rate is the speed at which the animation will be played and is measured in number of **f**rames **p**er **s**econd (fps). A slow frame rate makes the animation appear to stop and start, a very high frame rate can blur the detail in the animation.

A frame rate of 12 fps usually gives the best results on the web. QuickTime and AVI movies usually have a frame rate of 12 fps. An animation with a frame rate below 12 fps can appear jerky.

Examples of frame rates:

Animation on the Internet	12 fps
TV	25 to 30 fps
High-end video cards in computers	more than 100 fps

To determine the optimum frame rate for your animations, you would need to test your animation on a variety of players (which might not always be possible!). As a general rule, choose a frame rate between 12 fps and 18 fps.

An animation can play more smoothly with a slightly higher frame rate, e.g. 18 fps instead of the default 12 fps.

To change the Stage size for an existing document, ensure there are no objects selected on the Stage.

A higher frame rate means that there is a slightly increased demand on the user's computer to create the extra frames each second.

If you know the running time you need for an animation and the frame rate, you can calculate the number of frames you need as follows:

running time *x* frame rate = number of frames

Document size

Before you begin creating your animation, you should consider what an appropriate size would be for the type of animation and where it will be played. For example, for a banner that would be displayed horizontally on screen, a size of **600** pixels wide by **160** pixels high would be appropriate.

The default Stage size in a new Flash document is 550 pixels wide by 400 pixels high (19.3 cm wide by 14.04 cm high). You can change the size, background colour and other properties for a new or existing document.

The default unit of measurement is pixels but you can change this in the **Document Size** dialogue box by selecting the drop-down arrow for **Ruler units.** This will also change the ruler to centimetres which you will probably find easier to work with.

▶▶ HOW TO ... Set or modify the document properties

1 Click the **Modify** menu → **Document** → the **Document Properties** dialogue box will be displayed (refer to Figure 3.31).

2 Enter a **Title** and **Description** (optional).

3 Select the drop-down arrow for **Ruler units** and change the unit of measurement (optional).

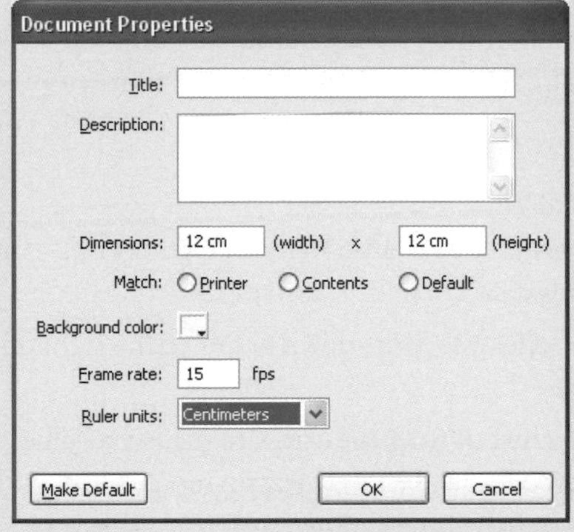

Figure 3.31 Setting document size, colour and frame rate

4 Enter the required **Dimensions** (width and height).

5 Click the drop-down arrow to the right of **Background color** to select a colour.

6 In the **Frame rate** box enter the required number of animation frames per second.

7 Click **OK**.

The document size will display in the **Properties** panel Size: 12 x 12 cm . Click this button to open the **Document Properties** dialogue box quickly.

Key terms

Morphing refers to an animation technique in which one image gradually turns into another. Morphing is short for metamorphosing.

SHAPE TWEENING

When you tween shapes, you create an effect similar to **morphing**. The shape appears to change into another shape over time.

With shape tweening, you set the properties for a shape in one keyframe. You then have two options:

1 If you want to draw another shape, insert a *blank keyframe* then draw the new shape.

2 If you want to modify the shape, insert a *new keyframe* then change the original shape properties and position (refer to the Info box on the right).

To create a new shape, you can also insert a new keyframe (instead of a blank keyframe), then for the second keyframe, delete the shape and create a new one.

▸▸ HOW TO … Create a shape tween

- Before you begin, make sure the **Properties** panel is displayed and expanded, and the **Selection Tool** is selected.

  Note: When creating a shape tween, at step 7 below, you have two choices:

  - either insert a *Blank Keyframe*. This blanks everything on the Stage, allowing you to create a new shape in the new keyframe or modify an existing shape,
  - or insert a Keyframe (as described in step 7 below). The shape remains displayed on the Stage. You can change the shape properties and position in the new keyframe.

  There is no 'right' or 'wrong' way. The choice is yours!

1 Set the document properties including the frame rate.

2 Rename the layer (optional).

3 In the Timeline, select the first keyframe (refer to Figure 3.32) – this is where the animation will start.

4 In the **Properties** panel, click the drop-down arrow to the right of **Tween** and select **Shape**.

5 Enter a value in the **Ease** box or drag the arrow to display a value.

6 Create the shape (or place the artwork) for the first frame of the sequence.

7 In the Timeline, right-click in a frame box the desired number of frames after the first keyframe → a menu is displayed → select **Insert Keyframe** (refer to Figure 3.33) or click once in the keyframe and press **F6**.

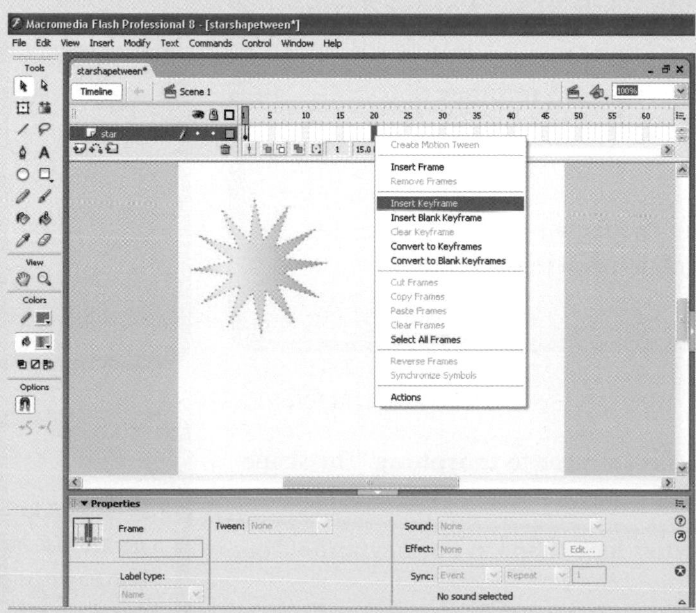

Figure 3.33 Inserting a keyframe

Keyframes are shown in the Timeline. An empty keyframe is represented by an empty circle before the frame (Figure 3.32). A keyframe with content is represented by a solid circle (Figures 3.33 and 3.34).

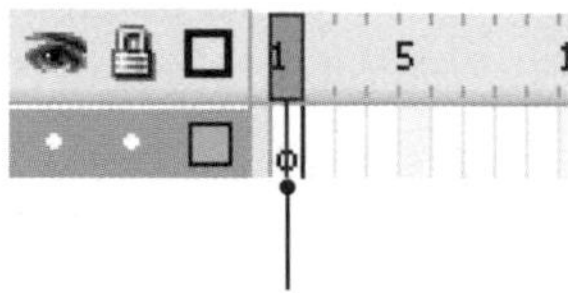

Figure 3.32 Selecting the first keyframe

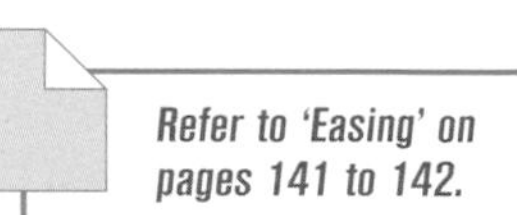

Refer to 'Easing' on pages 141 to 142.

Create keyframes only at those points where something changes.

TIP!

*To remove a keyframe, right-click on the frame in the Timeline → a menu is displayed → select **Remove Frame**.*

Continued ...

8 The shape will remain visible on the Stage and the Timeline will be displayed as shown in Figure 3.34.

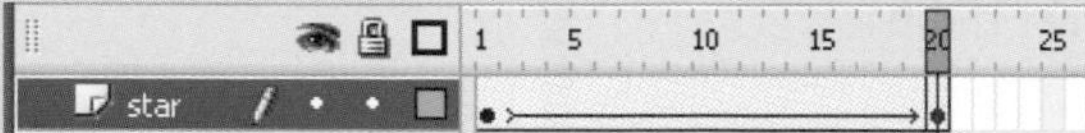

Figure 3.34 A new keyframe in the Timeline

If you get a dashed line as shown in the figure below, this indicates that the tween is broken or incomplete. You must correct this before moving on.

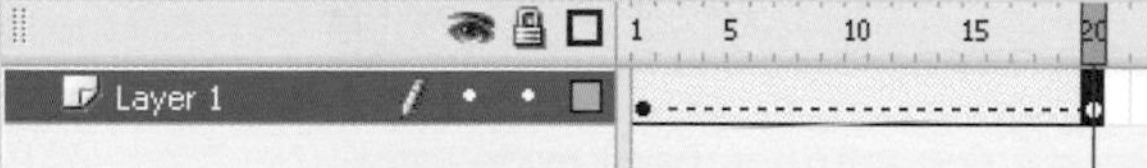

*Undo the new keyframe (**Ctrl + Z** or **Edit → Undo**) and ungroup the shape, or ensure it is not converted to a symbol. Then insert a blank or new keyframe (refer to steps 7 and 8). If you still get a dotted line, delete the shape, set the **Stroke Color** to **None** and repeat steps 7 and 8).*

9 Ensure the second keyframe is selected in the Timeline, then:

a) set the **Ease** value in the **Properties** panel
b) on the Stage, select the object and modify the shape using the options in the **Properties** panel and the tools in the Toolbox
c) move the shape to the new position.

10 You can insert another keyframe and change the shape or shape properties again by repeating steps 7 to 9. An arrow will be displayed between each keyframe as shown in Figure 3.35.

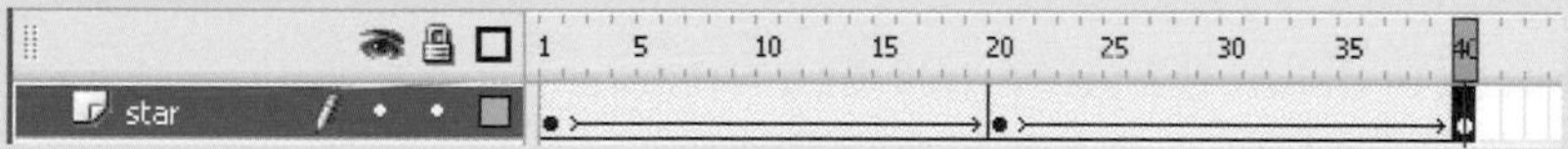

Figure 3.35 A third keyframe on the Timeline

11 Save the document in the Flash file (**fla**) format.

12 Press **Ctrl** + **Enter** to play the animation *or* **Control** menu → **Test Movie.** Close the new window.

You will learn to test and edit animations, and save in a format suitable for inclusion in a web page on pages 149 and 151.

Easing

The **Ease** value adjusts the rate of change between tweened frames. The default value of zero makes the rate of change between tweened frames constant. If you change the **Ease** value, you can create a more natural transformation of a shape, or a more realistic sense of motion of an object.

You should adjust the Ease value for shape, motion and frame-by-frame animations.

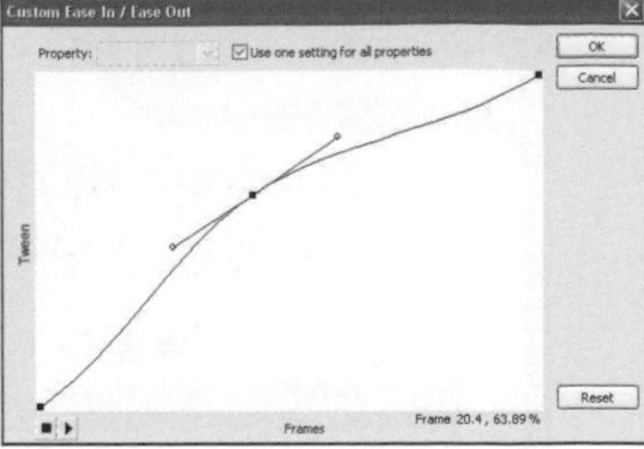

Figure 3.36 Setting custom easing

▸▸ HOW TO ... Adjust the easing

- Select the required keyframe in the Timeline, then in the **Properties** panel, adjust the **Ease** value:
- Enter a negative value between –1 and –100 to start the tween gradually then accelerate.
- Enter a positive value between 1 and 100 to start the tween quickly and slow down towards the end.
- For a motion tween or a frame-by-frame animation, to control the speed of the motion tween more precisely, you can either set the **Ease** value as described above or click the **Edit** button in the **Properties** panel, and set the **Custom Ease In/Ease Out** options (refer to Figure 3.36).

PRACTICAL TASK 3.8 Create a shape tween

Assessment objectives 1b, 1c, 2a, 2b, 2d, 2e

1. Open your saved document **clubanim**
2. On the layer containing the shape symbols, create a shape tween.
3. Set the **Ease** value as appropriate.
4. Save the document as a **fla** document.
5. Press **Crtl** + **Enter** to play the animation. Make a note of any modifications that need to be made.

MOTION TWEENING

To create a motion tween, you need to define the properties for an instance, grouped object or text in the starting keyframe, and then change the properties in a subsequent keyframe. Flash creates the animation from one keyframe to the next in the keyframes that are in between.

You can create a motion tween in two ways:

1. Create the starting and ending keyframes and select **Motion** as the **Tween** option in the **Properties** panel.
2. Create the first keyframe, insert the number of frames you want in the Timeline, then from the **Insert** menu, select **Timeline** and **Create Motion Tween**, and move the object to the new location on the Stage. Flash automatically creates the ending keyframe.

Method 1 is described in more detail on the next page.

▶▶ HOW TO ... Create a motion tween

- Before you begin, make sure the **Properties** panel is displayed and expanded, and the **Selection Tool** is selected.
- Ensure you have imported into the library any assets you intend to use.

1 Set the document properties including the frame rate.

2 Insert a new layer if required and select the appropriate layer. Rename the layer (optional).

3 In the Timeline, select the required keyframe.

Ensure you select the correct keyframe as the starting frame. The starting frame need not be keyframe 1.

4 In the **Properties** panel, click the drop-down arrow to the right of **Tween** and select **Motion**.

5 To create the first frame of the motion tween, do one of the following:
- Create a graphic object using the Toolbox tools then convert it to a symbol.
- Create an instance, group or text block on the Stage.
- Drag an instance of an existing symbol from the **Library** panel.

6 Insert a second keyframe in the Timeline: right-click and choose **Insert Keyframe**.

7 With the second keyframe selected in the Timeline, select the object on the Stage and modify it as required, for example:
- move the item to a new position
- modify the size, rotation or skew
- modify the item's colour (applicable to an instance or text block only).

8 Next, in the **Properties** panel, select the options required (refer to Figure 3.37).

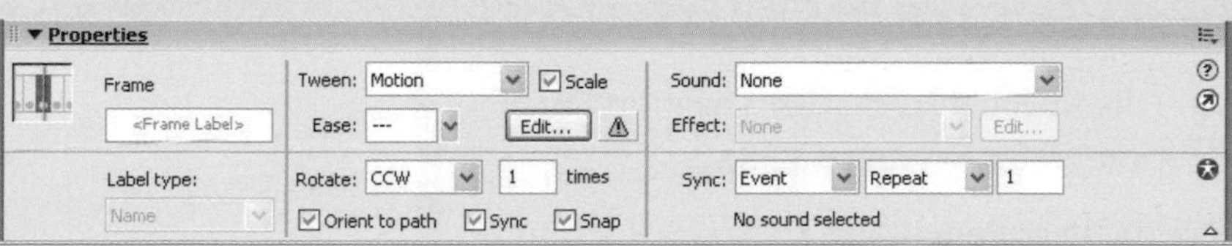

Figure 3.37 Setting the motion tween properties

9 Adjust the **Ease** value.

10 If you modified the size of the item, select the **Scale** check box.

11 To rotate the item while tweening, click the drop-down arrow to the right of **Rotate** and select an option:
- **Auto** to rotate the object once in the direction requiring the least motion

Continued ...

- **Clockwise** (CW) or **Counterclockwise** (CCW) to rotate the object as required, then enter a number to specify the number of rotations.

12 Select the **Sync** option to synchronise the animation of graphic symbol instances with the main Timeline.

13 If you are using or intend to use a motion path, select **Orient to Path** and **Snap**.

14 Repeat steps 4 and 5 if you want to insert more keyframes then modify the object. An arrow will be displayed between each keyframe as shown in Figure 3.38 on page 145.

15 Save the document in a Flash file (**fla**) format.

16 Press **Ctrl + Enter** to play the animation.

You will learn to edit animations, and save in a format suitable for inclusion in a web page on pages 149 and 151.

***Orient to Path** guides the baseline of the tweened element to the motion path.*

***Snap** attaches the tweened element to the motion path by its registration point.*

TIP!

To change the length of a tweened sequence, drag the last keyframe further to the right.

TWEENING MOTION ALONG A PATH

Motion guide layers allow you to draw paths along which tweened instances, groups or text blocks can be animated.

A motion guide is appropriate for motion-tweened animations but not for shape tweening.

▸▸ HOW TO ... Create a motion path for a tweened animation

- Start by creating a motion-tweened animation as described on page 143 and above in 'How to create a motion tween'.
- Select the **View** menu and ensure that **Snap to Objects** is selected.

1 Select the layer containing the animation to which you want to add a motion path.

2 **Insert** menu → **Timeline** → **Motion Guide.**

3 A new layer is created above the selected layer with a motion guide icon to the left of the layer name (refer to Figure 3.38).

4 On the new guide layer, use the **Pen**, **Pencil**, **Line**, **Circle**, **Rectangle** or **Brush Tools** to draw a path along which the item will move.

5 Select the first keyframe. Use the **Selection Tool** to drag the object's centre point to snap the centre point to the beginning of the motion path in the first frame. Repeat to align the object to other parts of the motion path. Remember, you can modify the object's properties in different keyframes.

The item will follow the motion path when you play the animation as shown in Figures 3.38 and 3.39.

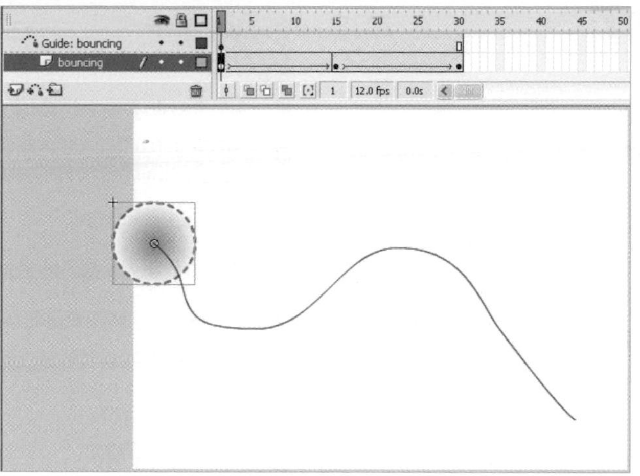
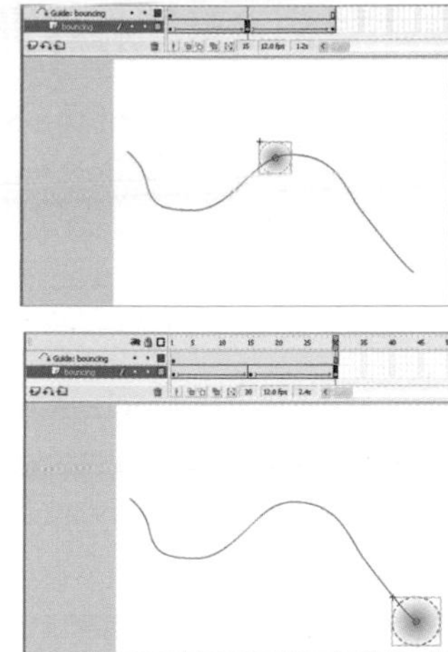

Figure 3.38 Motion path created using the Oval Tool. Object aligned to path at beginning, middle and end (bottom).

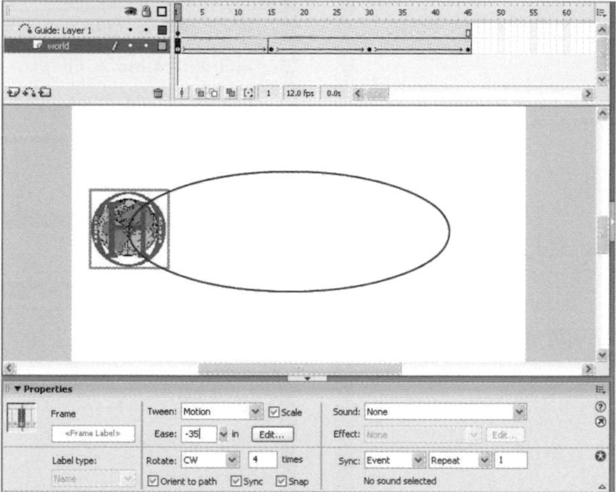
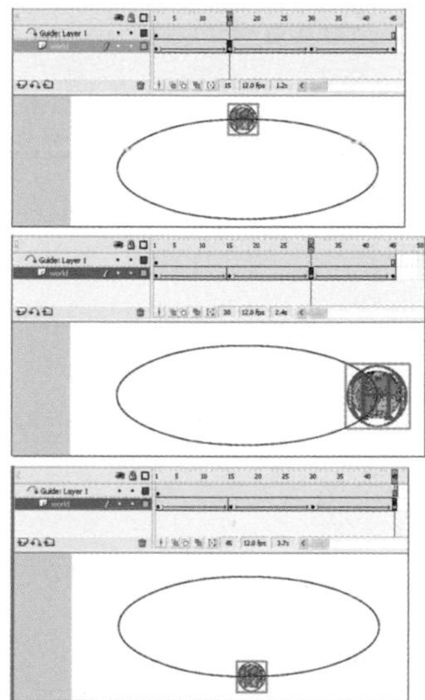

Figure 3.39 Motion path using Oval Tool. Object resized and aligned to path at left, top, right and bottom.

PRACTICAL TASK 3.9 Create a motion tween along a motion path

Assessment objectives 1b, 1c

1 In your saved document **clubanim** on a new layer, use your imported assets to create a motion tween along a motion path.

2 Play the animation. Make a note of any modifications that need to be made.

3 Save the document using the filename **clubanim2**

FRAME-BY-FRAME ANIMATION

In frame-by-frame animation the contents of the Stage are changed slightly in every frame. Frame-by-frame animation is best suited to complex animation in which an image changes in every frame instead of simply moving across the Stage as in shape tweening and motion tweening. Flash is better suited to tweened animation.

You can use a combination of animation techniques, e.g. shape tweening, motion tweening and frame-by-frame animation, in a single animation. If you do, you must insert and select layers carefully and ensure that you are working on the correct layer.

▶▶ HOW TO ... Create a frame-by-frame animation

- Before you begin, make sure the **Properties** panel is displayed and expanded, and the **Selection Tool** is selected.
- Ensure you have imported into the library any assets you intend to use.

1. Set the document properties including the frame rate.
2. Insert a new layer if required and select the appropriate layer. Rename the layer (optional).
3. Select a frame in the layer where you want the animation to start.
4. **Insert** menu → **Timeline** → **Keyframe**.
5. Create the object or insert the graphics for the first frame of the sequence.
6. Click the next frame to the right in the same row and select **Insert** → **Timeline** → **Keyframe** → this adds a new keyframe. The contents of this keyframe are the same as the preceding keyframe.
7. On the Stage, change the contents of the inserted keyframe slightly. For example, move the object *slightly* and/or change the properties such as colour or size.
8. Repeat steps 4 to 7 to complete your frame-by-frame animation sequence, until you have created the animation sequence.

You will learn to test and edit animations, and save in a format suitable for inclusion in a web page on pages 149 and 151.

The file size in frame-by-frame animation increases more quickly than in tweened animation.

Layers in animation

Your animation may consist of any number of layers. Often the background layer contains a static image or colour and each layer contains one separate animated object.

TIP!

To help you position the movement of objects more precisely, display rulers, grids and guides.

TIP!

To insert a keyframe, you could also right-click in the keyframe → a menu is displayed → select **Insert Keyframe**, or click in the keyframe and press **F6**.

PRACTICAL TASK 3.10 Use frame-by-frame animation techniques

Assessment objectives 1b, 1c, 2a, 2b, 2d

1 Refer to the assignment brief 'Cove Photography Club – Animation' on page 110.

2 In your saved document **clubanim2**, use a combination of your imported assets, symbols and/or instances and library items to create a frame-by-frame animation.

3 Ensure that this animation begins in the correct keyframe.

4 Insert text appropriate to the client's need. You will animate the text in Practical task 3.11.

5 Play the animation. Make a note of any modifications that need to be made.

6 Save the document using the filename **clubanim3**

ANIMATING TEXT

There are various ways of animating text. The 'correct' way is to break the text apart, and distribute the text blocks to separate layers as described below. You should then animate each text block separately. Refer to the guidelines for 'How to create a motion tween' and 'How to create a frame-by-frame animation'. A slightly quicker way is to apply a motion tween to all the layers at the same time as described below.

Refer to 'How to reshape a letter' on pages 183 to 184.

▶▶ HOW TO ... Break text apart and apply a motion tween to text

1 Enter and format the text. Using the **Selection Tool**, click in a text block.

2 **Modify** menu → **Break Apart** → each character is placed in a separate block.

3 Select the **Modify** menu again → **Timeline** → **Distribute to Layers** → each character is moved to a different layer → increase the height of the Timeline so that you can see all the layers (refer to Figure 3.40) → delete Layer 1 (this is empty).

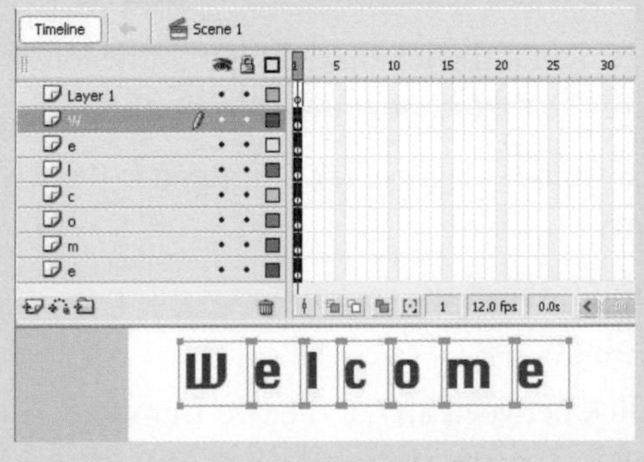

Figure 3.40 Text blocks distributed on separate layers

Continued ...

4 In the Timeline, click and drag down to highlight all the layers and drag across to the right up to a frame where you want to insert a new keyframe (as shown on the left of Figure 3.41).

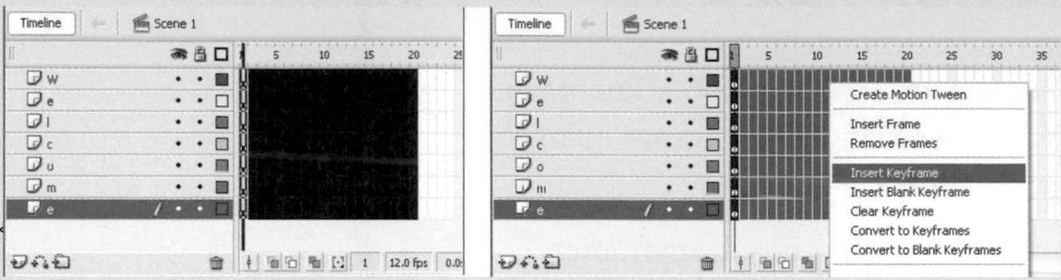

Figure 3.41 Highlighting multiple layers and inserting a keyframe in those layers

5 Right-click → **Insert Keyframe** (as shown on the right of Figure 3.41).

6 Right-click anywhere within the keyframes → **Create Motion Tween** (refer to Figure 3.42).

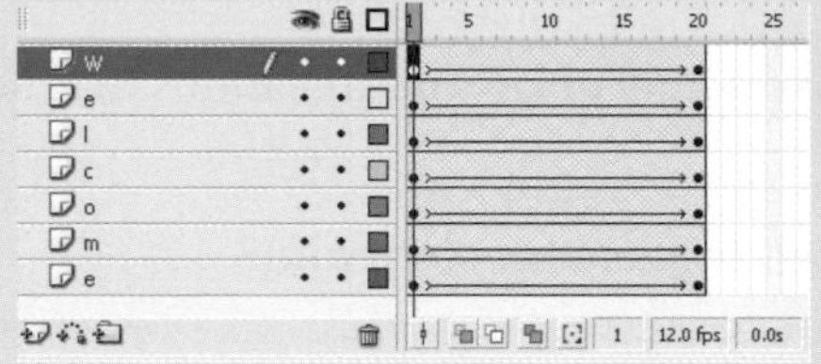

Figure 3.42 Creating a motion text for multiple text layers

7 Select the first frame of the layer containing the first letter → move the letter to the required position.

8 In the **Properties** panel, change the **Ease** value.

9 Repeat steps 7 and 8 for each letter.

10 Save and play the animation.

You will learn to test and edit animations, and save in a format suitable for inclusion in a web page on pages 149 and 151.

▶▶ HOW TO ... Animate text (a quick method)

The method described is a quick way of making text move in an animation.

1 Enter and format the text. Select the text and drag it to the left of the Stage to the grey work area so that no text is visible on the Stage.

2 On the Timeline, select a frame → right-click → a menu is displayed → select **Insert Keyframe**.

3 Click in the new keyframe → select the text and move it to the right, to the work area off the Stage.

4 In the Timeline, right-click between any of the two frames → a menu is displayed → select **Create Motion Tween** → in the **Properties** panel, set the **Ease** value.

5 Save the animation.

PRACTICAL TASK 3.11 *Animate text*

Assessment objectives 1c, 2a

1 Open the files named **text** and **clubanim3** that you previously saved.

2 In each file, animate the text on at least one of the layers.

3 Save the files retaining the filenames.

TESTING THE ANIMATION

You can test an animation at any time whilst you are creating it, even before you have saved it. You should always test it after you have completed it.

TIP!

When you test a tweened animation, if the speed of movement is not appropriate, select the keyframe in the Timeline and change the **Ease** value.

▶▶ HOW TO ... *Test an animation*

- **Control** menu → **Test Movie** *or* press **Ctrl** + **Enter** on the keyboard. The animation will play in a separate window.
- Click the red cross ☒ to close the window.
- To check the animated sequence on the Stage, drag the playhead in the Timeline. You can drag to the right and back again.

EDITING AN ANIMATION

After you create a keyframe, you can move it elsewhere in the active layer or to another layer, delete it or make other changes. Note that only keyframes are editable, tweened frames cannot be edited.

- To delete a frame or keyframe: select the frame → right-click → a menu is displayed → select **Remove Frames**.
- To move a keyframe: select the keyframe → drag it to the new location.
- To extend the duration of a keyframe: hold down the **Alt** key and drag the keyframe to the final frame of the new sequence.
- To change the frame rate: deselect any items selected on the Stage → **Modify** menu → **Document** to open the **Document Properties** dialogue box and change the frame rate.
- To copy and paste a frame: select the frame → **Edit** menu → **Timeline** → **Copy Frames**. Then select a frame → **Edit** → **Timeline** → **Paste Frames**.
- To reverse an animation sequence: check that there are keyframes at the beginning and end of the sequence → select the appropriate frames → **Modify** menu → **Timeline** → **Reverse Frames**.

When you test the animation, if the speed of movement is too slow, increase the **frame rate**, and vice versa, but do not deviate too much from the default 12 fps which is best for web playback.

USING EFFECTS

Flash has built-in Timeline effects that allow you to create complex animations very quickly or to add extra features to existing animations. Timeline effects can be applied to text, graphics, shapes, groups, graphic and button symbols and bitmap images.

For an OCR assessment, you are expected to use effects in your animation.

▶▶ HOW TO ... Add an effect to an object

1 Use the **Selection Tool** to select the object on the Stage to which you want to add an effect.

2 **Insert** menu → **Timeline Effects** → the effects available for the type of selected object will be displayed; others will be greyed out.

3 Select **Assistants**, **Effects** or **Transition/Transform** from the submenu then select an effect from the list → a dialogue box for the chosen effect is displayed.

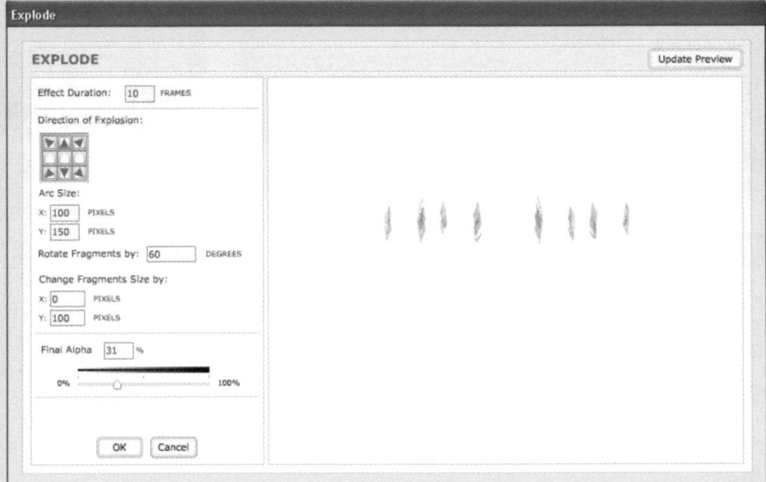

Figure 3.43 Adding effects

4 View the effect preview based on default settings.

5 Modify the default settings as you wish then click the **Update Preview** button to view the effect with the new settings → **OK**.

Depending on the effect chosen, a new layer is created and the object is transferred to that new layer (Figure 3.44).

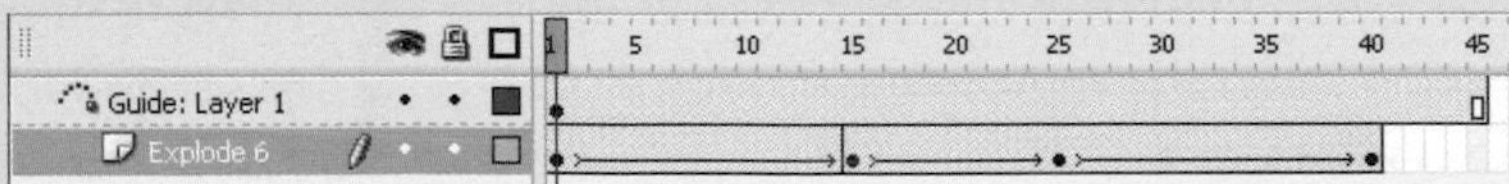

Figure 3.44 Effects shown in the Timeline

6 A folder with the effect's name is added to the library, containing elements used in creating the effect (Figure 3.45).

Key terms

Transition An effect that displays when one scene of an animation changes to another.

The object is placed inside the effect graphic and all tweens and transformations needed for the effect reside in the graphic on the new layer.

The new layer is automatically named with the effect type followed by a number representing the order in which the effect is applied in relation to other effects in the document.

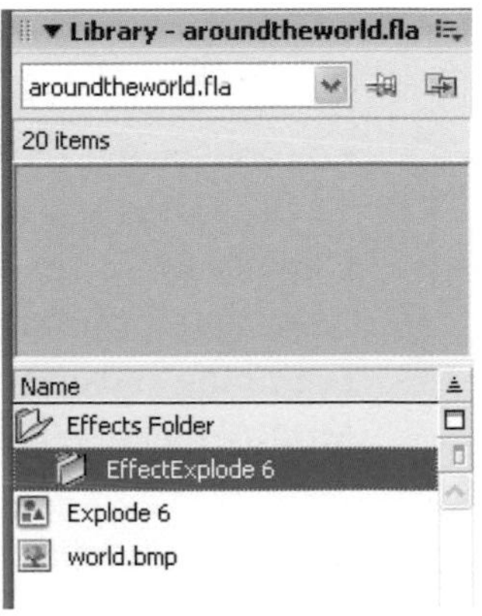

Figure 3.45 Effects shown in the library

PRACTICAL TASK 3.12 **Make modifications, use effects and complete the animation ready for publishing**

Assessment objective 2b

1 Refer to the notes you made when you played the animation at the end of Practical tasks 3.8, 3.9 and 3.10.

2 Modify the animation as required.

3 Apply at least one effect.

4 Save the document as a Flash document using the filename **clubanim_final**

When you have completed your animation, you need to save it in a file format suitable for the web e.g. **swf, htm** and **gif formats.** You should also save it as a Flash document in **fla** format. Do not delete this **fla** file in case you need to make any changes to the animation.

SAVING AN ANIMATION IN A FORMAT SUITABLE FOR THE WEB

Once you have created your animation, you need to save the Flash file (**fla** format) in a format suitable for inclusion in a web page. To do so, you need to **publish** the document.

Flash offers eight different options (eight different file formats) for publishing an animation as shown in Figure 3.46. Of these, the most common formats are:

- **swf** format (**S**hock**w**ave for **F**lash)
- **html** format
- **gif** format.

▶▶ HOW TO ... **Prepare your animation for publishing on the web (how to Save as a swf, html and gif file)**

1 **File** menu → **Publish Settings** → the **Publish Settings** dialogue box is displayed (Figure 3.46).

Although animations can be saved in other formats, this is not common. Refer to Unit 1, for an explanation of different file formats.

swf files play on a Flash Player. This software needs to be installed on the computer on which the file is played.

An animation published as an **HTML** file will be embedded in an HTML page.

You can also export **fla** files in several formats. Exporting **fla** files is similar to publishing in different file formats, except that the settings for each file format are not stored with the **fla** file.

Continued ...

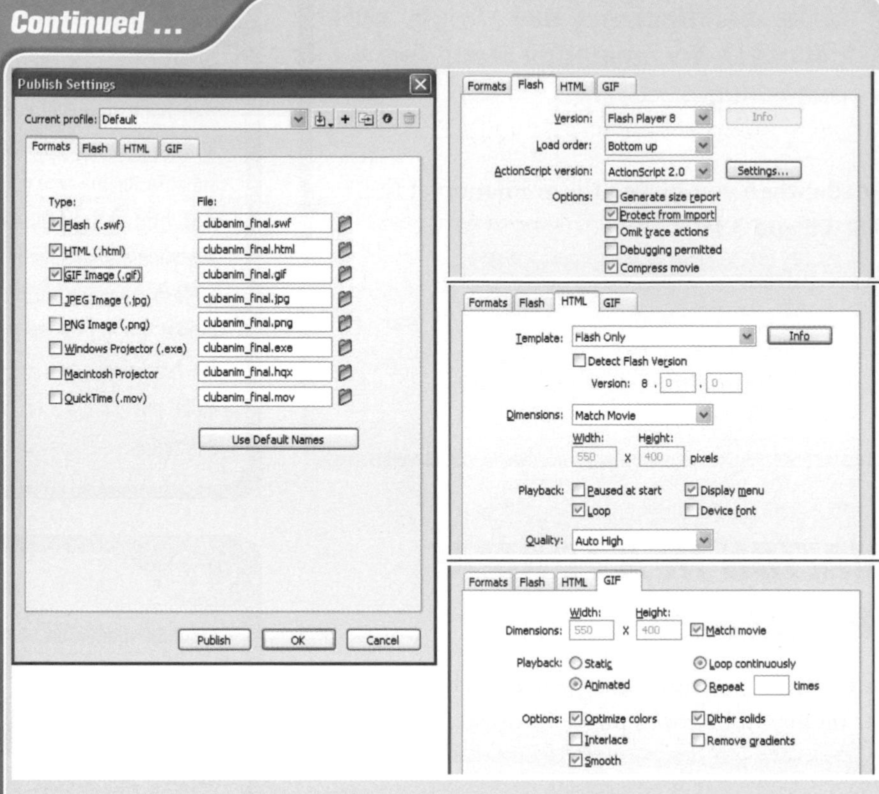

Figure 3.46 Saving in swf, html and gif format

2 In the **Formats** tab, ensure the **Flash (.swf)** and **HTML (.html)** checkboxes are selected. Tick the box for **GIF Image (.gif)**.

3 Select the **Flash** tab → to the right of **Version** ensure that **Flash Player 8** is selected. Retain the tick for **Compress Movie**.

4 Select the **HTML** tab → to right of **Template** ensure that **Flash Only** is selected. **Quality** sets the rendering quality at which your animation will play. Selecting **Auto High** allows Flash to change the quality of the animation if it is run on slower computers.

5 For motion tweened and frame-by-frame animations, select the **GIF** tab and select the button for **Animated** (you *must* change the default option of **Static**).

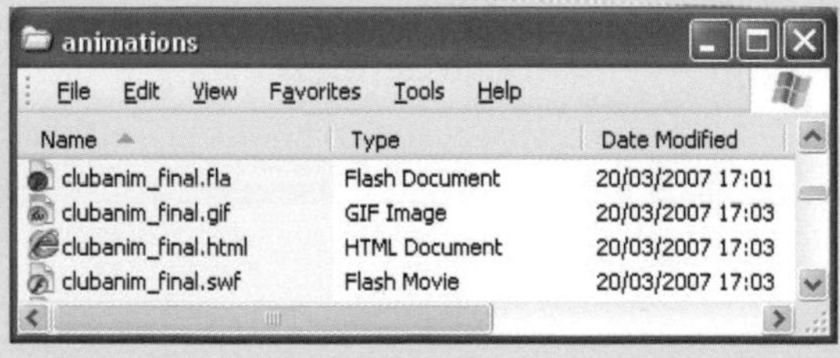

Figure 3.47 An animation saved in multiple formats

6 Click **Publish** → **OK**.

7 Flash will save a copy of your document in the selected formats in the same folder that contains your saved **fla** file (Figure 3.47).

Flash will optimise an animated gif file, storing the frame-to-frame changes.

Shape tweened animations cannot be saved in gif format.

In the Publish Settings dialogue box, each file format has an associated tab. The Flash and HTML formats are the default so these tabs are normally displayed. When you select another format (e.g. gif) that tab is added.

Select the most recent version of Flash Player.

PRACTICAL TASK 3.13 Prepare the animation for publishing

Assessment objective 2e

1 Save your document **clubanim_final** as a **swf** and **htm** file. You may also save it in **gif** format if you wish.

2 Play the **swf** and **htm** (and **gif** if appropriate) animations to ensure they play correctly.

PRACTICAL TASK 3.14 Review work against original brief

Assessment objective 3b

1 Refer to 'Reviewing your work' on page xxi of the 'Common Skills' chapter.

2 Collate all your evidence (e.g. saved files, scanned copies of any printouts, screen prints, Storyboard, planning notes, feedback received).

3 Refer to the Assignment Brief for the 'Cove Photography Club – Animation ' on page 110.

4 Review all your evidence, including your animations, against the assignment brief. You may have a discussion with your tutor.

5 Ensure that you have carried out all the tasks required in the assignment brief.

6 Obtain a copy of an Evidence Checklist (ask your tutor for a copy).

7 Complete the Evidence Checklist.

8 Identify at least two constraints that influenced your project e.g. asset manipulation, file formats. Note these in your Planning and Review Form or in a separate document.

9 Comment on the quality of your finished animations and their fitness for purpose.

10 Explain how the animation for the Cove Photography Club fulfils the original client brief.

11 Back up all your files on to a removable medium.

You should now have all the skills, knowledge and understanding required to complete an OCR iMedia sample or live assessment for this unit.

UNIT 4

INTERACTIVE MULTIMEDIA CONCEPTS

INTRODUCTION

This unit is designed to introduce you to multimedia technologies, applications and design processes. You will investigate how multimedia is used effectively in a range of existing professional products. You will develop knowledge and skills to creatively design and implement elements of a multimedia product using multimedia-authoring tools.

LEARNING OUTCOMES

After studying this unit you will be able to:

- understand the use of multimedia in a variety of professional applications
- understand the technology and techniques employed to generate such multimedia material
- produce, author and evaluate multimedia content from a variety of sources including image, sound, video and text.

RESOURCE TOOLKIT

Hardware

- Computer with CD/DVD writer
- Access to the Internet
- Printer
- Speakers

Software

- Macromedia Flash 8 (with Flash Player)
- Word-processing software

Other

- A variety of CD-ROMs/DVDs
- Pencil and paper
- Planning and Review Form
- Evidence Checklist

Optional

- Video recorder
- Microphone
- Digital still camera
- Mobile phone with camera
- Web camera
- Joystick

In this unit you will be looking at the technology required to produce a multimedia product – the hardware, software and peripheral devices. You will investigate sources and examples of multimedia applications, including online, CD-ROM, DVD, kiosks, games and TV, and understand the reason for their use.

Before you can create a multimedia product, it must first be planned. You will look at ways of identifying what the customer requires and the different planning methods that can be used.

You will understand the different elements used to create multimedia content, such as text, graphics, interactivity and video, and how to use authoring software to import these into a multimedia product. You will follow good practice for naming and storing these assets on the computer. You will publish the multimedia presentation and understand how to optimise and publish for different formats, e.g. on the web, CD, DVD.

Finally you will review your completed multimedia product against the original assignment brief and obtain appropriate feedback (e.g. from peers or your tutor). You will need to identify any parameters or constraints that influenced your choices regarding asset manipulation, file formats or compression techniques used.

The Student Review activities and Practical Tasks in this chapter will allow you to develop your understanding of the requirements for an OCR assessment and practise the skills required for the Unit 4 syllabus. The multimedia product you create in this chapter **CANNOT** be submitted for assessment purposes.

ASSESSMENT FOR UNIT 4

Assessment of this unit takes the form of practical activities which are assessed by your tutor and are then externally moderated by an OCR Examiner-Moderator. The assessment may be an OCR-set assessment or one which has been locally devised by your tutor.

In order to achieve a pass in the unit, you must demonstrate skills in each one of the assessment objectives.

Assessment tasks

You will be required to complete tasks that address all of the assessment objectives and you must provide evidence that shows where and how the assessment objectives have been met. Your assessment work should be submitted to OCR via e-portfolio. You should therefore save all evidence in electronic format. Any hard copy evidence should be scanned and saved electronically.

Evidence

You will need to:

- provide copies of the work you produce as part of the tasks
- provide a copy of the final product
- complete a Planning and Review Form provided by OCR to show how you have planned and reviewed the final presentation
- complete an Evidence Checklist to identify where and how the assessment objectives have been met

SOFTWARE

In this unit you will use a software program called Macromedia Flash version 8 which is part of the Macromedia Studio 8 suite (education version). From now on in this chapter, we will refer to it as Flash. Flash allows you to create interactive presentations that can be viewed on the web, saved as a stand-alone movie for distribution on a CD or DVD or in a format suitable for mobile devices.

ABOUT THIS CHAPTER

The chapter for this unit is divided into four sections. You must work through the sections in sequence.

- In Section 1 you will learn how to select appropriate hardware, software and peripheral devices for multimedia development and plan the multimedia product to a specified brief.
- In Section 2 you will learn how to evaluate multimedia sources and content and understand basic multimedia design principles for creating multimedia assets.
- In Section 3 you will learn how to use multimedia-authoring software to produce and import drawings, text, animation, images, sound and video. You will also learn how to add effects, interactivity and navigation to your multimedia presentation.
- In Section 4 you will learn how to publish the multimedia presentation in different formats. You will also review the finished product against the original brief.

AOs 1a, 1b, 1c, 3a

AOs 2a

AOs 2b

AOs 2c, 3b

Assessment objectives 3a (plan the multimedia product to a specific brief) and 3b (review the multimedia product against the original brief) and the corresponding knowledge, skills and understanding criteria are covered in the 'Common Skills' chapter. In addition to the planning skills covered in that chapter, producing a navigation map, which forms part of Assessment objective 3a, is covered in the current chapter.

Refer to 'Planning your work' and 'Reviewing your work' sections on pages xiv and xxi of the 'Common Skills' chapter.

SECTION 1 • Select appropriate hardware, software and peripheral devices for multimedia development

The following assessment objectives will be covered in this section:

1a Select appropriate hardware for multimedia development

1b Select appropriate software for multimedia development

1c Select appropriate peripheral devices

3a Plan the multimedia product to a specific brief

Note: most of objective 3a is covered in the 'Common Skills' chapter.

The following knowledge, skills and understanding criteria corresponding to assessment objectives 1a, 1b and 1c will be covered:

- *Current computer hardware*
- *Network and Internet connections*
- *Platforms*
- *Available software and minimum hardware specifications*
- *Peripheral devices used in multimedia production*

WHAT IS MULTIMEDIA?

Multimedia is the combination of many different types of media, e.g. text, images, animation, sound, narration, music and video. This media is then presented using one medium to communicate ideas.

Each media type has been with us for many years but previously each had its own medium for delivery. Text was printed and read in the form of books and newspapers; images were printed and viewed as photographs or illustrations, in magazines, newspapers and books; moving images were recorded on film and viewed on television sets or at the cinema; voice and music were converted to sound waves and listened to on a radio. Each of the different communication channels developed separately and did not share content with each other. For example, you could not see pictures on the radio, or listen to music in the newspaper.

Figure 4.1 Filmstrip: red line shows it is viewed only in a linear way

Some media types can also be multimedia. For example, a TV programme or film can include sound effects, music, text and still images. A book can include sketches and photographs as well as text. However, the information is presented to you in a *linear* format (see Figures 4.1 and 4.2). You receive the information passively; you have no control over the way the information is presented and you cannot give any feedback.

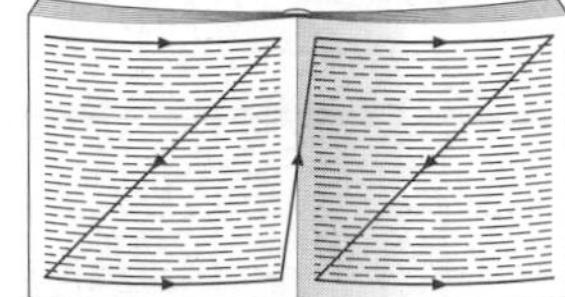

Figure 4.2 Book: red line shows the linear direction of reading

Older forms of communication were more interactive, e.g. a storyteller could see the faces of the listeners as they told the story; even today, actors on the stage in live theatre can respond to the reactions of an audience.

The first personal computers were mono-media. They only displayed text and were not capable of playing sounds or displaying complex graphics. Advances in computer technology in the 1980s and the growth of the World Wide Web in the 1990s changed the way in which the communication of ideas could be presented. Each of the different types of media could now be **digitised**. This is the process of converting information into a series of numbers that can be read by the computer. For example, scanners could be used to convert pictures, and sound could be digitised by a process called sampling.

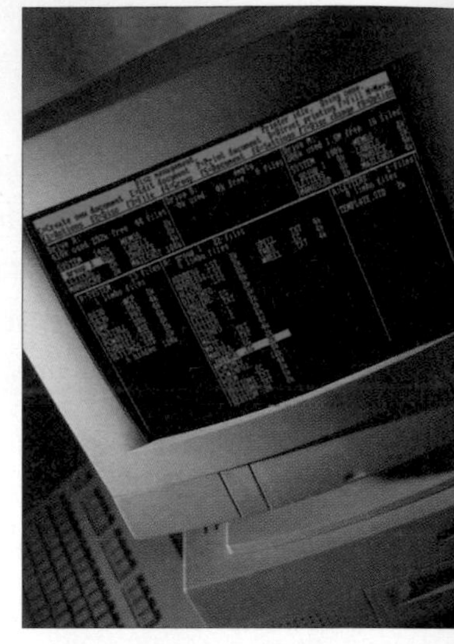

The development of the CD-ROM in the mid-1980s offered computer users massive storage capacity; often 20 times more than the hard disk of a typical personal computer of the time. This massive storage capacity made the CD-ROM an ideal medium for distributing multimedia encyclopaedias and reference titles.

What makes digital multimedia more powerful is **interactivity**. With interactive multimedia, you are in control, deciding how and when to access the information. Clicking on predefined areas, known as hotspots, will take you to a linked file which may be another window with more information, an image, a sound or a video clip (see Figure 4.3). You can explore information at your own pace and in any order you choose.

*The word **digitise** is derived from the Latin word **digit** meaning finger. Just as we count on our fingers, computers count digits.*

Refer to 'How to capture sound' on page 211.

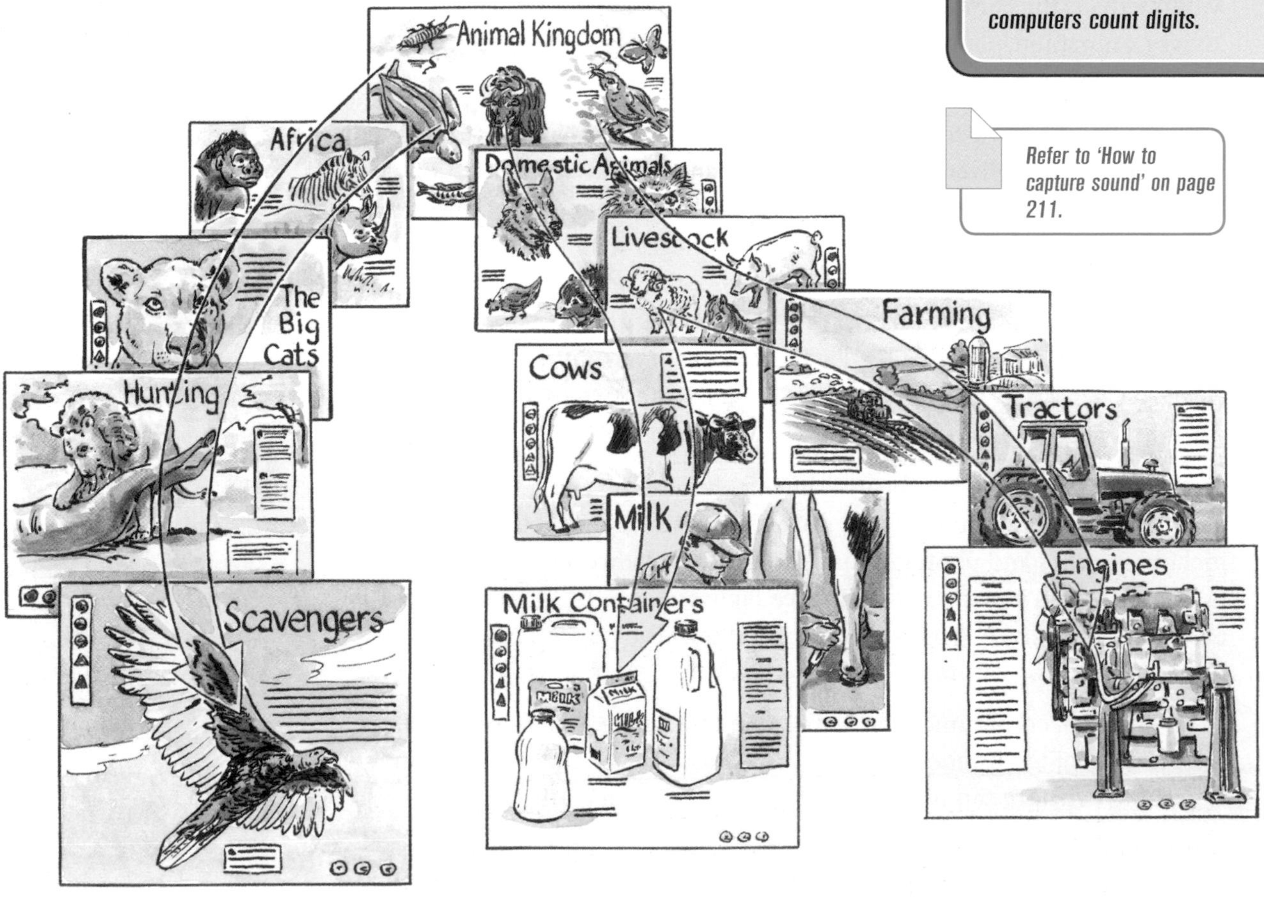

Figure 4.3 Using interactive multimedia

Student review 4.1 – Research media types

Assessment objective 1a

1 *Make a list of the different individual media types you have at home, e.g. CD player, VCR, radio, books.*

2 *In a table, identify the types of media each one receives. Remember some may include more than one type of content.*

3 *Are any of the media types interactive? If so, indicate these in the table.*

Types of multimedia:

- *Text*
- *Images*
- *Sound*
- *Music*
- *Video*
- *Animation*
- *Narration*

Assignment brief

Magnificent Bowl – Interactive Presentation
You work for a digital media company as an Assistant Multimedia Developer. Your line manager is the Multimedia Developer who assigns you work but allows you to develop your own creative ideas.

Your company has been asked by Magnificent Bowl to produce an interactive presentation to show the locations of their six clubs in the UK. These are located in Newcastle, Preston, Birmingham, Cambridge, London and Plymouth.

Magnificent Bowl has asked for the following to be included in the product:

- A map of the UK to show the location of each of the clubs
- Images to show the facilities at the clubs
- Suitable sounds
- A contacts page

The product must be an interactive presentation to include text, images, sound and/or video, and navigation and will be presented to the company on CD-ROM/DVD.

For an OCR assessment for this unit, you will be required to develop 4–6 screens of the multimedia product. You will be given a brief similar to this.

In an OCR assignment, when planning your work, you must use the Planning and Review Form to write down all the required information.

Before starting work on the production of the multimedia presentation, you must first plan your work. To help you to do this you will also be provided with an outline storyboard, similar to that shown in Figure 4.4 on the next page, which will show the layout and outline content for the prototype multimedia product. This outline storyboard also includes details on the screen size, the published format for the product and the platform it is to be developed for.

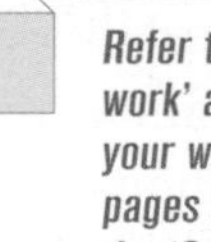

Refer to 'Planning your work' and 'Reviewing your work' sections on pages xiv and xxi of the 'Common Skills' chapter.

Outline storyboard – Layout and content for prototype multimedia product

Screen size: 1024 x 768
Published format: CD-ROM or DVD
Platform: Cross platform

Introduction Screen Video Navigation link to enter the presentation Screen 1	Home screen Map of UK (location of clubs indicated on map) Navigation to each of the clubs Screen 2
Locations 1 – 6 Images Descriptive text Background music Navigation to home page or other locations Screen 3	Contacts screen Images Addresses Telephone numbers Emails contacts Website address Screen 4

Figure 4.4 Storyboard

SELECTING APPROPRIATE HARDWARE FOR MULTIMEDIA DEVELOPMENT

The hardware requirements for developing a multimedia presentation are far more demanding than those needed to view the final product.

Sound, video and image files need large amounts of storage during their preparation because they are often in an uncompressed format until the final stage when high compression is applied. Therefore, you will need a computer with a large hard disk capacity, powerful graphics cards, high-speed data buses, large main memory as well as a high-resolution monitor capable of displaying millions of colours.

A high performance desktop PC may have a specification similar to that shown in Table 4.1.

CPU	Quad core processor
RAM	2–4 GB
Hard Drive	300 GB, 7,200 rpm **or** 2 separate hard drives
Optical storage	20× dual layer DVD burner CD-RW
Graphics card	With 728 MB RAM, **DVI** and **TV** out
Audio	Sound card supporting 5.1 speaker system
TV card	To receive broadcast TV and radio and to allow transfer of analogue videos from a VCR to your PC through an S-video connection

Table 4.1 Specification of a high performance desktop PC

Key terms

DVI **D**igital **V**ideo **I**nterface A connector for a digital monitor.

TV out Provides a connection for an alternative device, e.g. a TV set.

DVDs were first developed in 1995. Originally DVD stood for Digital Video Disk as they were intended as a replacement for VHS tapes for the distribution of video. As the disks could be used for storing any digital media, the name was changed to Digital Versatile Disk. A DVD has a much higher storage capacity than a CD-ROM but they have not been used as a substitute for CD-ROMs. They are mainly used for their original purpose of distributing high quality digital video and are also often used for distributing software.

UNDERSTANDING NETWORK AND INTERNET CONNECTIONS

There are two main methods of delivering a multimedia product to the target audience – online and offline. You may be required to distribute your multimedia product *offline* on a CD or DVD or you may be asked to prepare the multimedia product for distribution *online* over a network or the Internet.

The delivery of multimedia over a local area network (LAN) or the Internet can present technical difficulties. As already discussed, sound, video and image files can be very large and, depending on the **bandwidth** of the connection you have, this could result in very slow transfer or download times.

In a LAN the most widely used method of connecting computers, printers and other devices is by Ethernet cabling and protocols. This allows almost any kind of computer to be connected; so Apple Macs and Windows PCs can be connected on the same network. Using an Ethernet-based fibre optic network connection, data can currently be transferred from one computer to another on a LAN at the rate of 10 Gbit/s (10 gigabits per second). This year a 100 Gbit/s Ethernet is being developed.

WiFi is the registered trademark of the WiFi Alliance, an organisation that tests and certifies that equipment is compliant with wireless standards. WiFi (Wireless Fidelity) was originally developed as a standard for wireless local area networks (WLAN) for connecting laptops to networks. Many airports, hotels and trains offer the public access to WiFi networks so they can log on to the Internet and receive emails. The locations where this is available are known as hotspots.

Key terms

Bandwidth In computing terms, is the rate per second at which data is transmitted over a communications channel.

WiFi is also increasingly being used in the home to connect non-computer devices such as televisions, DVD players and digital cameras. Gaming devices such as Nintendo Wii, Playstation Portable are WiFi compatible and others can be made WiFi compatible by adding a wireless adaptor. WiFi networks can transfer data at speeds up to 54 Mbit/s (54 megabits per second).

Bluetooth is a wireless technology that enables devices such as personal digital assistants, mobile phones and computers to communicate over a short-range (approximately 10 metres) radio link.

When Bluetooth-enabled devices come within range of each other they set up a personal area network (PAN) or piconet. Data can be transferred between devices at speeds up to 3 Mbit/s. Bluetooth is suitable when two or more devices are in close proximity to each other and don't require a high bandwidth. However, a high speed, high data rate option is being developed to allow transfer of large amounts of data. This will enable high quality video and audio applications to be transferred using portable devices.

Bluetooth was named after Harald Bluetooth, who was King of Denmark between 940 and 981, because one of his skills was getting people to talk to each other.

There are still home computers that connect to the Internet using a 'dial-up connection'. This type of connection uses a modem and a telephone line to provide a temporary connection between the home computer and the Internet. There are two speeds of modem connection, a slow modem with a maximum download speed of 28.8 Kbit/s, and a fast modem with a maximum download speed of 56 Kbit/s.

Broadband connections make use of digital telephone systems or cable TV networks. In data communication terms, broadband is used to describe data transmissions, where multiple pieces of data are sent at the same time over a wide range of channels, thereby increasing the rate of transmission. Typical broadband connections can transfer data at speeds up to 10 Mbit/s depending on the type of service you have. The speed quoted by ISPs (Internet Service Providers) is the download speed of the connection (which is much faster than the upload speed). Download speeds are generally faster as most people do more downloading (viewing web pages, downloading files, etc) than uploading of files to the Internet. For example, with a 2Mbit connection, the download speed may be 1.98 Mbit/s, but the upload speed may only be 192Kbit/s.

Key terms

Smartphone A mobile phone that can include personal computer capabilities, email, personal organiser, Internet access, camera – still and/or video, and Global Positioning System (Satellite Navigation).

When authoring multimedia content for the web, you cannot control the platform on which the consumer will view the final multimedia product. It could be a Windows, Macintosh or Unix based computer, with an Intel or AMD processor; a personal digital assistant or a **smartphone**. Each device has different characteristics, i.e. screen size and resolution, colour capability, video and audio capabilities. This is a challenge when developing multimedia content for the web because you must provide content that is accessible to both desktop computers and mobile devices.

The W3C group are developing a solution to the problem of access by mobile devices with the introduction of DIAL (Device Independent Authoring Language). This is an authoring language that will provide filtering and presentation of web page content depending on the characteristics of the mobile device and software applications being used. Further details can be obtained from www.w3.org/TR/dial .

In this unit we are using Macromedia Flash Professional 8 which has a template for building applications for mobile phones. For further information about this visit the Mobile & Devices Developer Center at www.macromedia.com/devnet/devices/

SELECTING APPROPRIATE PERIPHERAL DEVICES

When producing multimedia products, you may also require access to specialised peripheral devices such as those listed in Table 4.2.

Graphics tablet with a pressure sensitive pen	For graphical work such as hand drawings
Scanner	For capturing images from photographs or magazines
Digital camera	For taking photographs that can be transferred directly to the computer
Video camera	For capturing moving images and sound
Microphone	For capturing narration and sound
Speakers	For listening to music and sounds

Table 4.2 Specialised peripheral devices for use in multimedia development

For more details on digital cameras, refer to 'Component parts of a digital camera' on page 7.

For more information on sound equipment, refer to 'Sound recording devices' on page 205.

For more information on video, refer to 'Selecting appropriate equipment for video capture' on page 248.

SELECTING APPROPRIATE SOFTWARE FOR MULTIMEDIA DEVELOPMENT

By visiting the software company's website, it is possible to find out the hardware you will need to be able to run certain software. For example, if you visit www.adobe.com/uk/products/flash/flashpro/ and follow the links for **system requirements** you will find the minimum hardware and operating system requirements needed to run Flash Professional 8 – as listed in Table 4.3. Before embarking on a multimedia project, you should check that the software and hardware you intend to use are compatible.

PLATFORM	Windows®	Macintosh®
PROCESSOR	Minimum 800 MHz Intel® Pentium® III or equivalent	Minimum 600 MHz PowerPC® G3 and processor
OPERATING SYSTEM	Windows® 2000, WindowsXP	Mac OS® X 10.3, 10.4
MEMORY	256 MB RAM (1 GB recommended to run more than one Studio 8 product simultaneously)	
MONITOR	1024 × 768, 16-bit display (32-bit recommended)	1024 × 768, thousands of colours display (millions of colours recommended)
HARD DISK	710 MB available disk space	360 MB available disk space

Table 4.3 Minimum hardware and operating system requirements required to run Flash Professional 8

Student review 4.2 – Identify hardware specifications

Assessment objectives 1a, 1b

1 Connect to the Internet.

2 Identify the minimum hardware specifications for each of the following software titles:

- Microsoft PowerPoint
- Macromedia Director
- Digital Workshops OpusPro
- Adobe Premiere
- Adobe Audition
- Adobe Photoshop

3 Record the information in a table similar to Table 4.3.

PRACTICAL TASK 4.1 Identify client requirements and produce planning documentation

Assessment objectives 1a, 1b, 1c, 3a

1 Refer to 'Planning your work' and 'Reviewing your work' on pages xiv and xxi in the 'Common Skills' chapter.

2 Obtain a copy of the Planning and Review Form.

3 Refer to the 'Magnificent Bowl – Interactive Presentation' assignment brief on page 159.

4 Identify the client and their requirements.

5 State the target audience and how the multimedia product will be delivered.

6 Produce a plan outlining the activities you will undertake and note any deadline dates.

7 Using a table similar to Table 4.3, identify the specification of the computer system you will be using to produce the multimedia product.

8 Identify the peripheral devices you will have access to when completing this task.

9 Make a note the software you will be using to produce the multimedia product.

SECTION 2 • Understand multimedia design principles and plan the multimedia product

The following assessment objectives will be covered in this section:

2a Create multimedia assets

3a Plan the multimedia product to a specific brief

The following knowledge, skills and understanding criteria corresponding to assessment objective 2a will be covered:

- *Sources and examples of multimedia applications*
- *Mobile technology*
- *Main multimedia elements*
- *Basic multimedia principles*
- *Reasons for use of multimedia*
- *Limitations*

The following knowledge, skills and understanding are covered in Units 1, 5 and 6:

- *Creating multimedia assets – digital images, sound and video*

The following knowledge, skills and understanding are covered in the 'Common Skills' chapter:

- *Good practice in file management and naming conventions*

Multimedia elements

- *Text*
- *Graphics*
- *Video*
- *Sound effects*
- *Animation*
- *Music*
- *Narration*
- *Navigation*

UNDERSTAND THE PURPOSE OF MULTIMEDIA PRODUCTS

Multimedia products are created for many different purposes. One of the biggest areas where interactive multimedia is used is for games and entertainment. In the home, multimedia CD-ROMs or DVDs are used for reference, e.g. encyclopaedias, atlases. Educational multimedia titles allow learners to carry out exercises at their own pace and promote learning through creative activities and adventure games. In the workplace, businesses use multimedia products to train their workforce, for example, in the use of software. Multimedia can also be used to train staff through simulation where it may be too dangerous to complete the training in the real world. Multimedia can also be used to provide local information, for example, at kiosks in train stations or museums to provide a guide to services. CD-ROMs are often used for marketing purposes and can include interactive catalogues.

Web-based examples of interactive multimedia include sites that allow you to play games as if you were a contestant on one of the TV programmes, learn new skills and obtain the latest news.

Student review 4.3 – Research web-based interactive multimedia

Assessment objective 2a

1 Connect to the Internet.

2 Log on to the BBC website www.bbc.co.uk/

3 Click on the link to **Entertainment**.

4 Follow the links to **The Weakest Link** game (or alternative game show).

5 Make a list of the multimedia content and interactivity.

6 Return to the home page and click on the link to **Learning**.

7 Follow the links to any of the learning programs available.

8 Make a list of the multimedia content and interactivity.

9 Log on to the BBC news website http://news.bbc.co.uk/

10 Follow the links to find the latest news for today.

11 Make a list of the multimedia content and interactivity.

CD-ROMs are a popular medium for interactive multimedia. They can be used for interactive encyclopaedias, e.g. the Encyclopaedia Britannica, or for training materials, e.g. learning a new language. A CD is often included on the front cover of a magazine to distribute free software or provide additional information or resources.

Student review 4.4 – Research CD-based interactive multimedia

Assessment objective 2a

1 Collect a number of CDs from the covers of magazines.

2 Identify the type of multimedia content on each CD.

3 Is the CD passive or interactive?

4 Record your findings in a table using the following headings:
- Title of CD
- Topic
- Multimedia content
- Interactive Y/N?

DVDs are more popular today than VHS tapes. In addition to the main film, many DVDs include additional features such as out-takes and interactive features that allow you to navigate to specific frames of the film. If a DVD contains multiple recordings, part of the navigational features often include being presented with a frame of each recording with menu options for playing the recording or navigating to specific frames in the recording.

Student review 4.5 – Identify DVD interactive features

Assessment objective 2a

1 Load a DVD of your choice.

2 Make a list of the interactive features available to you.

3 Identify the menus that are available and the navigation features.

4 Present your findings to your tutor.

An obvious source of interactive multimedia is games. These are available both online and offline. They come in various formats, e.g. simulation, adventure, action.

Student review 4.6 – Research interactive multimedia in games

Assessment objective 2a

1 Obtain a CD/DVD based game.

2 Identify the multimedia content and interactivity included in the game.

3 Connect to the Internet.

4 Log on to www.citycreator.com

5 Identify the multimedia content and interactivity included in the game.

6 Connect to the Internet.

7 Search for games in the following genres – simulation, adventure, action.

8 List three games titles for each genre.

Television programmes and advertisements may include many different media types making them multimedia. But in broadcast television this is presented to you in a linear format. Digital TV allows you to enjoy watching television in more ways through enhanced and interactive services. For example, with digital TV you can choose which football game to watch or the angle from which you view it. Through the 'red button' you can join in with quizzes and access enhanced information services. True two-way interactive services are also available, such as text messaging, email, joining in with auctions, games, shopping and banking services.

Interactive multimedia is available through kiosks such as in shops where you can view the latest promotions and obtain printed vouchers for discounts and money off products within the store. Kiosks are also used to provide tourist information and offer banking services.

Interactive multimedia applications can also been found on mobile phones, personal digital assistants and hand-held games consoles.

UNDERSTANDING THE MAIN MULTIMEDIA ELEMENTS

Text

Text is perhaps the easiest of all multimedia elements to manipulate. You will have had experience of working with text in a word-processing application and will be familiar with working with different fonts and font sizes.

When using text in a multimedia application follow these basic rules:

- Be concise. Reading text on a computer screen or mobile device can be difficult and tiring.
- Use appropriate fonts. The fonts used in the invitation on the left in Figure 4.5 would probably appeal to a younger audience. The font used in the invitation on the right is formal and is more difficult to read on screen.
- Make sure the text is readable, particularly when setting a coloured font against a coloured background.
- Be consistent. For example, if several screens have similar headings use the same font, size and style for all these headings.

Key terms

Fonts

Sans Serif Fonts without any extensions.

Serif Fonts that have a line or curve extension from the end of a letter.

Decorative Fonts that are more stylish and formal and are best used for emphasis.

Peter and Mary request the pleasure of your company at their wedding
on
October 26th at 10 a.m.
at
The Astoria Hotel

rsvp
Mr & Mrs Lawson

Zapf Chancery Font

Figure 4.5 Examples of fonts

SANS SERIF	SERIF	DECORATIVE
Arial	Times New Roman	Airstream
Verdana	Garamond	Oz handicraft
Comic Sans MS	Palatino	KidTypePaint
Tahoma	Minion	MYTHOS

Table 4.4 Examples of sans serif, serif and decorative fonts

Graphics

Graphical images are used in multimedia to add emphasis, direct attention or to illustrate concepts. There are two types of graphic that can be used – vector and bitmap. Vector graphics represent the image as a geometric shape made up of straight lines, ovals and arcs; bitmap graphics represent the image as an array of pixels.

For further details on bitmap images and vector graphics refer to 'Types of digital graphic' on page 4.

Graphical images can be obtained from various sources, for example:

- clip art supplied with the software
- stock photographs supplied with the software
- the Internet
- CDs and DVDs.

You could capture the images yourself using a digital camera, web camera or mobile phone. You could also use a scanner to capture an image from a magazine or a book.

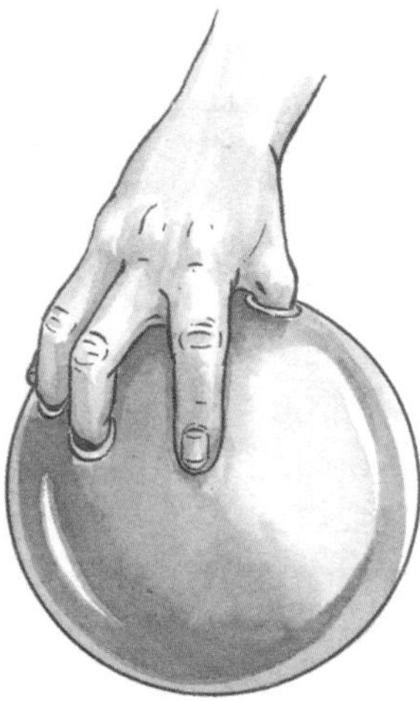

Figure 4.6 Examples of clip art

Video

Video images can be transferred to the computer from video tapes or can be obtained from the Internet. You could capture the footage yourself using a digital video recorder, mobile phone, web camera or a digital camera. Screen capture programs are available that will record actions on the computer screen, such as the movement of the mouse to point to a menu. These are useful if you are preparing a multimedia product to provide training in how to use computer software. An example of this type of software is HyperCam which is available from www.hyperionics.com/hc/ .

When using any image or sound in your multimedia product, you must always acknowledge the copyright.

Including a video clip can make the multimedia product more exciting but it can also be disappointing. Playing back video files from a CD-ROM takes a great deal of computing power. In order for the video to be played back on a low-specification PC, the quality of the video may have been compromised with reduced frame rates and small windows. Viewing video from a web page may also be slow depending on the bandwidth of the connection.

Refer to pages 243–5, starting with 'How video works'.

Sound

Music, narration and sound effects are used in multimedia to enhance drama and to make what you are seeing more realistic. For example, in games, sound effects may be used to create the sound of footsteps as an alien creeps up on you and music may be played in the background. In an educational title, narration may be included to explain a process as it is being shown on the screen or in a CD for learning a new language you may hear how a word is pronounced.

When saving your assets always use appropriate naming conventions and file formats. Refer to 'File organisation and file naming' on page viii in the 'Common Skills' chapter, and 'Different file formats and file extensions' on page 10.

If you plan to include audio in your multimedia product it should be produced using the best quality sound equipment. Audio can be used to add narration to your product providing additional commentary that will not obscure the information on the screen. You can also use audio to add music to your screen to create a mood or provide a sample of what something sounds like. If you do include sound, you must be careful not to confuse the user by providing competing information; people cannot read text and listen to spoken audio at the same time.

Refer to 'How to capture sound' on page 209.

As part of the planning process in an OCR assessment, you will be required to identify the assets you are going to use in the production of the multimedia product. This will include all image files, sound clips, video clips, animations and text. You must also include information on the source of the assets together with details of the size and format of each of the assets. You may have produced some of the assets yourself whilst completing other units for this qualification. Others may need to be obtained from other sources such as magazines or the Internet. If you have obtained assets from other sources you must log any materials needing copyright permission on the Planning and Review Form.

You must include a minimum of three multimedia elements, one of which must be the use of appropriate interactivity, e.g. hyperlinks, buttons or rollovers. You may use appropriate recorded sound and any video included must be edited and compressed.

For an OCR assessment you will be required to use a minimum of four images; two of these images must be captured using a digital camera, web camera, mobile phone or video camera, and two can be from other sources such as the Internet, magazines, CDs or books. The multimedia product must be created for a screen size of 640 × 480 unless otherwise specified in the assignment brief.

PRACTICAL TASK 4.2 Identify and record details of assets to be used

Assessment objective 3a

1 Refer to the 'Magnificent Bowl – Interactive Presentation' assignment brief on page 159.

2 Using the same Planning and Review Form from Practical task 4.1, state the purpose of the multimedia product.

3 Identify the assets you will use.

4 Include details of size, format and the source of each of the assets.

5 Log any assets needing copyright permission.

UNDERSTANDING MULTIMEDIA NAVIGATIONAL STRUCTURES

When planning the multimedia product you must take into account basic multimedia design principles which include the structure and navigation of the product, the screen design, user interface, and the use of colour, sound and video.

Your multimedia product will consist of a collection of screens connected by links which will allow the user to interact with the product and navigate through the pages. A well-designed multimedia product will have a clear structure and a means of navigation that is easy to understand.

There are four primary navigational structures used in multimedia:

- Sequential
- Totally connected
- Hierarchical
- Composite

Sequential

A simple linear structure (see Figure 4.7) may be appropriate for a multimedia product, for example, where a game has a story with a beginning, middle and end, or in a training title where the user needs to move through the instructions step by step.

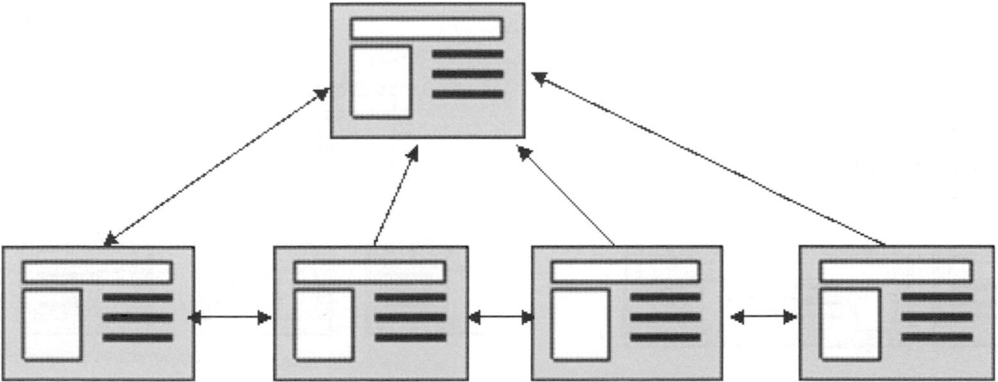

Figure 4.7 Linear structure (sequential)

The only navigation you need to provide in a sequential structure is to allow the user to move to the next screen or back to the previous screen. You might also decide to provide the option to return to the home screen from any of the screens in the linear presentation. Linear titles often include buttons or graphics such as arrows for navigation. To keep users interested when using a linear navigation structure you may want to include some interactivity such as clicking on an object to hear a sound, play an animation, or watch a video clip.

Totally connected

This is a non-linear structure where users can navigate through the screens and content freely without any restrictions (see Figure 4.8).

In this type of structure you would provide a link on each screen to every other screen. This type of structure would need a large number of links and would be difficult to draw for a large complex multimedia product. However, for a small, short product it could be the best way of organising the content because you could provide a standard navigation bar on each screen, containing a set of links to each of the other screens. This would also help to provide a consistent layout for your multimedia product.

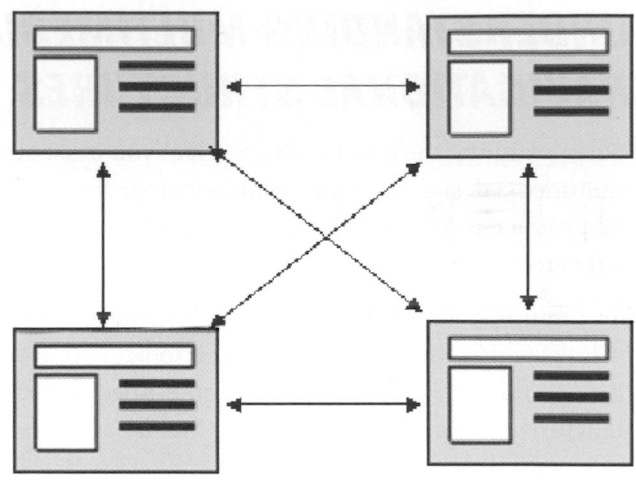

Figure 4.8 Non-linear structure (totally connected)

Hierarchical

A hierarchical, or topical, structure (see Figure 4.9) is the most popular structure for large multimedia titles such as encyclopaedias, interactive catalogues or information kiosks. In this type of structure there are often several layers depending on the number of topics. The home screen will

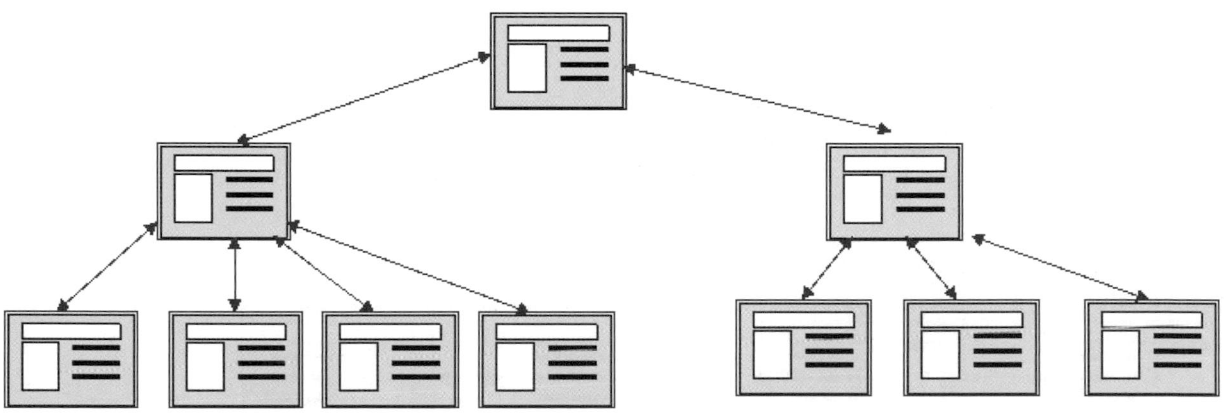

Figure 4.9 Hierarchical structure

include links to a sub-set of home screens. These in turn contain links to the screens or content for that section of the multimedia title.

Composite

In a composite, or hybrid, structure, you may navigate freely but you are sometimes constrained to a sequential presentation or to information that is arranged in a hierarchy (see Figure 4.10).

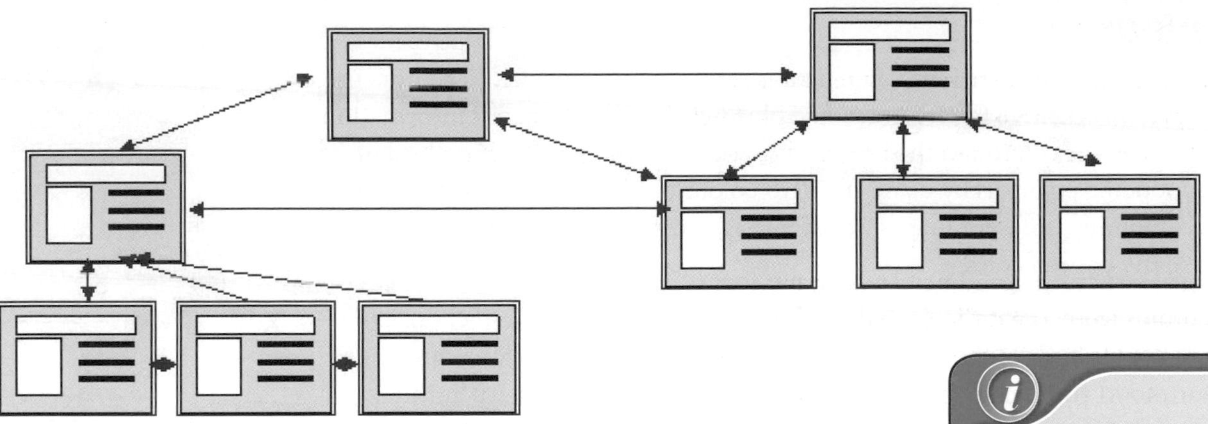

Figure 4.10 Composite structure

Mapping the structure of the multimedia product should be started early in the planning stage. The navigation map outlines the links between the various areas of your product and helps you to organise your content.

When drawing a navigational map (Navmap) you should indicate where the navigation is forward and back by using a double arrowhead.

UNDERSTANDING MULTIMEDIA DESIGN PRINCIPLES

Screen design

When you are designing the screens for your multimedia product you need to try and understand what look and feel would attract your intended audience. The product should have a purpose; it may be used to try and sell something, or it could be communicating or informing the audience about something. Whatever the purpose is, make sure that any graphics and text you use on your screens will enhance that purpose.

When designing your screens you should aim to arrange the multimedia elements so that the screen is balanced and no one part of the screen is overpowering. Harmony is achieved by blending the elements to give an integrated appearance, for example, by using the same background colour or buttons on each screen.

If you want to attract the audience's attention or make an element stand out you need to add emphasis. This could be achieved by applying a larger font to the text, or animating an image. However, emphasis should be used sparingly otherwise you will find that your pages will look garish and nothing will appear to be emphasised at all.

Contrast and variety will add interest to your screens. This could be achieved by using contrasting colours for screen titles or using graphics of different shapes and sizes.

Colour

Colour is what the eye sees when light is reflected off an object. Receptors in the eye are sensitive to red, green and blue light and can transmit information on millions of colours to the brain. On a computer monitor one method of reproducing colour is by using the RGB colour model. This represents colours by combining different intensities of red (R), green (G) or blue (B) light to make the desired colour.

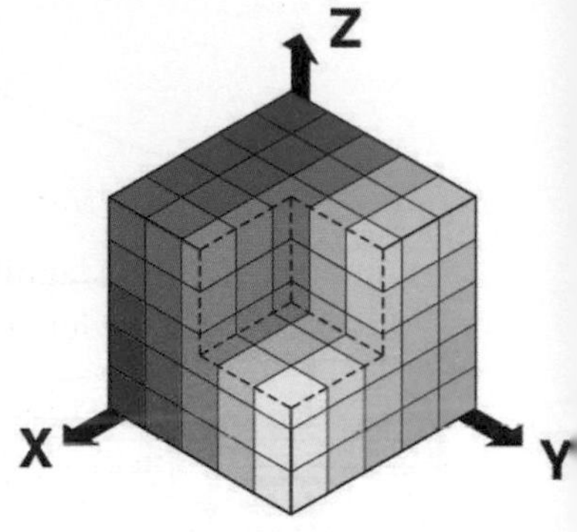

Figure 4.11 RGB colour cube

In multimedia, colour is a vital component and it is important to choose the right colour and combinations of colour for your product. Colour can affect your mood and in some cultures has special meaning. In western cultures, red means stop and green means go; red means hot and blue means cold. Red can be used to represent anger or danger. In eastern cultures, red is the colour of happiness and is often used in Chinese restaurants to make them happy places. In western cultures, black is the colour of death and white the colour representing birth whereas in eastern cultures, white is symbolic of a funeral.

Figure 4.12 Colour associations

Colour schemes

When planning your multimedia product, you should decide on a colour scheme.

Monochromatic colour schemes use different values of one colour, for example, dark blue, blue and light blue. This type of colour scheme looks clean and elegant; it can be used to create an overall mood and looks balanced. However, it is not very exciting, lacks colour contrast and can be difficult to highlight important elements.

An analogous colour scheme is one which uses colours that are adjacent to each other on the colour wheel (Figure 4.13), such as gold, orange and red. One colour would be used as the main colour and the others would be used to add contrast.

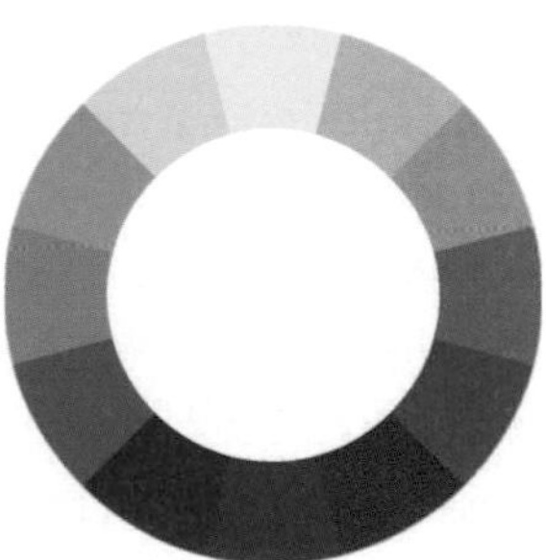
Figure 4.13 Colour wheel

A complementary colour scheme is one that uses two colours that are opposite each other on the colour wheel. This colour scheme can provide stronger contrasts than monochromatic or analogous colour schemes and draw the user's attention to your pages. However, it should be used with caution.

Both Macintosh and Windows use graphical user interfaces that are simple and easy to use. When designing your user interface it is best to use conventions that are easily recognised and understood by your potential audience, for example, a house to indicate returning to the home screen, arrows to indicate movement to the previous or next screen. The user interface controls should not confuse your audience.

PRACTICAL TASK 4.3 Produce a navigational map and screen layouts

Assessment objectives 2a, 3a

1 Refer to the 'Magnificent Bowl – Interactive Presentation' assignment brief on page 159.

2 Sketch a navigational map to show the navigation structure for the multimedia product.

3 Sketch the layout for your screen designs.

4 Identify a suitable colour scheme and note down details of this on your screen designs.

5 Note the multimedia content that will be included on the screens and identify fonts to be used for text.

6 Identify the position and type of the interface controls.

7 Attach the navigational map and screen designs to the Planning and Review Form from Practical task 4.2.

UNDERSTANDING THE LIMITATIONS ON DELIVERY OF MULTIMEDIA CONTENT

When creating a multimedia product you must be aware of how it will be delivered to your audience. If it is to be delivered over the Internet there are technical considerations that must be taken into account when deciding on the multimedia elements to include.

When requesting a web page, your user will want it to appear in a relatively short amount of time. The length of time it takes for a page to download will depend on the bandwidth of the user's connection to the Internet, the Internet Service Provider's capacity and speed and the size of the files being requested. The only part of this that is in your control is the size of the files. Therefore, if your product is to be delivered over the Internet you should limit the use of graphics, sound, animation and video. You should note that dial-up connections using a modem are not able to handle the required data rate to download video successfully.

If the media you have included in your multimedia web pages is to be seen it may be necessary for the browser to make use of additional software. The web browser will be able to display text and images but elements such as audio, video and some document formats will usually require plug-in applications. These are software modules that will be loaded by the browser when it starts. Plug-ins, or helper applications such as Adobe Acrobat Reader, RealAudio and QuickTime, assist the browser in presenting the data in an appropriate way. If the user does not have the required plug-in installed, then the media will not play. If the user wants to view the files, they must first download and install the necessary helper application. This could be a problem because some users may not want to download the plug-in, may not know how to download the plug-in, may make an error when downloading or their local area network may not allow such downloads for security reasons.

This problem can be avoided by delivering the multimedia product in a 'stand-alone' form that needs no additional software. Flash has the capability of saving a multimedia product as a 'projector' that can be delivered on a CD-ROM and will play on a computer, or in any browser or other movie-playing program.

There are also non-technical limitations that need to be considered when producing multimedia products. There are many costs associated with producing multimedia including:

- production – salaries, consumables, content gathering fees, graphics, audio and video production costs
- testing – salaries, editing
- distribution – salaries, documentation, packaging, marketing, advertising.

When estimating the cost, there are also hidden costs such as administration, the time taken for you to learn the software, and the time taken to liaise with the client.

The specification, or brief, that you have to work to may have a low budget, may have a tight deadline or may require that the product be for delivery on a mobile device. This may mean that you may not be able to include all the multimedia elements that you would like. You will need to make sure that the content you do include in your product is suitable for the intended target audience and that the final product meets the requirements of the original specification – is it fit for the purpose for which it was intended?

PRACTICAL TASK 4.4 **Identify possible limitations in the production of the presentation**

Assessment objectives 2a, 3a

1 Refer to the 'Magnificent Bowl – Interactive Presentation' assignment brief on page 159.

2 Identify any limitations there may be involved in the delivery of the multimedia product.

3 Record this on the Planning and Review Form from Practical task 4.3.

The making of a multimedia product can involve many different software tools and skills. For this unit you need to know how to create multimedia assets using the appropriate hardware and software. Professional quality multimedia production will usually involve a team of people, each of whom will have skills in different areas. If you have completed Units 1, 3, 5 and 6 you will have covered many of the skills needed to produce multimedia assets.

Before moving on to the next section in this unit, you should make sure that you are familiar with the following.

DIGITAL IMAGES

- Obtaining images by scanning and from a digital camera
- Manipulating images, e.g. cropping
- Compressing images

DIGITAL VIDEO

- Obtaining digital video using a webcam or digital video recorder
- Editing video
- Compressing video

For details on file management, refer to 'File organisation and file naming' on page xi in the 'Common Skills' chapter.

DIGITAL SOUND

- Recording sound effects, narration and music
- Editing sound files
- Compressing sounds

When collecting your assets you should create a suitable folder structure in which to save the different files and use appropriate file naming conventions.

SECTION 3 • Use Flash to create multimedia content

The following assessment objective will be covered in this section:
2b Create multimedia content

The following knowledge, skills and understanding criteria corresponding to assessment objective 2b will be covered:

- *How to use multimedia authoring software to import assets*

To create the multimedia presentation we will be using Macromedia Flash 8 which is part of Macromedia Studio 8 suite. Flash is an authoring tool that allows you to create interactive multimedia presentations. These presentations are suitable for delivery over the web, distributed on a CD or DVD, or can be saved in a format suitable for playback on mobile devices.

In this section you will learn how to use Flash to create your multimedia presentation. You will not be creating the assets required for the multimedia presentation as it is expected these will have already been created. To learn more about how to create assets using Flash, refer to Unit 3, Digital Animation. You will use Flash to enter small amounts of text for the different screens but you will not be using Flash to create any other content. You should make sure that you have already prepared the content that you need, i.e. sound, video, animations, images. You may have prepared some of this content when working in other units for this qualification.

▶▶ HOW TO ... Start Flash

1 Click on **Start** → **All Programs** → **Macromedia** → **Macromedia Flash 8**.

2 The Flash 8 Start Page will be displayed (Figure 4.14).

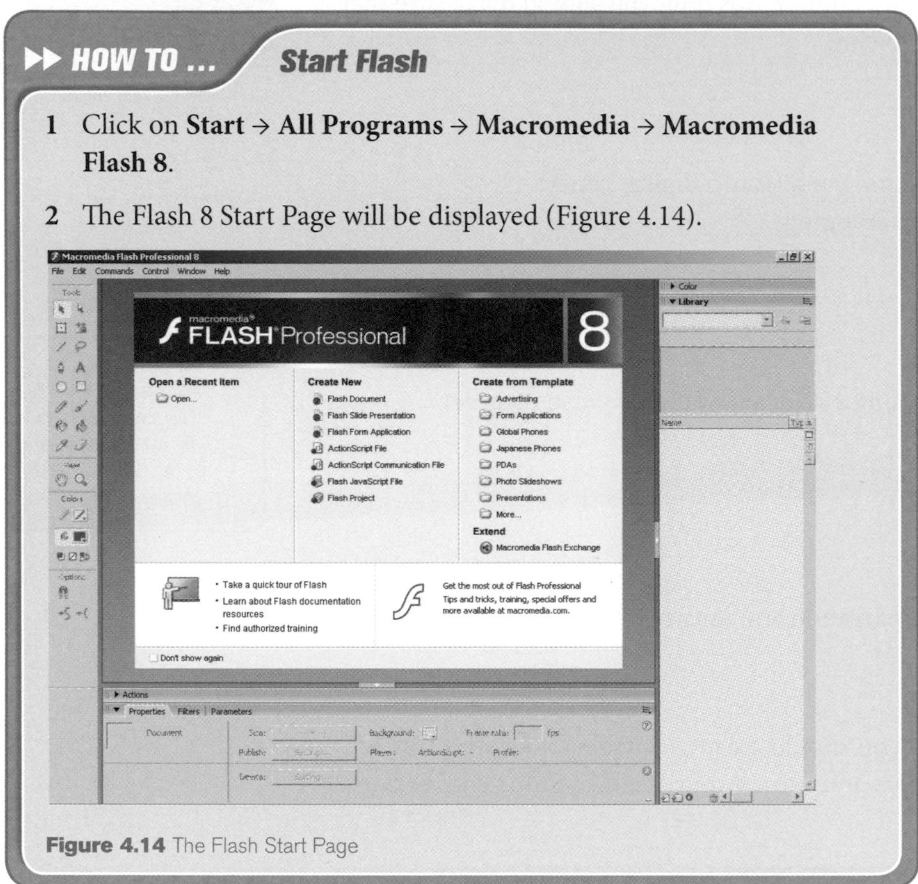

Figure 4.14 The Flash Start Page

Continued ...

3 In the **Create New** section, click on **Flash Document**.

4 The Flash screen will be displayed (Figure 4.15).

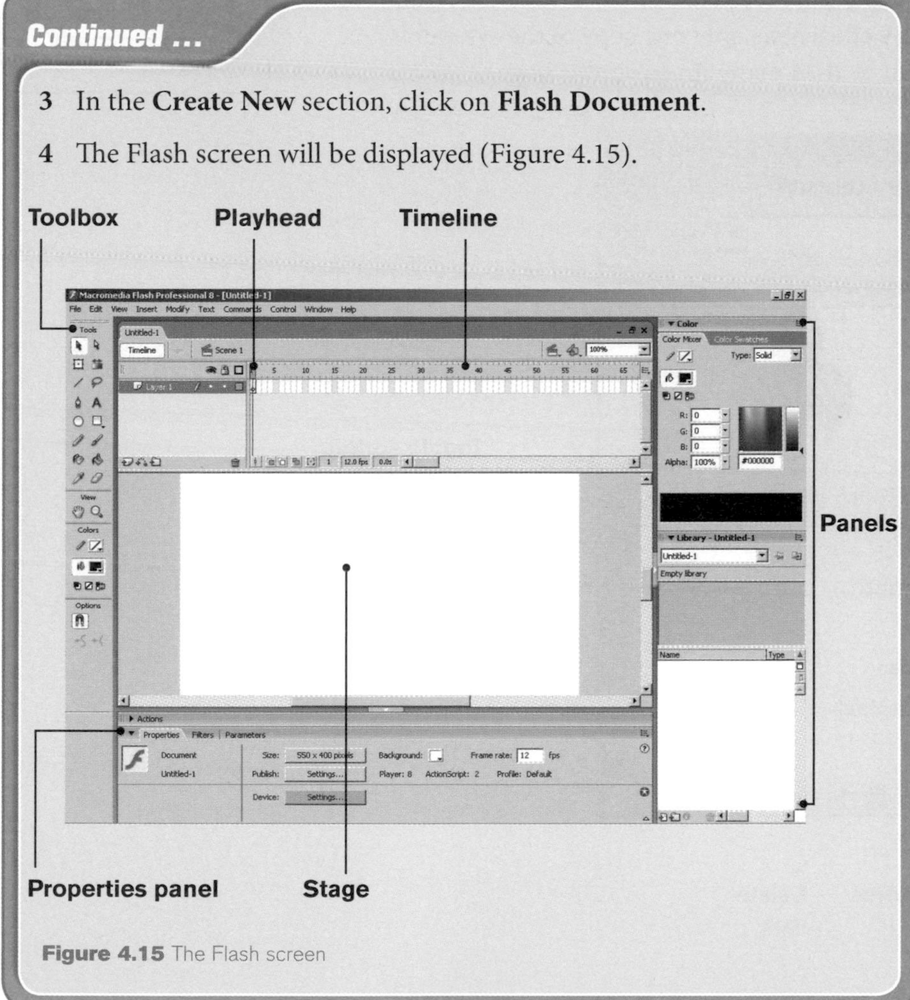

Figure 4.15 The Flash screen

TIP!

If the Start Page is not displayed, go to the **File** menu and select **New** → **Flash Document**.

WORKING WITH FLASH

The development environment in Flash uses a movie metaphor: you create scenes on a stage and the scenes run in frames on a timeline. You create the scenes by arranging objects such as text and graphics on the Stage. You animate the objects using the Timeline. You can play the movie on the Stage or you can test it in a browser. When the movie is complete, you will export it in the required format.

The Toolbox, Timeline, Stage and **Properties** panel (**Property inspector**) are explained in more detail on page 113 in Unit 3, Digital Animation.

For further information on the Flash screen refer to 'Understanding the Flash screen' on page 113.

The Library panel

When working on larger projects, it is important to understand the function of the **Library** panel (Figure 4.16). The library is where imported files such as video clips, sound clips and bitmap images, and symbols are stored. The library items can be organised into folders and sorted by type. Items stored in the library are referred to as assets. Each document has its own library referred to as the Document Library.

Symbols and instances

A symbol is a graphic, button, or movie clip that you create once and can reuse multiple times. When a symbol is copied to the Stage it is referred to as an instance.

When a symbol is used on the Stage it is referred to as an **instance** of the symbol. This makes Flash very efficient as only one copy of the symbol is stored in the library, but it can be used many times on the Stage.

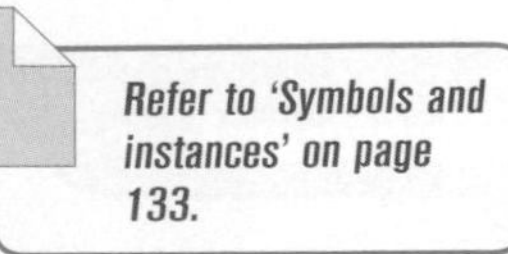
Refer to 'Symbols and instances' on page 133.

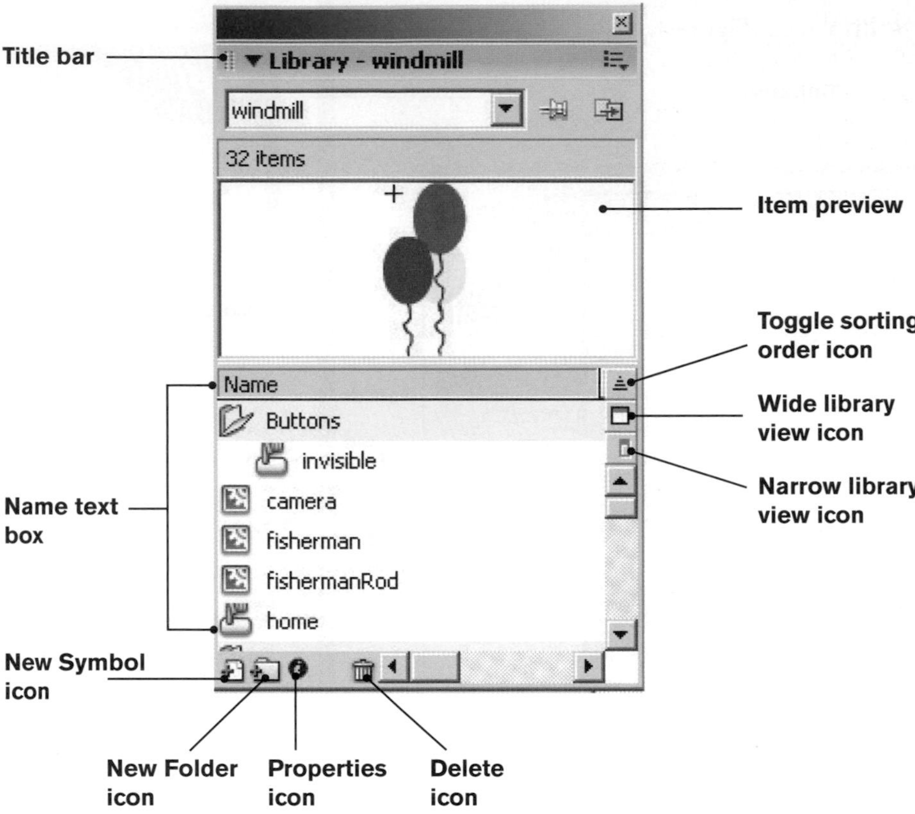

Figure 4.16 The Library panel

If the **Library** panel is not displayed, go to **Window** menu → **Library**.

UNDERSTANDING FLASH DOCUMENTS

All Flash files are called movies. When you save a Flash file it will be saved with the file extension **fla**. Files with the **fla** extension can only be opened in Flash. After you have opened the file, it can be edited in Flash and resaved.

In Section 4 you will learn to optimise and publish the Flash file in formats for distributing your movie using different mediums.

When you create a new Flash document (movie) you should set the document properties. This includes setting the size of the window the movie will play in, the background colour and the speed at which the movie will play, in frames per second.

The default size for a document in Flash is 550 pixels wide by 400 pixels high. For an OCR assessment the screen size should be set to 640 × 480 unless otherwise stated in the outline storyboard. This size is the most common size because it supports a wide variety of screen sizes and resolutions.

▸▸ HOW TO ... Set the document properties

1 Click on the **Modify** menu → **Document** → the **Document Properties** dialogue box will be displayed (refer to Figure 4.17).

2 In the **Title** box, enter a title for the document.

3 In the **Description** box, enter information about the document.

4 In the **Dimensions** section, enter the required width and height for the document.

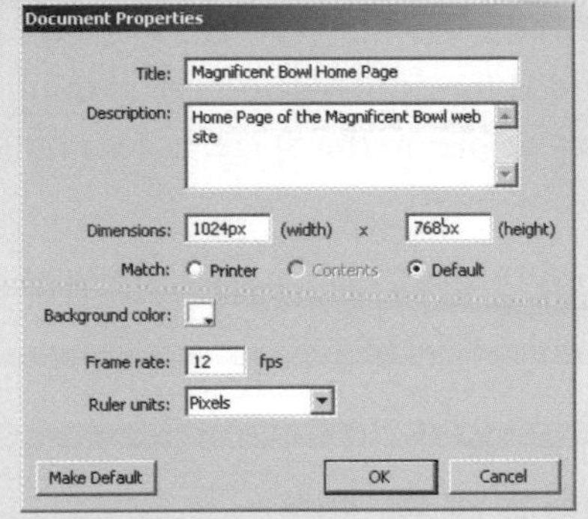

Figure 4.17 The Document Properties dialogue box

5 After entering the required width and height in pixels, you may find it easier to work on the screen in centimetres. If you would prefer to work in centimetres, select the drop-down arrow for **Ruler units** and change the unit of measurement (optional).

6 Click on the drop-down arrow to the right of **Background color** to select a colour for the Stage.

7 In the **Frame Rate** box, enter the required frame rate.

8 Click **OK** to close the **Document Properties** dialogue box.

The size of the document and the background colour will be displayed in the **Properties** panel (refer to Figure 4.18).

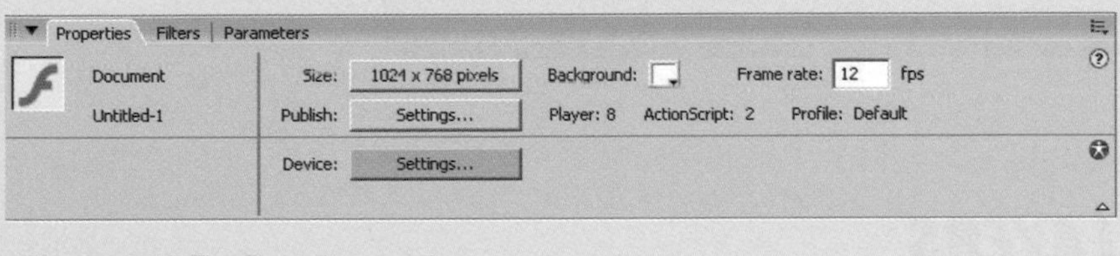

Figure 4.18 The Properties panel

> **TIP!**
>
> You can access the **Document Properties** by clicking on the button displaying the document size, which is to the right of the label **Size**.

▸▸ HOW TO ... Display the rulers

You may find it helpful to display the rulers.

1 **View** menu → **Rulers**.

2 To align items precisely, click on the ruler → drag the ruler guide to the Stage.

HOW TO ... Display the grid

You may also find it helpful to display the grid. The grid comprises lines that can be used as a guide for drawing and positioning objects on the Stage. The grid is only visible on the Stage; it does not display in your completed movie.

- **View** menu → **Grid** → **Show Grid**.

HOW TO ... Set snapping options

To automatically align items with each other or with the grid or ruler guides, use the snapping options.

- **View** menu → **Snapping** → select the required option.

HOW TO ... Save a Flash movie

- **File** menu → **Save As** → navigate to your user area → enter a suitable filename → **Save**.

HOW TO ... Close a Flash movie

- **File** menu → **Close**.

WORKING WITH LAYERS

Flash organises objects in two ways: the position of the object on the Stage and the stacking order of the objects. Layers are used as a way of organising the stacking order of the objects. Layers are like transparent sheets stacked on top of each other on the Stage. You can import, draw or edit objects on a layer without affecting the objects on other layers. Also, each layer has its own Timeline which makes it easier to control (Figure 4.19).

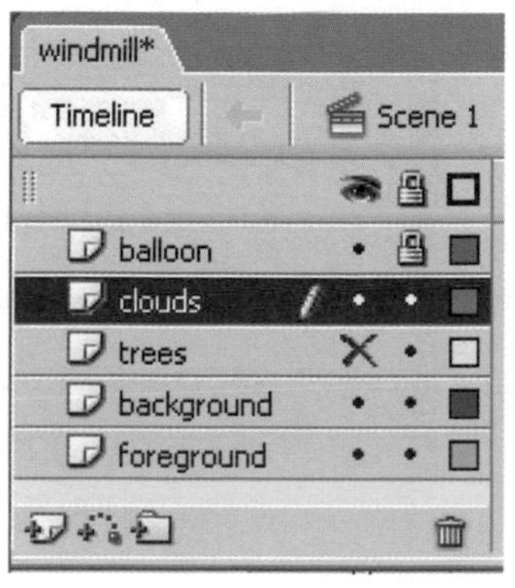

Figure 4.19 The Layers section of the Timeline

When you create a new Flash document, it contains only one layer. You can insert new layers using the **Insert Layer** icon located at the bottom left of the Timeline. The number of layers you can create is limited only by your computer's memory, and layers do not increase the file size of your published file. Only the objects you place into layers add to the file size.

You can change the order of the layers by clicking on the layer and moving it to the new position.

You can delete a layer by selecting the layer and then clicking on the **Delete Layer** icon at the bottom left of the Timeline.

You should always rename the layers with suitable names. The name of the layer should be a guide to the objects on that layer. To rename a layer, double-click on the layer name – the name field will be highlighted, type the new name.

You can temporarily hide a layer so that it is not visible on the Stage. Below the **Show/Hide Layers** icon, click the black dot in the required layer. In the **Layers** section of the Timeline shown in Figure 4.19, the **trees** layer has been hidden, as indicate by the red cross. You should note that a layer that has been hidden while you are working on a document will be visible when the document is published.

You can lock a layer so that it cannot be accidentally edited. To lock a layer, click the black dot in the required layer under the **Lock/Unlock Layers** icon. In the **Layers** section of the Timeline shown in Figure 4.19, the **balloon** layer has been locked.

If you want to lock all layers, or hide all layers, click on the icons at the top of the columns.

The pencil icon indicates which layer is active and can be edited. In Figure 4.19, this is the **clouds** layer. If the current layer is locked, the pencil icon will have a red line through it.

WORKING WITH TEXT

As a text block is an object, it can be transformed using the **Free Transform Tool**.

Refer to 'Transforming objects' on page 125.

Figure 4.20 Skewed text

Figure 4.21 Broken apart text

TIP!

When aligning objects, use the arrow keys on the keyboard.

▸▸ HOW TO ... Reshape a letter

You can select an individual letter and reshape it.

1 Click on the **Subselection Tool** and then click on the letter to be reshaped.
2 Click on the **Modify** menu → **Break Apart** (see Figure 4.21).
3 Click on the letter again to display the segment handles.
4 Drag the handles to reshape the letter (refer to Figure 4.22).

Figure 4.22 Reshaped letter

HOW TO ... Group letters

1 Click on the **Selection Tool** → drag the **Selection Tool** to select all letters.

2 Click on the **Modify** menu → **Group**.

You can convert the text to a graphic symbol and it will automatically become part of the Document Library. You will then be able to use the graphic on other screens in your multimedia product.

Refer to 'Symbols and instances' on page 133.

Student review 4.7 – Enter and manipulate text

Assessment objective 2b

1 *Open a new document.*

2 *Set the document properties.*

3 *Display the rulers and grid.*

4 *Use the* ***Text Tool*** *to enter your name on the Stage.*

5 *Using the* ***Properties*** *panel, experiment with different text attributes.*

6 *Transform your text by using the rotate and skew options.*

7 *Try reshaping some of the letters.*

8 *Rename the layer using a suitable name.*

9 *Convert your text block to a graphic symbol.*

10 *Save your movie using an appropriate filename.*

11 *Close the movie.*

IMPORTING ASSETS

As previously discussed, when you import assets they are stored in the Document Library. The library stores the assets that you import along with any symbols that you create within Flash.

Flash supports a large number of file formats including those shown in Table 4.5.

GRAPHICS	SOUND	VIDEO
bmp gif jpg/jpeg png psd tiff	aiff au mp3 wav	avi dv mov mpg/mpeg wmv

Table 4.5 File formats supported by Flash

Refer to 'Vector graphics' on page 5.

Importing graphics

HOW TO ... Import graphics

1 Click on the **File** menu → **Import** → **Import to Library**.

2 Navigate to the folder that contains the file → select the file → click **Open**.

3 You will see the graphic in the Document Library. If the library is not displayed click on **Window** menu → **Library**.

Flash is a vector-based application which results in small file sizes. When you import bitmap images, the file size of your movie will increase.

HOW TO ... Position and size assets on the Stage

1 To place an asset on the Stage, select the imported image in the library and drag it onto the Stage.

2 Click on the **Selection Tool** and select the graphic on the Stage (refer to Figure 4.23).

3 You can move the graphic on the Stage by dragging it to the required position.

4 You can modify the size of the graphic by selecting the **Free Transform Tool** → select the graphic → click on the **Scale** button in the **Options** section. You can now resize the object by dragging the handles around the graphic (refer to Figure 4.24).

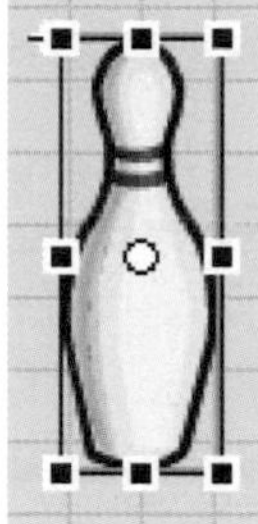

Figure 4.23 Object selected

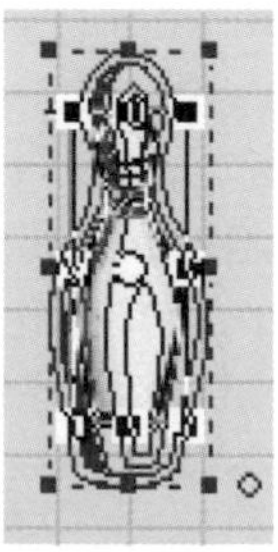

Figure 4.24 Object being scaled

Importing sound

You can add different types of sounds to a multimedia presentation. You could add CD quality sound to play in the background of the movie, you could add a narration to help explain what is being shown on the screen or you could add sounds that played to confirm an action, such as when the user clicked a button.

When you import a sound it is placed in the Document Library.

If you look in the **Properties** panel you will see that you can modify the height and width of the graphic as well as the X and Y position on the Stage. The X and Y coordinates match the position of the upper left corner of the graphic. Use the **Properties** panel when you want to place an object in a specific position.

▶▶ HOW TO ... Add sound to the movie

1 Click on the **File** menu → **Import** → **Import to Library**.

2 Navigate to the folder that contains the file → select the file → click **Open**. You will see the sound file in the Document Library.

3 Insert a new layer in the Timeline for the sound. Rename the layer.

4 Select the sound layer → drag the sound from the **Library** panel onto the Stage. The sound is added to the current layer.

5 In the **Properties** panel, click on the arrow to the right of the **Sound name** box → select a sound file from the **Sound** pop-up menu.

6 In the **Effects** section, click on the arrow to the right of the **Effects box** → select an effect from the **Effects** pop-up menu (optional).

7 In the **Synchronisation** section, select **Start** → **Repeat** → **1**. This starts the sound playing when its starting keyframe is reached. If the keyframe is reached again, and the sound is still playing, no new instance of the sound file will start playing.

You should place each sound you use in a movie in a separate layer. When the file is published, the sounds on all layers are combined.

Importing video

You can import video material into your movie in several different ways. The option you choose may depend on the size of the video clip. You can embed a video clip into the Timeline, but this is only recommended for very short clips with no audio track. If you embed a video clip this will increase the size of your movie file. Table 4.6 shows the most appropriate way of dealing with different sized video clips.

VIDEO CLIP SIZE	EMBEDDED	PROGRESSIVE	STREAMING
Under 10 seconds (no audio)	✓		
10 to 30 seconds		✓	✓
Over 30 seconds			✓

Table 4.6 How to deliver different sized video clips

If you attempt to import a file format that is not supported or you do not have the required additional software installed, a warning message will be displayed indicating that the operation cannot be completed.

When you import video into your movie using the Video Import Wizard, Flash encodes the video in the Flash Video format and saves it as an **flv** file. The Flash video can then be used just like any other media type and is displayed as an integral part of the movie.

▶▶ HOW TO ... Import video

1 Click on the **File** menu → **Import** → **Import Video**. The Import Video Wizard will start.

2 Follow the instructions in the **Import Video Wizard**.

PRACTICAL TASK 4.5 **Set document properties, create movies and import assets**

Assessment objective 2b

1 Refer to the 'Magnificent Bowl – Interactive Presentation' assignment brief on page 159 and your Planning and Review Form from Practical task 4.4.

2 Open a new Flash document for the first screen of your multimedia product.

3 Set the document properties and display the rulers and grid.

4 Save the movie using an appropriate filename, e.g. **Intro**

5 Save the movie again using a different filename for each of the screens in your multimedia product, e.g. home, location, contact. This will ensure that all screens have the same document properties.

6 Close all movies.

7 Open only the movie **Intro**

8 Import the assets for the screen into the Document Library.

9 Create any text required for the heading and convert this to a graphic symbol.

10 Place the assets for the first screen on the Stage. Remember to create new layers for each of the assets. Name the layers and the instances appropriately.

11 Save your movie keeping the filename **Intro**

To encode Flash video files (flv) you need Flash Professional 8. Flash Basic 8 only provides encoding for use with embedded video. For some video file formats you will need QuickTime and DirectX9 installed on the computer to be able to play back the files.

Note when using progressive or streaming options the Flash video file is saved separately from the movie file and the playback controls (the 'skin'). The playback controls are saved in the Document Library. When publishing your multimedia product you must remember to also include the Flash video file.

USING SYMBOLS IN MORE THAN ONE MOVIE

You have already learned that symbols from a library can be used more than once in your movie. You can also use the symbols in any other movie by dragging the assets from one document library and dropping them on to the Stage of a different movie.

For information on how to add animation and effects to the Stage, refer to Unit 3, Digital animations in particular page 137 onwards.

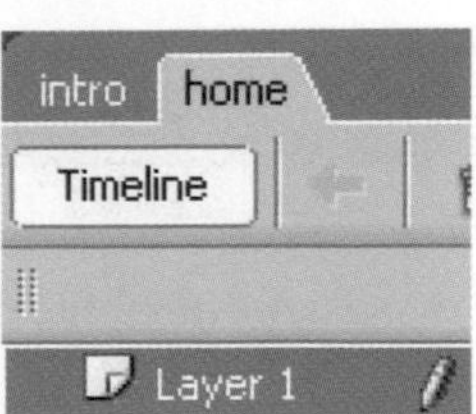

Figure 4.25 Two tabs will be displayed

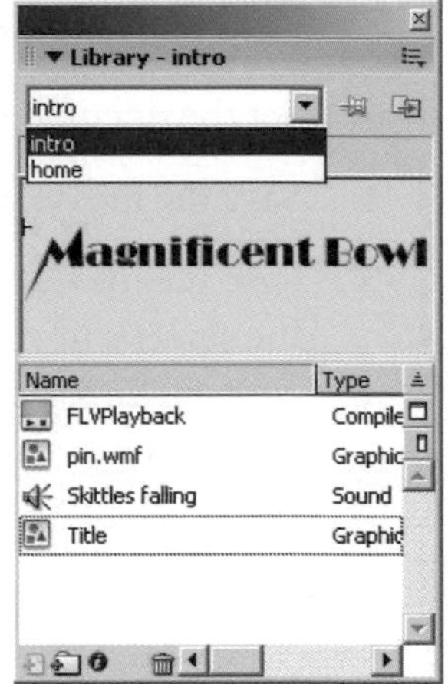

Figure 4.26 Switching between Document Libraries

▶▶ HOW TO ... Use symbols in more than one movie

1 **Open** a new movie → **Import** the assets into the Document Library → **Save** the movie. Do not close the movie.

2 Open a second new movie. You now have two movies open in the Flash window. You can move between the two movies by clicking on the appropriate tab (refer to Figure 4.25 on the right).

3 Click on the tab for the second movie.

4 In the **Library** panel, click on the drop down arrow under the library name box (refer to Figure 4.26 on the right) and select the library for the first window. The assets for the first window will be displayed.

5 Place an asset in the second movie by dragging and dropping the asset on to the Stage. The asset will also be placed in the Document Library for the second movie.

6 Save all movies: click on **File** menu → **Save All**.

PRACTICAL TASK 4.6 Open movies, place assets on the stage

Assessment objective 2b

1 Open the movies you created in Practical task 4.5.

2 Using the library for the **Intro** movie, drag any assets you need to use in other movies on to the Stage for the relevant movie.

3 Import or create all further assets that will be required for each movie into the associated library. Remember to create assets on separate layers in each movie.

4 Save all the movies you have open.

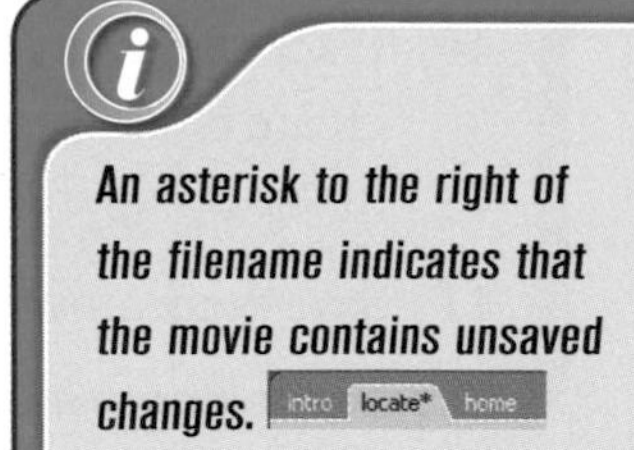

An asterisk to the right of the filename indicates that the movie contains unsaved changes.

ADDING NAVIGATION AND INTERACTIVITY

You now have a series of individual movies that need to be linked together. To do this you need to add the navigation elements to each of the movies. Buttons provide interactivity. When the user clicks on a button, an action occurs. This action could be to start an animation or to jump to another movie.

To create this interactivity Flash uses ActionScript. This is the programming language that allows you to write instructions that the movie will follow. Actions can be added to the Timeline, a movie clip or a button. You will be using ActionScript to add an action to a button. This will say what action will take place when the button is clicked.

To be able to use ActionScript, Flash needs to know which symbol to apply the action to. Therefore, each instance of a symbol has to be identified by giving it an **instance name**.

Flash recognises particular naming conventions when naming instances. The instance name must be followed by a suffix which identifies the instance type as shown in Table 4.7.

INSTANCE TYPE	NAMING CONVENTION
Movie clip	Name_**mc**
Text	Name_**txt**
Button	Name_**btn**

Table 4.7 The naming convention for instance types

▸▸ HOW TO ... Name instances

1 Use the **Selection Tool** to select the object.

2 In the **Properties** panel, click in the **Instance Name** box (refer to Figure 4.27) → enter the name of the instance followed by _ and the appropriate suffix (refer to Table 4.7).

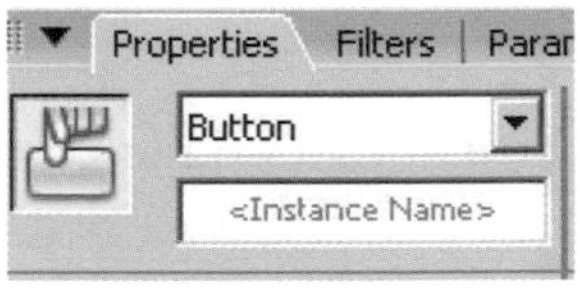

Figure 4.27 Instance Name box in Properties panel

Any object can be converted into a button; they can be animated or they can be invisible. Buttons have four states, therefore, the Timeline for a button has only four frames labelled Up, Over, Down and Hit (refer to Table 4.8).

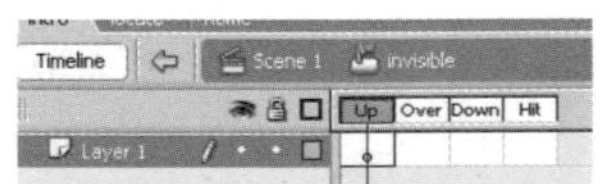

Figure 4.28 Timeline for button

Up	Represents how the button will look when the mouse pointer is not over it
Over	Represents how the button will look when the mouse pointer is over it
Down	Represents how the button will look when it is clicked by the mouse
Hit	Represents the area of the button that responds to the mouse click

Table 4.8 Button states

▸▸ HOW TO ... Create a button

1 Draw an object, or choose an object to be used as the button.

2 Use the **Selection Tool** to select the object.

3 Click on the **Modify** menu → **Convert to Symbol** → enter the name for the symbol → in the **Type** area, select **button** → click on **OK**.

▶▶ HOW TO ... Edit the button symbol

1 Use the **Selection Tool** to select the button.

2 Click on the **Edit** menu → **Edit Symbols**. This displays the Timeline for the button.

3 The original button symbol has been placed in Frame 1 – the **Up** state. You need to decide how the button will change for each state.

4 Click in Frame 2 (**Over**) and insert a keyframe. Click on the **Insert** menu → **Timeline** → **Keyframe**. This automatically places a copy of the button from Frame 1 into Frame 2.

5 Alter the appearance of the button for the **Over** state.

6 Repeat steps 4 and 5 for Frame 3 (**Down**).

7 Click in Frame 4 (**Hit**) and insert a keyframe.

8 Click the **Oval Tool** in the Toolbox → hold down the **Shift** key and draw a circle that covers the button.

9 Click on the **Edit** menu → **Edit Document** to return to the main timeline.

TIP!

You can insert a keyframe by pressing **F6** on the keyboard.

TIP!

You can insert a new symbol by pressing **Ctrl + F8** on the keyboard.

▶▶ HOW TO ... Preview the button

1 Click on the **Control** menu → **Enable Simple Buttons**.

2 Move the mouse over the button to see the different states.

▶▶ HOW TO ... Return to editing mode

- Disable the button: **Control** menu → **Enable Simple Buttons** to remove the check.

▶▶ HOW TO ... Add sound to a button

You can add sound to the different states for the button.

1 Click on the button in the **Library** panel, click on the **Options** button located in the top right corner of the panel → **Edit**.

2 In the button's timeline, add a new layer for the sound → rename the layer.

Continued ...

3 In the sound layer, in the Frame where you want to add the sound, add a **Blank Keyframe** → click in the keyframe you have created → in the **Properties** panel, click on the arrow to the right of the **Sound name** box → select a sound file from the **Sound** pop-up menu.

4 In the **Synchronisation** section, select **event** → **Repeat** → **1**.

To add a different sound to each of the button's events, repeat steps 3 and 4.

▶▶ HOW TO ... Create invisible buttons (hotspots)

1 Click on the **Insert** menu → **New Symbol** → name the symbol → make sure **button** is selected. The Timeline now shows **Scene1** and the name of the button, and also shows the button's timeline (refer to Figure 4.28).

2 In the centre of the Stage is the registration point for the button (a small cross +), and the button and the button icon are displayed in the Document Library.

3 In the Timeline, select the **Hit** frame and insert a **blank** keyframe. Click on the **Insert** menu → **Timeline** → **Blank Keyframe**.

4 Select the **Oval Tool** with a fill colour → draw a circle over the registration point → click on the **Edit** menu → **Edit Document**.

5 On the main timeline, **insert a new layer** → rename the layer **buttons**.

6 Select **Frame 1** of this layer → drag the invisible button from the library and place it over the object you want to use as a hotspot → give the instance an appropriate name.

7 Save your movie.

TIP!

*You can insert a blank keyframe by pressing **F7** on the keyboard.*

▶▶ HOW TO ... Test a movie

- Click on the **Control** menu → **Test Movie**.

TIP!

*You can test the movie by pressing **Ctrl + Enter** on the keyboard.*

Student review 4.8 – Create a button and a hotspot

Assessment objective 2b

1 *Open a new document.*

2 *Draw a shape on the Stage.*

3 *Convert the shape to a button symbol.*

4 *Create the button.*

5 *Give the layer and the instance of the symbol appropriate names.*

6 *Preview your button to make sure it reacts as it should.*

7 *Import an object into the library and add it to the Stage.*

8 *Create an invisible button and place it over the object to create a hotspot.*

9 *Test your movie.*

10 *Save your movie using an appropriate filename.*

PRACTICAL TASK 4.7 Add appropriate navigation features to movies

Assessment objective 2b

1 Open the movies you created in Practical task 4.6.

2 Refer to your navigation chart on the Planning and Review form.

3 Add appropriate buttons.

4 Save all your movies.

Understanding the Actions Panel

The Actions Panel lets you create and edit action code for a timeline, movie clip or object. If the Actions Panel is not displayed, click on the **Window** menu → **Actions**.

TIP!

*You can display the Actions Panel by pressing **F9** on the keyboard.*

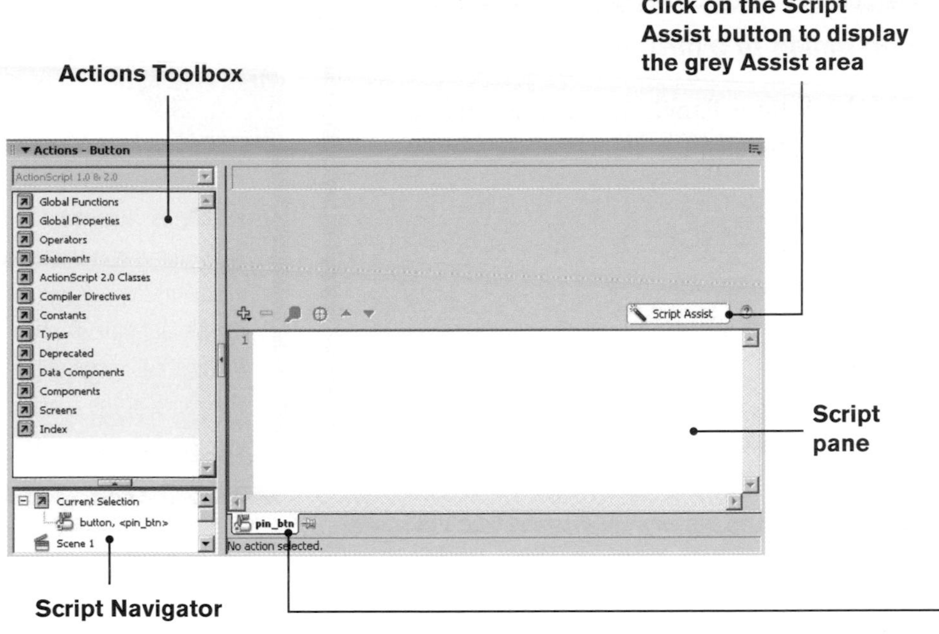

Figure 4.29 The Action Panel

Make sure you have the button selected by checking the tab at the bottom of the Actions panel.

The **Actions Toolbox** contains a list of all the ActionScript language elements. You can browse the list and add the script to the script pane by double-clicking. The **Script Pane** is where you can type in code. The **Script Navigator** displays a hierarchical list of the Flash elements that contain ActionScript. If you click on an item in the **Script Navigator**, the ActionScript will be displayed in the **Script Pane**.

Adding interactivity to the buttons

You are now going to add some simple ActionScript to the buttons to allow you to navigate between the different movies. The script will tell Flash what to do when the button is pressed, i.e. load another movie. However, Flash can only load **swf** files which are the files that are created when the movie is published.

Flash can only load **swf** files. It will not load **fla** files.

HOW TO ... Create the swf files

- Click on the **File** menu → **Publish Preview** → **Flash**.

▶▶ HOW TO ... Add an action to a button

1 Select the button → open the **Actions Panel**→ make sure you have the button selected by checking the name in the tab at the bottom of the Actions panel.

2 In the **Script Pane** enter the following script.

```
on(press) {
    loadMovieNum("name.swf",0);
}
```

3 Repeat the above action for each of the buttons.

You must enter the code **exactly** as it appears using the same case and including the quotation marks, but you should replace name.swf with the name of the movie you want to load.

PRACTICAL TASK 4.8 Add actions to link movies

Assessment objective 2b

1 Open the movies you saved in Practical task 4.7.

2 Refer to your navigation chart on the Planning and Review Form.

3 Save your movies to create the **swf** files.

4 Add actions to the buttons to link the movies.

5 Test the buttons.

6 Save all your movies.

SECTION 4 • Publish and review the multimedia presentation

The following assessment objectives will be covered in this section:
2c Publish a multimedia presentation
3b Review the multimedia product against the original brief

The following knowledge, skills and understanding criteria corresponding to assessment objective 2c will be covered:

- *Optimise and publishing to different formats*

The following knowledge, skills and understanding are covered in the 'Common Skills' chapter:

- *Reviewing the quality of the finished product*
- *Fitness for purpose*

Once you have linked all your movies you need to save the movies in a suitable format.

For an OCR assessment, you may be required to save the product for distribution on CD/DVD, over a local computer network, for publishing on the web or for distribution on a mobile device.

Flash has templates that you can use to create multimedia products suitable for publishing to different formats (see Figure 4.30).

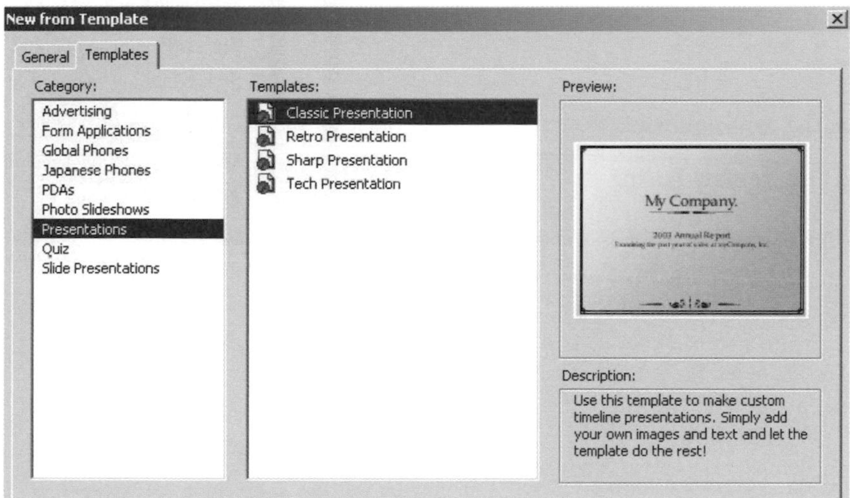

Figure 4.30 New from Template dialogue box

PUBLISHING THE MULTIMEDIA PRESENTATION

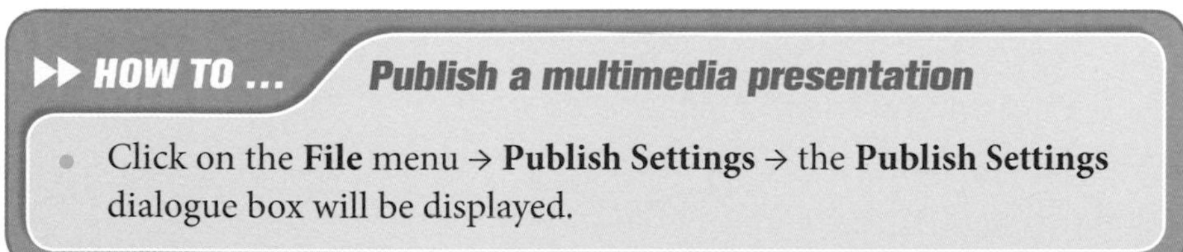
HOW TO ... **Publish a multimedia presentation**

- Click on the **File** menu → **Publish Settings** → the **Publish Settings** dialogue box will be displayed.

For details on the Publish settings, refer to 'Saving an animation in a format suitable for the web' on page 151.

The multimedia product will be saved in Flash (**swf**) format and HTML (**html**) format.

You can also save the files in a format that may not involve online delivery. The files can be saved as a **projector** for either Windows (**exe**) or Macs (**hqx**). Projector files maintain the movie's interactivity. Alternatively, you can use **File** → **Export** to export the movie in **avi** and **mov** formats. These files are not interactive.

The projector files and non-interactive files can be played directly from a computer or can be delivered on a CD or DVD.

PRACTICAL TASK 4.9 Save, test and review the interactive multimedia product

Assessment objectives 2c, 3b

1 Refer to the 'Magnificent Bowl – Interactive Presentation' assignment brief on page 159.

2 Save your movies in the required format.

3 Test the movies to make sure they operate correctly.

4 Save all your movies.

5 Review your product against the original brief.

6 Record this on the Planning and Review Form.

Refer to 'Reviewing your work' on page xxi of the 'Common Skills' chapter.

You should now have all the skills, knowledge and understanding required to complete an OCR iMedia sample or live assessment for this unit.

UNIT 5
DIGITAL SOUND

INTRODUCTION

This unit of the iMedia qualification relates to your understanding of digital sound files. In this unit you will develop an understanding of what sound is and how it is produced. You will be able to evaluate digital sound content from a variety of sources and applications such as the web, CD-ROMs and entertainment.

LEARNING OUTCOMES

After studying this unit you will be able to:

- understand the technology required to produce digital sound files
- analyse the effective use of digital sound content in a range of existing professional applications
- use computer software to create digital sound content.

RESOURCE TOOLKIT

Hardware

- Computer with sound card
- Microphone
- Speakers
- Access to Internet
- Printer

Software

- Windows
- Windows Media Player
- Audacity
- Word-processing application

Other

- Pencil and paper
- Audio CD
- Planning and Review Form
- Evidence Checklist

ABOUT THIS UNIT

In this unit you will be looking at the technology required to produce digital sound files: the computer hardware and appropriate peripheral devices such as microphones, speakers, mini-disk recorders and mixing equipment.

You will plan the sound files you need to capture using various planning methods, e.g. conceptualisation, visualisation and/or storyboarding.

You will use computer hardware and software to capture and create digital sound files including music, sound effects and voice-overs. You will follow good practice for naming and storing these files on your computer.

Finally you will review your final sound files against the original assignment brief and obtain appropriate feedback (e.g. from peers or your tutor). You will need to identify any parameters or constraints that influenced your choices regarding asset manipulation, file formats or compression techniques used.

The Student Review activities and Practical Tasks in this chapter will allow you to develop your understanding of the requirements for an OCR assessment and practise the skills required for the Unit 5 syllabus. The sound files you create in this chapter **CANNOT** be submitted for assessment purposes.

ASSESSMENT FOR UNIT 5

Assessment for this unit takes the form of practical activities which are assessed by your tutor and are then externally moderated by an OCR Examiner-Moderator. The assessment may be an OCR-set assessment or one which has been locally devised.

In order to achieve a pass in the unit, you must demonstrate skills in each one of the assessment objectives.

Assessment tasks

You will be required to complete tasks that address all of the assessment objectives and you must provide evidence that shows where and how the assessment objectives have been met. Your assessment work should be submitted to OCR via e-portfolio. You should therefore save all evidence in electronic format. Any hard copy evidence should be scanned and saved electronically.

Evidence

You will need to:

- *provide copies of the sound files you capture as part of the tasks*
- *provide a copy of the final sound file(s)*
- *complete forms provided by OCR to show how you have planned and reviewed the final sound file*
- *provide evidence of editing the sound files, adding effects and saving in an appropriate format*
- *complete an Evidence Checklist to identify where and how the assessment objectives have been met*

SOFTWARE

For this unit you will be using Windows XP, Windows Media Player and a software program called Audacity which is a free **cross-platform** audio editor that allows you to manipulate digital audio waveforms. If you do not have a copy of this software it is available for download from http://audacity.sourceforge.net/.

Key terms

Cross-platform software that can run under different operating systems, e.g. Windows 98, Windows XP, Mac OS, Unix, Linux

ABOUT THIS CHAPTER

This chapter for Unit 5 is divided into three sections. You must work through the sections in sequence.

- In Section 1 you will learn what sound is, and why it is used. You will also learn how to select appropriate hardware and peripheral devices used to capture sound and you will plan the sound files you will need to capture.
- In Section 2 you will learn how to capture sound and use digital sound software to import sound files to your computer.
- In Section 3 you will learn how to create and edit sound files, save the files in an appropriate format and review the final sound files against the original brief.

AOs 1a, 1b, 2a, 3a

AOs 2a, 2b, 2c, 2d

AOs 2a, 2b, 2c, 2d, 3b

SECTION 1 • Understand the technology required to create digital sound files

The following assessment objectives will be covered in this section:

1a Select appropriate hardware

1b Select appropriate peripheral devices

2a Use sound in professional applications

3a Plan the sound files to a specific brief

The following knowledge, skills and understanding criteria corresponding to assessment objectives 1a, 1b, 2a and 3a will be covered:

- *Computer hardware*
- *Peripheral devices*
- *Sources of sound*

The following knowledge, skills and understanding are covered in the 'Common Skills' chapter:

- *Ways of identifying client requirements*
- *Planning methods*

WHY IS SOUND USED?

Sound is used in many products that are used for entertainment, education or business.

In the world of entertainment, sounds are added to games for many reasons, for example, to enhance actions, as background music, to confirm choices.

In education, sounds could be added to a multimedia CD to let people hear the sounds made by different instruments, or the different sounds made by exotic birds. In quizzes they could be added to confirm correct or wrong choices to answers. The spoken word can be added to an electronic dictionary to help with the pronunciation of words or to help in learning a foreign language. It is also used as an aid to visually impaired people.

In business, sound may be added to company information held on CDs or the Internet to help to identify the company. For example, a short musical chord or a collection of notes could be used as a musical logo – known as a **jingle**. An example of this can be heard whenever an advert appears on television for a computer that contains an Intel processor. When the word 'Intel' is said you will hear a short sound of approximately four notes. This short sound has become associated with Intel even if the name is not mentioned.

Key terms

Jingles *A memorable, engaging melody that is constructed to stay in memory – 'ringing a bell'.*

WHAT IS SOUND?

Before we look at the technology needed to produce digital sound files, it is important to understand what sound is and how it is produced.

Sound is created when an object vibrates causing the air molecules around the object to move in patterns causing waves of pressure. If you could see these waves of pressure they would look like the ripples caused in a still pool of water when a pebble is thrown in. We hear the sounds because our ears are sensitive to the changes in pressure in the air.

Sound waves vary in **amplitude** and **pitch**. The amplitude of a sound is measured in decibels (dB) and the pitch of the sound is measured in hertz (Hz). The wavelength of a wave is the length of one complete wave cycle.

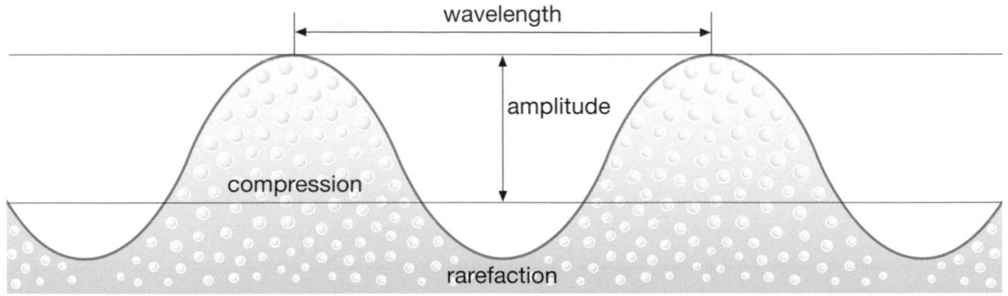

Figure 5.1 Sound wave diagram

Different sounds are represented by unique sound waves. Some examples of different sound waves are shown in Figure 5.2.

Key terms

Amplitude *The amount of energy in the sound wave which determines the loudness or volume of a sound.*

Pitch *Describes how high or low a note is. This depends on the frequency of the sound.*

Frequency *The number of vibrations per second. This determines the pitch of the sound which may be in a range from low or high.*

Tone *A musical or vocal sound considered with reference to its quality in terms of pitch and volume.*

Timbre *Also referred to as the tone colour, this is the quality of the tone of a sound that distinguishes it from other sounds. For example, two different instruments playing the same note, at the same pitch, will have different sound qualities – this difference is the timbre of the sound.*

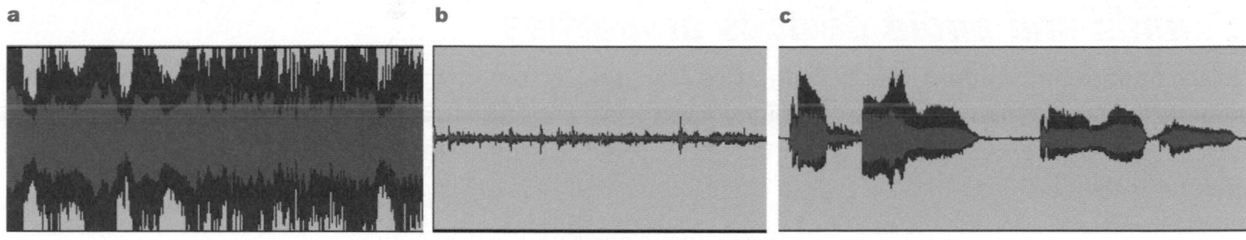

Figure 5.2 Sound wave for: **a)** the sound of a 'didgeridoo' **b)** trickling water **c)** the phrase 'OCR iMedia'

SELECTING APPROPRIATE HARDWARE

A computer system consists of three main parts: input devices such as a keyboard, mouse, microphone; output devices such as a monitor, printer, headphones or speakers; and the system unit which houses the electrical and storage devices such as a hard disk, memory (RAM), CD-ROM drive and sound card.

You can discover the CPU speed of your computer and how much RAM there is by checking the system information.

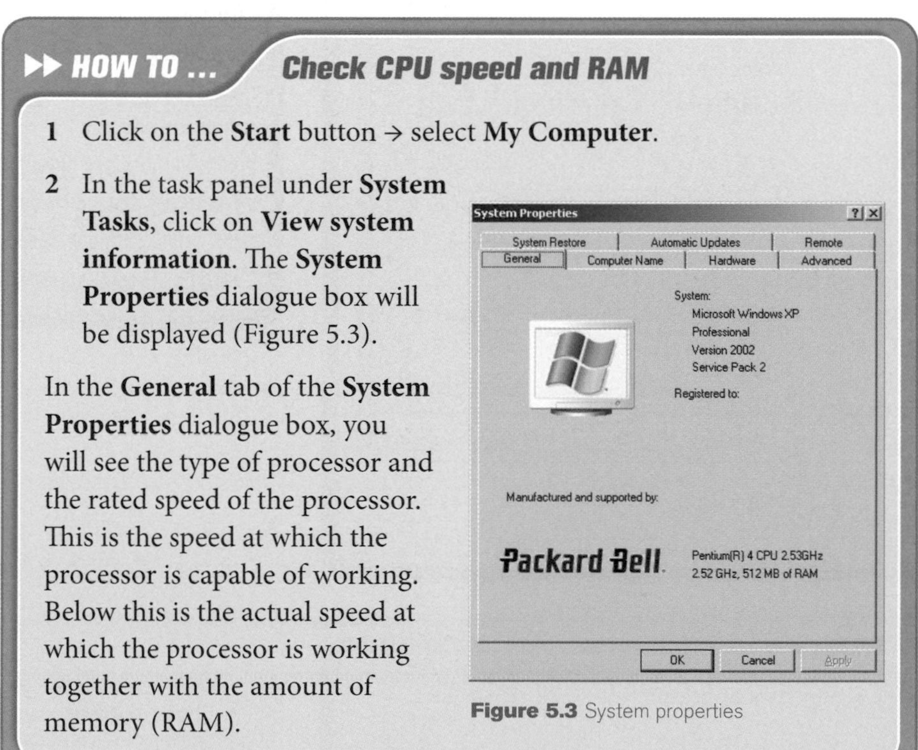

HOW TO ... Check CPU speed and RAM

1 Click on the **Start** button → select **My Computer**.

2 In the task panel under **System Tasks**, click on **View system information**. The **System Properties** dialogue box will be displayed (Figure 5.3).

In the **General** tab of the **System Properties** dialogue box, you will see the type of processor and the rated speed of the processor. This is the speed at which the processor is capable of working. Below this is the actual speed at which the processor is working together with the amount of memory (RAM).

Figure 5.3 System properties

Sound cards

In order to be able to record and play sound files on a computer you must have a sound card. Most home computers come equipped with a sound card and may also be supplied with a microphone. This enables the computer to output sound through speakers, record sound input from a microphone connected to the computer and manipulate sounds that are stored on a disk.

Sounds and audio devices properties

In the **Sounds and Audio Devices Properties** dialogue box you can assign sounds to some system events. For example, if you try to copy files to a floppy disk and if there is no disk in the floppy disk drive you can assign a sound to play to warn you.

The Sounds and Audio Devices Properties dialogue box also allows you to change the default volume of the sound card, the volume of the speakers, the type of speakers, e.g. mono, stereo, headphone, surround sound, and the option to place a volume icon in the notification area of the Taskbar.

▶▶ HOW TO ... Open the Sounds and Audio Devices Properties dialogue box

1 From the Taskbar, click on **Start** menu → select **Control Panel**.

2 Select **Sounds, Speech, and Audio Devices.**

3 Then select **Sounds and Audio Devices.**

4 The **Sounds and Audio Devices Properties** dialogue box is displayed (Figure 5.4).

5 Click on the **Audio** tab to display the name of the default device for sound recording and playback.

6 Click on the **Voice** tab to display the name of the default device for voice recording and playback.

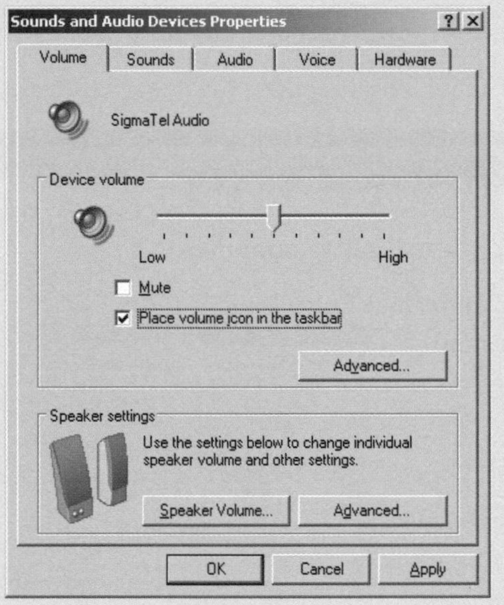

Figure 5.4 Sounds and Audio Devices Properties dialogue box

*The options available in the **Sounds and Audio Devices Properties** dialogue box may be different to those shown in Figure 5.4 depending on the sound card you have installed in your computer.*

Student review 5.1 – Identify sound and audio device properties

Assessment objective 1a

1 *Open the **Sounds and Audio Devices Properties** dialogue box.*

2 *Look in the **Audio** tab and make a note of the default device (usually the sound card) used for sound playback and sound recording.*

If your computer network will not allow you access to this, you can check the name of your sound card through Audacity. Refer to 'How to check the preferences' on page 213.

Volume and recording control

The **Sounds and Audio Devices Properties** dialogue box allows you to control the volume of recordings as well as playbacks. It also enables you to select different recording devices depending on the peripherals connected to your computer.

In this unit you will be controlling the volume of recording using Audacity software.

You will look at this in more detail in Sections 2 and 3.

PRACTICAL TASK 5.1 Identify and record the hardware specification

Assessment objective 1a

The following table shows the specification produced by the Multimedia PC Working Group in June 1995 for a level 3 multimedia PC. It has never been updated. Using a similar table, identify the hardware you will use and say why. Make a note of this on a Planning and Review Form.

CPU	75 MHz Pentium
RAM	8 MB recommended
Disks	3.5-inch 1.44 MB floppy drive and 500 MB fixed drive minimum.
Optical storage	4 × CD-ROM drive
Audio	CD-ROM quality audio output
Video	Display of 64k colours at 640 × 480 and fast enough for video at full frame rate in 15-bit colour
Inputs	101-key keyboard, two-button mouse
Input/Output	Serial port, parallel port, MIDI I/O, joystick port
System software	Binary compatibility with Windows 3.11

SELECTING APPROPRIATE PERIPHERAL DEVICES

A peripheral device is anything that is added to the computer to extend its functionality. Peripheral devices can be external, e.g. a scanner, or internal, e.g. a wireless LAN card. Originally a peripheral device was defined as anything that was not part of the main computer, i.e. the memory and microprocessor. However, a monitor, keyboard and mouse are considered to be essential parts of a modern personal computer and these devices are no longer considered to be peripheral devices.

Peripheral devices

- Disk drive
- Printer
- Scanner
- Microphone
- Speakers
- Camera
- Wireless LAN card
- Joystick
- Webcam
- Bar code reader
- Data glove
- Light pen
- Graphic tablet

Microphone

Different types of microphone

Your computer may have been supplied with a microphone for you to record voice messages directly to your PC. However, you may wish to record sounds away from the computer, for example, the sound of a bird in the garden, or the background noises of people talking and laughing in a café. To record these sounds you will need a microphone connected to a portable recorder.

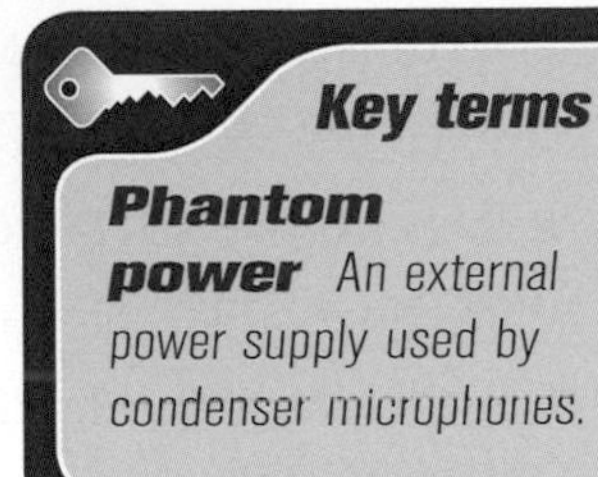

A microphone is a transducer which converts sound waves into electrical signals. Three popular transducer types are **condenser**, **dynamic** and **ribbon**.

A condenser microphone (Figure 5.5) uses a freely suspended thin plastic film diaphragm and a stationary backplate which are charged to form a capacitor. They can be charged by **phantom power** or by a permanently charged electret material in the backplate or diaphragm. The distance between the two plates varies as the sound waves strike the diaphragm and the sound is converted into electrical signals.

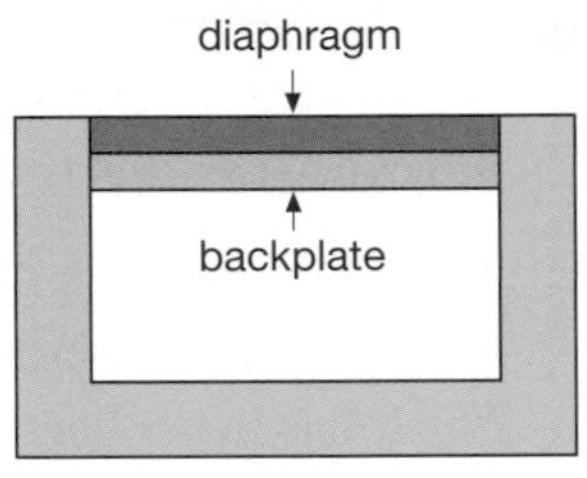

Figure 5.5 Condenser microphone

A dynamic microphone (Figure 5.6) does not need an external power source. It uses a magnet and a diaphragm with a coil of wire attached. This thin coil of wire, known as the voice coil, is suspended from the diaphragm into an air gap in the magnet. As the sound wave strikes the diaphragm, it vibrates causing the voice coil to move in the magnetic field thereby generating an electrical signal.

A ribbon microphone works in a similar way to a dynamic microphone. The sound wave moves a metallic ribbon suspended in a magnetic field in the head of the microphone.

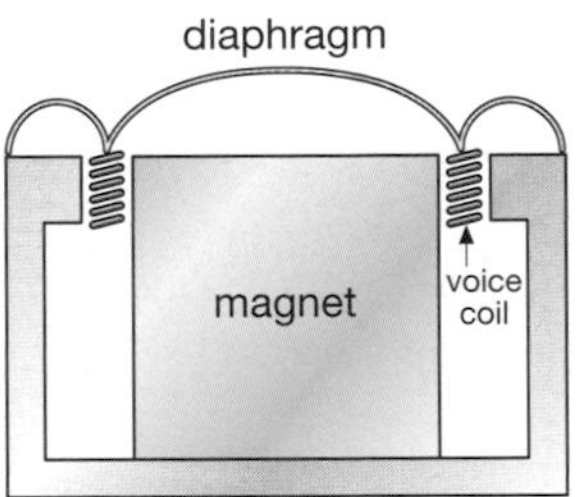

Figure 5.6 Dynamic microphone

Microphone polar patterns

Microphones also differ in their sensitivity to sounds coming from different directions. The **polar pattern** of a microphone shows diagrammatically how the sensitivity varies with direction.

Omnidirectional (Figure 5.7) microphones can pick up sounds from all directions and are suitable for both interviewing and recording atmospheric sounds. They are useful when interviewing outdoors as they are less sensitive to wind noise and explosive breath sounds, known as popping. They are generally lower in cost than other types of microphone.

Unidirectional (Figure 5.8) microphones pick up sounds from only one direction and are good at rejecting sounds from other directions. This makes them suitable as speech microphones. The most common unidirectional microphone is the cardioid microphone which has a 'heart-shaped' polar pattern; it picks up sound at the front of the microphone but rejects sounds at the back.

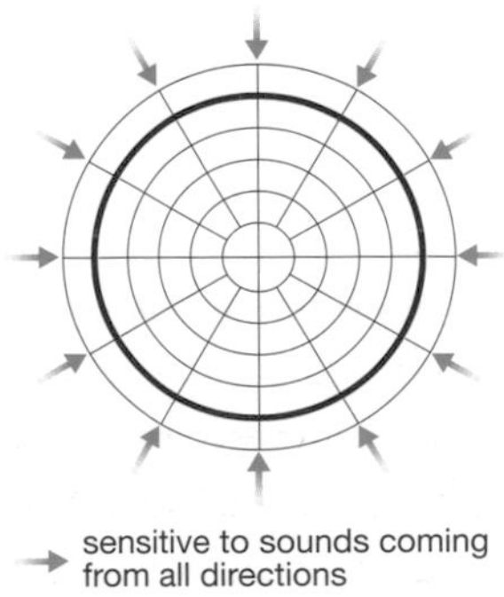

Figure 5.7 Omnidirectional polar pattern

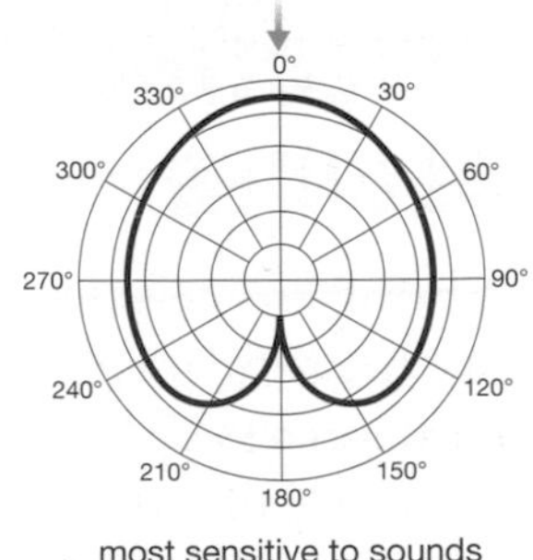

Figure 5.8 Unidirectional polar pattern

Bidirectional (Figure 5.9) microphones receive sound from two directions, the front and back, but reject sounds from the sides.

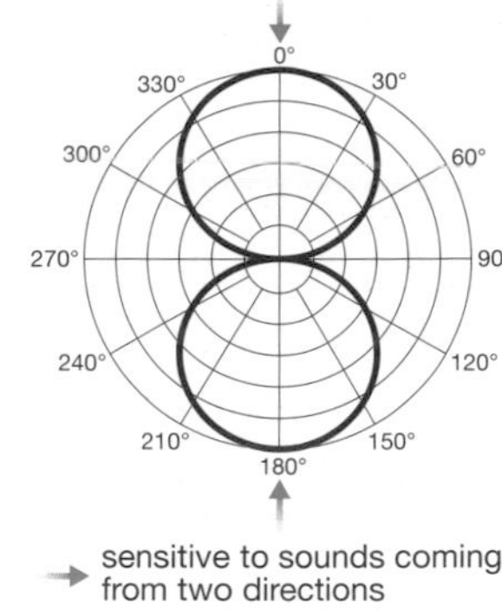

Figure 5.9 Bidirectional polar pattern

Forms of microphone

Microphones come in different shapes and sizes and the type of microphone you use will depend of the type of sound you want to capture.

A hand-held microphone is portable and can be useful for conducting interviews. It can also be attached to a microphone stand.

Personal microphones, known as a lavalier or clip-on mic, are small microphones that can be clipped on to a piece of clothing, usually a tie or jacket lapel, of the person speaking. These are good microphones for dialogue because they pick up the sounds from the chest.

Shotgun mics have the most highly directional polar pattern and are used for picking up dialogue from a distance.

Microphones often pick up noises that you may not hear, so it is useful to wear headphones when you are recording so that you can hear what the microphone is picking up. Some microphones supplied for computers also have headphones attached.

Student review 5.2 – Use a microphone

Assessment objective 1b

Visit www.bbctraining.com/modules/2857/1.asp to find the answers to the following questions.

1. *How should you hold a microphone?*
2. *What should you not do when holding a microphone?*
3. *What noises might the microphone pick up if interviewing someone indoors?*
4. *What tips could you give someone for interviewing in a large room?*
5. *What noises might the microphone pick up if interviewing someone outdoors?*
6. *Where should you position your microphone when interviewing?*

Sound recording devices

MiniDisc recorder

MiniDisc (MD) technology was announced by Sony in 1991 and was introduced in 1992 as a disc-based digital medium originally intended for storing digital audio. When introduced the MiniDisc was seen as a replacement for cassette recorders but it was overtaken by the recordable CD. In 1993 Sony introduced MD Data for storing computer data which has been overtaken by the USB flash pen.

In January 2004, Sony introduced Hi-MD. This was a revamp of the original MiniDisc system to include the ability to work with three different types of disc making it possible to store files of different types.

MEDIUM	STORAGE CAPACITY
Conventional MiniDisc	160 MB Audio 140 MB in Data mode
Conventional MiniDisc formatted to Hi-MD	305 MB
Hi-MD	1 GB

Table 5.1 Hi-MD storage capacities

A microphone can be connected directly to a MiniDisc making it popular as a portable recording device.

MiniDiscs store audio signals using a **compression** technique called ATRAC (Adaptive TRansform Acoustic Coding) which provides near CD-quality recordings. However, each time it is copied, the data is recompressed and this reduces the quality of the recording over time.

> **Key terms**
>
> **Compression** The process of removing redundant data from a digital media file to reduce its size or the bandwidth used.

Digital Audio Tape (DAT)

Digital Audio Tape recorders are widely used in professional broadcasting because of the high quality recordings they produce. They make digital recordings onto 6 mm tape cartridges at 44,100 or 48,000 samples per second. A DAT recorder is usually capable of digital output so that the recordings can be transferred digitally to a computer.

Mixing equipment

A mixing desk (Figure 5.10), or sound desk, is a device that can be used to balance or combine sounds from different sources. It has two main sections: an input section and an output section. A number of microphones can be connected to the input section, e.g. of singers in a group. The mixing desk is then used to balance and combine the sounds from each of the microphones before sending it to a device, e.g. a loudspeaker connected to the output section.

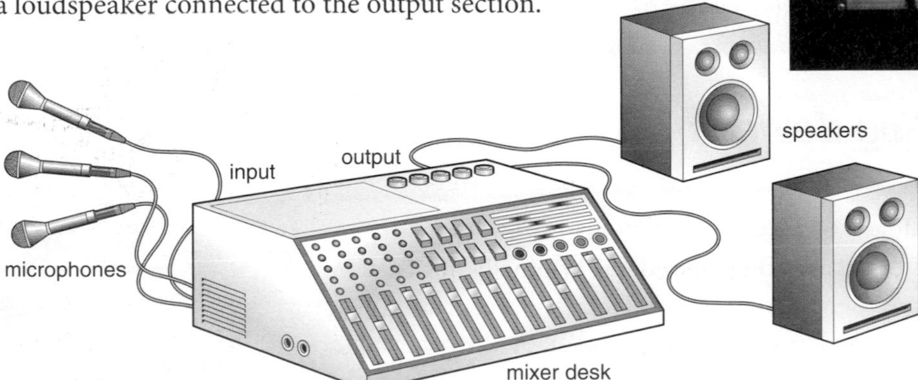

Figure 5.10 Mixing desk with microphones and speakers

Some mixing desks can also be used to:

- add sound effects
- produce stereo sound from mono signals by adjusting the **pan** and balance controls
- provide the phantom power required by condenser microphones
- interface with computers or other recording equipment.

Key terms

Panning Spreading a signal to be output over a number of different speakers.

Throughout this unit we will be using the following scenario which is similar to an OCR brief. We will use the scenario to develop the knowledge, skills and understanding you will require in order to complete an OCR-assessed assignment.

Assignment brief

Magnificent Bowl – Soundtrack

You work as an assistant sound recordist at a local radio station preparing sound materials for use in adverts and jingles.

The local ten-pin bowling alley, Magnificent Bowl, has approached the radio station to produce a series of adverts to promote the facilities at the bowling alley. They would like a series of adverts that would help to create an audio **ident**.

You have been asked to prepare the following sound materials to be used in this advertising campaign:

- Appropriate background music
- Sounds of people laughing and enjoying themselves
- An appropriate sound effect
- A short voice-over giving contact details

Key terms

Ident A simple statement that helps identify the company.

Refer to 'Planning your work' on page xiv of the 'Common Skills' chapter.

PLANNING THE SOUND FILES TO A SPECIFIC BRIEF

When planning the sound files for the brief, you should first consider what sounds you will need and how you will obtain the sample sounds. In an OCR assignment you will be expected to do all of the following:

- **Capture** (i.e. record) at least one original sound of approximately 3–5 seconds in length.
- Use digital software to **create** (i.e. modify or amend) existing sound files of approximately 10–15 seconds in length.
- Capture or create a voice-over of approximately 15–30 seconds.

For an OCR assessment you will be required to obtain at least six different sounds. Not all sounds will be used, but you should record your initial ideas for the files you will be obtaining on the Planning and Review Form.

In the 'Magnificent Bowl – Soundtrack' assignment brief, you may decide that you need the following sounds:

- Background music
- Sounds of people laughing
- The sound of a bowling ball rolling down the alley
- The sound of a bowling ball rolling down the gulley
- The sound of the pins falling over
- A voice recording of someone reading out the contact details
- A **stab/sting** after a strike (where all ten pins fall in a single bowl)

Key terms

Stab/sting *A single chord or sound that adds dramatic impact to an event, e.g. a bell ring after a strike.*

You may be able to think of other sound that would be suitable, e.g. the sound of drinks glasses, announcements over the public address system, a phone ringing or the sound of the ball being returned.

When obtaining sound you must remember to observe copyright laws. You must acknowledge the source of your files and record this on the Planning and Review Form. You will be required to reference any sounds that you have not captured yourself.

SOURCES OF SOUND

It is possible to purchase CDs with royalty-free music. This means that you can use the music without making any further payments. There are also many online web-based sites that hold samples of copyright free sounds. You may also be able to obtain sound from broadcast TV or radio but when using these sources you must observe copyright laws.

One of the sounds that you will be working with may be one that has been obtained from a sound library. Many sound libraries charge for their sounds but it is possible to obtain royalty-free sounds.

Student review 5.3 – Locate sources of sound files

Assessment objective 2a

1. *Connect to the Internet and visit www.findsounds.com .*
2. *Search for bowling alley sounds.*
3. *Review the sounds, and save any that you think may be suitable for use in the advertising campaign.*
4. *Record the names and file types on the Planning and Review Form.*
5. *Make sure that you acknowledge any copyright.*

SECTION 2 • Use computer hardware and software capture and save digital sound

The following assessment objectives will be covered in this section:

2a Use sound in professional applications

2b Capture sound

2c Create digital sound content

2d Save sound files

The following knowledge, skills and understanding criteria corresponding to assessment objectives 2a, 2b, 2c and 2d will be covered:

- *Main elements of sound*
- *Why it is used*
- *Limitations*
- *How to capture sound*
- *How to use digital sound software to create, produce and import sounds*
- *File management*

To capture and create the sounds needed for the bowling alley, you are going to use an audio editing program called Audacity which can be downloaded free of charge from **http://audacity.sourceforge.net/**

HOW TO CAPTURE SOUND

Capturing or recording sound means working with a sound system. This could be a simple microphone that came with your computer or it could involve using a studio with expensive microphones, mixers and other recording equipment. No matter what equipment you are using, they all use the same concept for capturing the sound. This involves converting sound waves into an analogue electrical signal and then into digital information that can be stored on a computer.

When a sound wave is captured by a microphone, the vibrations are converted into an analogue electrical signal. Recording these signals onto a tape recorder is an example of an analogue recording.

If the microphone is connected to a computer, the analogue signal is converted into a digital recording. For recordings, this conversion is performed by an Analogue-to-Digital Converter (ADC) which is part of the sound card in the computer.

The ADC captures the electrical signal at regular intervals (Figure 5.11) and represents this as a digital number that can be saved on the computer. This process is called sampling. The more samples that are taken, the better will be the quality of the recording. By capturing the signal thousands of times a second you can get a very good quality sound. For example, a **sample rate** of 44,100 times per second (44,100 Hz) will produce CD-quality sound. This is

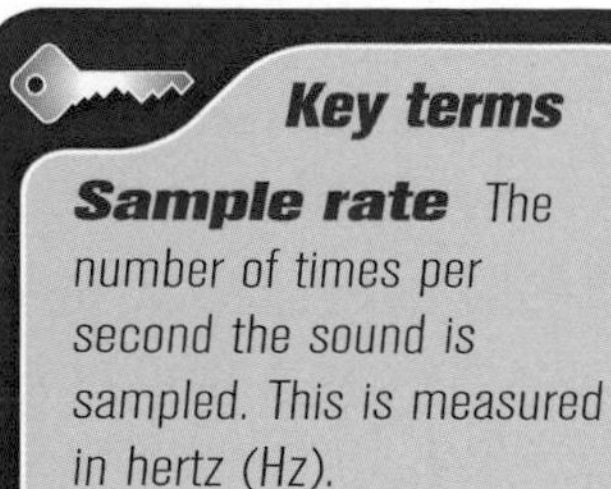

Key terms

Sample rate The number of times per second the sound is sampled. This is measured in hertz (Hz).

the standard sampling rate chosen for audio CDs because it includes all the frequencies that the human ear can detect.

The **sample format** (or bit rate) refers to the number of bits that will be used each second to represent the sound signal. The bit depth refers to the amount of data that is stored for each sample. For CD quality recordings this is usually 16 bit. The bit rate is represented in thousands of bits per second (kbit/s) and directly affects the file size and the sound quality of the recording. A high bit rate will give better sound quality and a larger file size. Lower bit rates will result in poorer sound quality and smaller file sizes. The recommended bit rate in Audacity is 32-bit float.

Key terms

Sample format This represents the number of digits that will be used to represent the sample.

To playback digital audio a Digital-to-Analogue Converter (DAC), also part of the sound card, reads the sample and recreates the signal (Figure 5.11).

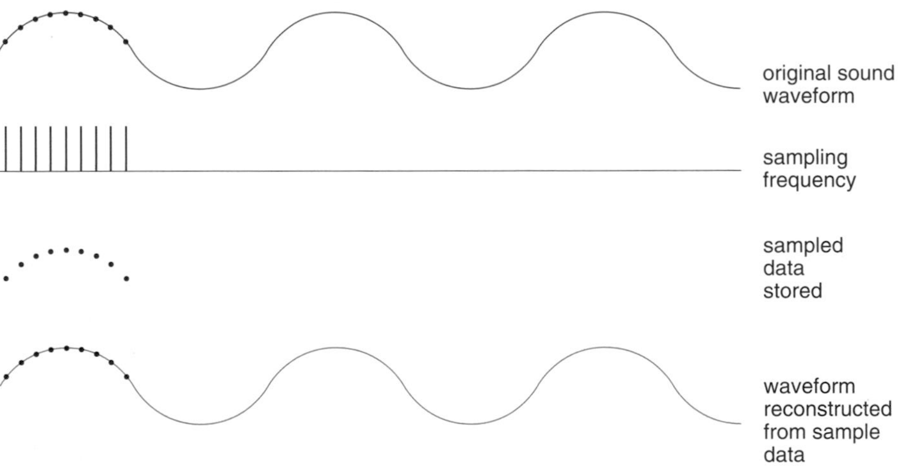

Figure 5.11 Sound sampling diagram

FILE FORMATS

When creating sound files for use in multimedia, it is not always necessary to record the sounds in CD-quality stereo. This is because playing high quality sound on a computer often slows the computer down, and also the files take up a large amount of disk space or space on the CD.

The size of a sound file can be made smaller in a number of ways. A CD-quality sound, recorded in stereo at 44,100 samples per second, can be halved in size by combining the two stereo channels to make one mono channel. Also, halving the number of bits used to measure each sample from 32 bits to 16 bits will result in a smaller file size. However, the quality of the sound will also sound grittier.

The most effective method of reducing the file size is to use a compression technique. Sound files are stored on a computer as a list of numbers, ones or zeros. These numbers can be stored in either an uncompressed or compressed format. An uncompressed sound file contains the original list of numbers from the recording. These files can be very large, 5–20 MB for each minute,

Refer to page 211 for a description of these file types.

depending on the quality of the recording. **wav** and AIFF are examples of uncompressed audio files.

There are two types of file compression – lossy and lossless:

- **Lossy compression** uses a technique to reduce the size of a file by throwing away some of the information contained in the sound file. The information that is lost is not noticeable to the human ear, and so the quality of the sound is not usually affected. Compressing a file using this technique can reduce the size of a file to one-tenth of its original size. This form of compression is used when transferring files over the Internet and for storing large collections of digital audio. **mp3** and Ogg Vorbis are examples of files using lossy compression formats.
- **Lossless compression** reduces the size of a file without losing any of the original information or quality. The file will be compressed to about one-half of the original size and therefore take up less disk space. When the file is uncompressed the playback will sound exactly the same as the original. FLAC is a popular open format file type that employs lossless compression, but this is not supported by Audacity.

Sound files can be saved in different formats. Audacity can work with the following file formats:

- wav – short for Waveform. Developed by Microsoft, this file format usually contains uncompressed audio in **PCM** format. This is the default audio format for Windows computers.
- AIFF – Audio Interchange File Format. Developed by Apple, this file format also contains uncompressed audio in PCM format. This is the default audio format for Macintosh computers.
- Ogg Vorbis – This is a compressed audio format that was developed as a free alternative to **mp3**. They are about the same size as **mp3** files but they are not as common.
- mp3 – MPEG1 Layer 3. This is a compressed audio format which compresses audio files to one-tenth of their original size without losing the quality of the recording.

Key terms

PCM Pulse Code Modulation The standard audio format for CDs sampled at 44,100 Hz. It uses a lossless storage method which keeps all of the samples of the audio track.

The **mp3** format is patented and cannot be used in free programs. However, Audacity can use existing mp3 encoders that can be downloaded separately. The first time you try to export **mp3** files, Audacity will ask for the location of the mp3 encoder. Refer to the Audacity web page http://audacity.soundforge.net for further information.

Audacity will not work with the following file types:

- **wma** (**W**indows **M**edia **A**udio) a compressed audio file format developed by Microsoft.
- **aac** (**A**dvanced **A**udio **C**oding) digital audio compression used by Apple for the iPod and on iTunes.

Before we start capturing and creating the sounds, you will need to make yourself familiar with the Audacity screen.

▶▶ HOW TO … Start Audacity

1 Click on the **Start** button.

2 Click on **All Programs**.

3 Click on **Audacity**.

Audacity will open and the Audacity screen is displayed (Figure 5.12).

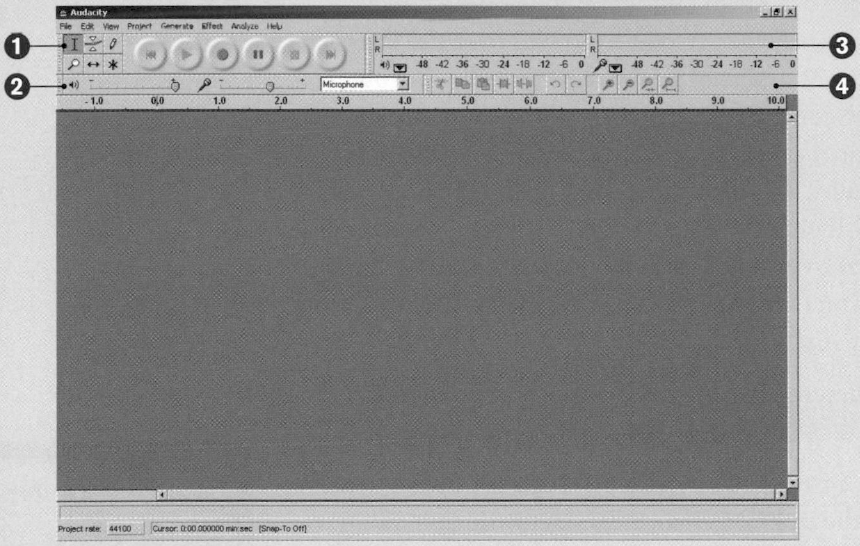

Figure 5.12 The Audacity screen

There are four toolbars:

1 Control toolbar
2 Mixer toolbar
3 Meter toolbar
4 Edit toolbar

WORKING WITH AUDACITY

Audacity writes all the recorded and changed audio to a file called *projectname_data*. This file will be located wherever you save the project. It is very important to create a new project before recording or importing audio files.

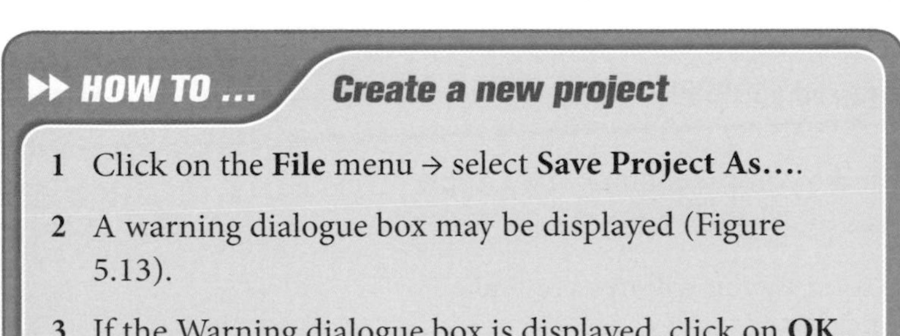

▶▶ HOW TO … Create a new project

1 Click on the **File** menu → select **Save Project As…**.

2 A warning dialogue box may be displayed (Figure 5.13).

3 If the Warning dialogue box is displayed, click on **OK**.

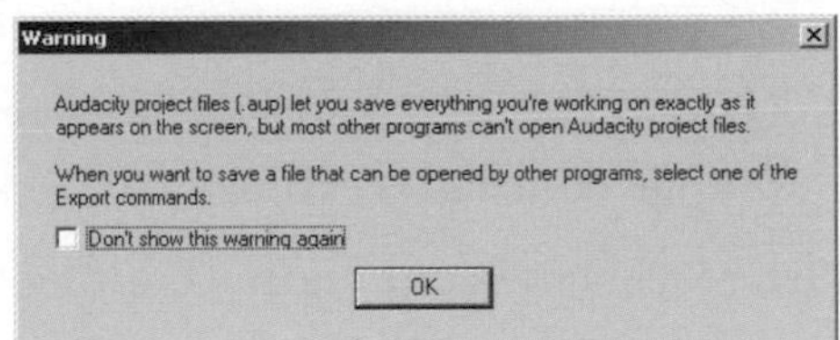

Figure 5.13 Warning dialogue box

Continued ...

4 Make sure the name of the folder where you want to save your files is displayed in the **Save in** section of the dialogue box.

5 In the file name box, give the project a suitable name.

6 Click the **Save** button.

HOW TO ... Check the preferences

1 Click on the **Edit** menu → select **Preferences....**

2 Click on the **Audio I/O** tab → this displays the name of the device (sound card) used for recording and playback of audio files.

3 Click on the **Quality** tab → this displays the default sample rate and sample format for the audio files.

4 Click the **Cancel** button.

It is very important to check the preferences before starting to work on your project.

PRACTICAL TASK 5.2 Identify client requirements, peripheral equipment and sounds to be used for the Magnificent Bowl brief

Assessment objectives 1b, 2a, 2b, 3a

1 Read through the 'Magnificent Bowl – Soundtrack' assignment brief on page 207.

2 Identify the peripheral equipment you will use for this project.

3 State the purpose of the sounds required by the brief.

4 Note down your initial ideas of the sample sounds that will be produced.

5 Identify which of your sounds will be captured and which will be created.

6 Find out the name of the Audio I/O device on your computer and determine the default sample rate and sample format that will be used for the audio files.

7 Record all your findings in the Planning and Review Form.

When opening, or importing, uncompressed audio into Audacity there are two ways in which this can be done:

- **Make a copy of the original before editing** Audacity will copy the entire audio file into the project data folder. This method is slower and uses more disk space, but it is a safer method should anything happen to the original file, e.g. accidentally deleted. It is also easier to back up the project because all the files are contained in the project data folder.

- **Read directly from the original file** Audacity will read the original data file and save only the changes in the project data folder. During playback, all data that remains unchanged will be played from the original file. This method is faster and uses less disk space.

▶▶ HOW TO ... Set the file format preferences

1 Click on the **Edit** menu → select **Preferences....**

2 Click on the **File Formats** tab.

3 Select the required option.

Student review 5.4 – Decide the method for importing files

Assessment objective 2c

1 *Discuss with your tutor which method of importing files you should choose and set the preferences for this.*

2 *On the Planning and Review Form give reasons for your decision.*

▶▶ HOW TO ... Import a file into the Audacity project

1 Click on the **Project** menu → select **Import Audio**.

2 Locate the file you want to open.

3 Select the file.

4 Click the **Open** button.

When you open a file in Audacity it is displayed in the window as a waveform. This is the default way of visualising audio. It is possible to change the display to a spectrogram, which shows the amount of energy in different frequency bands.

Student review 5.5 – Import a sound into Audacity

Assessment objective 2c

Create an Audacity project called **bowling** *and import one of the sounds that you have saved.*

Figure 5.14 shows a stereo waveform. The top waveform is for the left channel and the bottom one is for the right channel. A mono track would only show one waveform. To the left of the waveform is the track Control Panel (Figure 5.15).

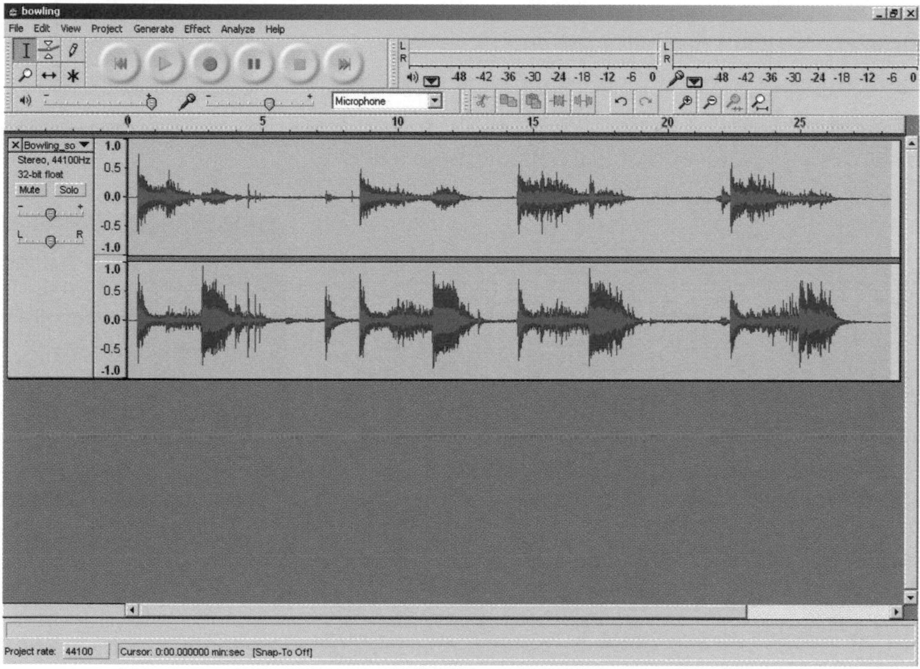

Figure 5.14 Stereo channels

>> **HOW TO ... Display the Track pop-down menu**

- Click on the down arrow to the right of the track title.

The Track menu allows access to special commands that apply to the individual tracks, such as:

- renaming the track
- changing the order of tracks
- changing the display from waveform to spectrum
- splitting a stereo track so that each separate track can be modified independently
- changing the track from stereo to mono
- changing the track from mono to stereo
- changing the sample format
- changing the sample rate.

On the track Control Panel (Figure 5.15), below the track title, is information about the track. The **Mute** button is used to stop the track from playing and will be displayed blue when it is selected. Clicking on the play button plays only those tracks where the **Solo** button has been selected – this will be displayed in blue if selected.

>> **HOW TO ...**

Select the entire track

- Click in the grey area of the Control Panel below the sliders.

>> **HOW TO ...**

Close the track

- In the Control Panel, click on the cross to the left of the track title.

The track will be removed but the Audacity window, and any other tracks, will remain open.

The top slider is the gain control. This affects the volume of the track. The bottom slider is the pan control. This affects the balance of the output between the left and right speakers.

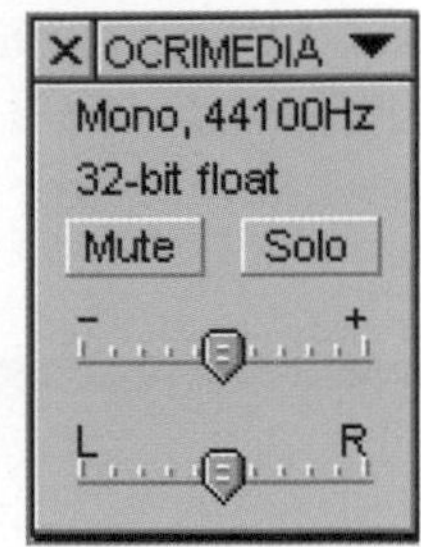

Figure 5.15 Track Control Panel

To the right of the track Control Panel, just before the waveform, is the vertical ruler (see Figure 5.14). This gives a guide to the loudness of the sound you see in the waveform. This is expressed in decibels (dB) and the level is shown relative to 0 dB which, in Audacity, represents the hearing of someone with an undamaged ear. A range of –1.0 dB to 1.0 dB is the maximum recommended because any part of the waveform that lies outside these levels will be **clipped**. As you can see in Figure 5.16, parts of the top wave have been clipped.

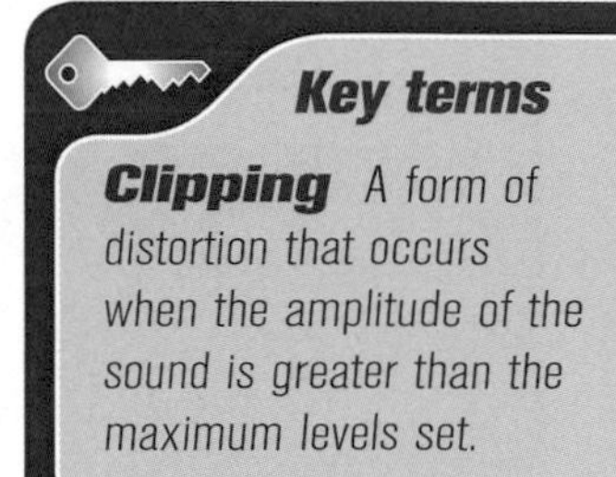

Key terms

Clipping A form of distortion that occurs when the amplitude of the sound is greater than the maximum levels set.

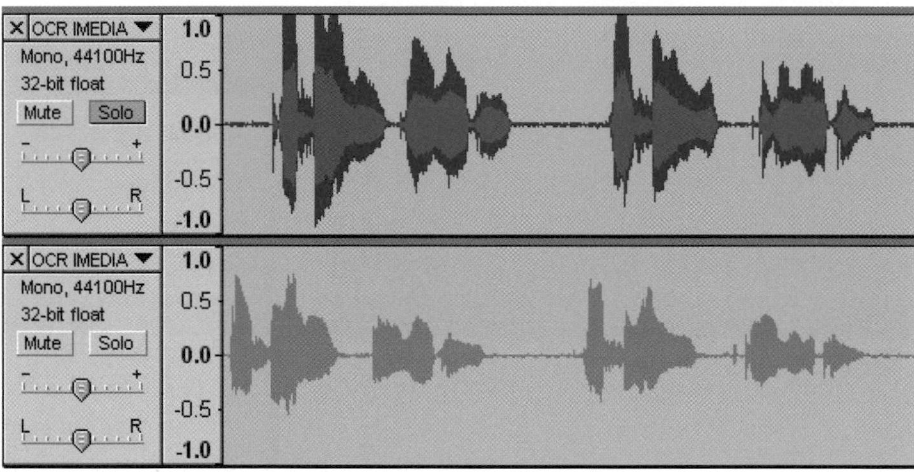

Figure 5.16 Example of a clipped waveform

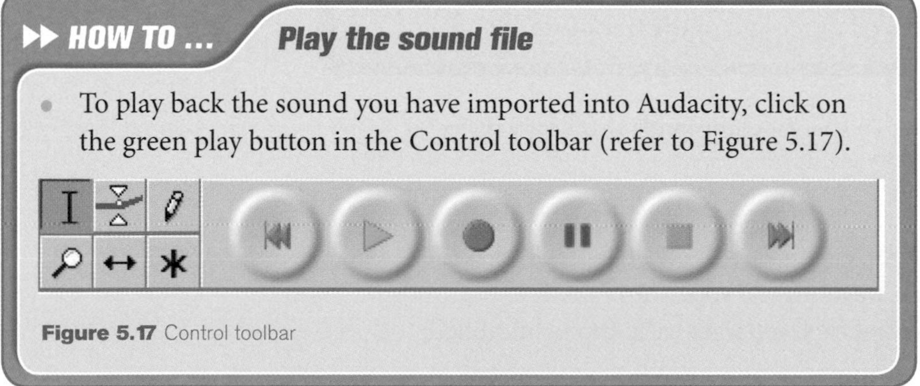

HOW TO ... Play the sound file

- To play back the sound you have imported into Audacity, click on the green play button in the Control toolbar (refer to Figure 5.17).

Figure 5.17 Control toolbar

The six small buttons on the left of the Control toolbar are the editing tools. The six round buttons on the right of the Control toolbar are the audio control buttons. These work just the same as the buttons on a video recorder.

Saving/naming conventions

Audacity creates a project file, an **aup** file, which is a format that has been optimised for Audacity so that it can open and save projects quickly. If you are working with large sound files, Audacity breaks these files into smaller pieces and places them in a directory with a similar name to the project. For example, if you are working on a project called *bowling*, Audacity will create a project file called *bowling.aup* (where the general information about your project is stored) and will store the audio files in a folder called *bowling_data*. This file cannot be read by other programs, so it is important that, when you have finished editing your audio file, you use the export command to save the file in the required format.

TIP!

When you import a compressed file, e.g. **mp3**, edit it and then export it in a lossy format, it will be compressed again, and lose additional information. To avoid this, use lossy formats, i.e. **mp3** and Ogg Vorbis, **only** for finished recordings.

Naming an audio track

To help you identify the tracks in a project, it is good practice to name each individual track.

HOW TO ... Name a track

1. In the track Control Panel, click on the down arrow to the right of the track title.
2. Click on **Name**.
3. In the dialogue box that appears, give the track a suitable name and click the **OK** button.

Student review 5.6 – Name a soundtrack and save a project

Assessment objective 2d

1. *Using a suitable name, rename the soundtrack you imported in Student review 5.5.*
2. *Save your project keeping the name* **bowling**

HOW TO ...

Save the project

- Click on the **File** menu → select **Save Project**.

SOUND CATEGORIES

Digital sound encompasses a hierarchy of sound categories which include natural sounds, ambient sound, foley effects (see pages 218 to 219) and voice-overs.

The first recorded sound effect was of Big Ben striking. It was recorded on 16 July 1890 and is now available in the public domain.

Natural sound

Natural sounds are those that occur naturally such as those made by water, air, fire, the earth, animals, insects, fish and sea creatures.

Sound effects

Natural sound effects can be categorised as hard or soft effects. Hard effects are effects that need to be timed to coincide with on-screen actions such as a door slamming, a car driving by or someone stirring a cup of tea. Soft effects are those that do not need to synchronise with a particular action on-screen such as the wind, falling rain or the sound of a bird singing. These soft sounds are often referred to as **background sound effects** or ambient sound. The sound of many people in a crowded situation, where the speech is indistinguishable and the language unrecognisable is known as a 'walla'.

Key terms

Background sound effects Sounds used to indicate a setting, e.g. a rain forest. Background sounds are also called 'ambience' or 'atmos' (atmosphere).

Other sound classifications

Other classifications of sound include the following:

- **Human sounds**, e.g. those made by the voice, body or clothing
- **Cultural sounds**, e.g. in a city environment, a domestic environment, factories and offices
- **Mechanical sounds**, e.g. office machinery, kitchen appliances, transportation, demolition
- **Signals**, e.g. bells, horns, whistles, warning signals
- **Quiet and silence,** e.g. room tone, night time, only heart beating, only breathing

Student review 5.7 – Capture and create sounds

Assessment objectives 2a, 2b, 2d

1. *Connect to the Internet and, using a search engine, search for the first recorded sound effect of Big Ben striking.*
2. *Save the file using a suitable filename.*
3. *Using a microphone and recording device, try to capture the following sounds:*
    - *Natural sounds of weather, e.g. wind, rain*
    - *Animal sounds, e.g. dogs barking, ducks quacking*
    - *Bird sounds*
4. *Transfer these sounds from your recorder to the computer saving them in an appropriate file format in a suitable location.*

PRACTICAL TASK 5.3 **Capture ambient sounds**

Assessment objectives 2a, 2b, 2d

In the assignment brief for the 'Magnificent Bowl – Soundtrack' on page 207 you need to include some ambient sounds of people enjoying themselves and laughing.

1 Think of places you could record this ambient sound, e.g. in the college/school refectory, at your local youth club or even at a bowling alley.
2 Use your recording equipment to record these sounds. You may want to make more than one recording.
3 Transfer these sounds to your computer, saving them in an appropriate file format and location.

When capturing or creating sounds, it is useful to keep a log of the sounds. This should include the date, what the sound is and the environment in which it was recorded. Keeping this metadata about each sound will help you to identify the sounds and to assess their suitability for use in future projects.

PRACTICAL TASK 5.4 **Produce a log of sounds**

Assessment objective 2d

1 Produce a log of the sounds you have captured/created for the bowling alley.
2 Make a note of the details on the Planning and Review Form.

Foley sounds

Foley sound is a technique named after Jack Foley who was a sound engineer at Universal Studios in the 1930s. These are sounds that are recorded in a studio after the filming of a scene has taken place. They are used to emphasise a movement or action. Such effects could be the sound of a bunch of keys jangling, footsteps in the snow, the unzipping of a jacket or the sound of a shirt ripping. They are recorded by specialists in foley effects called foley artists.

Creating sound effects

Sometimes these sound effects are created naturally but some may be created artificially. Some examples of how to create sound effects artificially are shown in Table 5.2 on the next page.

SOUND	CREATED BY
Fire	Crumpling cellophane paper
Eagle taking off	Flapping a pair of leather gloves
Marching army	Shaking a box full of small rocks
Heavy footsteps	Falling bags of sugar
Rain	Salt sprinkled onto paper
Hailstones	Rice sprinkled onto paper
Thunder	Beating the lower strings of a piano
Quill pen writing on parchment	Plastic spoon scratched on rough paper
Crunching snow (footsteps on soft snow)	Tease a ball of cotton wool apart
Water running over stones	Straw blowing into a glass of water
Horses hooves	Half coconut shells on hard surface

Table 5.2 Artificial ways to create sound effects

To create the right sound effect you may need to experiment with everyday objects.

Simple sound effects are easy to recreate, however more elaborate sound effects such as machine-gun fire, a police siren or an explosion are not so simple. For these more elaborate sounds, sound libraries may be used.

Sound that is used in games, on educational CDs or on the Internet, may be played as a result of a trigger, i.e. user interaction, such as a button click, a mouse moving over an object, or a number of points being earned.

When recording sounds to be used on web pages, consideration must be given to the size of the file. There are two ways that the file can be delivered; it can be downloaded from the server to the user's computer or by streaming, where the file is delivered bit by bit and starts to play as it is being downloaded. The speed at which these downloads take place is determined by the bandwidth.

Bandwidth is used to describe the width of the range of frequencies or sound waves that an electronic signal occupies on the transmission medium. In digital systems it describes the rate at which data can be transmitted over a given period of time expressed as megabits per second (Mbit/s).

PRACTICAL TASK 5.5 — RECORD FOLEY SOUNDS

Assessment objectives 2a, 2b, 2d

From the assignment brief for the 'Magnificent Bowl – Soundtrack' on page 207, you need to include some additional sounds.

1 With your tutor, or peers, discuss types of sounds that could be included.
2 Using foley techniques, try to create and record the sounds.
3 Experiment with different everyday objects to try and create the sounds.
4 Use your recording equipment to record these sounds. You may want to make more than one recording.
5 Transfer these sounds to your computer.
6 Save them in an appropriate file format and location.

SECTION 3

- Use computer software to create digital sound content and review the sound files

The following assessment objectives will be covered in this section:

2a Use sound in professional applications

2b Capture sound

2c Create digital sound content

2d Save sound files

3b Review the sound files against the original brief

The following knowledge, skills and understanding criteria corresponding to assessment objectives 2a, 2b, 2c, 2d and 3b will be covered:

- *Best practice sound principles*
- *How to capture sound*
- *How to use digital sound software to create, produce and import sounds*
- *File management*

The following knowledge, skills and understanding are covered in the 'Common Skills' chapter:

- *Reviewing the quality of the finished product*
- *Fitness for purpose*

RECORDING VOICE-OVERS

Many adverts or audio promotions will include some narration or dialogue. This may be recorded by the sound recordist or a member of the production team. However, professional productions often use the services of a professional voice artist. These voice artists fall into two categories – character actors and narrators. Character actors are used to bring life to animated characters, whilst narrators present documentary information using a **clean voice** with little, or no accent. A narrator usually speaks from a pre-prepared script, timing the delivery to within a fraction of a second of the required length.

Key terms

Clean voice When speaking, the sound should be free from hissing 's' sounds (sibilance), the sound of the tongue touching the palate of the mouth, or the sound of loud breaths between words (popping).

Recording directly into Audacity using a microphone

Sometimes you may want to record directly to the computer. Before making a recording it is important to check that the preferences are set to the required sample format and sample rate. You should also check that the file formats are set as required. When you are recording directly to Audacity, you should use the settings shown in Table 5.3.

Sample rate	44,100 Hz
Sample format	32-bit
Channels	Mono
Uncompressed export format	**wav** (Microsoft 16-bit PCM)

Table 5.3 Audacity settings for direct recordings

Recording the voice-over in mono will save disk space whilst still producing a high-quality recording.

Student review 5.8 – Check audacity settings

Assessment objective 2c

Check the settings in Audacity and, if necessary, change the settings for the sample rate, sample format, number of channels and uncompressed export format to those specified in Table 5.3.

Setting up the microphone

To make a recording directly into Audacity you will need a microphone connected to the computer. This should be connected using the input jack socket which is usually labelled with the word 'mic' or will have a small microphone symbol. It is usually colour-coded pink.

Before you start recording, check the Audio I/O preferences to make sure Software Playthrough (Play new track while recording it) is not checked.

▸▸ HOW TO ... Check the Audio preferences

1 Click on the **Edit** menu → select **Preferences....**

2 Select **Audio I/O** tab.

3 Click in the box next to **Software Playthrough (Play new track while recording it)** to remove the tick and then click the **OK** button.

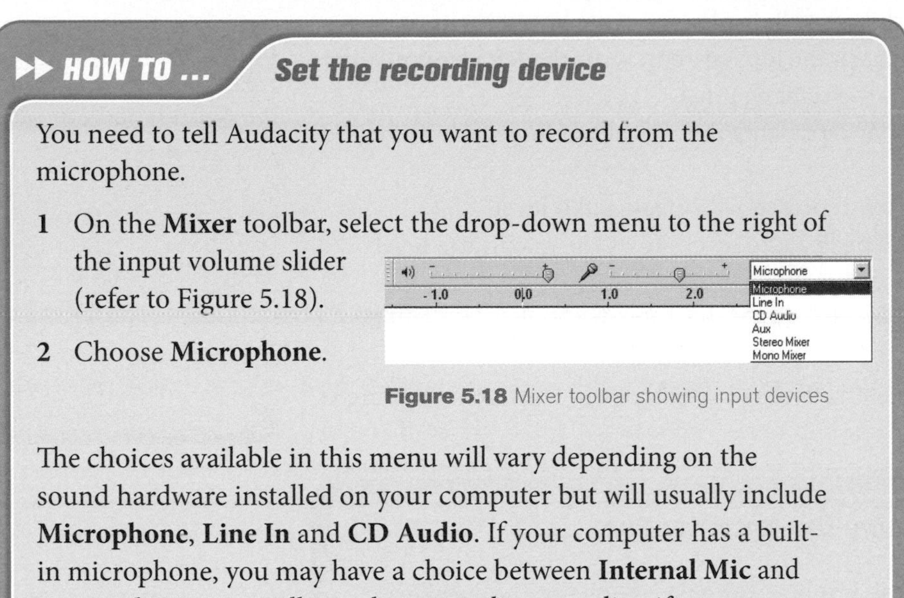

HOW TO ... Set the recording device

You need to tell Audacity that you want to record from the microphone.

1 On the **Mixer** toolbar, select the drop-down menu to the right of the input volume slider (refer to Figure 5.18).

2 Choose **Microphone**.

Figure 5.18 Mixer toolbar showing input devices

The choices available in this menu will vary depending on the sound hardware installed on your computer but will usually include **Microphone**, **Line In** and **CD Audio**. If your computer has a built-in microphone, you may have a choice between **Internal Mic** and **External Mic**. You will get a better quality recording if you use an external microphone.

The slider controls on the **Mixer** toolbar (see Figure 5.18) allow you to set the input and output volume levels. The left slider is the output volume and the right slider is the input volume for the input device.

The **Meter** toolbar (Figure 5.19) gives a visual representation of the levels of audio going into and out of Audacity. The left (green) bars show the output (playback) and the right (red) bars show the input (recording).

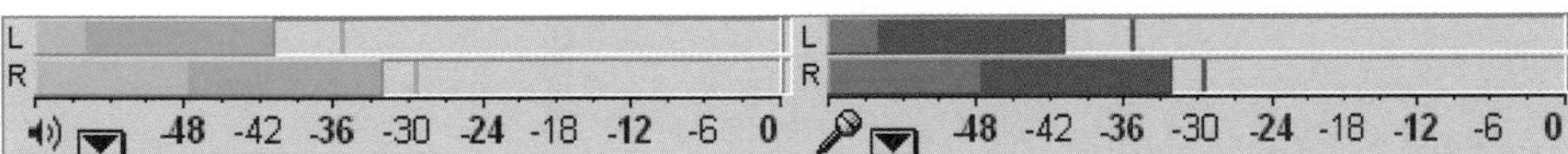

Figure 5.19 Meter toolbar

The meters are active when you play or record audio. You can also monitor input levels before you start recording by selecting **Monitor input** from the pop-down menu to the right of the microphone, as shown in Figure 5.20.

When recording you should aim to record at around –12 dB and should peak as close as possible to the 0 dB mark. Going over the 0 dB mark will result in the sound being distorted and will cause audible clicks and crackles.

Figure 5.20 Input menu

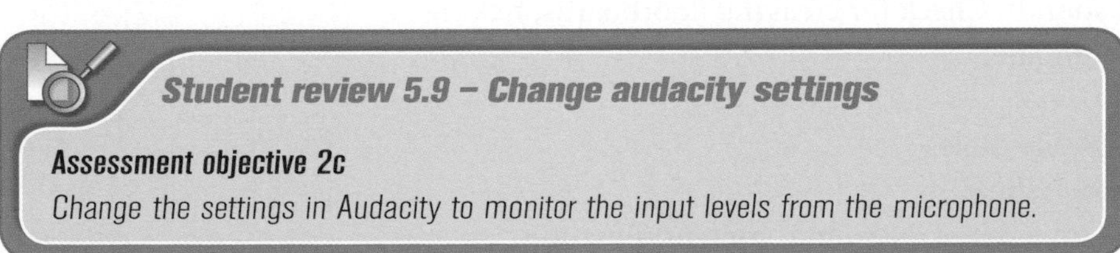

Student review 5.9 – Change audacity settings

Assessment objective 2c

Change the settings in Audacity to monitor the input levels from the microphone.

The meters in the **Meter** toolbar (Figure 5.19) show several characteristics of the audio:

- The left-hand end of the meter represents silence.
- For mono recordings, the level will be shown in only the top bar.

- For mono playbacks, both bars will display the same level of output.
- For stereo recording/playback the top bar represents the left channel and the bottom bar represents the right channel.
- The lighter shade on the bar represents the average audio level with regard to loudness.
- The darker shade on the bar represents the peak audio level.
- The line to the right of the peak audio level shows the maximum level achieved in the last 3 seconds.
- The right-hand end of the meter shows the point at which audio will be clipped.
- At the far right of each meter, clipping indicators will light up if clipping is detected.

▶▶ HOW TO ... Disable the Meter toolbar

1 Click on the arrow to the right of the microphone or the speaker.

2 From the pop-down menu, select **Disable**.

If you are using an older, slower computer, disabling the **Meter** toolbar may help to speed up Audacity's processing of the audio.

▶▶ HOW TO ... Show the Meter toolbar again

1 Click on the **Edit** menu → select **Preferences....**

2 Select the **Interface tab.**

3 Click on the option to **Enable Meter Toolbar**.

Before you start recording set the recording level for the microphone.

Tips for creating good quality sound recordings

- Turn off all mobile phones and watch alarms.
- Monitor sound while you are recording using a set of headphones so you will be able to hear what the microphone is picking up.
- Eliminate any unwanted sounds. Check for creaking floorboards, ticking clocks, the sound of the computer.
- Do not move around.
- Do not handle the microphone cable.
- If possible, use a microphone stand.
- Keep sound records – the time of the recording, content, situation, equipment used etc.

HOW TO ... Record directly from the microphone

1 Click on the red **Record button** on the Control toolbar, or press the **R** key on the keyboard. 

2 If there is clipping in the output meters you should make the track quieter by using the input volume slider.

3 When you have finished recording, click on the yellow **Stop button** on the Control toolbar, or press the spacebar on the keyboard. 

TIP!

If clipping is detected, you should stop recording, lower the volume of the input source and then start recording again.

HOW TO ... Save your file to disk

1 Click on the **File** menu → select **Export as Wav** (for Windows) *or* **Export as AIFF** (for Mac).

2 Give the file a suitable name.

3 Click on **Save**.

Student review 5.10 – Record narration

Assessment objectives 2b, 2c

1 *Think about a topic you are interested in.*

2 *Record yourself speaking about this topic as if you were talking to a friend.*

3 *Make the recording directly in Audacity.*

4 *Experiment with disabling and enabling the **Meter** toolbar. Did this affect the speed at which Audacity processed the audio file?*

5 *When you have finished recording, transcribe the recording.*

6 *Work through the script and try to improve it.*

7 *Record the script again.*

8 *Give the audio track a suitable name.*

9 *Save your project file giving it a suitable name.*

Tips for writing a good script

Before recording a good quality voice-over, it is important to write a good quality script.

When writing your script here are some tips to follow:

- Write conversationally as if you are speaking to one person.
- Use an informal tone.
- Don't use very long sentences.

- Vary the length of the sentences.
- Mark on the script where you will take your breaths.
- Talk about only one idea in each sentence.
- Make sure your ideas flow from one sentence to the next.
- Check everything you write by reading it out loud before recording.
- Write everything the way you would say it, for example, pound for £, one hundred for 100, et cetera for etc.
- Use 'we' or our' to make the narrator appear as part of the audio production, company or program.
- Rehearse your script before making the recording.

PRACTICAL TASK 5.6 **Write a script for a voice-over**

Assessment objective 2a

For the 'Magnificent Bowl – Soundtrack' assignment brief on page 207, write a script informing people about the facilities at the club and giving information about the opening hours and membership details. You could also include the address and telephone number and any information about special offers. The length of your voice-over should be approximately 15–30 seconds.

Rules for creating and using voice-overs

When recording your voice-over, you should try to make a 'clean' recording. The following tips may help you to avoid recording some unwanted sounds when using a microphone:

- Reduce the effects of 'breaths' and 'pops' by using a pop shield between the speaker and the microphone.
- Position the microphone about 3"–6" away from your mouth. Move closer to the mic to improve the sound of the recording and make your voice more intimate. Moving further away increases the pick up of sound from the room around you and will make your voice sound distant.
- Record in a quiet environment. Position the microphone away from your computer or monitor to avoid unwanted noise.
- When you are ready to record, turn away from the microphone and take a deep breath, exhale, take another deep breath and then turn to the microphone and start to speak. Using this technique will help to avoid the sound of your intake of breath being recorded at the start of the recording.
- Speak clearly and keep an even pace.
- Don't close your mouth at the end of a sentence because this will create a popping sound.
- If the microphone picks up unwanted 'breaths', try speaking above the microphone rather than directly into it.

TIP!

A pop shield can be made using an embroidery ring and a stocking.

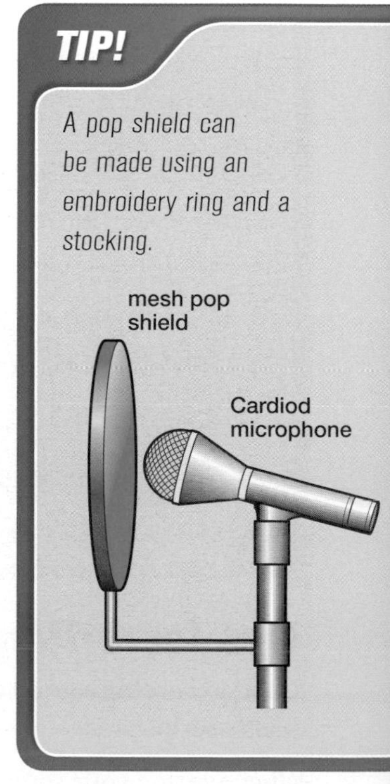

PRACTICAL TASK 5.7 **Record a voice-over**

Assessment objectives 2b, 2c, 2d

1 Open the **bowling** project file.

2 For the 'Magnificent Bowl – Soundtrack' assignment brief on page 207, record a voice-over using your script created in the Practical task 5.6.

3 Experiment with the position of the microphone.

4 Give the voice-over audio track a suitable name.

5 Save the **bowling** project file.

IMPORTING MUSIC FROM A CD

The assignment brief has asked for appropriate background music. You will need to identify the music you are going to use. This music could be recorded from an audio CD, although you will have to be aware of copyright issues.

When you place an audio CD into the computer's CD or DVD drive, Windows Media Player (Figure 5.21) usually starts, and the first track on the CD will start to play. You will need to stop the track from playing until you are ready to make your recording.

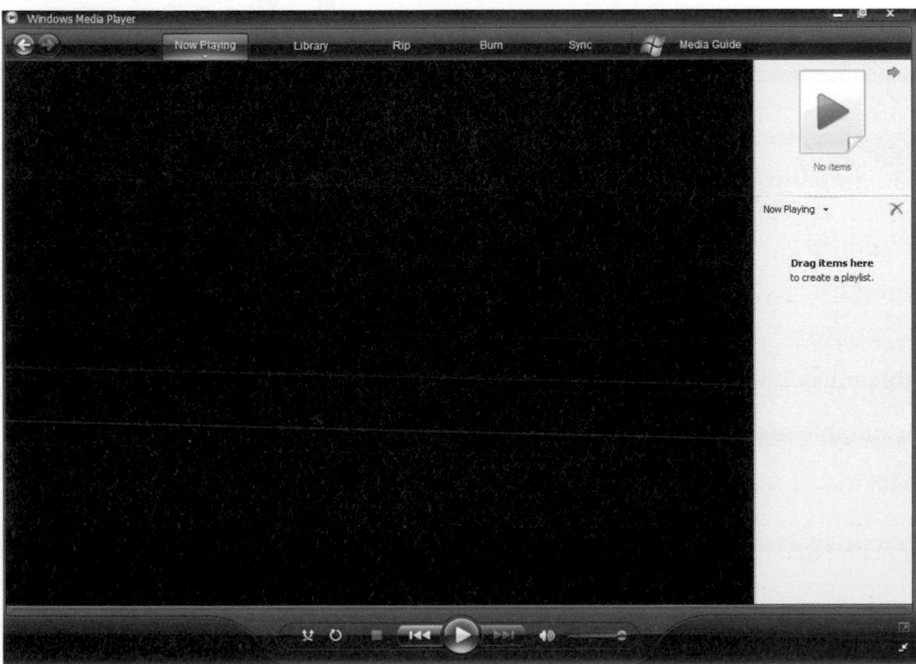

Figure 5.21 Windows Media Player

Windows Media Player will be easier to manage if you enable the mini player mode. This displays the playback controls on the Taskbar when Windows Media Player is minimised (see Figure 5.22).

Figure 5.22 Mini player mode

▶▶ HOW TO ... Enable mini player mode

1 Right-click on a blank area of the Windows Taskbar (e.g. click below the clock) but not on a Taskbar button for any program that is running.

2 Select **Toolbars** from the pop-up menu.

3 If **Windows Media Player** is not ticked, select it from the sub-menu. If it is already ticked, click outside the menu to close it.

▶▶ HOW TO ... Set the recording device

1 On the **Mixer** toolbar, select the drop-down menu to the right of the input volume slider.

2 Choose **CD Audio**.

▶▶ HOW TO ... Record the music

1 Select the track you want to record in Media Player.

2 Minimise Media Player by clicking on the **Minimize** button.

3 In Audacity, click on the **Record** button.

4 In the Media Player playback controls, click on the **Play** button.

▶▶ HOW TO ... Stop recording the music

1 In Audacity, click on the **Stop** button.

2 On the Media Player playback controls, click on the **Stop** button.

PRACTICAL TASK 5.8 Capture music

Assessment objectives 2b, 2c, 2d

1 Open the **bowling** project file.

2 For the assignment brief for 'Magnificent Bowl – Soundtrack' on page 207, record suitable music.

3 Give the music track a suitable name.

4 Save the **bowling** project file.

Observing copyright

When making recordings from audio CDs it is important that you observe copyright laws. Always record details of the artist, name of track and date. This should be recorded on the Planning and Review Form.

EDITING A SOUND FILE

Editing a sound file can involve cutting, copying, pasting, moving, adding effects and adjusting the volume.

The most basic editing is to cut and paste. The sound you have saved may be longer than you require. You may want to edit the sound to leave only the part you require. For example, in the sound file that contains the dialogue 'OCR iMedia', you may want to remove the sound of 'OCR' and keep only the sound for the word 'iMedia'. To do this you would need to listen to the sound file to find where the word 'OCR' appeared. You would then need to select this section of the sound file and cut it from the original sound file as shown in Figure 5.23.

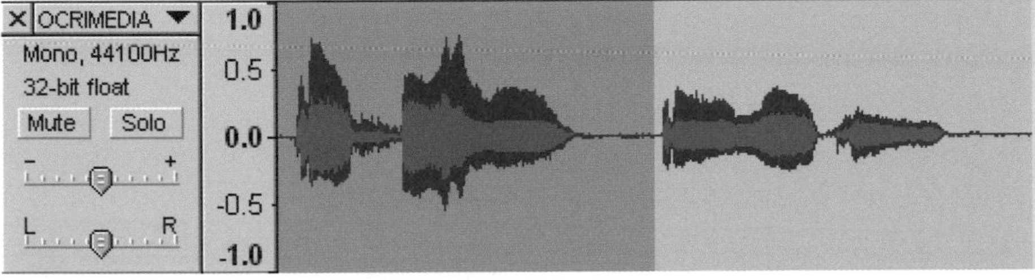

Figure 5.23 Selecting a section of a sound file

▶▶ HOW TO ... Select a section of the sound file

1 In the **Control** toolbar, click on the **Select** tool [I].

2 Drag the cursor over the section of the audio clip that you want to select.

3 The selection will appear darker (refer to Figure 5.23).

When you have made the selection, any actions will only apply to this selection.

Refer to Figure 5.12, the Audacity screen, on page 212.

▶▶ HOW TO ... Delete the selection

- Click on the **Edit** menu → select **Delete**.

▶▶ HOW TO ... Copy the selection

1 Click on the **Edit** menu → select **Copy**.

2 Move the cursor to the position on the track where the selection is to be copied.

3 Click on the **Edit** menu again → select **Paste**.

▶▶ HOW TO ... Replace the selection with silence

- Click on the **Edit** menu → select **Silence**.

▶▶ HOW TO ... Create a new sound track containing only the selection

- Click on the **Edit** menu → select **Duplicate**.

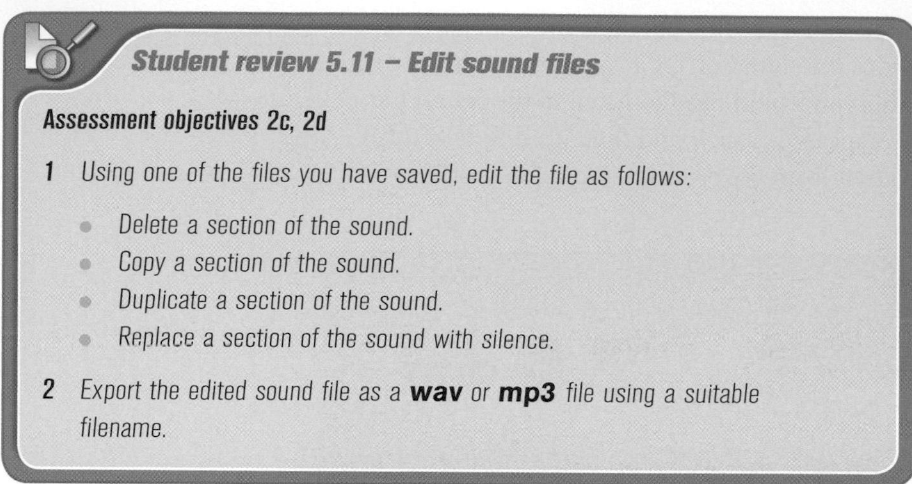

Student review 5.11 – Edit sound files

Assessment objectives 2c, 2d

1 *Using one of the files you have saved, edit the file as follows:*

- *Delete a section of the sound.*
- *Copy a section of the sound.*
- *Duplicate a section of the sound.*
- *Replace a section of the sound with silence.*

2 *Export the edited sound file as a* **wav** *or* **mp3** *file using a suitable filename.*

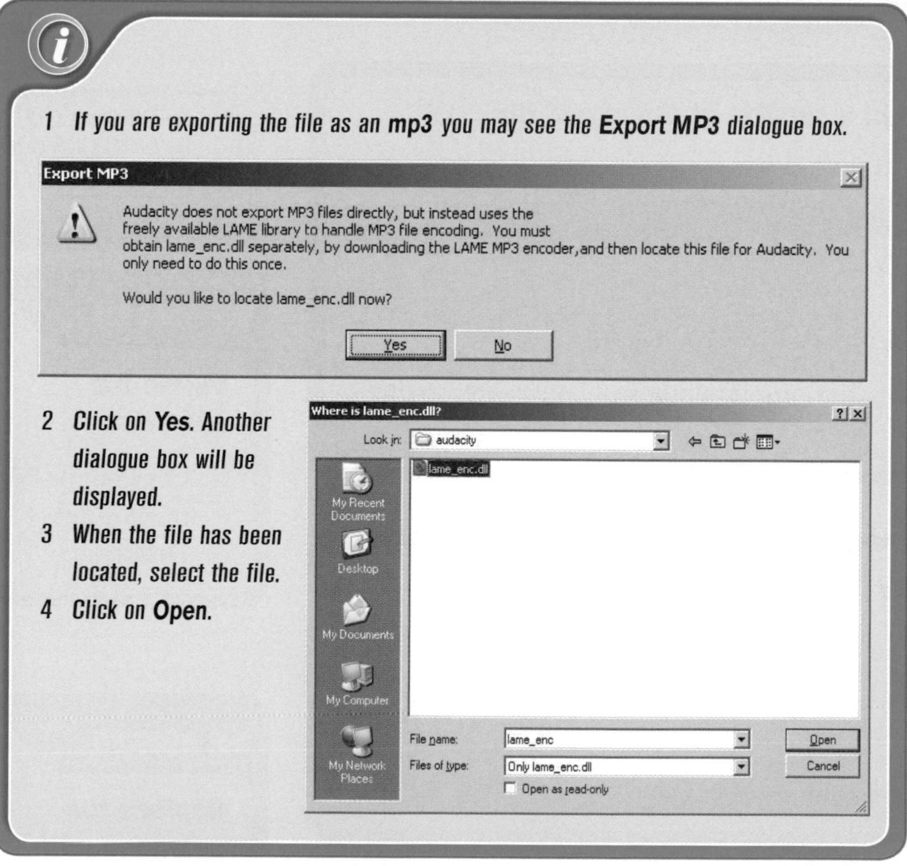

1 ***If you are exporting the file as an*** **mp3** ***you may see the*** **Export MP3** ***dialogue box.***

2 ***Click on*** **Yes**. ***Another dialogue box will be displayed.***

3 ***When the file has been located, select the file.***

4 ***Click on*** **Open**.

If exporting the file as an mp3 file, refer to Page 233.

Figure 5.24 shows the sound file for a bowling alley. This includes the sound of the ball rolling down the alley, and then hitting the pins and the pins falling. For the advertising campaign we need to split the sound so that we have the sound of the ball rolling down the alley and a separate file of the pins being hit and falling over. To do this we need to identify the different parts of the sound. In this sound file, the sound of the bowling ball rolling down the alley is in the left channel and the sound of the skittles falling is in the right channel. The sounds are repeated.

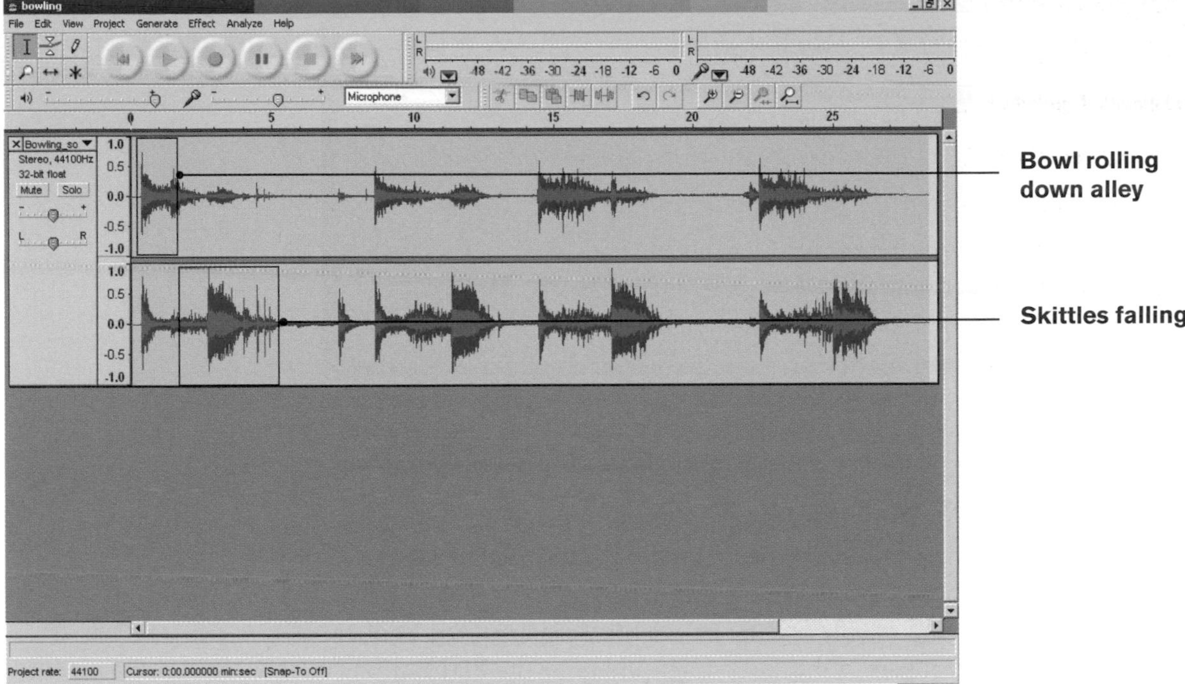

Figure 5.24 Sound file for a bowling alley

▶▶ HOW TO ... Split a stereo track

If you have a stereo sound, to be able to edit the sounds separately in the left and right channels you will need to split the stereo track.

1 Click on the down arrow to the right of the track title.

2 Select **Split stereo track**.

You will now be able to edit each of the channels separately.

▶▶ HOW TO ... Change the tracks from stereo to mono

You may want to change the individual tracks from stereo to mono.

1 Click on the down arrow to the right of the track title

2 Select **Mono**.

To listen to only one of the tracks, click on the **Solo** button for the track you want to listen to.

Refer to Figure 5.15 on page 216.

Student review 5.12 – Split channels

Assessment objective 2c

1. *Using one of the audio files you have saved for the bowling alley project, experiment with splitting a stereo track and changing the individual tracks to mono.*
2. *Listen to each track individually. If it is a long recording you may be able to identify different sounds.*

If you have a long recording you may want to split the audio file into several pieces and save each piece as a separate file or you may want to identify separate sounds in the recording.

To find where one sound ends and another begins, you may need to use the **Zoom** tool to enlarge the view of the waveform and identify pauses in the recording. A pause is usually visible as a flat line in the waveform. You could use the **Select** tool to select part of the audio track and press the **Play** button to listen to that part of the track. When you have located the place where one sound ends and the next begins, click in the audio track to place the cursor at this position.

▸▸ HOW TO ... Add a label to the audio track

1. Position the cursor in the audio track at the beginning of the sound.
2. Click on the **Project** menu → select **Add Label At Selection**.
3. A **Label Track** will appear below the audio track(s).
4. Type the name of the sound in the label track.

Repeat this process to add labels for the different sounds in your audio track.

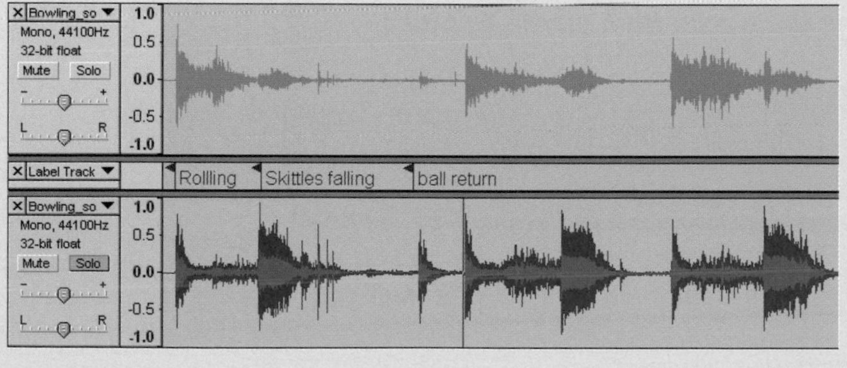

Figure 5.25 Adding labels to an audio track

In this figure, the Label Track has been moved above the audio track.

▶▶ HOW TO ... Move the position of the Label Track

1 Click on the down arrow to the right of the Label Track title.

2 Select **Move Track Up**.

▶▶ HOW TO ... Change the font of the Label Track text

1 Click on the down arrow to the right of the Label Track title.

2 Select **Font**.

3 Scroll through the list of fonts available until you find the required font.

Student review 5.13 – Use the label track

Assessment objectives 2c, 2d

1 *Record six sounds on one track, e.g. introductions to songs from an audio CD.*

2 *After recording the first sound, click on the* ***Pause*** *button, move to the introduction of the next song, before clicking on the* ***Record*** *button again.*

3 *Repeat this process until you have recorded all six sounds.*

4 *Use the label track to identify the start of each of the songs.*

5 *Save your file using a suitable filename.*

If you want to save each of the sounds as a separate file, Audacity can use the labels to name each of the files.

If you choose to export the files as ***wav*** *files, the files will be exported and a dialogue box will appear to confirm* ***Successfully exported x number files.***

If you choose to export the files as ***mp3*** *files, a dialogue box will appear* ***Edit the ID3 tags for all MP3 files.*** *Click on* ***OK.*** *The files will be exported and a dialogue box confirming* ***Successfully exported x number files*** *will appear.*

▶▶ HOW TO ... Export the sounds as separate files

1 Click on the **File** menu → select **Export Multiple**.

2 An **Export Multiple** dialogue box (Figure 5.26) will be displayed.

3 Set the required **Export format** and the **Export location**.

4 Under **Split files based on**, make sure that **Labels** is selected.

5 Under **Name files**, make sure **Using Label/Track Name** is selected.

6 Click on the **Export** button.

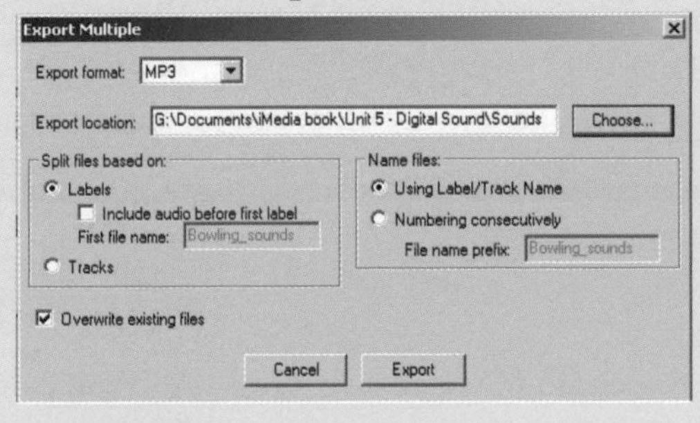

Figure 5.26 Export Multiple dialogue box

Student review 5.14 – Export multiple sounds

Assessment objective 2d

Using your audio file created in Student review 5.13, save the individual songs as separate files using **Export Multiple**.

Envelope editing

Using the **Envelope** tool you can change the volume of a track gradually over time (Figure 5.27) by adding a series of control points. Each control point you add will set the volume at that point.

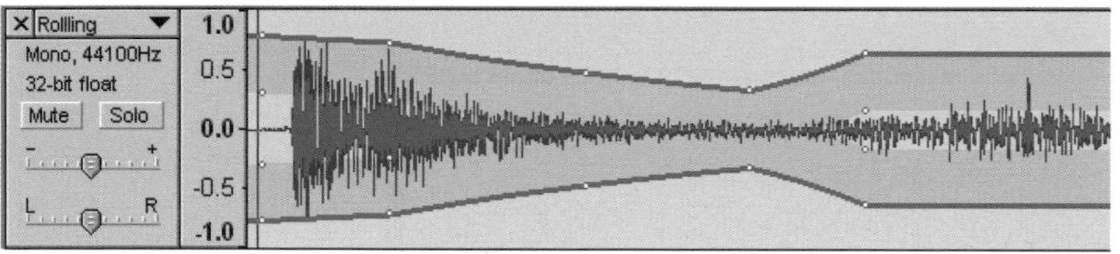

Figure 5.27 Envelope editing

▸▸ HOW TO ... Move the control point

1 Click on the control point.
2 Drag it to the new position.

Student review 5.15 – Use the envelope tool

Assessment objective 2c

1 *Using one of your song tracks from Student review 5.14, use the* **Envelope** *tool to add five control points to change the volume of the track, starting at 0, gradually increasing in volume and then reducing in volume back to 0.*
2 *Play the track and listen to the results.*
3 *Edit the control points so that the track starts loud and reduces in volume towards the middle.*
4 *Remove one of the control points so that only four remain.*
5 *Save your file using a suitable filename.*

▸▸ HOW TO ... Create a control point

- Click where you want the control point to appear on the audio wave.

▸▸ HOW TO ... Remove a control point

1 Click on the control point
2 Drag it off the track.

Effects

Effects can be applied to the entire audio file or to selections only. You can only apply effects from the **Effect** menu when a piece of audio has been selected. Audacity does not have any real-time effects which means that the audio must be selected, the effect applied and then you can listen to the results. However, many of the effects do have a preview button which allows you to listen to approximately 3 seconds of the audio so that you can hear the result of the effect.

If, after you have applied the effect, you are not happy with the result you can undo the action.

>> **HOW TO ...**

Undo an action

- Click on the **Edit** menu → select **Undo** (effect name).

Noise removal

All recordings will contain noise, a background 'hiss'. This is caused by the recording being made at too low a level, so that when the volume is increased for playback, you also raise the noise level.

TIP!

To reduce noise, record at the highest level that does not distort the sound, and lower the volume on playback.

The 1890 sound recording of Big Ben (Figure 5.28) contains noise that makes it difficult to hear the recording.

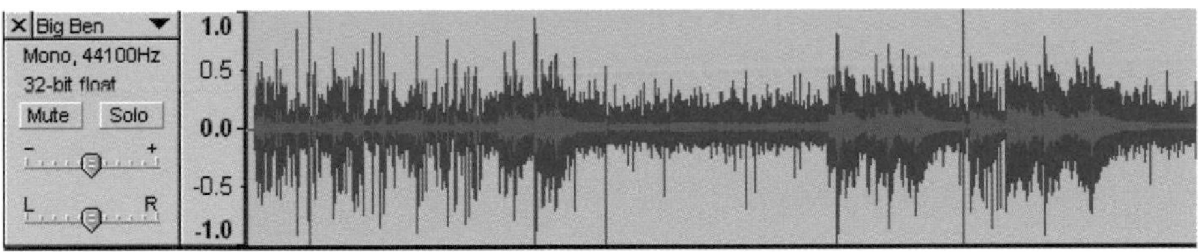

Figure 5.28 The sound of Big Ben

You can clean up noise from a recording by using the noise removal effect.

>> **HOW TO ... Remove noise**

1. Select a piece of the audio that is silent, except for the noise you want to remove.
2. Click on the **Effect** menu → select **Noise Removal** → the **Noise Removal** dialogue box is displayed (Figure 5.29).
3. In the dialogue box, click on the **Get Noise Profile** button.
4. Select all of the audio you want to filter. If this is the complete file, click on the grey area in the track Control Panel.
5. Click on the **Effect** menu → select **Noise Removal**.
6. From the dialogue box that appears, click on the **Remove Noise** button.

Noise Removal

Noise Removal by Dominic Mazzoni

Step 1

Select a few seconds of just noise so Audacity knows what to filter out, then click Get Noise Profile:

Get Noise Profile

Step 2

Select all of the audio you want filtered, choose how much noise you want filtered out, and then click Remove Noise.

Less More

Preview Remove Noise

Close

Figure 5.29 Noise Removal dialogue box

The waveform in Figure 5.30 is the same Big Ben sound with the noise removed.

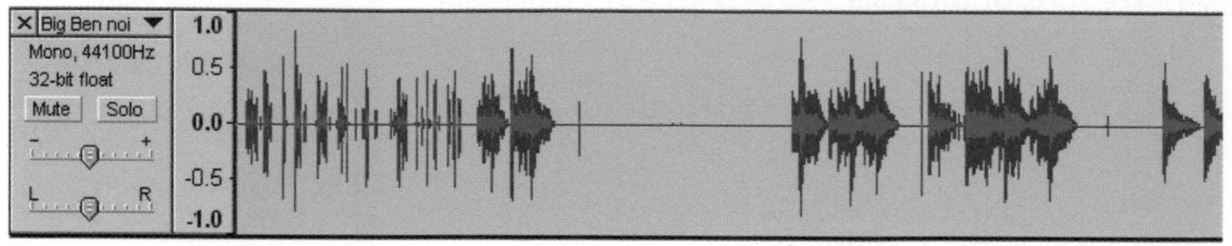

Figure 5.30 The sound of Big Ben with the noise removed

Noise removal works best when the audio signal is much louder than the noise. However, noise removal can cause some distortion.

▶▶ HOW TO ... Remove clicks

If your audio file contains clicks or pops these may be removed using the **Click Removal** tool.

1 Select the section of audio you want to filter.

2 Click on the **Effects** menu → select **Click Removal.**

3 Adjust the threshold sliders as appropriate.

4 Click **Preview** to listen to the effects of the change.

5 Click **Remove clicks** to remove the clicks.

Student review 5.16 – Remove noise from a sound

Assessment objective 2c

1 *Using the Big Ben sound effect (or a sound of your choice), try to clean up the sound by removing some of the background noise.*

2 *After removing the noise, you may be left with long periods of silence. You may want to remove this silence to reduce the length of the audio track.*

3 *If there are any clicks or pops in your file, use the* **Click Removal** *tool.*

Other effects

From the **Effects** menu you can change:

- the speed of playback of your audio file
- the tempo without changing the pitch
- the pitch.

These effects can be changed by a specific speed, tempo (beats per minute) or pitch, or they can be changed by a percentage in relation to the original recording.

The following are some further effects that are available from the **Effects** menu:

- **Amplify** This will change the volume of the selected audio. Make sure that the 'Allow Clipping' box is **not** selected. If this box is checked, your audio may be amplified beyond the range of the waveform which will result in the sound being distorted.
- **Fade in** This effect 'fades in' the audio sound, starting from silence and gradually increasing the amplitude over a period of time.
- **Fade out** This effect is similar to fade in but gradually reduces the amplitude of the sound over a period of time until there is silence.
- **Echo** This effect repeats the selection, sounding like a series of echoes. It does not alter the length of the selection so it is advisable to add some silence to the end of the selection before applying this effect.

HOW TO ... Add silence

1. Click in the audio file where you want the silence to appear.
2. Click on the **Generate** menu → select **Silence**
3. In the dialogue box, enter the **Length (seconds)** of silence, e.g. 5.
4. Click on the **Generate Silence** button.

Creative effects can be added to your sound by using the phaser or wah-wah effects.

PRACTICAL TASK 5.9 Apply effects to sounds

Assessment objectives 2c, 2d

1. Using one of the sound files that you have saved for the bowling alley, apply an effect to either the entire file or part of the file.
2. On the Planning and Review form, identify the effect you have used, giving a reason for your choice.
3. Using one of the other audio files you have saved, apply two different effects, e.g. fade in/fade out.
4. Save your amended files using suitable filenames.

FILE MANAGEMENT

Before submitting your work for an OCR assignment, you will need to check that you have captured/created the required number of files. These files should be saved using appropriate filenames and should all be saved in the same folder.

You should record the names of these files, including the file attributes and file formats using the Planning and Review Form.

Finally, you should review your sound files against the original brief, and keep a record of this on the Planning and Review Form.

Refer to 'Reviewing your work' on page xiv of the 'Common Skills' chapter.

PRACTICAL TASK 5,10 Review your sound files

Assessment objective 3b

1 Review your sound files for the bowling alley against the original brief.
2 Make a note of this on the Planning and Review Form.

You should now have all the skills, knowledge and understanding required to complete an OCR iMedia sample or live assessment for this unit.

UNIT 6
DIGITAL VIDEO

INTRODUCTION

This unit is designed to provide you with an understanding of the skills required to prepare and capture digital video. While studying this unit you will investigate the technology used in the production industry. You will also learn the techniques for using a digital video camera to capture footage. You will use basic editing tools and the features of appropriate software to store, edit and produce the assembly cut of a video sequence.

LEARNING OUTCOMES

After studying this unit you will be able to:

- understand the technology required to produce digital video
- use a digital video camera to obtain video footage
- use computer software to store digital video
- edit and export the assembly cut of a digital video clip for a particular purpose.

RESOURCE TOOLKIT

Hardware
- Digital video camera
- Computer with capture card
- Microphone
- Speakers
- CD/DVD writer
- Access to the Internet

Software
- Windows
- Windows Movie Maker
- Access to a word-processing application

Other
- Blank CD/DVD
- Planning and Review Form
- Evidence Checklist

In this unit you will be looking at the technology required to produce digital video: looking at the hardware for capturing and manipulating video then selecting and using appropriate equipment for recording video.

For an OCR assignment, you will need to plan what needs to be captured, generate ideas for the video, and record these on a Planning and Review Form, showing the initial concept for the video and your planning methods e.g. visualisations and storyboards. You will also prepare a script/screenplay. Using your plans as a guide, you will create the source video and audio footage.

You will use software to transfer the raw footage from the capture device and save it to the hard drive of your computer.

You will create a new project, import the saved video and edit the video to produce an assembly cut of the video. You will then export the movie in different formats suitable for use in different environments.

Finally you will review your completed assembly cut of the video against the original assignment brief and obtain appropriate feedback (e.g. from peers or your tutor). You will need to identify any parameters or constraints that influenced your choices regarding content, file formats or compression techniques used.

The Student Review activities and Practical Tasks in this chapter will allow you to develop your understanding of the requirements for an OCR assessment and practise the skills required for the Unit 6 syllabus. The assembly cut movie you create in this chapter **CANNOT** be submitted for assessment purposes.

ASSESSMENT FOR UNIT 6

The assessment for this unit takes the form of practical activities which are assessed by your tutor and are then externally moderated by an OCR Examiner-Moderator. The assessment may be an OCR-set assessment or one which has been locally devised.

In order to achieve a pass in this unit, you must demonstrate skills in each one of the assessment objectives.

Assessment tasks

You will be required to complete tasks that address all of the assessment objectives and you must provide evidence that shows where and how the assessment objectives have been met. Your assessment work should be submitted to OCR via e-portfolio. You should therefore save all evidence in electronic format. Any hard copy evidence should be scanned and saved electronically.

Evidence

You will need to:

- *provide copies of the raw footage you captured as part of the tasks*
- *provide a copy of the assembly cut video you produce*
- *complete forms provided by OCR to show you have planned and reviewed the video*
- *provide evidence of editing the video files, adding effects and saving in an appropriate format*
- *complete an Evidence Checklist to identify where and how the assessment objectives have been met*

SOFTWARE

In this unit you will be using Windows Movie Maker. This application is an accessory available with Windows XP. If you do not have this software, it can be downloaded free of charge from www.microsoft.com/windowsxp/downloads/updates/moviemaker2.mspx.

ABOUT THIS CHAPTER

This chapter for Unit 6 is divided into four sections. You must work through the sections in sequence.

- In Section 1 you will learn about the hardware and equipment needed to capture and manipulate digital video.

  AOs 1a, 1b, 1c

- In Section 2 you will learn how to plan pre-production of the video and about the techniques used to create source video footage.

  AOs 2a, 2b

- In Section 3 you will learn how to use software to capture and save video footage to the computer, creating a new project and arranging the workspace window.

  AOs 3a, 3b, 3c, 3d

- In Section 4 you will learn how to use the software tools to edit the video, add effects, and export the final video in different formats. You will also review the finished product against the original brief.

  AOs 4a, 4b, 4c, 4d, 4e

SECTION 1 • Understand the technology required to produce digital video

The following assessment objectives will be covered in this section:

1a Select appropriate hardware for capturing and manipulating video

1b Select appropriate equipment for video capture

1c Demonstrate how to use basic video technology

The following knowledge, skills and understanding criteria corresponding to assessment objectives 1a, 1b and 1c will be covered:

- *Computer hardware*
- *Equipment*
- *Understanding what digital video is and why it is used*
- *The impact of DVD, interactive TV and the Internet on digital video*
- *Genres and audiences*
- *Video standards, resolutions and aspect ratios*
- *Audio settings*

WHAT IS DIGITAL VIDEO AND WHY IS IT USED?

Analogue technology was really about the developments in magnetic tape. Film-makers relied on 16 mm film to produce high quality films. VHS tape did not provide the quality required so it was never used as a replacement for 16 mm film. The main disadvantage of analogue video is that it has **noise** which can blur the colours and distort the quality of the picture. Also, each time you make a copy, the copy becomes less clear than the original.

Key terms

Noise A disturbance that affects the signal, such as interference from an external source that can cause 'hissing' sounds or a 'snowy' picture.

Digital video is so called because it records the information as a series of numbers: ones and zeros. The images can still be recorded onto magnetic tape but the information is easier to read than measuring the strength of magnetism and is therefore more accurate.

The introduction of digital video technology has brought about a change in the film-making industry. Gone are the days when the only way to make a professional film was to use projectors and rolls of film. The introduction of affordable digital cameras, editing equipment, powerful personal computers and a connection to the Internet makes it possible for anyone to become involved in the film-making business. You can shoot a short film on any subject and distribute it over the Internet, showing it to a global audience.

Creating a DVD was once a costly exercise. Now DVD burners are included in every new personal computer and authoring software is inexpensive or often comes free with the video camera.

Advantages of digital video

- The picture resolution of digital video is about double that of a VHS recording.

- Digital video can be copied without any degradation in the quality.
- The colour rendition is closer to what the camera originally recorded and the colours are cleaner.
- Sound recording on digital video can be of CD quality.

Key terms

Genre A set of conventions used to categorise commercial films.

FILM GENRES

Before you capture a movie or video, you will have an idea of the style you want to use to tell the story. Films and videos are often categorised by **genre**.

SETTING	crime, historical, science fiction
MOOD	action, comedy, horror
FORMAT	live action, animation
TARGET AUDIENCE	children, family, adult

Table 6.1 Different ways of categorising films

Table 6.1 shows some examples of categorising films, but often films can cross the boundaries into more than one genre.

Other methods of categorising films can be by director, e.g. Steven Spielberg, Martin Scorsese, or film style such as the way it is edited, e.g. Lynda La Plante's *Trial & Retribution* where the screen is often split into four different scenes.

Student review 6.1 – Research film genres

Assessment objective 1c

1. *Connect to the Internet and search for different film genres.*
2. *Present your findings in a table similar to the one shown above.*

How video works

In capture and in playback, each frame in a video is built up, or drawn, line by line. The number of lines in a frame is known as the video resolution. Digital Video (DV) format is capable of approximately 550 lines of resolution.

During playback, most standard definition televisions reproduce the image using a technique called interlacing. This is where alternate lines of the image are drawn; the odd numbered lines are drawn first, from the top of the screen to the bottom, and then the even numbered lines are drawn, again from the top of the screen to the bottom. This method of playing back video was first introduced in the 1930s to improve picture quality on TV screens where images were created by phosphors that glowed after being hit by a beam of electrons. On these screens, the phosphors only glowed for a short time, and by the time the last lines of the frame had been scanned, the first lines at the top of the image had started to fade and looked darker.

Computer monitors and modern LCD and plasma screens use a method of recreating the frames called progressive-scan. This method does not use interlacing; each frame in the video is recreated in one pass, drawing the lines for each frame in sequence.

Video standards

Most countries around the world use one of three video broadcast standards: NTSC, PAL or SECAM, none of which is compatible.

STANDARD	NTSC (National Television System Committee)	PAL (Phase-Alternating Line)	SECAM (Sequential Colour with Memory)
COUNTRY	Americas and parts of East Asia	Europe (except France)	France
LINES	525	625	625
FRAMES PER SECOND	30	25	25

Table 6.2 Video standards

NTSC has a lower number of pixels on the screen but operates at a faster frame rate than PAL and SECAM. PAL and SECAM are closer in the way they operate, but PAL transmits colour information sequentially.

Even though a video format may be digital, such as that used in DVDs, it is still based on these standards.

High Definition Television (HDTV) is the biggest revolution in television since the development of colour television. This involves a type of broadcasting that gives realistic picture quality and digital surround sound. To receive high definition content a television must have:

- an XGA screen with a minimum of 720 horizontal lines
- an HDMI or DVI connection compliant with high-bandwidth digital content protection (HDCP)
- a component video input.

The term 'aspect ratio' (or frame shape) relates to the ratio of image width to image height (Figure 6.1). The standard 4:3 aspect ratio produces a frame size that is almost a square. The measurement of the 4:3 aspect ratio is 720 × 576 pixels for video monitors. However, computer monitors have a slightly different ratio, 768 × 576, which is used to take into account the computer's square pixels. If you are shooting film for the web, these are almost always shown in a 4:3 ratio.

The aspect ratio designed for high definition television is 16:9 which produces a narrower rectangle shape. The purpose of this was to match the aspect ratio used in feature film production so that the audience would see all of the film as if they had seen it at the cinema.

TIP!

Try to shoot your video in the same aspect ratio (screen shape) as you want to edit in.

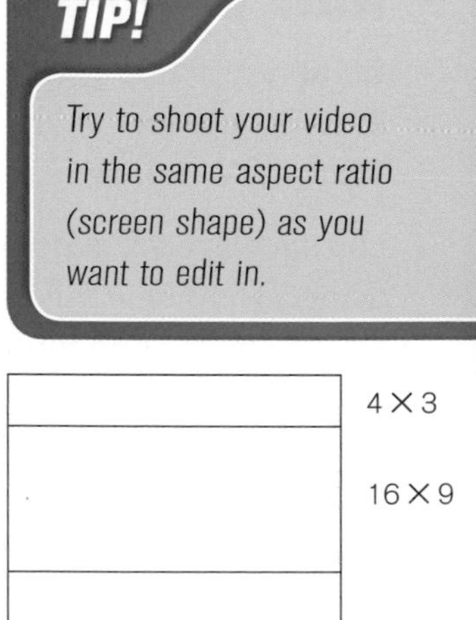

Figure 6.1 Aspect ratio

Recording sound

The built-in microphone on the camera is the easiest way to record sound. If you require professional sound with your video recordings you should use an external microphone. If you are recording sound with your filming, a mono recording would be sufficient.

In this unit you are not required to create separate audio for your digital video. However, you should be aware of the audio that may be captured whilst you are recording the video images.

How compression works

There are many different devices that can be used to view a video – CD, DVD, Internet, PDA, mobile phone. Video files are huge and to enable the files to be viewed on these small devices, the size of the files must be reduced. This is achieved using a technique called compression.

Compression techniques look at each individual frame and assess which parts are the same in each frame. Any part of the frame that is the same as the previous frame will be discarded. For example, if six frames in a sequence all have the same blue sky, all six frames would be given the same code for the sky.

When compressing video, compression techniques perform the following:

- Analyse the video signal
- Decide which parts of each frame the human eye would not miss
- Code the process

This technique is used to reduce the sizes of videos for DVDs, CD-ROMs, Internet gaming, mobile phones and web broadcasts.

However, with any compression, there must be the ability to decompress or uncompress the file so that it can be viewed again. This process is called 'compression-decompression' and is often shortened to **'codec'**.

The word codec is used to describe the various methods that are available for compressing-decompressing files. These various methods have been developed by different companies. Different codecs are best used for different applications. Some of the popular codecs are shown in Table 6.3 on the next page.

CODEC	USES
MPEG1	Encoding video for CD-ROM or VCD Web video MPEG-1 Layer 3 is the most widely used format for compressing music files (**mp3**)
MPEG2	Development of MPEG1 Used to compress video for set-top digital TV boxes Performs well with HDTV
MPEG4	Gaming Broadcasting via the web and mobile devices Gives the user the choice to opt for compression rate depending on type of connection
MPEG7	Ideal for web-based video Allows the user to personalise and filter content
H.263	Used for video conferencing
Cinepak	Small image sizes More suited to CD-ROMs
RealG2	Good for web work

Table 6.3 Codecs

SELECTING APPROPRIATE HARDWARE FOR CAPTURING AND MANIPULATING VIDEO

Digital video can be captured using small hand-held video cameras, digital still cameras, web cameras and mobile phones. However, you need a very powerful computer to be able to work with the video on your desktop due to the demands of the non-linear editing (NLE) software that is used.

Video editing produces large data streams that have to be processed by the computer at a constant rate in order to produce good quality images. One hour of DV compressed video requires approximately 13 GB of hard disk space.

If you are buying a computer for digital video editing you should aim for the best-equipped computer you can afford. There are three basic elements that make up your computer: the CPU (Central Processing Unit), the RAM (Random Access Memory) and the hard disk drive.

As a minimum, you should aim for the specifications listed in Table 6.4.

	WINDOWS PC	MAC
Processor	Pentium 4	G4
RAM	512 MB	512 MB
Operating system	Windows XP	OS X 10.3 or later
Hard disk	120 GB	120 GB
Video card	128 MB RAM	128 MB RAM
DVD recorder	Dual format	Dual format

Table 6.4 System specifications

It is also advisable to have a second hard drive – internal or external – on which to save your video clips and **rendered** movies.

Key terms

Render The process of turning clips and transitions into the final video.

You can discover the CPU speed of your computer and how much RAM there is by checking the system information.

To check system information, refer to 'How to check CPU speed and RAM' on page 201.

Your computer must also be fitted with a capture card. This enables you to connect your video camera to the computer to 'capture' the images. A basic capture card will allow you to transfer your digital images to the computer; a more expensive card can encode analogue video into digital and may also allow you to send digital films back to analogue VHS tape.

The capture card should also include an IEEE 1394 port, commonly referred to as a Firewire or iLink port, which is used to capture digital video. This port uses either a four- or six-pin connection and is often fitted as standard on modern computers. It provides a fast connection between the video camera and the computer. When video is transferred to the computer through a Firewire cable, nothing is changed – it is a digital copy identical to the original.

USB is a cheaper alternative to Firewire and is ideal for the home market and small businesses creating short commercial videos for viewing on the Internet. USB works with a screen size of approximately 320 × 420 pixels. If you try to enlarge the image to make it full screen size, there will be a significant loss in quality. Video transferred using a USB connection is smoother, the smaller it is displayed.

Some capture cards are fitted with a TV tuner for terrestrial broadcasts which enables you to make digital recordings of broadcasts on your computer. It is also possible to make digital recordings on a DVD recorder connected to a television and play these recordings on the computer.

You will need a good quality monitor to display your work; preferably a 17" monitor with a resolution of 1,280 pixels. The video card will look after the task of controlling the monitor, leaving the computer memory free for the editing tasks. If you intend to do a lot of video editing, it may be worth investing in a second monitor that can be used to test the effects and transitions that have been applied to the video footage.

Most modern computers will have enough power and memory capacity to handle DV editing tasks, but the more RAM you have the better. The more powerful your computer is will mean less time is taken rendering the editing effects that you apply to the raw footage. Depending on the processor speed of the computer, the number of effects applied and the final output format, rendering the final movie could take as much as one hour for every minute of video.

PRACTICAL TASK 6.1 **Identify the specification of your computer and record the details on a Planning and Review form**

Assessment objective 1a

1 Using a table similar to Table 6.4, identify the system specifications of the computer you are using.

2 Identify the computer hardware that you will need to use.

3 Record all this information on a Planning and Review Form.

For an OCR assessment you will be given a brief similar to the one below.

Assignment brief

Magnificent Bowl – TV Commercial
You work for a video production company as an assistant to the head of creative concepts.

The local ten-pin bowling alley, Magnificent Bowl, has asked your company to produce a television commercial to promote the facilities at the bowling alley which include a virtual reality gaming area and a café bar as well as the bowling lanes.

You have been asked to plan and capture the following clips to be used in this advertising campaign:

- Interior shots of the facilities
- A shot of the company name and contact details
- A simple voice-over, sound effects or music

You are required to deliver the concept for the commercial and to produce a **rough cut** of the final idea. The video must last for approximately 30 seconds and should be aimed at a target audience aged 16–30. You may deliver an **animatic** or real-time footage but must include:

- a minimum of three edits (preferably more)
- a minimum of two different camera movements
- a simple voice-over, appropriate sounds or music
- a closing screen with the company name and contact details.

Key terms

Rough cut *A draft; the first stage in which the film starts to resemble the final product.*

Animatic *A filmed version of the storyboard. Sometimes a sound track is added to the sequence of still images to test if the images and sound work together. Most commonly used for television commercials.*

SELECTING APPROPRIATE EQUIPMENT FOR VIDEO CAPTURE

As part of an OCR assessment you will also be required to identify the equipment you will use to capture the video. You may capture the video using a digital still camera or a mobile phone, but the most popular way of capturing video is by using a video camera.

Cameras

Digital video cameras are smaller and lighter than older analogue models. They produce digital quality pictures and sound that can be easily transferred to your computer for editing.

There are a number of different types of digital video camera that use different recording mediums for storing the digital images. Some of the most popular are:

- **Mini DV** This is one of the most popular recording mediums. A mini DV tape is about the size of a matchbox and holds approximately 60 minutes of recording. The tapes are long-lasting and usually give high quality images.

- **DVD** Digital video cameras that record directly onto disk are not as compact as those that use mini DV tape. The disks are 8 cm (2/3 size of a standard DVD) and have the advantage of immediate playback on your DVD player, computer or laptop. The disadvantage is that spinning the disk and powering the laser quickly runs down the battery.

- **HDD** With this type of video camera there is no need for tapes or disks as they record directly on to a high capacity hard disk drive which can store over 25 hours of video footage.

- **High Definition (HD) video cameras** can use mini DV tapes or SD (Secure Digital) memory cards. The advantage of these cameras is that they produce superb high-definition video capture and, if using a SD memory card, the cameras can be very small and lightweight. Cameras using SD memory cards have no moving parts so consume very little power from the battery pack. Although the SD memory cards are limited in memory and can be expensive, they can be reused thousands of times.

Mobile Phones

Some **3G** mobile phones provide the user with high quality video capturing capabilities which can produce up to 90 minutes of video of near DVD quality. The phones have a built-in camera complete with **optical zoom** and **digital zoom** which allows you to get close-up pictures without losing quality. Some mobile phones also allow the user to edit the video footage and add effects.

Key terms

3G *The third generation of developments in wireless technology which allows high speed data transfer.*

Optical zoom Allows you to zoom in on your subject without any loss of picture quality.

Digital zoom *Allows you to magnify specific parts of a picture but you may lose some quality because it reduces the resolution of the image.*

Many video cameras have a built-in microphone. However, these microphones are more likely to pick up noise from the camera than an external microphone. If you want good quality sound with your video you should record the sound separately. This could be recorded using a MiniDisc player.

For details on MiniDisc players, refer to 'Sound recording devices on page 205.

For an OCR assignment, if sound is required, it is acceptable for it to be recorded using the microphone built in to the video camera.

Lighting

When shooting a video, you may be able to obtain your footage using only the light that is available but by using extra lights you can improve the look or change the mood of your scene.

Lighting is used to:

- pick out relevant details or figures in a scene like a spotlight
- create mood and atmosphere
- aid the camera.

Filters

Filters are placed over the lens of the camera to alter the images entering the camera. The most common filter used is a plain UV filter which is used to protect the lens of the camera and should be kept on the camera at all times. Other filters can be used to add special effects, increase the intensity of colours where there are shiny surfaces, add colour tints to create changes in the mood of lighting or graduated filters to change the effect in only one area in order to correct imbalances.

Batteries

Modern video cameras have low power requirements and modern batteries are very efficient. This can result in a battery providing sufficient power for many hours of recording. It is always worth having a spare battery; the batteries themselves are small so can easily be carried in your pocket. Battery power will be used more quickly if you are using the zoom on the camera, or you are viewing your footage on an LCD screen.

TIP!

Battery care

- *Discharge a battery fully before recharging. This prolongs the life of the battery.*
- *Keep the contacts clean and do not expose to moisture because this can cause corrosion to develop.*
- *Do not expose the batteries to extreme temperatures – hot or cold.*
- *Do not leave the battery attached to the video camera for long periods when not in use because this could affect the battery's ability to be re-charged.*

Tripods

Tripods are used to achieve a steady shot. They are not only vital when interviewing or shooting a static shot, but are also used when filming movement such as a horse galloping along a beach.

Tripods also help to create smooth camera movement, because even the most basic model will have a pan and tilt head. Some tripods are fitted with a spirit level to show when the tripod is level.

PRACTICAL TASK 6.2 Identify equipment to be used for video capture

Assessment objective 1b

1 Referring back to the Magnificent Bowl – TV Commercial assignment brief on page 248, identify the equipment you will be using for video capture.

2 Record these details on the Planning and Review Form you used in the previous task.

SECTION 2 • Use a digital video camera to obtain video footage

The following assessment objectives will be covered in this section:

2a Plan pre-production

2b Create source video footage

The following knowledge, skills and understanding criteria corresponding to assessment objectives 2a and 2b will be covered:

- *Generating ideas*
- *Planning methods specific to video*
- *Preparing a script and/or characters*
- *Selecting location*
- *Production design*
- *Capturing video and audio on tape/disc*

The following knowledge, skills and understanding criteria are covered in the 'Common Skills' unit:

- *Ways of identifying client requirements*
- *Planning methods*

PLANNING PRE-PRODUCTION

For an OCR assessment you will be required to plan the pre-production of the video using conceptualisation, visualisation and/or storyboarding techniques.

Before you start shooting your video footage, you will need to plan what you need to do.

The first part of the planning stage is to develop your ideas, writing down the concept of the video. This will include identifying the genre, the target audience and a general outline of what you plan to do. This may be in the form of one or two sentences.

For general information about planning, refer to 'Planning your work' on page xiv of the 'Common Skills' chapter.

PRACTICAL TASK 6.3 Generate ideas for the magnificent bowl brief

Assessment objective 2a

1 Write down your ideas for the 'Magnificent Bowl – TV Commercial' assignment brief on page 248.

2 Remember to include a general outline of what will happen in the advertisement; include the genre and the target audience.

3 Record this information on the Planning and Review Form you used in the previous task.

The next stage in planning the production is to translate your words into images – visualising. This involves sketching your ideas to show as much information as possible about the shot, including the arrangement of objects or people, the camera angles, the direction of light, and text layered over the image. Visualisation allows you to quickly develop ideas.

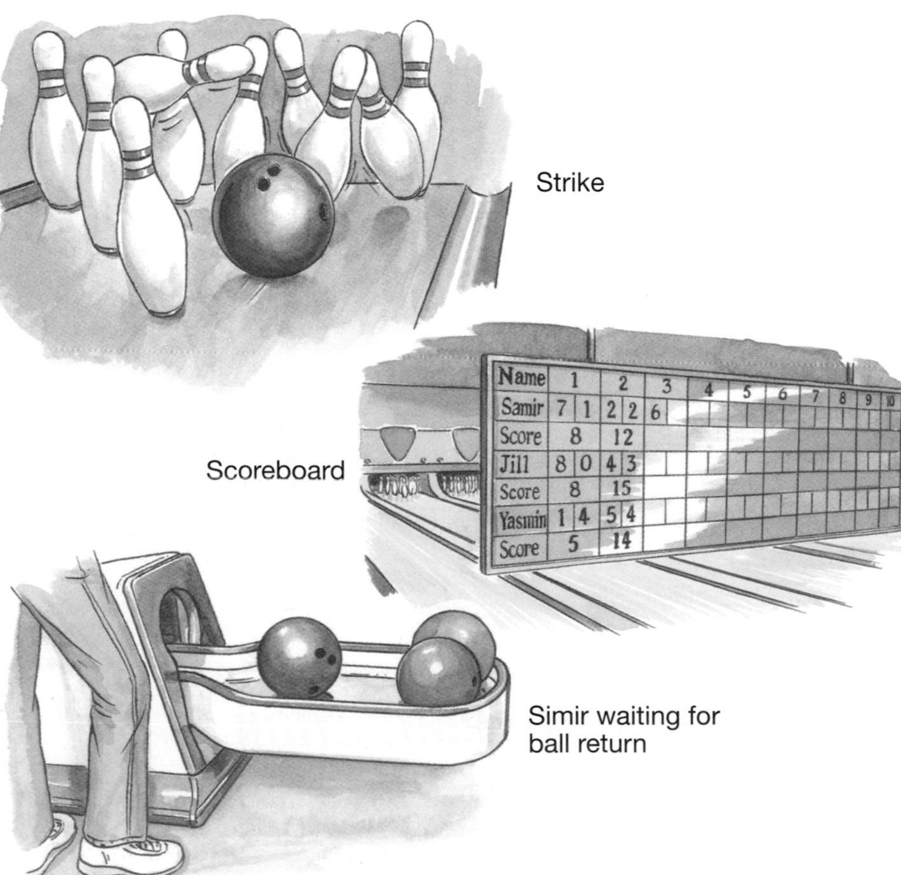

Figure 6.3 Visualisations for the 'Magnificent Bowl' advertisement

PRACTICAL TASK 6.4 Visualise your ideas for the magnificent bowl brief

Assessment objective 2a

1 Develop your concept for the ten-pin bowling advertisement by sketching the visuals for some of the shots.

2 Attach your sketches to your Planning and Review Form.

The next stage in the planning process is to collate your visual ideas into the required sequence for the video. This is shown in a storyboard. The example storyboard shown in Figure 6.4 has the frames down the left side of the page and the information relating to the frame, such as location, camera movement, props and dialogue, on the right side of the page.

You do not have to be a great artist to produce a storyboard; you can use stick figures to represent people. Each frame of your storyboard should indicate the action for the scene and the camera angles.

There is software available for producing storyboards that allows you to enter shot titles, descriptions, camera angles, shot tips etc. Atomic Learning's Storyboard Pro is free software (freeware) that can be used to produce storyboards, or print blank copies of a storyboard. It is available for download from www.atomiclearning.co.uk/storyboardpro.

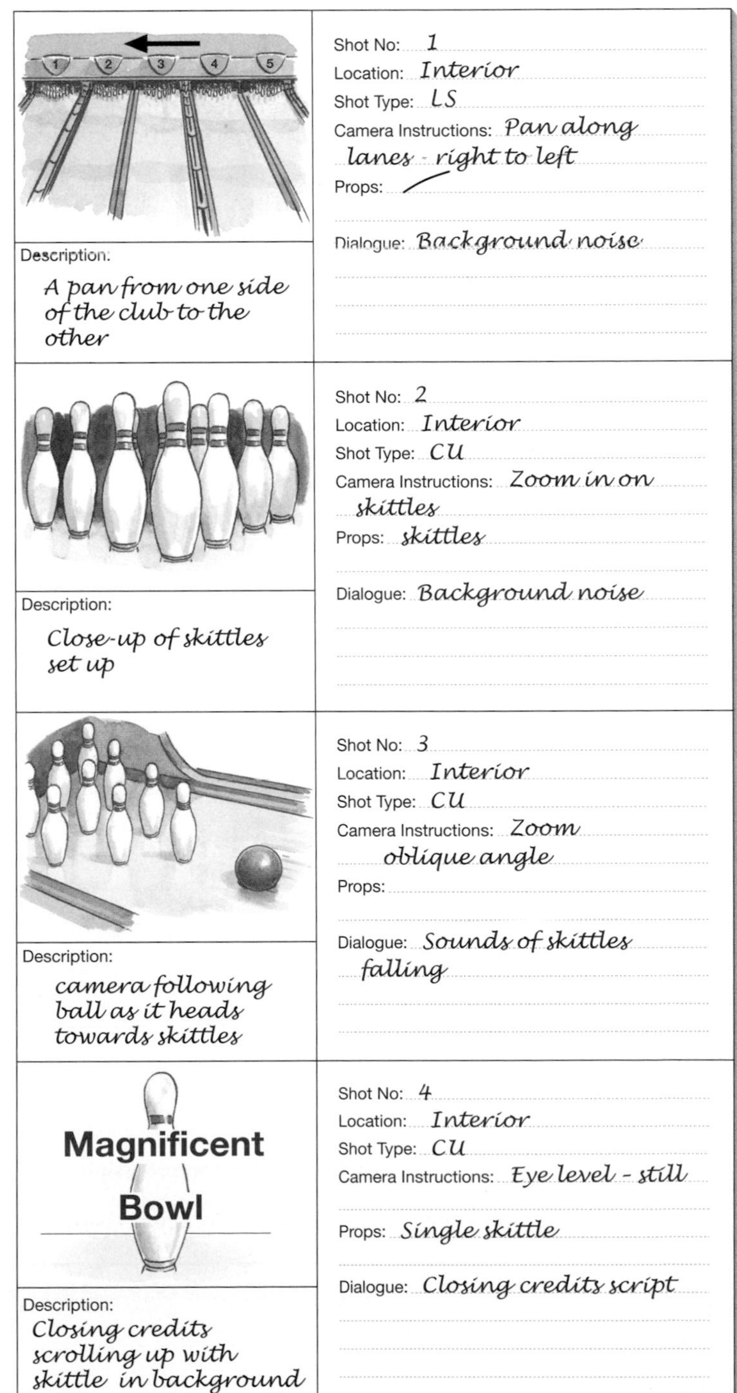

Figure 6.4 Storyboard

PRACTICAL TASK 6.5 *Create a storyboard*

Assessment objective 2a

Using the visuals you sketched out in Practical task 6.4, create a storyboard for the Magnificent Bowl brief.

Key terms

Screenplay Contains the script, but also includes directions for the crew, e.g. interior or exterior location, lighting, camera angles, timings.

Before you start shooting your video footage, it may be necessary for you to prepare a script. This is the text that the characters or the narrator will say and will often contain information on how the words are to be delivered, e.g. in a whisper, or cues for when to start speaking, e.g. after the skittles have fallen. A character could also be an object, e.g. the scoring screen in the bowling alley. In this case the script will contain the information that will be displayed on the screen.

Example of a screenplay and script

ACTION:

Three friends are at the bowling alley. Two are sat on the seats looking up at the scoring screen; the third is waiting next to the ball return for his bowling ball.

LOCATION:

INTERIOR – BOWLING ALLEY

(Camera – low angle) Camera shows the scoring screen the two friends are looking at

SCORING SCREEN

Name	1	2	3	4	5	6	7	8	9	10										
Samir	7	1	2	2	6															
Score	8		12																	
Jill	8	0	4	3																
Score	8		15																	
Yasmin	1	4	5	4																
Score	5		14																	

(Camera – eye level) Camera **cuts** to shot of Samir waiting for his bowling ball to be returned.

NARRATOR

(As Samir is waiting for the bowling ball to be returned)

"At Magnificent Bowl, we like to make sure our guests have a good time …"

TIP!

When shooting a person at eye-level, make sure the camera is at their eye level not yours.

When describing different camera shots, you should take into account:

- the length
- the angle
- any movement.

LENGTH		
Long shot (LS)	This can be used for scene-setting where the audience can see the context and surroundings. It often shows an exterior, e.g. the outside of a building.	
Close-up (CU)	This shows very little background. It concentrates on either a face or on one aspect of a scene. It can be used to show the importance of an object, suggest intimacy or even claustrophobia.	
ANGLE		
High angle	This shows a scene from high above the action. This makes the object or character seem smaller and less significant. It can suggest vulnerability and suggests that the viewer is more powerful than the subject.	
Eye level	This angle is one of the most commonly used shots and is the one that causes the least discomfort because this is the way we see things. The camera is positioned to give the viewer the feeling of being part of the actual scene.	
Low angle	This shot will make the object or character appear taller. It gives the viewer a sense of powerlessness within the scene. The background to the shot is often just sky or the ceiling which can cause confusion for the viewer.	
Oblique/ canted angle	This shot is where the camera is tilted. This type of shot suggests imbalance, instability or that something is not quite right.	
MOVEMENT		
Pan	A movement that scans a scene horizontally. Used to follow a moving object, e.g. a ball thrown from one person to another.	
Tilt	A movement that scans a scene vertically. Can be used to show a tall building by starting at the bottom and moving up to the top.	
Zoom	The zoom lens is used to move closer to a subject. It can be used to change from a long shot to a close-up. Reverse zoom can be used to move from a close-up to a long shot.	
Dollying (Tracking)	The camera is placed on a moving vehicle and follows alongside the action.	

Table 6.5 Camera shots

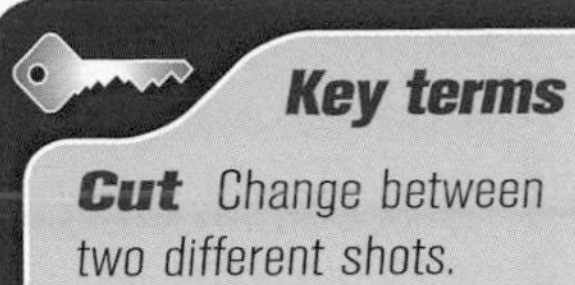

Key terms

Cut Change between two different shots.

TIP!

Use movement sparingly. Start your shot on a stationary subject, use the pan/tilt/zoom, then end on a stationary subject.

Rapid camera movements can cause a viewer to experience motion sickness and the video to blur.

PRACTICAL TASK 6.6 Write a script

Assessment objectives 2a, 2b

Write a script and/or screenplay for the 'Magnificent Bowl' advertisement including the camera shots.

You will need to find a suitable location for your filming, which may be inside or outside depending on the subject of your video. When choosing your location you should consider the camera angles you will be using, and decide what will be seen in the background of the shot and any sound effects you may need to add.

You will also need to consider what will be seen in the shot. You may need to add props (theatrical property) to put across a point. For example, in a shot for the bowling alley you may want to include drinks glasses, cups or food such as burgers to show that the club also has a café bar.

When planning your shots, use the rule of thirds and place any objects that you want to emphasise in the position where the lines intersect.

Refer to 'Rule of thirds' on page 6.

Before you start filming in a public place, you must obtain the necessary permissions. You may think you are in a public place, such as a shopping mall, but this may be privately owned. You may record an object that is in public view and has been photographed many times. However, if that object is to feature in your video, you should seek permission from the owner. If filming in public places, you should also seek the permission of people who feature in the film, and it may be necessary to obtain 'model releases'. If a person is 'caught' on your video whilst you are filming, this can be used provided that you do not show that person in a derogatory manner.

For an OCR assessment you will be required to log all materials requiring copyright permissions on the Planning and Review Form.

PRACTICAL TASK 6.7 Obtain permissions and acknowledge copyright

Assessment objective 2a

1 Using your Planning and Review Form, make a list of any permissions that you may need to obtain before you start your filming.

2 Make sure that you acknowledge copyright permissions of items that you will be including in your video.

CREATING SOURCE VIDEO FOOTAGE

For an OCR assessment you will be required to create a minimum of three edits (preferably more) that will be combined to create the final product.

When creating your video you must make sure that there is sufficient light. If you are shooting outdoors in daylight, this is usually not a problem. However, light changes throughout the day and weather conditions may change so you may find that will need additional lighting.

When shooting indoors, modern video cameras do not always need additional lighting. However, ambient lighting, the natural light from a light bulb or the sun shining through the window, may not always create the required atmosphere. In such cases additional lighting may be needed.

Most video cameras are fitted with a built-in light but you should avoid using this wherever possible because this lights the subject from the front and can throw shadows.

The lens of the video camera is the point at which light from the subject passes into the camera. The iris in the lens will control the amount of light that enters the video camera. The amount of light needed is determined by the **CCD** chip. If there is too little light, the CCD will add its own information, creating 'noise', which can result in a grainy image.

Key terms

CCD charge-coupled device A silicon device (chip) situated near the lens of the video camera which converts the light received from the subject into digital information.

Modern video cameras are small and lightweight but because they are so light, it can be difficult to shoot a steady picture. Some cameras offer image stabilisation which will reduce the effects of camera shake on the image. Another way to reduce camera shake is to use a stabiliser, which has a weight which acts as a counterbalance when the camera is held at the centre of gravity.

Video cameras, like digital still cameras, have a white balance feature that removes unrealistic colour casts so that objects that appear white to the naked eye will appear white in the video. A household light bulb will give off light that has an orange tint. The human eye will automatically adjust and compensate for this. Video cameras use the white balance feature to ensure accurate colour recording.

For examples of camera movement, refer to Table 6.5 on page 255.

Refer to the documentation for your video camera so that you become familiar with the camera settings and how your video camera works.

When creating the source video footage you will need to show evidence of camera movement.

TIP!

When shooting video footage, start your recording before the action starts and continue to record after the action has finished. This will help when you come to edit the footage.

Student review 6.2 – Use a video camera

Assessment objective 2b

Using your video camera and referring to the manual, familiarise yourself with the automatic features and the operation of the camera.

PRACTICAL TASK 6.8 Record the source video for the Magnificent Bowl advertisement

Assessment objective 2b

Using the storyboard and script you prepared in previous practical tasks, create the source video footage required to create the advertisement video for the 'Magnificent Bowl' assignment brief on page 248.

SECTION 3 • Use a computer program to store digital video

The following assessment objectives will be covered in this section:

3a Select appropriate software for editing and producing video

3b Creating a new project

3c Arrange workspace window for video capture

3d Capture and save video footage to computer

The following knowledge, skills and understanding criteria corresponding to assessment objectives 3a, 3b, 3c and 3d will be covered:

- *Equipment*
- *Selecting appropriate project and video settings*
- *Arranging windows and panels*
- *Connecting hardware*
- *Movie capture*

SELECTING APPROPRIATE SOFTWARE FOR EDITING AND PRODUCING VIDEO

In this unit we are using Windows Movie Maker to edit the video. This is a **NLE non-linear** editing software program that is supplied as an accessory with Windows XP. With the Apple Mac, iMovie is available. Video editing software is also often supplied with the video camera.

Other editing software includes Adobe Premier, Apple Final Cut, and Ulead VideoStudio.

Key terms

NLE non-linear editing Software that allows you direct access to any part of a movie.

With Windows Movie Maker you can combine video, audio and still images and use special effects to create a movie.

Before you use Movie Maker you will need to connect and install the equipment you have used to create your video content. Refer to your computer/video camera documentation for details.

PRACTICAL TASK 6.9 **Identify the video editing software**

Assessment objective 3a

1 Identify the NLE system that you will be using to edit the video footage.

2 Make a note of this on your Planning and Review Form.

ARRANGING WORKSPACE WINDOW FOR VIDEO CAPTURE AND CREATING A NEW PROJECT

HOW TO ... **Start Movie Maker**

1 Click on the **Start** button.

2 Select **All Programs**.

3 Select **Accessories**.

4 Click on **Windows Movie Maker**.

The Windows Movie Maker screen will appear displaying a new untitled movie project (Figure 6.5).

Before you start Movie Maker you must connect your video camera to the computer so that Movie Maker detects it as a capture device.

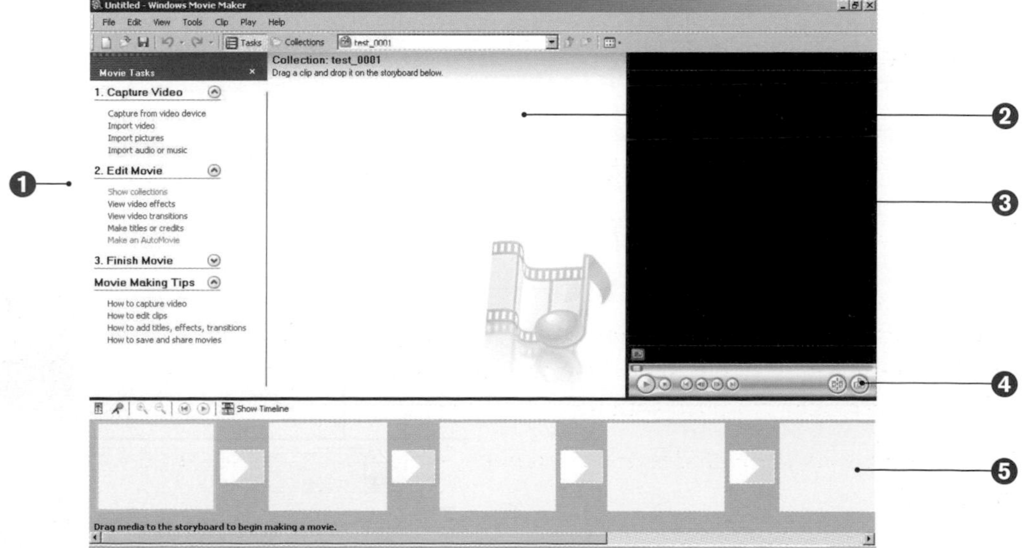

Figure 6.5 Windows Movie Maker window

The numbers in this list refer to the key features of the Movie Maker window shown in Figure 6.5:

1. The **Movie Tasks** pane lists the common tasks you may need to do.
2. The **Contents** pane displays the video clips, audio, still images, transitions and effects that can be added to the Timeline or Storyboard and included in the project.
3. The **Monitor** is where individual clips or a movie are displayed.
4. Below the Monitor are the **Seek bar** and **Playback controls** (refer to Figure 6.6) – the controls for video playback and buttons for splitting a clip and taking a picture.
5. The **Storyboard** displays the sequence or order of the clips in the project and any video effects or video transitions that have been applied.

Figure 6.6 The Seek bar and Playback controls

Movie Maker terminology

Source files	The digital media files (video, audio) or images that you import into your project.
Collection	A collection helps you organise the source files that you have imported into Windows Movie Maker. All clips in a collection will appear in the **Collections** pane.
Project	A project contains the arrangement and timing information of audio and video clips, video transitions, video effects and titles that have been added to the Storyboard. When you save a project it is saved with the file extension **mswmm**. You can open a project file at a later time and continue working in it from where it was last saved.
Storyboard	The Storyboard is the default view in Windows Movie Maker. The Storyboard displays the order of the clips, and shows any video transitions or effects in your project. It does not display audio clips.
Timeline	The Timeline also displays all the clips in your project, including audio. You can use the Timeline to modify the timing of clips, recording narration or adjusting the audio levels. Time is displayed as hours:minutes:seconds: hundredths of a second (h:m:s:hs).
Movie	This is the final project that is saved using the Save Movie Wizard. The movie can be saved to computer, CD, DVD or, if you have your DV camera connected to the computer, the movie can be recorded onto the DV tape and viewed on your camera or a TV.

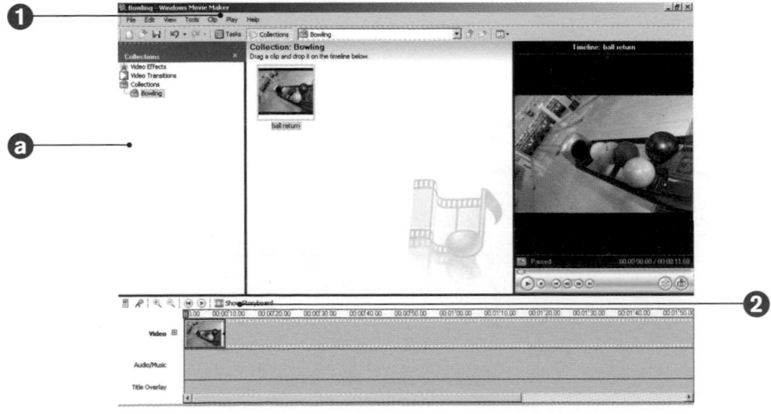

Figure 6.7 The Collections pane and Timeline

These numbers/letter refer to features annotated in Figure 6.7:

❶ Clicking on the **Collections** button will display the **Collections** pane (ⓐ).

❷ Clicking on **Show Timeline** will display the Timeline. Note that when the Timeline is displayed, this button will be **Show Storyboard**.

The **Contents** pane will display your clips for the Collection that is selected. The **Collections** pane also contains the video effects and video transitions that are available.

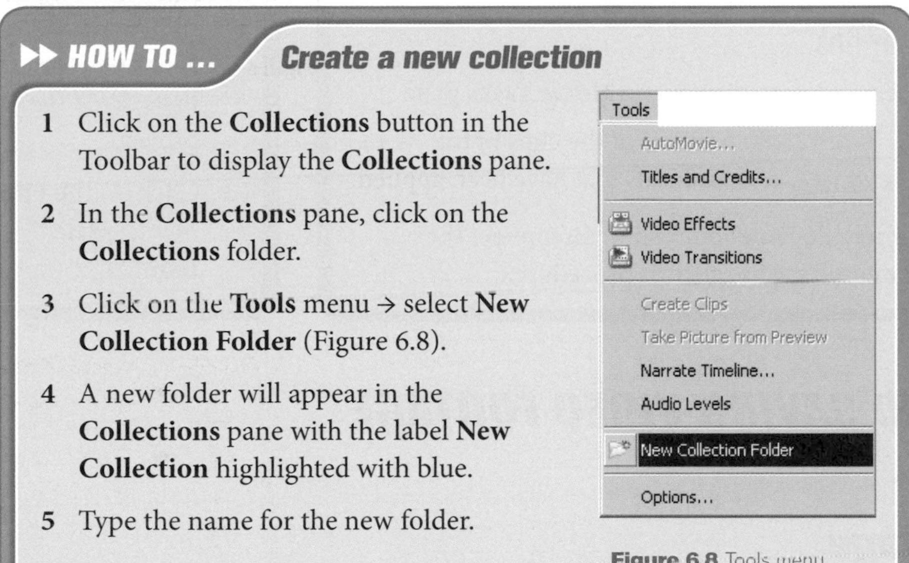

▶▶ HOW TO ... Create a new collection

1 Click on the **Collections** button in the Toolbar to display the **Collections** pane.

2 In the **Collections** pane, click on the **Collections** folder.

3 Click on the **Tools** menu → select **New Collection Folder** (Figure 6.8).

4 A new folder will appear in the **Collections** pane with the label **New Collection** highlighted with blue.

5 Type the name for the new folder.

Figure 6.8 Tools menu

The **New Collection Folder** option will appear grey and will not be available if the **Movie Tasks** pane is displayed at the left of the screen.

If you want to make the new collection a sub-folder of an existing collection, click on the collection name at step 2.

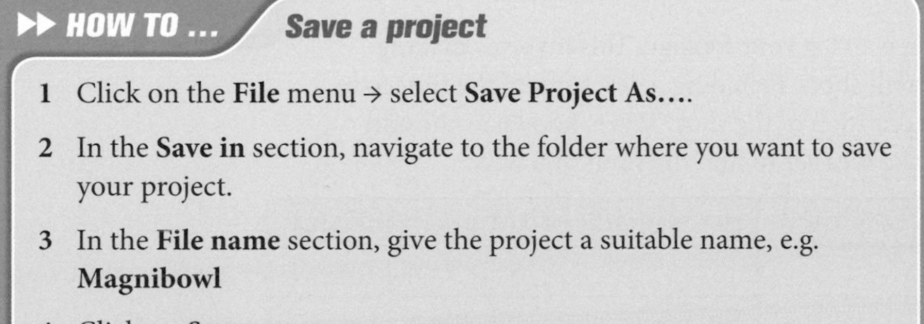

▶▶ HOW TO ... Save a project

1 Click on the **File** menu → select **Save Project As....**

2 In the **Save in** section, navigate to the folder where you want to save your project.

3 In the **File name** section, give the project a suitable name, e.g. **Magnibowl**

4 Click on **Save.**

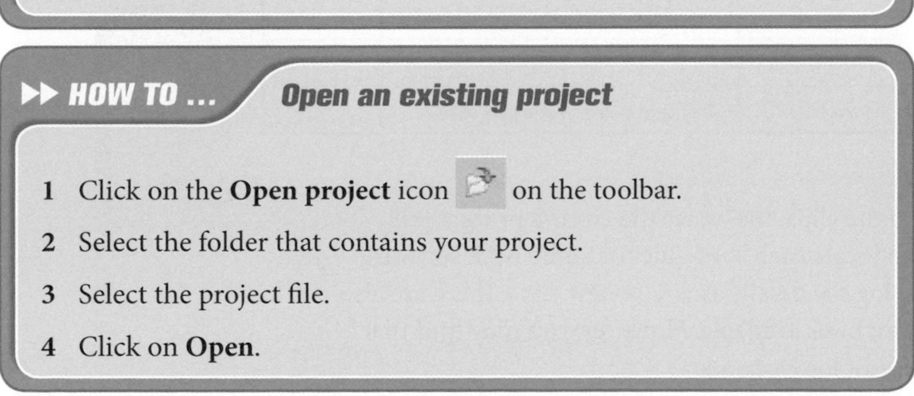

▶▶ HOW TO ... Open an existing project

1 Click on the **Open project** icon on the toolbar.

2 Select the folder that contains your project.

3 Select the project file.

4 Click on **Open.**

PRACTICAL TASK 6.10 Name a new collection and arrange the workspace window

Assessment objectives 3b, 3c, 4b

1 Connect your video camera to the computer.
2 Start Windows Movie Maker.
3 Create a new collection for your clips.
4 Name the collection **bowling**
5 Arrange the workspace window to display the **Movie Tasks** pane and the **Storyboard**.
6 Save the project using a suitable filename.
7 Refer to your video camera documentation and disconnect the camera from the computer using the correct procedure.

▶▶ HOW TO ...

Close Movie Maker

1 Make sure you have disconnected the video camera using the correct procedure.
2 Make sure you have saved the project.
3 Click on the **File** menu → select **Exit**.

CAPTURING AND SAVING VIDEO FOOTAGE TO COMPUTER

Logging the footage

Before you **capture** and save your video footage to a computer, you will need to review and log the raw footage. If you recorded your video following a script you had prepared this should be a straightforward process. If, on the other hand, you recorded everything, 'just in case', you will have a lot of footage that you will not need, or may not fit into your storyline.

Key terms

Capture To record audio, video or still images as digital data in a file.

The first stage in video editing is to log your footage. This involves making detailed notes about the different shots, including a description, the timecode start and end points, and the duration of the shot. This is known as the edit log, the aim of which is to make it easier to find the shots you want.

TIMECODE	DESCRIPTION OF VIDEO	DESCRIPTION OF AUDIO	ORDER
00:10:00	LS outside of club		
00:20:15	LS of lanes inside club	Background music and laughter	
00:24:10	CU of Samir collecting ball		
00:27:12	Samir preparing to throw ball		
00:30:09	LS of ball rolling down lane	Sound of ball on wooden lane	

Table 6.6 An example of an edit log

The more thoroughly you log the clips, the easier the editing process will be because you will be able to locate each shot quickly. Some NLE software programs have the facility to log the details as you review clips; there are also specialist logging software programs available. However, you may find that you will need to produce the edit log by hand.

From the edit log you will be able to make decisions as to which clips you want in the final movie and the order in which you want to show them. The new order can be shown in the Order column of the edit log. Alternatively, you can produce an edit decision list (EDL) by cutting and pasting the clips in the edit log into the correct running order. The EDL is a useful tool which will help save time when capturing the clips on to a computer.

PRACTICAL TASK 6.11 **Review video footage on the camera and produce an edit log and edit decision list**

Assessment objective 3d

1 Using the display on the video camera, review the raw video footage you have captured.

2 Using a word-processing application, produce an edit log similar to that shown in Table 6.6.

3 From your edit log, produce an edit decision list.

Capturing video

To capture audio and video directly into Windows Movie Maker you must have a capture device correctly connected to the computer and it must be detected by Movie Maker. A capture device could be a digital video camera, an analogue video camera, a web camera, a video recorder (VHS) or a TV tuner card. Audio can be recorded by connecting a microphone, CD or audio tape.

▶▶ HOW TO ... **Capture video from a connected video**

1 Make sure your video camera is connected to the computer.

2 Open Windows Movie Maker.

3 Click on the **Collections** button on the Toolbar to display the **Collections** pane.

4 Select the collection you want to save your clips to, e.g. **bowling**

5 Click on the **Tasks** button on the Toolbar to display the **Movie Tasks** pane.

6 On the video camera, select the play mode.

7 In the **Movie Tasks** pane, click on **Capture from video device**. If the options are not displayed you will need to click on the down arrow for **Capture Video** to display them.

8 The first screen of the Video Capture Wizard will be displayed (Figure 6.9).

TIP!

If you have more than one capture device connected to the computer you may need to select the device you want to capture from.

Continued ...

9 In the box under **Enter a file name for your captured video**, enter the name for your captured video.

10 In the section **Choose a place to save your captured video**, click on the **Browse** button to select a location to save your captured video.

11 Click on the **Next** button → the next step of the Video Capture Wizard will be displayed (Figure 6.10).

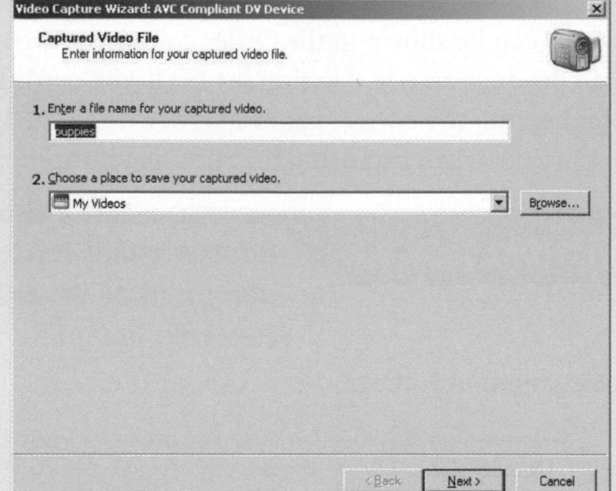

Figure 6.9 First step of Video Capture Wizard

This step of the Video Capture Wizard lets you choose the settings you want to use when capturing video and audio. The video setting you choose will determine the quality and file size of the captured video file.

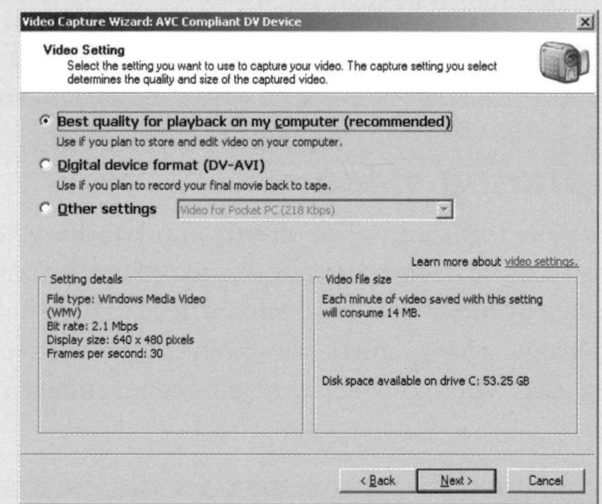

Figure 6.10 Second step of Video Capture Wizard

You should consider the file size along with the main purpose for your captured video when choosing the video setting. It is generally most efficient to choose the setting that provides the smallest file size while producing the quality level you require. Therefore, when choosing the video settings you should consider the following:

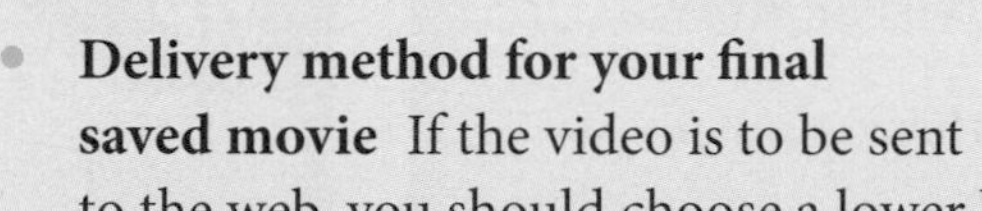

- **Delivery method for your final saved movie** If the video is to be sent to the web, you should choose a lower bit rate setting so it can be easily viewed. If the movie is to be saved to a recordable CD you can choose a higher bit rate setting which will increase the quality of the movie. If you have captured your video from a DV video camera and you plan to save the edited movie back to the DV tape, you should choose the digital device format (DV-AVI) because this lets you capture the video as an **avi** file which is suitable for recording back to tape.
- **Capturing quality** The quality of your final movie will depend on the quality of the captured video and audio. Therefore, you should choose a higher video setting when capturing. You can always save your movie at a lower setting. However, capturing the video at a higher setting than the setting used for the original recording will not improve the overall quality.
- **Hard disk space available** If you have a lengthy video to capture, this can create quite a large file even though it will be highly compressed by Windows Media Format. If you have limited hard disk space, try to use the smallest file size available for the quality required for your final movie.

Continued ...

- **Video and audio content** Video that contains a lot of motion and audio requires a higher video setting, which will increase the file size. Video that contains little action can be saved at a lower video setting without affecting the quality of the video.

The **Settings details** section displays additional information about the video being captured at the current setting, as explained in Table 6.7.

File type	The file type for the saved video: Windows Media Video (**wmv**) or Audio-Video Interleaved (**avi**)
Bit rate	The total bit rate of the captured video and audio – a higher bit rate will result in smoother motion
Display size	The size of the picture, width × height, in pixels
Frames per second	The higher the number will result in smoother motion
Video format	NTSC or PAL. This is displayed when capturing video as a DV-AVI video file.

Table 6.7 Video settings

The **Video file size** section gives an estimated file size for the movie if you save it with the chosen settings, along with the disk space available on your computer. For settings that are based on the quality of the video and audio, the file size estimate is not available.

12 Using the information provided here to help you, select the settings you require.

13 Click on the **Next** button.

If you are capturing video from a DV video camera or other DV device, the Video Capture Wizard will display the dialogue box shown in Figure 6.11.

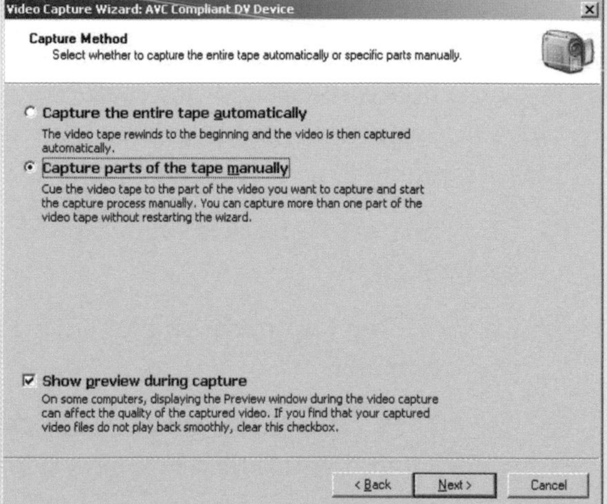

Figure 6.11 Capturing video from a DV device

The options available in this dialogue box allow you to capture the entire tape automatically or capture only parts of the tape manually:

- If you select the option to capture the entire tape, the tape in the capture device will be rewound to the beginning and the video will be captured automatically.
- If you want to capture only part of the video, you should rewind the tape to where you want to start capturing.

You can choose to see a preview of the video, but this may affect the quality of the captured video. If the captured video files do not play back smoothly, you should clear the check from this box and recapture the video.

14 Click on the option you require.

15 Click on the **Next** button.

Continued ...

If you are capturing content live or from tape, Video Capture Wizard will display the dialogue box shown in Figure 6.12.

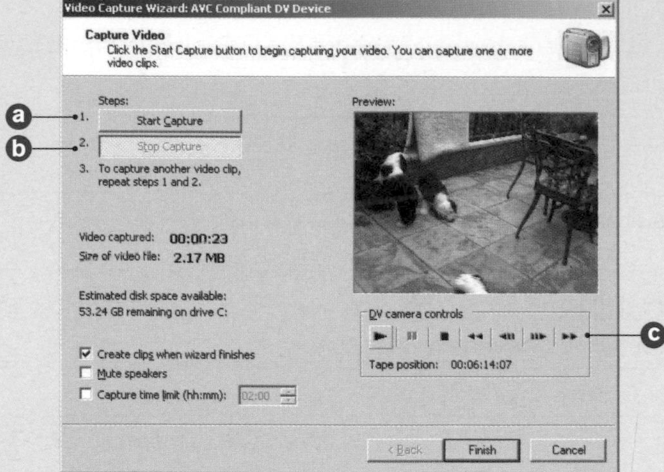

Figure 6.12 Capturing content live or from tape

You can choose to start and stop capturing individual parts of the video manually which reduces the amount of unnecessary video that is captured to your computer.

ⓐ Click on **Start Capture** to begin capturing audio and video to your computer.

ⓑ Click on **Stop Capture** to stop capturing audio and video to your computer.

ⓒ Use the **DV camera controls** to locate the next part of the video you want to capture and then repeat steps a and b.

The information and options available on this screen are:

- **Video captured** indicates the amount of time for the current capture.
- **Size of video file** indicates the file size as the video is being captured.
- **Estimated disk space available** shows the amount of space available on the hard drive of the computer you are using.
- **Create clips when wizard finishes** separates the captured video into manageable sized clips. How the clips are created is determined by the video capture device and is based on the timecode information set by the DV camera when the video was recorded. If you don't choose to create clips, the video appears as one large clip when you have finished capturing.
- **Mute speakers** If this box is selected, audio will not be played back on the speakers. If the box is left clear, background sounds from the computer may be heard and captured if you are capturing live content.

Regardless of the number of times you start and stop capturing, the captured video is saved in one file.

Key terms

Timecodes *The smallest unit of video that you can work with in NLE is a frame. This is identified by a standard code called the timecode. It is written as hours:minutes:seconds: frames. Some cameras only show the timecode as minutes:seconds:frames. Therefore a display of 12:34:24 would indicate 12 minutes, 34 seconds and 24 frames from the beginning of timing.*

Continued ...

- **Capture time limit** specifies whether there is a capturing time limit. If this box is selected, capturing stops automatically when the specified time limit has been reached.
- **DV camera controls** provides buttons to control your DV camera from your computer.

16 Using the information provided here to help you, select any settings you require.

17 Click **Start Capture** to start capturing a video clip; click **Stop Capture** to stop capture.

18 When you have finished capturing your clips, click on the **Finish** button.

19 The message box shown in Figure 6.13 will be displayed to confirm that the file is being imported into Movie Maker.

TIP!

Import your shots as separate video clips and give them appropriate names so you will be able to locate them easily on the computer.

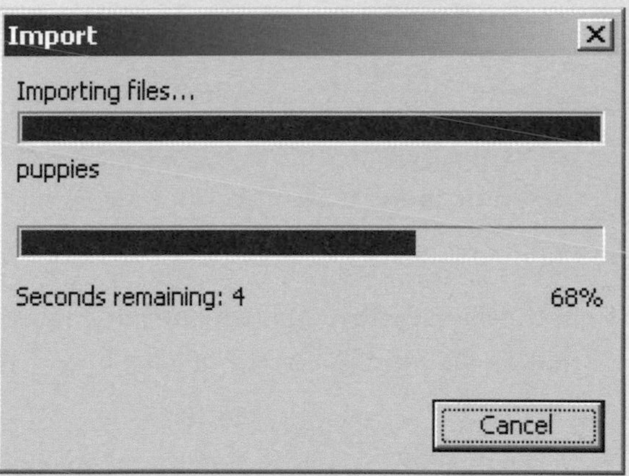

Figure 6.13 Import message box

Importing files into Movie Maker

If you already have the video, audio or still image file saved on your computer or on a CD, you can import them into Movie Maker to include in your movie.

HOW TO ... Import video already saved on the computer or CD

1 Click the **Tasks** button on the toolbar to display the **Movie Tasks** pane.

2 In the **Capture Video** section, click **Import Video**.

3 Select the drive and folder that contains the video to be imported.

4 Select the file and click the **Import** button.

TIP!

To import audio or music files, follow the procedure above, but at step 2:

- *to import audio, click on **Import audio or music***
- *to import pictures, click on **Import pictures**.*

You can import files with the file extensions listed in Table 6.8.

AUDIO FILES	PICTURE FILES	VIDEO FILES
aif aifc aiff asf au mp2 mp3 mpa snd wav wma	bmp dib emf gif jfif jpe jpeg jpg png tif tiff wmf	asf avi m1v mp2 mp2v mpe mpeg mpg mpv2 wm wmv

Table 6.8 List of files that can be imported into Movie Maker

If your source files are saved with file extensions that are not included in the lists in Table 6.8, you will need to use additional software to convert the files. A search on the Internet will usually provide the information you will need.

Creating stills from video

You can take a still picture of a frame from a previously imported video, save it as a file and import it back into Movie Maker.

▶▶ HOW TO ... Save a frame as a picture

1 Select the video clip you want to take a picture from.

2 Below the Monitor, move the playback indicator on the Seek bar to the frame of the video that you want to capture as a picture.

3 On the Playback controls, click the **Take Picture** button .

4 In the **Save Picture As** dialogue box, click on the drop-down arrow next to the **Save in** box. Locate the folder where you want to save the picture.

5 In the box next to **name**, enter a suitable name for the picture.

6 Click on **Save**.

Refer to Figure 6.6 on page 260.

Student review 6.3 – Save frames as still pictures

Assessment objective 4b

1 *Using clips you have previously imported, save approximately six individual frames as pictures using suitable filenames.*

2 *Import a music file that can be used as a background track to your movie.*

SECTION 4 • Edit and export the assembly cut of a digital video clip for a particular purpose

The following assessment objectives will be covered in this section:

4a Arrange workspace window for basic editing

4b Import media

4c Use editing tools to edit the video

4d Render the movie

4e Evaluate the assembly cut against the original brief

The following knowledge, skills and understanding criteria corresponding to assessment objectives 4a, 4b, 4c, 4d and 4e will be covered:

- *Workspace windows and panels*
- *Importing saved video into project*
- *Managing multiple files within a project*
- *Assembling tracks on the timeline*
- *Editing tools*
- *Export formats*
- *Exporting movies for different multimedia environments*

The following knowledge, skills and understanding are covered in the 'Common Skills' unit:

- *Reviewing the quality of the finished product*
- *Fitness for purpose*

ORGANISING CLIPS IN A COLLECTION

Collections are just like folders. The contents of a selected collection are displayed in the **Contents** pane. You can change the way in which your clips are displayed:

- In **Details** view (Figure 6.14), you can view all the properties about each clip.
- In **Thumbnails** view (Figure 6.15), you can view an image of the clip and its title.

To see the layout of the Movie Maker window, refer to Figure 6.5 on page 259.

▶▶ HOW TO ... View a collection

1 Click on the **Collections** button on the Toolbar.

2 Click on the name of the Collection folder you want to view.

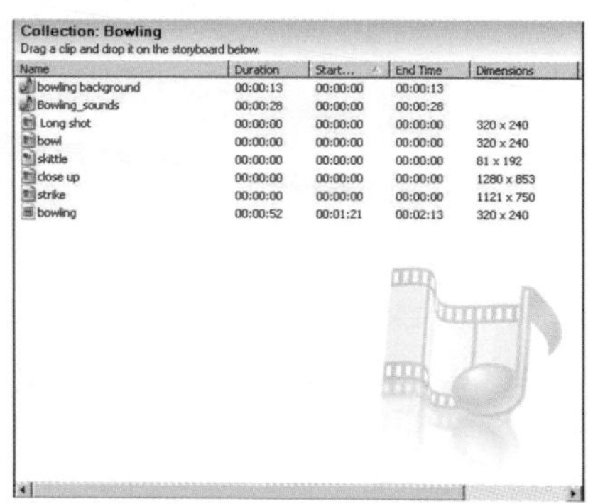

Figure 6.14 Details view

Collection: Bowling
Drag a clip and drop it on the storyboard below.

ball return | bowling background | bowl | lanes | ball return | skittle

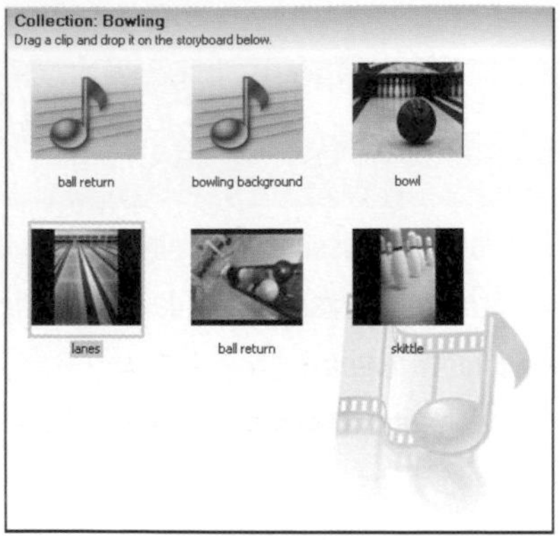

Figure 6.15 Thumbnails view

▸▸ HOW TO ... View the clip details

- Click on the **View** menu → select **Details**.

▸▸ HOW TO ... View the clip as a thumbnail

- Click on the **View** menu → select **Thumbnails**.

You can choose to organise your clips in different ways, just as you would files in Windows Explorer.

▸▸ HOW TO ... Arrange clips

1 Click on the **View** menu → select **Arrange Icons By**.

2 Select your preference from the list (Figure 6.16).

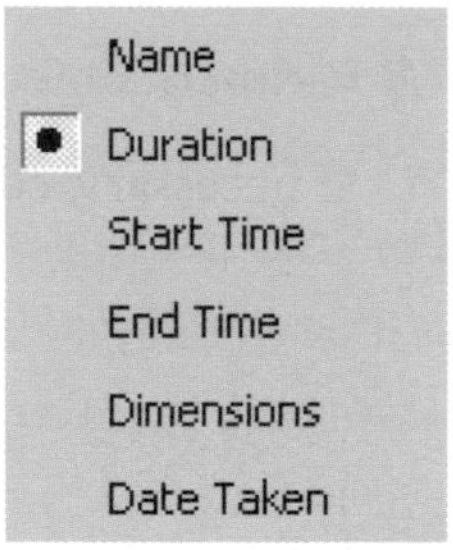

Name
● Duration
Start Time
End Time
Dimensions
Date Taken

Figure 6.16 Arrange options

▸▸ HOW TO ... Rename a clip

1 Right-click on the clip to be renamed.

2 Select **Rename** from the pop-up menu.

3 Type the new name of the clip.

▸▸ HOW TO ... Move a clip to a collection

1 Click on the **Collections** button on the Toolbar to display the **Collections** pane.

2 Click on the Collection folder that contains the clip.

3 In the **Contents** pane, click on the clip you want to move.

4 Drag the clip to the new Collection folder in the **Collections** pane.

▸▸ HOW TO ... Split a clip

If you have a long clip, you can divide it into smaller clips.

1 Click on the clip to be split.

2 Drag the Seek bar to the position (frame) where you want to split the clip.

3 In the Playback controls, click on the **Split the Clip** button .

▸▸ HOW TO ... Rename a collection

1 Right-click on the collection to be renamed.

2 Select **Rename** from the pop-up menu.

3 Type the new name for the collection.

▸▸ HOW TO ... Delete a media clip from a collection

1 Click on the clip to be deleted.

2 Press **Delete** on the keyboard.

▶▶ HOW TO ... Combine clips

1 Hold down the **Ctrl key** on the keyboard.
2 Click on each of the individual clips that you want to combine.
3 Click on the **Clip** menu → select **Combine**.

TIP!

In Timeline view you can drag the blue playback indicator line to locate the frame where you want to split a clip.

PRACTICAL TASK 6.12 Capture clips in movie maker, split clips and save in a collection

Assessment objectives 3d, 4b

1 If necessary, connect your video camera to the computer and start Windows Movie Maker.
2 Refer to the edit decision list you created in Practical task 6.11 and locate the position of the first clip on the camera.
3 Capture each clip as an individual file, give each clip an appropriate filename and save in the **bowling** collection in Movie Maker.
4 Make sure that you have saved all your clips for the 'Magnificent Bowl – TV Commercial' in the **bowling** collection.
5 If necessary, move the clips into the correct collection.
6 If you have any long clips, split the clips at suitable positions.
7 Make sure all clips and collections have been named with appropriate filenames.

Key terms

Transition Animation effect that shows how one clip moves to the next.

Effects Special enhancements that determine how the clips are displayed in the final movie.

Storyboard

The Storyboard (Figure 6.17) displays the order of the clips, and shows any video **transitions** or **effects** in your project. It does not display audio clips.

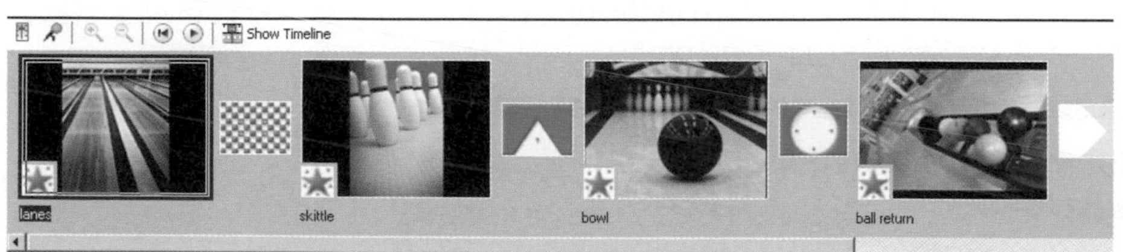

Figure 6.17 The Storyboard

Timeline

The Timeline (Figure 6.18) displays all the clips in your project; it also includes audio. All the clips, transitions and effects in the Timeline, define your project. You can use the Timeline to modify the timing of clips, trim the length of clips, record narration, add titles and credits, or adjust the audio levels. Time is displayed as hours:minutes:seconds:hundreths of a second (h:m:s:hs) along the top of the Timeline.

Figure 6.18 The Timeline

Figure 6.19 The Timeline buttons

The Timeline buttons (Figure 6.19) allow you to adjust the audio levels, record narration, zoom in and out of the Timeline, rewind to the beginning of the Timeline, play the Timeline or change the view of your project back to the Storyboard.

The Timeline displays the following tracks:

- **Video** shows the video clips or still images that have been added to the Timeline. Clicking on the ⊞ next to the track label expands the video track to reveal the transition and audio tracks. These tracks show any transitions that have been applied to the Timeline and any audio that is recorded with any of the video clips.
- **Audio/Music** displays audio clips that you have added to the project. You can also add video clips to this track if you want the audio, but not the video, to play in your project and final movie.
- **Title Overlay** displays any titles or credits that you have added to the Timeline. You can add multiple titles to this track at different points in your movie. The titles overlay the video as it is played.

IMPORTING MEDIA

To create a movie, you drag clips from the Collections area to the Storyboard or Timeline of the project. You can then arrange the clips in the order you want them to appear.

▶▶ HOW TO ... Import saved video/image clips into a project

1. Click on the Collections folder that contains the clips you want to use in your project.
2. Click on the clip you want to include in your project.
3. Drag the clip from the **Collections** pane to the first available box in the Storyboard.
4. Repeat steps 2 and 3 until you have included all the video/image clips you want to include.

▶▶ HOW TO ... Import saved audio clips into a project

1. Click on the Collections folder that contains the clips you want to use in your project.
2. Click on **Show Timeline**.
3. Click on the audio clip you want to include in your project.
4. Drag the clip from the **Collections** pane to the Audio/Music track in the Timeline.
5. Repeat steps 3 and 4 until you have included all the required audio clips.

▶▶ HOW TO ... Change the order of clips

1. Click on the clip to be moved.
2. Drag the clip to the new position.

PRACTICAL TASK 6.13 Import clips to the timeline and storyboard

Assessment objective 4b

1. In Windows Movie Maker, arrange the workspace to display the Storyboard and the **bowling** collection.
2. Import the clips you want to use in your final movie into the Storyboard or Timeline.
3. Save your project keeping the original filename, e.g. **Magnibowl**

TIP!

You can also trim a video clip by using the trim handles. Position the cursor on the left or right edge of the clip and drag the trim handles.

USING EDITING TOOLS TO EDIT THE VIDEO

In an OCR assignment you will be required to use a minimum of three editing tools. These tools can include the tracks in a project, trimming and cutting clips, rolling edits, split edits, audio editing, transitions and effects.

The 'Magnificent Bowl – TV Commercial' assignment brief states that the final video should last for approximately 30 seconds. Some of your clips may be longer than you want them to be, or contain content that you want to cut. You can easily trim the clips in the Timeline.

▶▶ HOW TO ... Trim (crop) a video clip

1. If necessary, display the Timeline – click on **Show Timeline**.
2. Click on the video clip you want to trim.
3. Drag the Seek bar to the position where you want the clip to start.
4. Click on the **Clip** menu → select **Set Start Trim Point**.
5. Drag the Seek bar to the position where you want the clip to end.
6. Click on the **Clip** menu → select **Set End Trim Point**.

You cannot trim still images.

▶▶ HOW TO ... Restore a clip to its original length

1 Click on the clip you want to restore.

2 Click on the **Clip** menu → select **Clear Trim Points**.

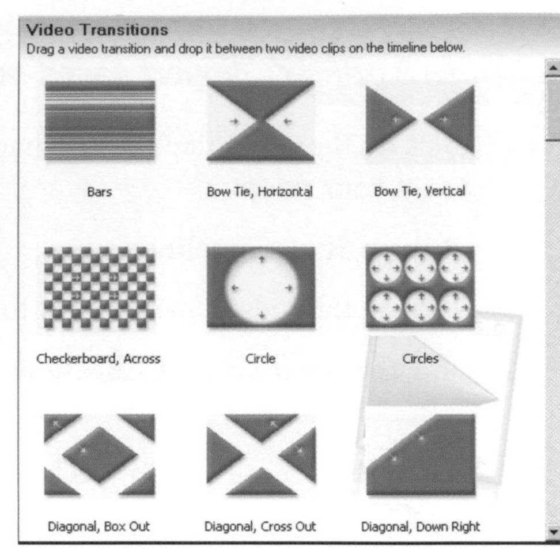

Figure 6.20 Video transitions available in Movie Maker

Adding transitions between clips

A transition is an effect that makes the change between two clips smoother. It can be added between two video clips, still images or titles. The transition will play before one clip ends and as the next clip starts to play. The choice of transitions available (see Figure 6.20) is displayed in the **Contents** pane when you click on **View video transitions**.

▶▶ HOW TO ... Add transitions to the movie in the Storyboard

1 Click on the **Tasks** button on the Toolbar to display the **Movie Tasks** pane.

2 In the **Movie Tasks** pane, in the **Edit Movie** section, click on **View video transitions**.

3 A representation of the transitions that are available will appear in the **Contents** pane.

4 Click on the transition that you want to use and drag it to the cell between the two clips.

! *You will not be able to add a transition if you have only one clip in the Storyboard.*

▶▶ HOW TO ... Add transitions to the movie in the Timeline

1 Follow steps 1–3 as above.

2 When you drag the transition to the Timeline, the Video track will automatically expand and allow you to place the transition on the Transition track.

TIP!

You can increase or decrease the duration of the transition in the Timeline:

- *Increasing the duration of the transition makes the transition effect slower.*
- *Decreasing the duration of the transition will make the effect quicker.*

▶▶ HOW TO ... Change the duration of the transition

1 If necessary, display the Timeline – click on **Show Timeline**.

2 To increase the transition duration, drag the beginning of the transition towards the beginning of the Timeline.

3 To decrease the transition duration, drag the beginning of the transition towards the end of the Timeline.

If you change your mind and you no longer want a transition effect in the movie, you can remove it.

TIP!

You can change the default transition duration.

Tools → **Options** → **Advanced Tab** → enter a value for **Transition duration** → **OK**.

HOW TO ... Remove a transition effect

1 Click on the transition to be removed.

2 Press **Delete** on the keyboard.

PRACTICAL TASK 6.14 Adding transitions to the movie timeline

Assessment objective 4c

1 Add transition effects to your movie.

2 Use the Monitor to preview the effects.

3 Experiment with the different effects until you are happy with the transitions applied.

4 Save your project keeping the same filename.

Adding video effects

A video effect determines how your clip is played in the movie, for example, fade in, blur, watercolour. You can add video effects to video clips, still images or titles in a movie project. When you add a video effect to a clip, it is applied for the entire duration of the clip. You can add more than one effect to a clip and you can change the order in which the effects appear.

Video effects are maintained when you split, cut, copy, or move a video clip or picture. For example, if you add the Blur effect, and then split the clip, the Blur effect will be applied to both clips. However, if you combine two video clips, the effects that were applied to the first clip are applied to the new combined clip, and the effects for the second clip will be removed.

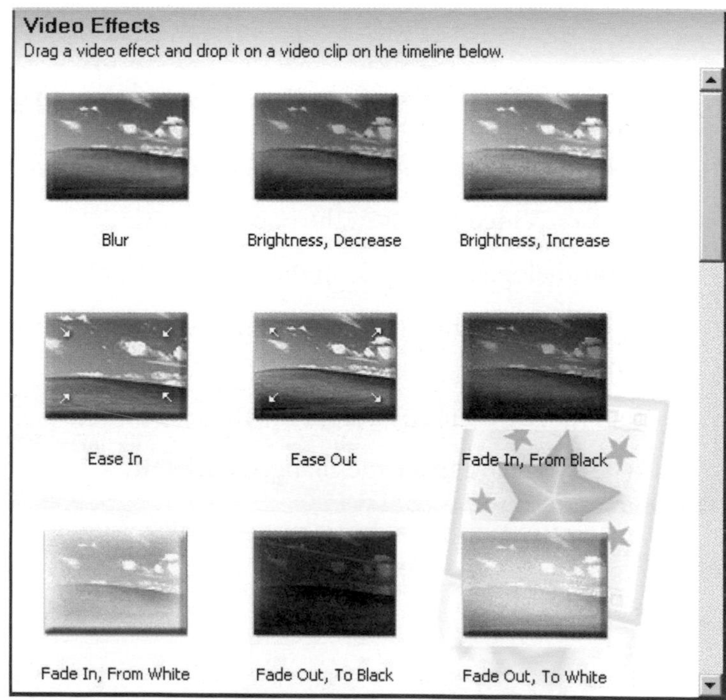

Figure 6.21 Video effects available in Movie Maker

▸▸ HOW TO … Add a video effect

1. Click on the **Tasks** button on the Toolbar to display the **Movie Tasks** pane.
2. In the **Movie Tasks** pane, in the **Edit Movie** section, click on **View video effects**.
3. A representation of each of the video effects that are available will appear in the **Contents** pane (Figure 6.21).
4. Click on the effect that you want to use and drag it on to the clip that you want it to apply to.

When you add a video effect to a clip, a blue star will be displayed. If a clip has more than one effect applied to it, two blue stars will be displayed.

Figure 6.22 Video effects shown in the Storyboard

Figure 6.23 Video effects shown in the Timeline

▸▸ HOW TO … Change the order or remove effects

1. Right-click on the clip that has the effects you want to change.
2. Click on **Video Effects** in the pop-up menu.
3. In the dialogue box, click on the effect you want to remove or move.
4. To change the order of the effect, click on the **move up** or **move down** button.
5. To remove the effect, click on the **Remove** button.
6. When you have made the changes, click **OK**.

PRACTICAL TASK 6.15 Add effects to movie clips

Assessment objective 4c

1 Add video effects to your clips.

2 Experiment with the different effects available, using the Monitor to preview the results.

3 On one clip, add more than one effect.

4 Try changing the order of the effects on the clip.

5 Save your project keeping the same filename.

Adding titles and credits

You can add text-based information to your movie to show a title at the beginning and credits at the end. You can also add text-based information in various places in the movie, e.g. a title at the beginning before the clips start to play, before or after a particular clip, at the end of the movie. The text can even overlay a clip.

▸▸ HOW TO ... Add a title or credit

1 If necessary, click on the **Tasks** button in the Toolbar to display the **Movie Tasks** pane.

2 In the **Edit Movie** section, click on **Make titles or credits.**

3 You will be asked where you want to create the title or credit:

- Title at the beginning of the movie
- Title before the selected clip
- Title on the selected clip
- Title after the selected clip
- Credits at the end of the movie

4 Click on the required option.

5 On the next screen, enter the text. A preview of this will be shown in the Monitor.

6 To choose an animation style, click on the link **Change the title animation** and choose from a list of available effects. A preview of your changes will be displayed in the Monitor.

7 To change the font attributes, click on the link **Change the text font and colour** and make your choices. A preview of your changes will be displayed in the Monitor.

8 When you have finished, click on **Done, add title to movie.**

You can change the duration of a title or credit, in the same way as you change the duration of a transition.

TIP!

To remove a title, select it and then press **Delete** on the keyboard.

PRACTICAL TASK 6.16 Add titles and animation effects

Assessment objective 4c

1 Experiment with adding titles to different places in your movie.
2 Try the different animation effects until you find one you like.
3 Add a title to the start of the movie and credits to the end of the movie.
4 Save your project keeping the same filename.

Adding a soundtrack

When you recorded your video, you may have recorded sound at the same time. The Video track on the Timeline includes the actual track that contains the images, a Transition section that would contain any transitions and the Audio section of the track that will display any sound that has been recorded with the video. When the video track is expanded, these three sections will be shown as separate tracks on the Timeline – though they are connected with a dotted line, as shown in Figure 6.24. (If the Video track is not expanded, you will not see the Transition and Audio sections of the video track.)

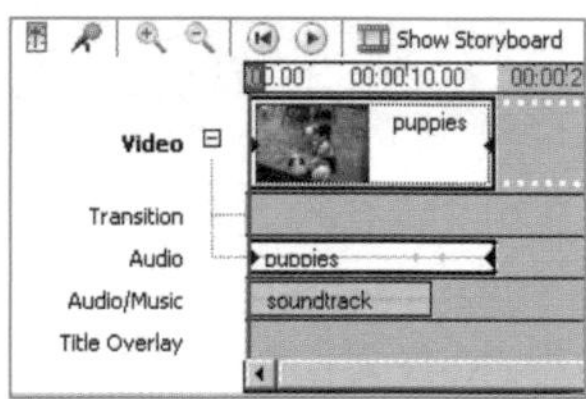

Figure 6.24 Tracks shown in the Timeline

You can also add separate sounds such as music or a narration. These will appear in the Audio/Music track of the Timeline (Figure 6.24).

HOW TO ... Add a soundtrack

1 Make sure you have the audio clip saved in your Collection.
2 If necessary, display the Timeline – click on **Show Timeline**.
3 Drag the sound clip onto the **Audio/Music** track at the location where you want the clip to play.

HOW TO ... Adjust the volume

1 Click on the **Set Audio Levels** button.
2 Play the Timeline.
3 Drag the audio levels slider to adjust the balance between the video clip and the soundtrack (refer to Figure 6.25).
4 Click on the **Set Audio Levels** button again to close the dialogue box.

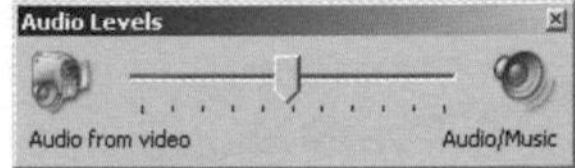

Figure 6.25 Audio Levels adjustment

Adding audio effects

You can add basic audio effects to your audio files, i.e. Mute, Fade in and Fade out. If you have a video track that has audio recorded with it and you do not want to hear the audio during playback, you can mute this in the audio track.

Audio effects are maintained when you split, cut, copy or move a clip. If you combine two audio clips, the audio effects that were applied to the first clip will be applied to the new combined clip, and the audio effects for the second clip will be removed.

▶▶ HOW TO ... Add an audio effect

1 If necessary, display the Timeline – click on **Show Timeline**.

2 Right-click on the audio clip.

3 Click on the required effect (**Mute**, **Fade In**, **Fade Out**).

▶▶ HOW TO ... Remove an audio effect

1 Right-click on the audio clip.

2 Click on the effect you wish to remove (to remove the tick).

PRACTICAL TASK 6.17 Add sounds and music

Assessment objective 4c

1 Experiment with adding sounds and music to different clips in your movie.

2 Try adding different audio effects.

3 Save your project keeping the same filename.

Adding narration

To add narration to your movie, you will need to have a microphone connected to your computer. The narration will be saved as a Windows Media Audio file with a **wma** file extension. By default, the audio narration file is saved in a Narration folder in the My Videos folder on your hard disk/network area. It will display in your current Collection and also in the Audio/Music track of the current Timeline.

Refer to 'Tips for writing a good script' on page 225.

Before you start to record your narration, you should prepare a script.

▶▶ HOW TO ... Add a narration

1 Make sure you have a microphone connected to your computer.

2 If necessary, display the Timeline – click on **Show Timeline**.

3 Drag the playback indicator to a blank position on the Audio/Music track where you want to start the narration.

4 Click on the **Tools** menu → select **Narrate Timeline…**.

⚠ *An audio narration can only be added in the Timeline view. If you are in Storyboard view, a warning dialogue box will be displayed. Click OK. You will be automatically switched to Timeline view.*

Continued ...

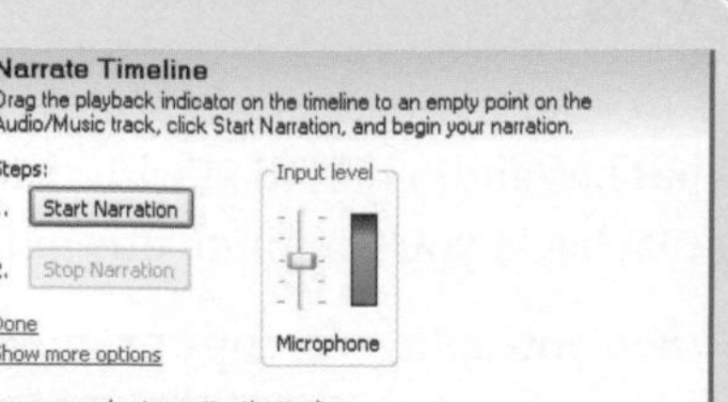

Figure 6.26 Narration options

5 The options shown in Figure 6.26 will be displayed in the **Contents** pane.

6 Click on the link **Show more options**.

7 In the box under **Input level**, make sure that **Microphone** is selected.

8 When you are ready to record, click on **Start Narration**.

9 When you have finished recording, click on **Stop Narration**.

10 Save the audio file using an appropriate name.

11 When you have finished recording your narration(s), click on **Done**.

If the playback indicator is overlapping another audio clip on the Audio/Music track, the Start Narration button will be grey. The playback indicator must be in a blank position on the track.

PRACTICAL TASK 6.18 ***Write a script and record the narration***

Assessment objective 4c

1 Write a script for a narrative piece for the beginning of your movie, to be played while the opening titles are being displayed.

2 Write a script for a narrative piece for the end of your movie, to be played while the credits are being displayed.

3 Record both your narrations and save with appropriate filenames.

4 Save your project keeping the same filename.

RENDERING A MOVIE CLIP

Before you save the project as a final movie, you may want to include some general information about your movie which will be displayed by the media player during playback.

▸▸ HOW TO ... Add project properties to your project

1 Click on the **File** menu → select **Properties**.

2 The **Project Properties** dialogue box will be displayed (Figure 6.27).

3 Enter the movie title, the author, any copyright information, the rating for the movie, and a description.

4 Click on **Apply** → **OK**.

Figure 6.27 Project Properties dialogue box

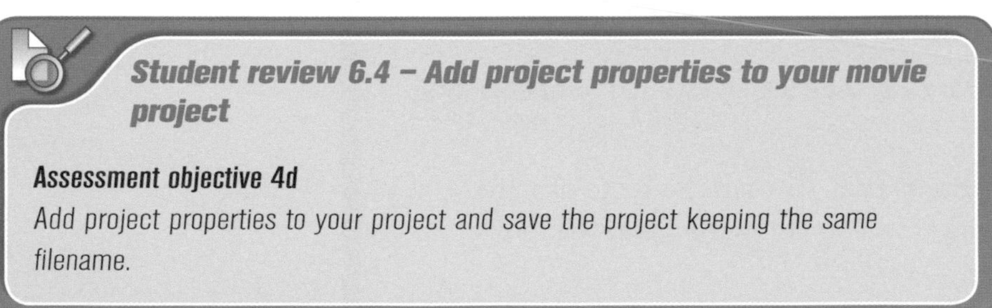

Student review 6.4 – Add project properties to your movie project

Assessment objective 4d

Add project properties to your project and save the project keeping the same filename.

When you are happy with the content and effects of your project, you are ready to save it as a final movie. This can be done using the Save Movie Wizard. Using this Wizard you can save the movie to your computer, a recordable CD, send it as an email attachment, save it and send it to the web or record it back to your video camera. When the movie has been saved in **wmv** format, you can play it in a media player or view it in a web browser.

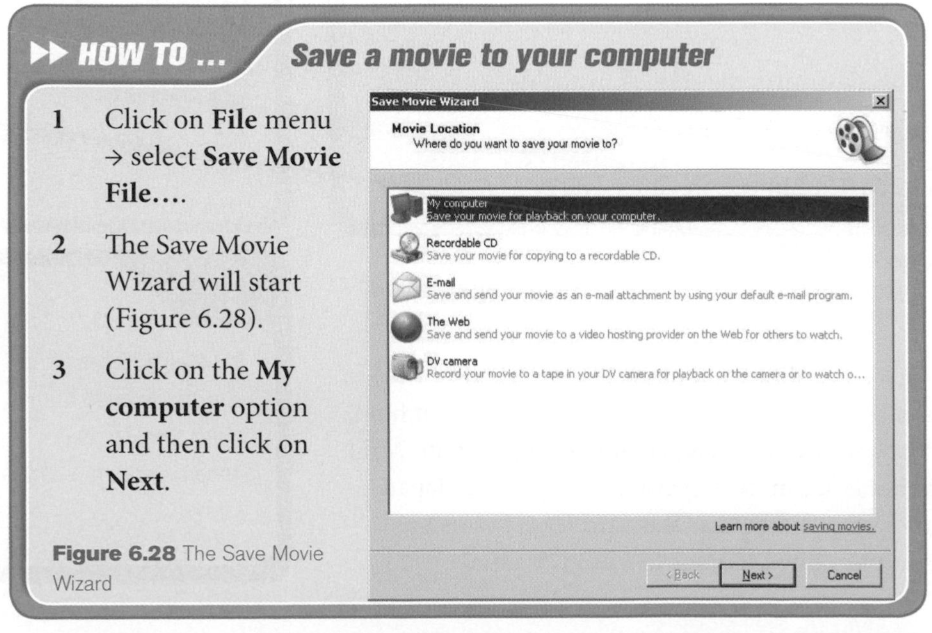

▸▸ HOW TO ... Save a movie to your computer

1 Click on **File** menu → select **Save Movie File....**

2 The Save Movie Wizard will start (Figure 6.28).

3 Click on the **My computer** option and then click on **Next.**

Figure 6.28 The Save Movie Wizard

Continued ...

4 Enter the name for the movie.

5 Browse to the location on your computer where you want to save the movie.

6 Click on **Next.**

7 The next step will show the movie settings (Figure 6.29).

8 Click on **Next.**

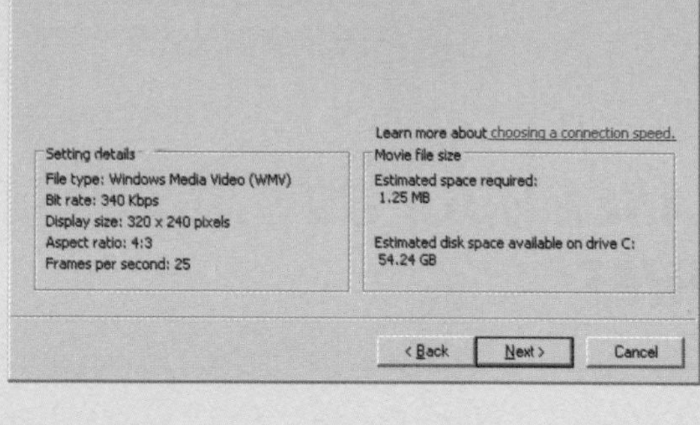

Figure 6.29 Movie Setting options

9 The Save Movie Wizard will save your movie, showing an estimation of how long this will take.

10 When the movie has been saved, you can choose to play the movie. Remove the tick if you do not want to play the movie.

11 Click **Finish.**

▶▶ HOW TO ... Save your movie to a portable PC

1 Follow steps from 1–7 for saving to a computer.

2 At Step 7, in the **Movie Settings** dialogue box, click on the link **Show more choices.**

3 Select **Other settings.**

4 Click on the down arrow to display the choices available.

5 Select **Video for Pocket PC.**

6 Then follow on with steps 8–11 in the previous 'HOW TO'.

TIP!

If you have difficulty saving your movie to a CD through Windows Movie Maker, try saving the file to your computer and using your usual copying software to copy the file to a CD.

For other saving locations, following the instructions in the dialogue boxes that appear on screen.

All Mini DV video cameras have the ability to output DV signals (DV-out) to a computer and models that also feature DV-in let you send videos that have been edited on a computer back to the video camera for recording onto Mini DV tape. In Europe these cameras are more expensive to buy, but in Japan, Asia and the USA video cameras have DV-in as standard. This is a useful feature if you want to archive your edited footage to Mini DV tape.

To be able to send your movie back to the Video camera, your camera must have DV-in enabled.

PRACTICAL TASK 6.19 *Save a project in different formats*

Assessment objective 4d

1 Save your project to your computer as a final movie.

2 Experiment with saving your project for use in different locations, e.g. sending as an email attachment, saving for viewing on the web.

3 Send your final movie to CD (or copy using your normal software).

REVIEWING THE ASSEMBLY CUT AGAINST THE ORIGINAL BRIEF

For an OCR assessment you are required to review your final movie against the original brief. You will need to identify how the movie you have produced meets the client's original specification and show that the final product is fit for purpose. You could review your final movie with your tutor acting as the client and identify good features and areas that could be improved.

Refer to 'Reviewing you work' on page xiv of the 'Common Skills' chapter.

PRACTICAL TASK 6.20 *Review your final movie*

Assessment objective 4e

With your tutor, review the final movie and record your findings on your Planning and Review Form.

You should now have all the skills, knowledge and understanding required to complete an OCR iMedia sample or live assessment for this unit.

Note: Page numbers in **bold** indicate location of key terms.